AND EDUCATION

University of Plymouth
Charles Seale Hayne Library
Subject to status this item may be renewed
via your Voyager account

http://voyager.plymouth.ac.uk
Tel: (01752) 232323

Encyclopedia of Language and Education

VOLUME 2: LITERACY

General Editor
Nancy H. Hornberger, *University of Pennsylvania, Philadelphia, USA*

The volume titles of this encyclopedia are listed at the end of this volume.

Encyclopedia of Language and Education

Volume 2

LITERACY

Edited by

BRIAN V. STREET

King's College London
Department of Education and Professional Studies
UK

and

NANCY H. HORNBERGER

University of Pennsylvania
Graduate School of Education
USA

 Springer

Volume Editors:
Brian V. Street
King's College London
Department of Education and Professional Studies
London, SEI 9NN
UK
brian.street@kcl.ac.uk

Nancy H. Hornberger
University of Pennsylvania
Graduate School of Education
Philadelphia, PA 19104-6216
USA
nancyh@gse.upenn.edu

General Editor:
Nancy H. Hornberger
University of Pennsylvania
Graduate School of Education
Philadelphia, PA 19104-6216
USA
nancyh@gse.upenn.edu

Library of Congress Control Number: 2007925265

ISBN-13: 978-0-387-32875-1 (hard cover)
ISBN-13: 978-90-481-9200-7 (soft cover)

The electronic version will be available under ISBN 978-0-387-30424-3
The print and electronic bundle will be available under ISBN 978-0-387-35420-0

Printed on acid-free paper.

9 8 7 6 5 4 3 2 1 0

springer.com

TABLE OF CONTENTS

VOLUME 2: LITERACY

*B. V. Street and N. H. Hornberger (eds), Encyclopedia of Language and Education,
2nd Edition, Volume 2: Literacy, v–vii.*
©*2010 Springer Science+Business Media LLC.*

NANCY H. HORNBERGER

GENERAL EDITOR'S INTRODUCTION [1]

ENCYCLOPEDIA OF LANGUAGE AND EDUCATION

This is one of ten volumes of the *Encyclopedia of Language and Education* published by Springer. The Encyclopedia bears testimony to the dynamism and evolution of the language and education field, as it confronts the ever-burgeoning and irrepressible linguistic diversity and ongoing pressures and expectations placed on education around the world.

The publication of this work charts the deepening and broadening of the field of language and education since the 1997 publication of the first Encyclopedia. It also confirms the vision of David Corson, general editor of the first edition, who hailed the international and interdisciplinary significance and cohesion of the field. These trademark characteristics are evident in every volume and chapter of the present Encyclopedia.

In the selection of topics and contributors, the Encyclopedia seeks to reflect the depth of disciplinary knowledge, breadth of interdisciplinary perspective, and diversity of sociogeographic experience in our field. Language socialization and language ecology have been added to the original eight volume topics, reflecting these growing emphases in language education theory, research, and practice, alongside the enduring emphases on language policy, literacies, discourse, language acquisition, bilingual education, knowledge about language, language testing, and research methods. Throughout all the volumes, there is greater inclusion of scholarly contributions from non-English speaking and non-Western parts of the world, providing truly global coverage of the issues in the field. Furthermore, we have sought to integrate these voices more fully into the whole, rather than as special cases or international perspectives in separate sections.

This interdisciplinary and internationalizing impetus has been immeasurably enhanced by the advice and support of the editorial advisory board members, several of whom served as volume editors in the Encyclopedia's first edition (designated here with*), and all of whom I acknowledge here with gratitude: Neville Alexander (South Africa), Colin Baker (Wales), Marilda Cavalcanti (Brazil), Caroline Clapham* (Britain),

---

[1] This introduction is based on, and takes inspiration from, David Corson's general editor's Introduction to the First Edition (Kluwer, 1997).

B. V. Street and N. H. Hornberger (eds), Encyclopedia of Language and Education,
2nd Edition, Volume 2: Literacy, ix–xi.
©*2010 Springer Science+Business Media LLC.*

Bronwyn Davies* (Australia), Viv Edwards* (Britain), Frederick Erickson (USA), Joseph Lo Bianco (Australia), Luis Enrique Lopez (Bolivia and Peru), Allan Luke (Singapore and Australia), Tove Skutnabb-Kangas (Denmark), Bernard Spolsky (Israel), G. Richard Tucker* (USA), Leo van Lier* (USA), Terrence G. Wiley (USA), Ruth Wodak* (Austria), and Ana Celia Zentella (USA).

In conceptualizing an encyclopedic approach to a field, there is always the challenge of the hierarchical structure of themes, topics, and subjects to be covered. In this *Encyclopedia of Language and Education*, the stated topics in each volume's table of contents are complemented by several cross-cutting thematic strands recurring across the volumes, including the classroom/pedagogic side of language and education; issues of identity in language and education; language ideology and education; computer technology and language education; and language rights in relation to education.

The volume editors' disciplinary and interdisciplinary academic interests and their international areas of expertise also reflect the depth and breadth of the language and education field. As principal volume editor for Volume 1, Stephen May brings academic interests in the sociology of language and language education policy, arising from his work in Britain, North America, and New Zealand. For Volume 2, Brian Street approaches language and education as social and cultural anthropologist and critical literacy theorist, drawing on his work in Iran, Britain, and around the world. For Volume 3, Marilyn Martin-Jones and Anne-Marie de Mejia bring combined perspectives as applied and educational linguists, working primarily in Britain and Latin America, respectively. For Volume 4, Nelleke Van Deusen-Scholl has academic interests in linguistics and sociolinguistics, and has worked primarily in the Netherlands and the USA. Jim Cummins, principal volume editor for Volume 5 of both the first and second editions of the Encyclopedia, has interests in the psychology of language, critical applied linguistics, and language policy, informed by his work in Canada, the USA, and internationally. For Volume 6, Jasone Cenoz has academic interests in applied linguistics and language acquisition, drawing from her work in the Basque Country, Spain, and Europe. Elana Shohamy, principal volume editor for Volume 7, approaches language and education as an applied linguist with interests in critical language policy, language testing and measurement, and her own work based primarily in Israel and the USA. For Volume 8, Patricia Duff has interests in applied linguistics and sociolinguistics, and has worked primarily in North America, East Asia, and Central Europe. Volume editors for Volume 9, Angela Creese and Peter Martin, draw on their academic interests in educational linguistics and linguistic ethnography, and their research in Britain and Southeast Asia. And for Volume 10, Kendall A. King has academic interests in sociolinguistics and educational linguistics, with work in Ecuador, Sweden, and the USA. Francis Hult, editorial assistant for the Encyclopedia, has academic interests in educational and applied linguistics and educational language policy, and has worked in Sweden and the USA. Finally, as general editor, I have interests in anthropological linguistics, educational linguistics, and language policy, with work in Latin America, the USA, and internationally. Beyond our specific academic interests, all of us editors, and the contributors to the Encyclopedia, share a commitment to the practice and theory of education, critically informed by research and strategically directed toward addressing unsound or unjust language education policies and practices wherever they are found.

Each of the ten volumes presents core information and is international in scope, as well as diverse in the populations it covers. Each volume addresses a single subject area and provides 23–30 state-of-the-art chapters of the literature on that subject. Together, the chapters aim to comprehensively cover the subject. The volumes, edited by international experts in their respective topics, were designed and developed in close collaboration with the general editor of the Encyclopedia, who is a co-editor of each volume as well as general editor of the whole work.

Each chapter is written by one or more experts on the topic, consists of about 4,000 words of text, and generally follows a similar structure. A list of references to key works supplements the authoritative information that the chapters contains. Many contributors survey early developments, major contributions, work in progress, problems and difficulties, and future directions. The aim of the chapters, and of the Encyclopedia as a whole, is to give readers access to the international literature and research on the broad diversity of topics that make up the field.

The Encyclopedia is a necessary reference set for every university and college library in the world that serves a faculty or school of education. The encyclopedia aims to speak to a prospective readership that is multinational, and to do so as unambiguously as possible. Because each book-size volume deals with a discrete and important subject in language and education, these state-of-the-art volumes also offer highly authoritative course textbooks in the areas suggested by their titles.

The scholars contributing to the Encyclopedia hail from all continents of our globe and from 41 countries; they represent a great diversity of linguistic, cultural, and disciplinary traditions. For all that, what is most impressive about the contributions gathered here is the unity of purpose and outlook they express with regard to the central role of language as both vehicle and mediator of educational processes and to the need for continued and deepening research into the limits and possibilities that implies.

Nancy H. Hornberger

BRIAN V. STREET

INTRODUCTION TO VOLUME 2: LITERACY

This collection of articles is intended to be both Encyclopaedia and something more. The chapters represent an Encyclopaedic account of current knowledge in the literacy field, in the sense that they cover a broad range of topics and regions by the leading researchers in the field. But they also aim to provide something more in that they are also cutting edge considerations of the nature of the field and how new concepts and ideas are being applied in different contexts. And that itself is a break through in literacy studies, in the sense that traditionally research in literacy has tended to focus on narrower issues, such as the acquisition of skills by those lacking literacy—mostly children but also encompassing 'illiterate' adults—and the measurement and recording of these skill 'levels'. Certainly national and international agencies have been concerned to address this category of people and to 'improve' their 'literacy rates' by enhancing methods of delivery, so requiring attention to pedagogy, curriculum and assessment. But recent research in the field has begun to step back from these assumptions and has asked 'what is literacy?' as a prior question to issues of delivery and learning. The answers to the question 'what is literacy?' have been some-times surprising. It turns out that literacy means different things to different people across different periods of time and in different places. So the concern for those 'lacking' literacy has first to be located in time and space and the practical and policy responses will differ accordingly.

To address these prior questions, we have asked historians, anthropologists, linguists, and educationalists to review what we know about literacy across these spans of time and space and to explain to readers in accessible language how we can come to understand what literacy means in these different contexts and from these different perspectives. The result is not simple answers but further complexity. The in-depth, scholarly accounts provided here indicate just how literacy varies as authors consider what it has meant in past times, whether in Europe and the USA (*Harvey J. Graff and John Duffy*), in Africa (*Pippa Stein*) or in South America (*Kwesi K. Prah*) or across different social con-texts, such as urban spaces in the UK (*Eve Gregory*) communities in Australia (*Trevor Cairney*) or Nepal (*Roshan Chitrakar and Bryan Maddox*) or Latin America (*Judy Kalman*). Or, to take another cut through the perspectives that scholars now bring to bear on literacy, some authors address what literacy means for children and parents in

B. V. Street and N. H. Hornberger (eds), Encyclopedia of Language and Education,
2nd Edition, Volume 2: Literacy, xiii–xxix.
©*2010 Springer Science+Business Media LLC.*

South Africa (*Pippa Stein*) or the USA (*Vivian Gadsden, Kathy Schultz, and Glynda Hull*). And this perspective raise further conceptual points, as researchers consider the relationship between literacies in and out of school (*Jabari Mahiri; Kathy Schultz and Glynda Hull; David Bloome; Alan Rogers*) and also in higher education (*Mary Lea*).

Nor is it just a matter of educational contexts, whether for children or adults, that are at stake in reviewing what we know about literacy. What we take literacy to be, whose definitions count and have power in different societies, lie at the heart of all of these accounts—as *Arlette Ingram Willis* brings out in her accounts of Critical Race Theory and *Gemma Moss* in considering Gender and Literacy. The issue of definitions and of power is also evident in chapters on language and literacy by *Jim Cummins, Marcia Farr* and *Constant Leung* and how we frame these social issues associated with the definitions and meanings of literacy are put into broader context for us by *Peter Freebody* in a review of the literature on Critical Literacy and by *Viniti Vaish* on Biliteracy and Globalization. Still, this does not exhaust the range of topics we need to take into account in considering literacy in the contemporary age. Inevitably, we have to look at the place of literacy in broader communicative patterns, notably recent developments in 'Literacy and Internet Technologies', which are explored in a chapter by *Kevin Leander and Cynthia Lewis* whilst *Brian Street* attempts an overview of these developments in his 'New Literacies, New Times' piece. But at the same time, more familiar considerations regarding how literacy is acquired remain important for our understanding of the field and a number of papers do address reading as a significant dimension of literacy practices, notably *John Edwards* in his chapter 'Reading: Attitudes, Interests, Practices' and also those papers already signalled that deal with literacies in and out of school, such as those by *David Bloome* and by *Kathy Schultz and Glynda Hull*.

This summary, then, has in a sense come full circle, starting with reference to 'traditional' concerns with literacy as reading acquisition, moving through varieties of time and space, attending to social categories such as gender and race, taking on board recent sophisticated considerations of language and language varieties as they relate to literacy, noting the significance of new technologies and finally reminding ourselves of the role that education and learning must play in addressing these issues. And that is probably the major significance of what the authors in this volume have to tell us—that if we wish to address issues of policy and practice with regard to literacy, including how we learn to use it, then we will need to take account of various combinations of all of these other issues and the complexity they indicate even as we address any one context and set of practices. How these issues and topics combine will vary, as the authors show in demonstrating the different literacies and policies and meanings to be found in Africa, Asia, the American continent and Europe and across different time spans. If that makes it harder for all of those involved—policy makers, educational-ists and researchers—then that is the job of an Encyclopaedia such as this, to help us to come to such topics in the full light of what is known rather than acting out of partial knowledge.

Having indicated some of the key themes and issues, we now pro-vide a brief summary of the 26 chapters included in this Volume, as a kind of map of the overall text. The first section of the volume is entitled 'Literacies and Social Theory' and attempts to provide the reader with some key theoretical frames and organising concepts before authors address more closely particular social institutions, in Section 2 and particular social and cultural experiences of literacy, in Section 3. The sections inevitably overlap but this organisation can provide one route through the volume for those who wish to move from the more theoretical to the more concrete and contextualised accounts of literacy. However, since the topic itself is literacy, we are acutely conscious that each reader will develop your own route through the text.

SECTION 1: LITERACIES AND SOCIAL THEORY

The volume begins with a piece by the editor, who suggests his own map of the field of literacy studies and how it is learning to deal with what he terms 'New Literacies, New Times'. He begins with an outline of the current theoretical frameworks, in particular work in New Lit-eracy Studies, in multi-modality, and in theories of technology and artefact. He then considers some of the educational responses evident in different countries as they come to terms with the challenges posed by new literacies. Anticipating the end rather than the beginning of the Volume, he also makes some suggestions as to why it is that policy in some countries—notably the USA and UK—seems to be facing in the opposite direction to that which the research base tells us is needed. We begin to see possible answers to this question straight away in the recognition by *Arlette Willis*, writing about the USA, that literacy can-not be separated from social position, which for many is a racialised position. In addressing Critical Race (CRT) Theory she argues, firstly, that this topic is not limited to some sub categories of society, such as African Americans' experience, or individual acts of prejudice. Rather, she suggests, activists and scholars have long believed that it is equally important to address epistemological and ideological racism along with psychological and emotional effects of racism situated in US social and political systems and institutions. And secondly, she argues that the acquisition and use of literacy can be seen as a key compo-nent of such epistemological and ideological positioning. To understand the nexus of CRT and literacy, she reviews the genesis, definitions, basic concepts, and tenets of CRT from legal studies, followed by its evolution in educational and literacy research. Pointing, as all of the chapters do, to 'Future Directions', she suggests that work by Literacy scholars will envisage CRT's 'emancipatory and transformative positioning' so that knowledge of racial/cultural positioning will be effected through use of narratives and voice and that this in turn will offer a more adequate route to examine race, racism, and power in society. Literacy, in the sense of narrative and voice, calling upon autobiography, biography, parables, stories, *testimonio*, voice infusing humor, and allegory can expose hidden truths and explicate and situate race, racism, and power within the experiences of people of colour. This, then, is a broader and more 'social' and power laden view of literacy than many accounts simply of acquisition or of reading have allowed.

Moving to another continent, *Kwesi K. Prah* provides a scholarly and detailed summary of Language, Literacy and Knowledge Production in Africa, that likewise brings home the significance of power relations and of different epistemological and language based definitions in understanding literacy. Kwesi locates our view of literacy within the larger purview of language and provides a detailed account of the different languages known to exist in Africa and how they have been mapped by linguists. This is partly in contrast with earlier and perhaps still dominant perspectives that are uncertain what we really know about Africa—the 'uncertainty principle lingers,' as Prah suggests. Following this account we should be less uncertain both about the actual languages but also about their social roles and their relationship to literacy. For instance, Prah indicates the difference to be observed between the languages of the elites and the languages of the broad societal majorities. Education and literacy, in the dominant languages (and in English), have a significant role to play in both reinforcing and challenging this divide. The relationship between oral and written channels of communication and bases for knowledge may not be as clear cut as earlier scholars such as Goody suggested or as superficial views of Africa may suggest—indigenous knowledge, embedded in oral cultures, plays a significant role even as literacy spreads. Following a scholarly summary of the impact of outside scripts and the development of indigenous scripts in Africa in the past century, Prah argues that African development requires the spread of literacy in African languages.

Prah's historical account of literacy development in Africa is complemented by an analysis by *Harvey J. Graff* and *John Duffy* of the development of literacy in western societies. Building on Graff's earlier historical work they argue that our understanding of these developments is often better characterised as 'Literacy Myths' and, like Prah, they throw doubt on Goody's and others' hypotheses that 'the acquisition

of literacy is a necessary precursor to and invariably results in economic development, democratic practice, cognitive enhancement, and
upward social mobility'. Problems of definition and measurement in
particular have undermined such claims. Despite this, as they show,
many public institutions continue to develop policy and practice based
on this myth. In keeping with many of the chapters, for which theirs provides a key conceptual framing, they argue that the myth 'is not so much
a falsehood but an expression of the ideology of those who sanction it
and are invested in its outcomes'. Building on this social analysis, they
document major elements of the myth over time—the myth of decline,
and the myth of the alphabet—and then consider its role in current public
policy. Like many authors in this volume they suggest that what research
can tell us, in terms of educational implications, is that 'there are multiple
paths to literacy learning'. They conclude that the reflections provided
in this chapter 'offer a more complex narrative than that of the Literacy
Myth. They may also point toward new and different ways of understanding, using, and benefiting from the broad and still developing
potentials that literacy may offer individuals and societies'.

Kevin Leander and *Cynthia Lewis* bring these historically based
arguments up to date in a chapter entitled 'Literacy and Internet
Technologies'. In keeping with the other authors, Leander and Lewis
recognise that such an account 'reveals as much about the current
theoretical and ideological paradigms operating in any time period as
it does about technology's relationship to literacy'. Nevertheless, we
learn a great deal about contemporary technologies and their uses in
literacy activity, such as interactive and networked computing media,
and the use of a range of semiotic modalities beyond just print in order
to make meaning, including sound, icons, graphics, and video. They
are particularly interested in 'how networked technologies fundamentally change the relationships of literacy to social relations' and the
chapter provides detailed examples of such practices in and out of
school, including inevitable reference to blogs, video games, multimedia
etc. Maintaining their focus, though, on the social contexts rather than just
the technologies, they point to the location of technologies in fanfiction
communities, in children's learning in and out of school, and in 'zones
of mobility for underserved youth' and argue for multidisciplinary
approaches to understanding such processes.

Jim Cummins has been one of the leading scholars in developing
theory about language development in educational settings and in
this chapter he addresses some of the criticisms that have been made
of his work as it relates to literacy theory. He takes us through the distinction he developed, that has provided the basis for much work in
education, between basic interpersonal communicative skills (BICS)
and cognitive academic language proficiency (CALP). He discusses

its relationship to other theoretical constructs, and shows how it has evolved such as with regard to studies of power relations between teachers and students and with respect to theories of multiple literacies. With regard to critiques that his distinction locates him within an autonomous model of literacy, Cummins argues that there is no contradiction between his theoretical interests and those of New Literacy Studies but that the BICS/CALP distinction has been specifically located in educational settings where likewise different literacies may be operationalised: 'One can accept the perspective that literacies are multiple, contextually specific, and constantly evolving (as I do) while at the same time arguing that in certain discursive contexts it is useful to distinguish between conversational fluency and academic language proficiency'. This latter stance is developed later in the volume in the account of 'academic literacies' by Mary Lea and what the argument indicates is that the authors in this Volume, whilst strongly grounded in the scholarship of their field, are using their chapters to develop key arguments and debates, not just providing lists of previous knowledge. In that spirit he concludes by seeing future directions in the field being dependent on 'teachers, students, and researchers working together in instructional contexts collaboratively pushing (and documenting) the boundaries of language and literacy exploration'.

John Edwards picks up exactly this nexus of researchers and practitioners as the site for development of our understanding of that dimension of literacy concerned with 'Reading: Attitudes, Interests, Practices'. He argues for the importance of the social psychology of reading, that attends to the 'questions of what people read, how much they read, and the purposes and effects of their reading' and not just the technical decoding skills that continue to dominate the literature and to influence policy and educational design. In this vein, he argues that 'in many modern societies, *aliteracy* is as much an issue as functional literacy. It is certainly more compelling in a social-psychological sense, because the question here is why some of those who *can* read *don't* read'. He summarises the research literature that considers what and why people read rather than more narrowly their cognitive skills, using surveys such as the Roehampton Institute's study of children's reading habits in the UK. He addresses through such studies, issues of gender differences in reading, the difficulty of measurement and questions of content and preferences such as fiction and non fiction, citing also his own survey of children's reading habits that combined large respondent numbers with detailed assessment instruments. Despite a long record of such work, he still sees 'future directions' as needing to move beyond descriptive to more robust theoretical perspectives. One possibility here might be the marrying of the more 'technical' approaches with the more social ones evident in his work and that of others in the volume.

A number of the chapters reviewed so far indicate that understanding of the relationship between gender and literacy is crucial to such new social and theoretical approaches. *Gemma Moss* provides an incisive overview of work in this field, linking it especially to educational interests. She notes that interest in gender and literacy has recently shifted from concern for girls to current worries about boys' underachievement. She links this to the current dominance of performance-management cultures and their aim of securing maximum homogeneity in outcomes from education. Literacy plays a leading role in these debates but, as we have seen with other chapters, its definition is contingent on both specific contextual issues and broader policy frames, such as the concern for 'homogeniety' identified by Moss. Moss firstly summarises debates in the field, notably the two strands represented by feminist concern with content on the one hand and those more focussed on literacy learning on the other. By the 1990s it was boys' underperformance that became a centre of attention and she provides close summaries of different perspectives on this theme, addressing views of what needed to be 'fixed'. Her own position focuses on what she sees as the 'turn in analysis from what the curriculum says directly about gender to how the curriculum orders its knowledge base and regulates knowers' and she wonders whether this might be the best direction for committed researchers to turn. New regimes of accountability and managerialism, she suggests, may create new struggles for gender politics and the role of literacy may take on a different hue in this context than it did in earlier ones.

Peter Freebody addresses many of the themes raised so far, under the heading of 'Critical Literacy Education' for which he provides a sub heading that indicates the focus of the chapter: On Living with 'innocent language'. What he means by this is that 'Socialization entails, among other things, using language as if its relation to material and social realities were innocent and natural—transparently determinable, fixed, singular, and portable'. It is this critical reflection on language that provides a grounding for likewise critical perspectives on literacy, a link that occurs in a number of other chapters in this Volume (e.g. *Sichra, Leung, Farr*). The educational dimension of this, especially, involves the contest between training students to critically think and providing regulatory frameworks. He summarises early accounts of this contestation and its significance for literacy in both theory and practice and then describes a 'loose affiliation of theories' that have particularly focussed on literacy in education. He then identifies some of the problems currently facing critical theories generally, notably their particular expressions in different disciplines, and 'tussles between these disciplines for the ownership of the essence of the critical literacy education project'. He lists a set of questions that critical literacy theorists will have to address and attempts to articulate in a succinct conclusion exactly what distinguishes the field:

"There is a positive thesis at the heart of critical literacy pedagogies, methodologies, and practices: Interpreting and producing texts is a way of rendering experience more understandable, of transforming experience through the productive application of epistemological, ideological, and textual resources, thereby re-visiting and re-understanding experience though active work on articulating the 'stuff' of experience and on re-articulating the experience of others"

An appropriate conclusion to the first Section of this Volume is provided by *Viniti Vaish* whose chapter 'Biliteracy and Globalization' brings together many of the themes raised, within the wider context of global movements. Building on Hornberger's seminal work on bi-literacy, she asks telling questions about who meets around what texts in the new global flows. More precisely, she asks 'What does a biliterate text in our globalizing world look like?', a question addressed (as do others in this volume) to both in and out of school. As a way of addressing these questions, she provides data from two countries where she conducted research—India and Singapore. In 'Early Developments' she provides a helpful summary of theoretical work in globalisation and in the field of biliteracy and raises a number of themes that emerge from putting these areas together: 'changing media of instruction in national school systems, new literacies required in the workplace, the threatened linguistic ecology of the globe, and finally biliterate textual practices influenced by the internet'. She concludes with a brief summary of some of the problems that work in these areas signals, notably what implications new texts and practices have for the bilingual classroom, a theme that complements the questions raised by Street in the opening chapter. Future directions will include studies of local workplaces and their relationship to global markets and what role schools play in providing the skills needed in these new contexts. Many of the chapters in subsequent sections of this volume address these issues from their own specific contexts and the theme of literacy, language and education runs throughout.

SECTION 2: LITERACIES AND SOCIAL INSTITUTIONS

In this Section authors consider many of the issues raised above in the context of specific social institutions in which literacy practices are located. Given the importance of educational institutions for the overall theme of this volume, a number of the chapters address educational issues both inside and outside of the formal institutions with which literacy is usually associated. We begin with a paper on Informal

Learning and Literacy by *Alan Rogers* who points out that formal institutions tend to have dominated not only education for children but also that for adults. In contrast, he explores the learning of literacy by adults outside of the formal learning process. He first reviews some of the developments in our understanding of informal learning, discusses some new findings from research into adult literacy learning in developing societies, and suggests some applications of this to literacy learning programmes in the future. These proposals include a greater emphasis on task-related learning; cyclic rather than linear; collaborative learning rather than individual; real literacy activities and texts drawn from the literacy learners themselves rather than imposed from outside; critical reflection on both the literacy learning tasks and the contents of the teaching-learning materials; changed relationships of the teacher and learners.

Constant Leung brings together two aspects of literacy learning that have sometimes been kept too separate: Second Language learning and Academic Literacies. He points out that literacy learning has often been seen as a matter of moving to a second language, frequently English in formal educational contexts in many parts of the world. However, the ability to communicate informally for social purposes in a second language does not automatically translate into effective academic use, particularly in relation to reading and writing. Some of the requirements of academic literacy, as we saw in Cummins' piece and as Mary Lea also points out in her paper, may be specific to that context and not easily derived from more everyday social uses of a second language (L2). Drawing upon communicative approaches to language learning he concludes that we need to move beyond general abstractions and take account of the actual ways in which students and tutors do things with language in context, as a way to then facilitate the learning of academic literacy in context.

Vivian Gadsden brings together many of the themes raised by other authors under the heading of Family Literacy. She notes the shift in this as in other such topic areas within the overall field of literacy, from a more normative perspective focused on an autonomous model of literacy to a more analytic approach based on the notion of multiple literacies. In particular she cites the traditional deficit views that informed family literacy policy and shows how more recent research has looked more broadly at the cultural and social dimensions of learning and the contexts in which it occurs. Future work, then, is likely to address a more in depth focus on and analysis of culture, attention to gender and identity, and recognition of the different learning environments for families and their literacies. Understanding of variation and difference seems to be the underlying theme here, as in many of the chapters. Gadsden concludes by recognising just what a challenge this shift of agenda and perspective entails.

Gadsden's reference to gender here echoes that by Gemma Moss in Section 1, which provided an overview of the ways in which gender issues have been raised in the context of literacy learning. *Anna Robinson-Pant* now provides an application of some of these themes in the field of Literacy and Development. She reviews early programmes that focused on Women in Development (WiD) and charts the change to a Gender and Development (GAD) approach. Current work in feminist and 'ideological' approaches to literacy, informed by the New Literacy Studies challenges the dominant agenda evident in the programmes of development agencies. She concludes by noting the slow movement towards a rights perspective on literacy and argues that the growing popularity of qualitative research approaches within this area suggests that a gendered perspective on literacy and development may be more evident in the future.

Still working within the development context, *Roshan Chitrakar and Bryan Maddox* describe A Community Literacies Project in Nepal in which many of the principles raised by authors so far, including by Anna Robinson-Pant who also worked in Nepal, are worked through in practice. They begin with the principle enshrined in the programme that local meanings and uses of literacy should inform the design and implementation of adult literacy programmes, and that literacy programmes should respond, and be flexible to people's expressed needs. They describe how this principle was worked through in a number of sites in Nepal, and indicate the problems this raised in particular concerning the tensions between the articulation of 'local' meanings of literacy within the wider national and international discourses of development. Indeed this raises questions about any reified use of the term community, since 'local' communities are always shot through with national and international politics and institutional politics, a theme that again runs throughout the Volume and is picked up in the next chapter by *Trevor Cairney*. He looks at Community Literacy Practices and Education in Australia, using the local case to make broader points beyond, for instance, the focus on 'family literacy' that has tended to dominate government agendas. Cairney is especially interested to identify variation in literacy practices within the community and draws upon the home school literature cited by authors in Section 1. One such variation is to be seen in the changing nature of communication and growth in multimedia, of the kind signalled earlier by Leander and Lewis and by Street, whilst another range of community literacy practices is signalled by work in critical theory, of the kind summarised by Freebody who also works in Australia. Building on these insights, Cairney offers a review of the literature that encompasses, firstly, early foundational research efforts that explored community literacy practices as well as the relationship of this work to major theoretical traditions. Secondly he summarises significant recent and current explorations that have acknowledged more complex definitions of literacy and community, with special consideration of work in Australia, including that on indigenous literacy. Finally he iterates the need to problematise the existing research literature in this area and map out possible future directions. These include again a recognition of how literacy varies across home, school and community contexts, and how these relate to other factors such as social disadvantage, gender, and language diversity.

Mary Lea moves from everyday community contexts to the role of literacy in higher education, applying many of the same theoretical and methodological principles as we have seen in other contexts. She explores the concept of Academic Literacies as a way of understanding student writing, which highlights the relationship between language and learning in higher education. She reviews early approaches that tended to see literacy as a unitary skill, looking at work in freshman composition in the USA and notes the shift there and elsewhere to a more social view of writing. Recent expansion of universities, in the UK amongst other countries, has led to concern there too for student writing and approaches from New Literacy Studies, notably the concept of 'academic literacies', have been added to the array of theoretical perspectives. Lea also notes the methodological issues involved here, as approaches shifted from simple 'measurement' of student attainment to new forms of data collection that are more qualitative and ethnographic. She locates current research in the larger context of globalisation and of changing media, of the kind already indicated by Leander and Lewis and by Vaish, amongst others. One new direction she indicates in these changing contexts is for researchers to pay more explicit attention to reading as part of writing, in both print based and virtual contexts and she suggests that this could be combined with research that addresses the lack of longitudinal ethnographic research in specific institutional settings.

Work on literacies in and out of school has already been signalled by a number of authors and *Kathy Schultz and Glynda Hull* look at research in this area in the USA, at the same time offering broader theoretical and practical frameworks for comparative work. They sketch the major theoretical traditions that have shaped research on the relationships and borders of literacy in- and out-of-school—the ethnography of communication, cultural historical activity theory, and the New Literacy Studies—and then introduce recent perspectives from cultural geography and semiotics. Their own previously published work has established a key benchmark for such approaches and they locate this in the longer history of approaches to literacy in both the in-school and the out-of-school traditions. They summarise the recent documentation of literacy practices across the boundaries of school and out-of-school

BRIAN V. STREET

contexts, noting such specific examples as Chinese immigrant youth in the USA, and youth uses of digital technologies and blogging. They conclude by expecting and encouraging research on several fronts: ever changing conceptions of space, place, and borders; multiple identities; and inequality and social reproduction. Many of the chapters in this volume offer ways of addressing these aims in specific contexts, in and out of formal education.

David Bloome then brings us back to Literacies in the Classroom, but now seen from a broader and more methodologically sophisticated perspective than usually serves to pronounce on mandated policy in this area. Whilst recognising the role of 'unofficial' literacies, he focuses here on 'official' literacies. He summarises research on the nature of classroom literacy practices; on the relationship of literacy practices outside of the classroom (in home and community) to literacy practices in classrooms; and on the use of classroom literacy practices for schooling, academic literacies, critique, and community action, many of which have been addressed in other chapters in this volume. His particular concern is with such questions as what is going on in the literacy classroom and how can we research it? He notes recent interest in the cultural and the power dimensions of such activity and cites research that has facilitated students themselves to reflect upon their own community literacies, using ethnographic methods. Such work points towards a way of handling the problems of the next generation, how to conceptualise and to teach literacy in changing times. For instance, communities will variously choose to resist, to adapt themselves, to balance between the local and the global, to incorporate globalisation within their own economic, cultural, and linguistic frames, or some combination. Such choices will affect classroom literacy practices as such choices shift the epistemological content and the context of social relationships. We cannot, then, avoid making the links across contexts for literacy learning and use that tend to be ignored in research and policy that detaches school from its wider context.

SECTION 3: LIVING LITERACIES—SOCIAL AND CULTURAL EXPERIENCE

In this section authors explore in greater depth the specific issues associated with literacy for people in different social and cultural environments, whether multilingual Chicago, post apartheid South Africa or South American communities. *Marcia Farr* opens the section with a classic linguistic survey of the city of Chicago and draws out the implications of such language variation for literacy uses and learning. An immediate link to the chapters we have been considering above is that she sees Chicago as a global city, closely linked to other places in the world economically, culturally, and linguistically. Another is that she addresses the issue of identities in such a context, as linked to the ways of using language and literacy. She takes us through historical accounts of the language map of the city, looks at current demographics that show the linguistic and ethnic diversity and the associated variations in scripts and uses of literacy. Amidst these general surveys she also focuses upon specific examples that indicate the relationship between identities and literacies, noting how use of proverbs constructs people in a Mexican transnational social network and how Chinese migrants use traditional Chinese writing systems. There are many populations in Chicago not yet studied in these ways and the links across communities also remain to be researched. Farr's work provides a model of how such future research could be conducted.

In a similar vein, *Inge Sichra* documents Language Diversity and Indigenous Literacy in the Andes. In particular she provides a review of indigenous literacy in the Andes centering on Andean languages that have managed to survive Spanish language rule and maintain certain functional spaces in national societies and she puts such local language variety in the broader context of national policies and of research interests. Local languages have increasingly come to symbolise ethnic identity and she notes how in this context literacy acquires a driving role in the social participation of sectors traditionally marginalised by their societies. She reviews the literature from seventeenth century Spanish conquest through to current post-Freirean debates, educational reforms and indigenous publishing. One ironic problem is that amidst all of this challenge to central hegemony of Spanish, the language of the conquest is still seen as the model for standards and for education by many in government. Against this and building upon new research directions that are more sensitive to multiple literacies, she sees two directions for research in this field: On the one hand, understanding and promoting indigenous literacy must take as a point of departure the indigenous languages themselves and their characteristic orality. On the other hand, multiple, complementary modes of literacy (alphabetic, graphic, textile) must be taken into account.

Jabari Mahiri shows the limitations of depending upon the traditional view, in this case within cities in the USA, where surprisingly similar issues emerge to those signalled by Sichra and others for different contexts. He looks at Literacies in the Lives of Urban Youth and pays particular attention to What They Don't Learn in School. He sees the urban youth he is concerned with as living in the new digital age, the new times signalled by authors in Section 1 and his work, both in this chapter and more broadly published, can be read as a concrete working through of the implications of some of those ideas. Again he associates local literacies for such youth with broader links to global culture

that involve particular styles of music, language, dress, and other practices linked to hip-hop culture and that serve for core representations
of meaning and identity. He takes us through shifts in literacy theory
as researchers have attempted to come to terms with these changes and
then focuses in on work that began to explore sociocultural contexts like
transnational communities and the uses of new media. In doing so he
draws upon ethnographic work amongst Mexican communities, Heath's
accounts of communities in the Piedmont Carolinas, Gutiérrez's notion
of 'third space' and the work of Richardson whose chapter in this
volume on Hip Hop literacies nicely complements that by Mahiri.
Indeed, his own current research is at the intersection of digital media
and hip-hop culture and he cites others who are building up a rich
pool of data in this field. A key direction, then, for future research
on the literacy and learning of youth is the centrality of practices of
meaning making and representation through musical texts and how
their selection enacts narratives.

Shifting continents again, *Pippa Stein* takes us to urban and rural
schools and out of school practices in South Africa, again pursuing
many similar themes. Her particular question in the context of literacy
and education is: what does it mean, in practice, to design a curriculum
which works towards integrated understandings of South African identities, despite the diversity of races, cultures, languages, religions, and
histories? To address this question she provides a selected overview
of research projects in South Africa which investigate alternative ways
of conceptualising literacy learning. For Stein, literacy is constructed as
a multiple semiotic practice, in keeping with the frequent references
by authors in the volume (Leander and Lewis, Literacy and Internet
Technologies, Volume 2; Street, New Literacies, New Times: Developments in Literacy Studies, Volume 2, etc.). She summarises, firstly,
work in post-colonial, cultural and historical studies that explores the
relations between indigenous cultural and linguistic forms in Southern
Africa, which were predominantly oral and performative in nature, and
their interaction with western cultural forms and epistemologies,
including literacy. She then looks at education policy initiated in the
post apartheid era and its implications for literacy learning. Here significant research projects have been conducted in and out of school to
address these changes and their implications in a multilingual and
multiethnic context. Stein herself has been involved in the Wits Multiliteracies Project that has developed classroom-based pedagogies
which are multimodal, multilingual and involve different kinds of
'crossings'. Pointing to future directions, she calls for not only a continuation of the research on out-of-school literacies that she has cited, but
also for research into 'in' school literacies which has been neglected: it
is time to look in much deeper ways into children's actual experience of

literacy learning across the curriculum (as Bloome, Literacies in the Classroom, does in Volume 2).

Switching continent again, *Judy Kalman* provides an overview of research into Literacies in Latin America. Complementing Sichra's account of Andean Literacies, Kalman likewise provides an overview of research traditions in the region known as Latin America and the Caribbean that includes not only the land mass stretching from Mexico to Argentina but also the small English, Spanish, and French speaking islands as well. Unlike many of the other regions mentioned in this volume, Latin America has high educational gender equality. Male and female enrolment is nearly equal and the difference between genders in adult literacy statistics is just 4%. However, indigenous peoples are more likely to be illiterate than other groups and, as with Andean literacies it is here in particular that research and policy are focusing. Kalman provides first an overview of the role of schooling in the region. With respect to literacy she notes that not all prehispanic languages were unwritten; in Mexico, for instance, writing developed around 600 B.C. and was passed on from one culture to another. In more recent times, the role of literacy has been located within national educational development programmes but research suggests that their attention to narrow technical features of acquisition was in practice offset by the importance of literacy classes as sites for socialisation. Again the broader view of literacy described by many authors in this volume points towards new understandings and indeed new data sets. There is now a small but growing body of research on literacy, schooling, and social practice in Latin America. Indeed, Kalman's own study from Mexico, documenting the dissemination of literacy in a semi urban township, recently won the UNESCO International Literacy Research Award. Ongoing discussions in Latin America and the Caribbean around the meanings of the term literacy and its representation in different languages and the recent UNESCO Global Monitoring Report have given more credence in policy circles to the notion of a 'literate environment' rather than simply individual skills and statistical accounts of 'literacy rates'. However, one direction for future research is to study literacy in indigenous communities which continues to be problematic and insufficiently understood. Like other authors, Kalman also notes that new literacies, including graffiti and murals and new technologies will become increasingly important in practice and therefore need to be taken into account in both educational policy and in research.

In the USA similar themes emerge as researchers look more closely at youth patterns of literacy use and their connections with other media of communication. *Elaine Richardson's* account of African-American Literacies complements both the kind of study indicated by Kalman for other continents and also the work on urban youth already signalled in the chapter by Mahiri. Focusing on African American literacies involves looking at how cultural identities, social locations, and social practices influence ways that members of this discourse group make meaning. She takes us through sociocultural approaches to African American literacy education advanced by the various subfields: including sociolinguistics, rhetoric and composition, and New Literacies Studies. Early developments in African-American literacies, as Willis showed in her piece on Critical Race Theory, inevitably involved issues of race and prejudice as the Civil Rights and Black Liberation Movements of the 1950s and 1960s struggled for access to educational and other institutions for African American people. The work of academic researchers played a part here as it showed the validity and power of local dialects, a perspective that has only recently begun to also play a part in the definition and consideration of local literacies. In this vein, researchers have sought to develop literacy curricula using well-documented research on African American language and culture as the basis of instruction. Making visible language and literacy practices that appeared hidden has been a major role of researchers in both educational environments and policy more broadly. The achievement gap for African American children in formal education may, from this new research perspective, have to be explained in terms other than cognitive 'deficit'. Work in progress includes attention to youth identities, links to other semiotic practices: again the role of music, hip hop—on which Richardson has just written a significant book—and new media play a key role. Richardson concludes by noting the contribution of the work on African American literacies to broader comparative study of the kind indicated by the authors in this volume.

Finally, *Eve Gregory* brings us back to the theme of cities, focusing on London where she has conducted ethnographic research on community literacies over a long period but also, like Richardson and others, linking this local knowledge with the broader themes articulated throughout the volume. Cities, she suggests, are the home of many of the world's great libraries, and have traditionally been recognised as a hub of both literacy and illiteracy. She provides, then, a review of existing literature documenting the history and development of 'city literacies', translated into 'literacies in cities'. This is followed by a more detailed account of recent major contributions to the field and trends in research in progress with special reference to individuals growing up and becoming literate at the beginning and the end of the twentieth century in London, one of the largest and most ethnically diverse cities in the world. Looking at early developments in the study of city literacies, she goes back to Athens around 500 B.C., gradually bringing us up to date with accounts of Renaissance cities and then the industrial revolution with its associated class and educational issues. Throughout, the theme has been of cities as both facilitating high levels of 'cultural' literacy and at the same time excluding a great many of their inhabitants. More recent debates have addressed inequality though largely in policy terms through surveys, tables indicating literacy rates and it is only now that the literacy lives of urban populations are being addressed in more qualitative and ethnographic terms. Gregory's own work (with Williams) entitled 'City Literacies' represents one amongst a small number of key contributions to this growing field (along with that of the Lancaster group in the UK and of a UK organisation Research and Practice in Adult Literacy and the recent publication by the UNESCO Institute of Education (UIE) of studies in *Urban Literacy*—see Rogers, Informal Learning and Literacy, Volume 2). New directions she signals will have to include taking account of the literacies brought by the many migrants who now move into cities from rural areas, bringing with them literacy practices developed in their own communities and sometimes perhaps not acknowledged by educators and policy makers. Here, as in Farr's and others' work, the issue of multi-lingual literacies will loom large, whilst in educational terms the key issue will be the 'many pathways to literacy' that such varied backgrounds involve, as well as new ways of addressing the relationship of literacies in and out of formal contexts. Finally new technologies may mean that libraries may no longer be the main repositories of information, giving way to new digital technologies which may be sited outside as well as within new urban contexts.

As with other papers and in keeping with the opening comments of this Introduction, we find that when we address a particular site of literacy practice—in this case urban literacy, but in others as we have seen it might embrace different continents and different time periods—we have to take into account a range of themes that until recently were considered extraneous to the study of literacy: gender, class, race; litera-cies in and out of school; language variety; new technologies and in particular their uses by youth; national policy and its relation to what ethnographic accounts tell us about actual uses and meanings of literacy on the ground. This volume, then, has pointed to such themes as key elements in future literacy research and practice.

Brian V. Street

CONTRIBUTORS

VOLUME 2: LITERACY

David Bloome
The Ohio State University,
School of Teaching and Learning,
Columbus, USA

Trevor H. Cairney
The University of New South Wales,
Sydney, Australia

Jim Cummins
University of Toronto,
Ontario Institute for Studies in Education,
Toronto, Canada

Roshan Chitrakar
Tribhuvan University, Research
Centre for Educational Innovation and
Development, Kathmandu, Nepal

John M. Duffy
University of Notre Dame, USA

John Edwards
St Francis Xavier University,
Department of Psychology,
Nova Scotia, Canada

Marcia Farr
Ohio State University, Columbus, USA

Peter Freebody
University of Sydney, Faculty of
Education and Social Work,
Sydney, Australia

Vivian Gadsden
University of Pennsylvania, USA

Harvey J. Graff
Ohio State University,
Department of English,
Columbus, USA

Eve Gregory
University of London, London, UK

Glynda Hull
University of California,
Graduate School of Education,
Berkeley, USA

Judy Kalman
Department de Investigaciones
Educativas–Cinvestav, Center for
Advanced Study and Research,
Mexico City, Mexico

Mary R. Lea
Open University, Institute of Education
Technology, Milton Keynes, UK

Kevin M. Leander
Vanderbilt University, Nashville, USA

Constant Leung
King's College London, Department of
Education and Professional Studies Centre
for Language, Discourse and
Communication, London, UK

Cynthia Lewis
University of Minnesota, Curriculum and
Instruction, Minneapolis, USA

Bryan Maddox
University of East Anglia, School of
Development Studies, Norwich, UK

Jabari Mahiri
University of California, Berkeley, USA

Gemma Moss
University of London, Institute of
Education, London, UK

Kwesi Kwaa Prah
The Center for Advanced Studies of African
Society, Cape Town, South Africa

B. V. Street and N. H. Hornberger (eds), Encyclopedia of Language and Education,
2nd Edition, Volume 2: Literacy, xxxi–xxxii.
©*2010 Springer Science+Business Media LLC.*

Elaine Richardson
The Pennsylvania State
University, Department of English
and Applied Linguistics,
University Park, USA

Anna Robinson-Pant
University of East Anglia, Centre for
Applied Research in Education,
Norwich, UK

Alan Rogers
University of East Anglia, Centre for
Applied Research in Education,
Norwich, UK

Katherine Schultz
University of Pennsylvania,
Graduate School of Education,
Philadelphia, USA

Inge Sichra
Universidad Mayor de San Simón,
PROEIB Andes, Cochabamba, Bolivia

Pippa Stein
University of the Witwatersrand,
Applied English Language Studies,
Johannesburg, South Africa

Brian V. Street
King's College, Department of Education
and Professional Studies, London, UK

Viniti Vaish
National Institute of Education,
Centre for Research in Pedagogy and
Practice, Singapore

Arlette Ingram Willis
University of Illinois at Urbana,
College of Education, Champaign, USA

REVIEWERS

VOLUME 2: LITERACY

Chris Abbott
Trevor Cairney
Peter Freebody
Vivian Gadsden
Nancy H. Hornberger
Francis M. Hult
Constant Leung
Gemma Moss
Elaine Richardson
Anna Robinson-Pant
Alan Rogers
Brain V. Street

Section 1

Literacies and Social Theory

BRIAN V. STREET

NEW LITERACIES, NEW TIMES:
DEVELOPMENTS IN LITERACY STUDIES

INTRODUCTION

This chapter attempts to survey briefly some of the new directions evident in literacy studies. I begin with an outline of the current theoretical frameworks in particular work in New Literacy Studies, in multimodality, and in theories of technology and artefact before considering some of the educational responses evident in different countries as they come to terms with the challenges posed by new literacies. I also make some suggestions as to why it is that policy in some countries—notably the USA and UK—seems to be facing in the opposite direction to that which this research base tells us is needed.

EARLY DEVELOPMENTS: LITERACIES ACROSS CULTURAL CONTEXTS

New Literacy Studies (NLS)

What has come to be termed New Literacy Studies (NLS) refers to a body of work that for the last 20 years has approached the study of literacy not as an issue of measurement or of skills but as social practices that vary from one context to another. In policy circles, on the other hand, dominant voices still tend to characterize local people as illiterate (currently media in the UK are full of such accounts, cf. Street, 1997), while on the ground ethnographic and literacy-sensitive observation indicates a rich variety of practices (Barton and Hamilton, 1998; Heath, 1983). When literacy campaigns are set up to bring literacy to the illiterate— light into darkness, as it is frequently characterized—those adopting the more ethnographic and culturally sensitive perspective of NLS first ask what local literacy practices are there and how do they relate to the literacy practices of the campaigners (see chapters in Volume 2 of this encyclopedia). In many cases, the latter fails to take; few people attend classes and those who do drop out (cf., Abadzi, 2003) precisely because they are being required to learn the literacy practices of an outside and often alien group. Even though in the long-run many local people do want to change their literacy practices and take on some of those associated with western or urban society, a crude imposition of the latter that

B. V. Street and N. H. Hornberger (eds), *Encyclopedia of Language and Education,*
2nd Edition, Volume 2: Literacy, 3–14.
©2010 Springer Science+Business Media LLC.

marginalizes and denies local experience is, from an NLS perspective, likely to alienate even those who were initially motivated.

Research, then, has a task to do in making visible the complexity of local, everyday, community literacy practices and challenging dominant stereotypes and myopia. Much of the work in this ethnographic tradition (Barton and Hamilton, 1999; Collins, 1995; Gee, 1999; Heath, 1993; Street, 1993) has focused on the everyday meanings and uses of literacy in specific cultural contexts and linked directly to how we understand the work of literacy programs, which themselves then become subject to ethnographic enquiry (Robinson-Pant, 2005; Rogers, 2005).

In trying to characterize these new approaches to understanding and defining literacy, I have referred to a distinction between an autonomous model and an ideological model of literacy (Street, 1984). The autonomous model of literacy works from the assumption that literacy in itself, autonomously, will have effects on other social and cognitive practices. The autonomous model, I argue, disguises the cultural and ideological assumptions that underpin it and that can then be presented as though they are neutral and universal. Research in the social practice approach challenges this view and suggests that, in practice dominant approaches based on the autonomous model are simply imposing western (or urban) conceptions of literacy onto other cultures (Street, 2001). The alternative, ideological model of literacy offers a more culturally sensitive view of literacy practices as they vary from one context to another. This model starts from different premises than the autonomous model. It posits instead that literacy is a social practice, not simply a technical and neutral skill, and that it is always embedded in socially constructed epistemological principles. The ways in which people address reading and writing are themselves rooted in conceptions of knowledge, identity, and being. Literacy, in this sense, is always contested, both its meanings and its practices, hence particular versions of it are always ideological; they are always rooted in a particular world-view often accompanied by a desire, conscious or unconscious, for that view of literacy to dominate and to marginalize others (Gee, 1990). The argument about social literacies (Street, 1995) suggests that engaging with literacy is always a social act, even from the outset. The ways in which teachers or facilitators and their students interact is already a social practice that affects the nature of the literacy learned and the ideas about literacy held by the participants, especially new learners and their positions in relations of power. It is not valid to suggest that literacy can be given neutrally and then its social effects only experienced or added on afterwards.

For these reasons, as well as the failure of many traditional literacy programs (Abadzi, 1996; Street, 1999), academics, researchers, and practitioners working in literacy in different parts of the world have come to the conclusion that the autonomous model of literacy, on which much of the practice and programs have been based, was not an appropriate intellectual tool, either for understanding the diversity of reading and writing around the world or for designing the practical programs this diversity required, which may fit better within an ideological model (Aikman, 1999; Doronilla, 1996; Heath, 1983; Hornberger, 1997, 2002; Kalman, 1999; King, 1994; Robinson-Pant, 1997; Wagner, 1993). The question this approach raises for policy makers and program designers is, then, not simply that of the impact of literacy, to be measured in terms of a neutral developmental index, but rather of how local people take hold of the new communicative practices being introduced to them, as Kulick and Stroud's (1993) eth-nographic description of missionaries bringing literacy to New Guinea villagers makes clear. Literacy, in this sense, is then already part of a power relationship and how people take hold of it is contingent on social and cultural practices and not just on pedagogic and cognitive factors. These relationships and contingencies raise questions that need to be addressed in any literacy program: What is the power relation between the participants? What are the resources? Where are people going if they take on one form of literacy rather than another literacy? How do recipients challenge the dominant conceptions of literacy?

Before addressing educational responses to these new perspec-tives I would like to signal two other theoretical frameworks that are helpful in considering the issues associated with literacy practices in the new conditions in which they operate in the contemporary. One perspective known as Multimodality is particularly associated with the work of Günter Kress in the UK and concerns technology and cultural artefacts.

WORK IN PROGRESS

Multimodality

Kress (2003) argues that educational systems in particular and western societies more broadly have overemphasized the significance of writing and speech as the central, salient modes of representation. It has been assumed that language is the primary site for meaning making and that therefore educational systems should concentrate on speech and writ-ing in training new generations. The work of Kress and his colleagues (cf., Jewitt, 2006; Kress and van Leeuwen, 1996; Kress, Jewitt, Bourne, Franks, Hardcastle, Jones, and Reid, 2005) has attempted to redress this emphasis in favor of a recognition of how other modes— visual, gestural, kinaesthetic, three-dimensional—play their role in

key communicative practices. As he and I say in the Foreword to a book
significantly entitled, *Travel Notes from the New Literacy Studies: Case
Studies of Practice* (Pahl and Rowsell, 2006):

> So one major emphasis in work on Multimodality is to
> develop a "language of description" for these modes that
> enables us to see their characteristic forms, their affordances
> and the distinctive ways in which they interact with each
> other. [Just as] those in the field of New Literacy Studies
> (NLS) have attempted to provide a language of description
> for viewing literacy as a social practice in its social environ-
> ments [so, in Multimodality] there is an intent to change
> many emphases of the past – especially in educational con-
> texts of the most varied kinds—from literacy as a static skill
> and to describe instead the multiple literacy practices as they
> vary across cultures and contexts. (Kress and Street, 2006,
> p. viii)
>
> Kress explicitly links his theoretical and research interest in
> the nature of signs and the shift towards more multimodal
> understandings, with concern for the kinds of social changes
> signalled by Luke in the opening quotation. He argues that
> there is now a burning need to link 'issues in representation
> and communication with the profound changes in the social,
> cultural, economic and technological world, issues for which
> there are as yet no answers'. (Kress and Street, 2006, p. ix)

The kinds of questions this approach opens up for those interested in
education and its role in these new times include: What *is* a mode,
how do modes interact, how can we best describe the relationship
between events and practices, and how do we avoid becoming the
agents producing the new constraints of newly described and imposed
grammars? These questions are different from those often being asked
in schools, as we shall see later, but they may be more relevant to
the age we live in than the kinds of questions that arise from the
autonomous model of literacy. On analogy with Literacy Studies, then,
those working with different modes may need likewise to develop an
ideological model of multimodality. It is in this sense that I am suggesting the present Chapter is concerned with the kinds of questions we ask
and the way we frame them rather than, at this stage, to posit definitive
answers. If we can begin to find answers that will serve us for educational purposes then, I argue, they will arise from having posed the
questions in this way.

There is one further set of questions and of new concepts that
I would like to address before looking at the ways in which educationalists are responding to the demands of new times. These I characterize
as artefacts in our cultural activity.

Globalization, Technology, and Literacy

One response to the growing role of technologies of communication in our lives is to overstate their ability to determine our social and cultural activity. This tradition has been evident in earlier approaches to literacy, where overemphasis on the technology of literacy (cf., Goody, 1977) has led to assumption about the ability of literacy in itself, as an autonomous force, to have effects, such as the raising of cognitive abilities, the generation of social and economic development, and the shift to modernity. All of these features of the autonomous model were rooted in assumptions about technological determinism that the ideological model and new social practice approaches to literacy have challenged and discredited. And yet, we now find the same array of distorting lenses being put on as we ask, what are the consequences of the present generation of new technologies, those associated in particular with the internet and with digital forms of communication? While these forms evidently do have affordances in Kress's (2003) sense, it would be misleading and unhelpful to read from the technology into the effects without first positing the social mediating factors that give meaning to such technologies. How, then, can we take sufficient account of the technological dimension of new literacies without sliding in to such determinism? A range of literature from different intellectual traditions has begun to provide answers which, I suggest, if linked with the frameworks provided by New Literacy Studies and by Multimodality, may begin to help us see the new literacies in a fuller and more rounded way (see Schultz and Hull, Literacies In and Out of School in the United States, Volume 2; Leander and Lewis, Literacy and Internet Technologies, Volume 2; and Mahiri, Literacies in the Lives of Urban Youth, Volume 2, for rich attempts to address exactly these issues).

Artefacts and "Figured Worlds"

One such way of seeing is put forward by Bartlett and Holland (2002) who, like Kress, link their account to the social dimension of literacy practices already being developed in New Literacy Studies. They "propose to strengthen a practice theoretical approach to literacy studies by specifying the space of literacy practice, examining in particular the locally operant figured world of literacy identities in practice, and artefacts" (p. 12). Drawing upon Holland's earlier work on figured worlds, they ask us to think about technology and artefacts as resources for seeing and representing the world, for figuring our identities in cultural worlds that, as Brandt and Clinton (2002) reminded us, may exist before we enter them:

Figured worlds are invoked, animated, contested, and enacted through artefacts, activities, and identities in practice. Cultural worlds are continuously figured in practice through the use of cultural artefacts, or objects inscribed by the collective attribution of meaning. An artefact can assume a material aspect (which may be as transient as a spoken word or as durable as a book) and/or an ideal or conceptual aspect. These objects are constructed as a part of and in relation to recognized activities. Artefacts meaningful to the figured world of literacy might include blackboards or textbooks (in the classroom), reading assessment scales, road-signs or signing ceremonies (in public space). Such artefacts "open up" figured worlds; they are the means by which figured worlds are evoked, grown into individually and collectively developed. ... Cultural artefacts are essential to the making and remaking of human actors. (Bartlett and Holland, 2002, pp. 12–13)

If, then, we think of artefacts as tools of self-management and as ways of figuring who we are and what is going on, then when we enter, say, a classroom we will see the artefacts available there—blackboards or textbooks—as not only functional but also symbolic in their ability to evoke the habitus of that social environment. The work of the classroom, its establishment of particular kinds of social relationships amongst participants—the role of teacher, the assumptions about being a learner, the rights to speaking and writing inscribed in situ—is partly done through artefacts. Not only do we enact all of these social practices through personal, human interaction but we also call upon objects that we, or others, have placed there to help stabilize and assure us of what kind of social practice is required. Brandt and Clinton (2002) make this point very clearly with respect to another such social space of literacy practice, a bank:

... if you enter a bank to arrange for a loan, your interaction with the loan officer is framed by a number of objects, beginning with the building itself; the furniture, and so on, proceeding to forms, files, documents, contract, calculator, computer, data bases, the presence of which enables you to interact as loan applicant to loan officer in a focused way. The objects help to stabilize a piece of reality so that even if the two of you engage in friendly banter about some other subject there is still no confusion about what the two of you are doing. Things hold you in place. (Brandt and Clinton, 2002, pp. 344–345)

One might apply similar analysis to the classroom and consider how the objects there help stabilize pedagogic interaction so that, for instance, even if teacher and pupils talk socially about last night's game or about some local gossip as part of their binding and stabilizing social relations, they all know the frame within which this social discourse takes place. The objects help assure them, as in the bank, that the underlying framing discourse is that of teaching and learning within specific institutional settings. Brandt and Clinton (2002) link this local use of objects to their interest in the broader, global features of literacy, using the bank example in ways that again we might extend to schooling:

> Moreover, these same objects—forms, files, contract, calculator, computer, data base—aggregate your loan transaction for use in other settings; you become part of somebody else's calculations—at the local bank, in a regional clearinghouse, maybe eventually (we hope not) in bankruptcy court, etc. Eventually, perhaps, your transaction, aggregated, enters into decisions by a distant stockholder or makes its way into a debate on the floor of the U.S. Senate. ... the interest rates, the disclosure language, the reporting mechanisms, the counting machines all will transform this local literacy event into somebody else's meaning and send it into somebody else's setting where the meanings of the original context will not matter. Objects especially provide for and speak to connections beyond the here and now. ... Our objects are us but more than us, bigger than we are; as they accumulate human investments in them over time, they can and do push back at us as "social facts" independent and to be reckoned with. We find this an accurate description of literacy in its historical, material, and especially technological manifestations. (pp. 337–356)

Similarly in the classroom the artefacts, including those of literacy, signify not only immediate and local purposes but also bring in messages from outside. The equivalent to the clearinghouse and the floor of the Senate may be the local educational authorities and the national ministries as well as broader, even more global notions of the role of education in new times, exactly the theme with which we are here concerned. These accounts of literacy as artefacts, and the references to habitus, practice and discourse can, then, provide us with a language of description, as Kress and van Leeuwen (1996) call for, in articulating and clarifying what is going on in new literacy practices and how they are linked to new social practices on the global stage. The language of phonics and of decoding may be helpful in helping children learn immediate aspects of the letter code (cf., Adams, 1993; Snow, 1998) but cannot provide much help in locating such activity in the broader frames that are continually impinging on our local practices.

PROBLEMS AND DIFFICULTIES; IMPLICATIONS
FOR EDUCATION

One of the most recent summaries of the literature in the field of
New Literacy Studies and the responses to it that we have been discussing here provides a helpful link between these academic studies and
their application, or take up, in educational circles. Reder and Davila
(2005) comment

> As ... theories of context and literacy continue to develop, it
> is important that they connect with issues of educational pol-
> icy and practice. Ethnographically-based literacy studies
> have inspired many teachers and literacy practitioners with
> their accounts of the diversity of learners, literacy practices,
> and contexts and with their insights about the ideological
> content of school-based literacy. But such literacy studies
> are open to criticism that they have not developed a practical
> alternative pedagogy for literacy ... Teachers may be con-
> vinced by the insights of NLS, but they must work within
> the increasingly narrow constraints of the school system ...
> while sociolinguists argue that varieties of literacy are struc-
> turally equal and practice theorists decry the arbitrary domi-
> nance of one form of literacy over another, practitioners
> must decide whether and how to teach dominant literacies
> without becoming complicit in the reproduction of power
> (Kim, 2003, pp. 182–183).

This is a major challenge for literacy educators, whether teaching in
K-12 schools or adult education programs, as contributors to this
volume make evident. Better theories about how contexts shape literacy practices should help teachers to see the literacy events in their
classrooms and programs in relation to the multiple contexts in which
they are situated, including the local classroom context and the broader
and more distant contexts of home, community, and beyond. Insights
derived from such research and the theory-building it would drive
can help educators to develop new models of language and literacy
education with applications to improved curricula and programs.

Educational Responses

How, then, have schools responded to both these insights and the social
changes that accompany them? Amongst the many studies of the links
between ICT and literacy, Abbott's (2002) study for the UK: National
Centre for Language and Literacy; in the UK, and Jim Gee's (2004)
work on video games and what they teach provide models for future
research and practice. One rather negative example of how schools

are responding is provided by Leander (2005), another of the leading
researchers in this field. He describes a US high school that appeared
to adapt to the new technologies by making available wireless access
to the Internet and giving laptops to all of its pupils. The difficulties
such a strategy can cause, as traditional pedagogies clash with new
frames of reference and new literacy practices, provides a case study
for many such encounters:

> Ever since it had implemented its laptop program, Ridgeview
> struggled with a number of contradictions between tradi-
> tional schooling and ubiquitous Internet access. As one
> teacher put it, "We have opened Pandora's box." Even as
> Ridgeview had heavily invested in providing Internet access
> to its students, it has also structured, over three years' time,
> an array of implicit and explicit means of closing this access.
> In short, Ridgeview was a contradiction of social spaces: on
> the one hand it presented itself and technically structured
> itself to be an "open" wired social space for 21st Century
> girls, while on the other hand, official school practices and
> discourses domesticated, or pedagogized (Street and Street,
> 1991), potential openings of space-time provided by the
> wireless network. In official school practice, the wireless net-
> work was "rewired" or closed off and anchored in ways that
> reproduce traditional school space-time (Leander, 2005, p. 1)

He wants to make it clear that it is not his intent to simply offer
a researcher critique of teachers. It is not that researchers understand
what is needed and schools are behind the times. The Ridgeview example precisely shows that schools are indeed aware of the needs of new
technology for their pupils. What the example brings out is the complexity of working with the contradictions such approaches entail.
Drawing upon the kinds of theorizing developed in the earlier part of
his paper, Leander tries to understand and explain those contradictions.
He notes how artefacts located in specific time-space contexts may
bring with them associations and identities that figure other worlds than
those with which many participants are familiar. And then, as the many
writers who refer to the notion of habitus make clear, those participants
draw upon cultural and epistemological values with which they are
familiar to handle these new worlds. It is these conflicting worlds and
their associated habitus that create the contradictions we see in this
example and the many others like it with which readers will be familiar.
This chapter, like Leander's (see also Leander and Lewis, Literacy and
Internet Technologies, Volume 2, and Schultz and Hull, Literacies In
and Out of School in the United States, Volume 2), is about trying to
understand and describe these issues rather than claiming already to
have answers. In this case, the questions circle around the meanings

of new technologies in time-space contexts accustomed to other values and practices. How will change come about?

These approaches to literacy and learning present a dilemma for those in policy circles, such as the "No Child Left Behind" framework in the USA (see critiques in Larson, 2003) or aspects of the National Literacy Strategy in the UK. Marsh (2004), a researcher at Sheffield University in the UK has done considerable research on issues of gender, social use, and Multimodality in UK schools. In the passage quoted here, she exposes the limitations of the official strategy on learning literacy in that country in contrast with what such rich and detailed accounts of social literacies might tell us:

> ... the National Literacy Strategy Framework privileges particular types of texts and producers of texts. All references to producers of texts use the words "writer", "author" or "poet", and there is no mention of producers, directors or creators. It could be argued that the term "author" is used in a generic sense to include authorship of televisual and media texts, but the word is most frequently used in conjunction with terms that relate to the written word. This privileging of the written word is clearly stated in supporting documentation. The *Teachers' Notes on Shared and Guided Reading and Writing at KS2* (Department For Education And Employment [DfEE], 1998b) suggest that, "Although the emphasis in the Literacy Hour is upon books, children should have plenty of opportunity to read a range of media texts" (DfEE, 1998b, p. 7). This marginalisation of media texts can also be identified in the current National Curriculum (DfEE/QCA, 1999). Media texts are not mentioned at all in the key stage 1 orders [ages 5–7] [and only marginally] at key stage 2 [ages 8–10]. ... [There] is a clear prioritisation of print-based texts, with media texts used merely to support children's understanding of the former. (pp. 249–262)

Marsh calls upon much of the literature cited here, such as Kress, NLS etc to propose an alternative approach to the literacy curriculum. She asks; "How might we identify the kind of popular, "socio-cultural literacy practices" evident in children's everyday lives and build upon themes in developing educational curriculum and pedagogy?"

New Directions

In this chapter I have suggested that the ethnographic approach adopted by many researchers and practitioners in the New Literacy Studies could fruitfully link with work in the field of Multimodality and of new technologies to inform policy and practice in education that could help us see and then build upon such practices. The development of an ideological model of multimodality may enable those working in these fields, with different modes and new technologies, to build on the insights developed in the literacy field, starting with the rejection of an autonomous model that might otherwise lead to mode or technical determinism. Drawing upon the rich insights by researchers and practitioners signalled earlier and evident in the chapters in this volume, we might begin to see how we could learn and teach the new (and the old) literacies we will need for the developing century.

REFERENCES

Abadzi, H.: 2003, *Improving Adult Literacy Outcomes*, World Bank, Washington, DC.
Abbott, C.: 2002, *ICT and Literacy*, National Centre for Language and Literacy, Reading, UK.
Adams, M.: 1993, 'Beginning to read: An overview', in R. Beard (ed.), *Teaching Literacy, Balancing Perspectives*, Hodder & Stoughton, London, pp. 204–215.
Bloome, D., Carter, S.P., Christian, B.M., Otto, S., and Shuart-Faris, N.: 2005, *Discourse Analysis and the Study of Classroom Language and Literacy Events: A Microethnographic Perspective*, Lawrence Erlbaum, Mahwah, NJ.
Brandt, D. and Clinton, K.: 2002, 'Limits of the local: Expanding perspectives on literacy as a social practice', *Journal of Literacy Research* 34, 337–356.
Brandt, D. and Clinton, K.: 2006, 'Afterword', in J. Rowsell and K. Pahl (eds.), *Travel Notes from the New Literacy Studies: Case Studies in Practice*, Multilingual Matters Ltd, Clevedon, pp. 254–258.
Cowan, P.: 2005, 'Putting it out there: Revealing Latino visual discourse in the Hispanic Academic Summer Program for Middle School Students', in B. Street (ed.), *Literacies Across Educational Contexts: Mediating Learning and Teaching*, Caslon Publishing, Philadelphia, pp. 146–148.
Department for Education and Employment: 1998a, *National Literacy Strategy*, Her Majesty's Stationery Office, London.
Department for Education and Employment: 1998b, *Teachers' Notes On Shared and Guided Reading and Writing At Ks2*, Her Majesty's Stationery Office, London.
Gee, J.: 2004, *Situated Language and Learning: A Critique of Traditional Schooling*, Routledge, London.
Goody, J.: 1977, *The Domestication of the Savage Mind*, University Press, Cambridge.
Jewitt, C.: 2005, 'Multimodality, "reading" and "writing" for the 21st Century', *Discourse: Studies in the Cultural Politics of Education, Sept*, pp. 315–331.
Jewitt, C.: 2006, *Technology, Literacy and Learning: A Multimodal Approach*, Routledge, London.
Kalman, J.: 1999, *Writing on the Plaza: Mediated literacy practices among scribes and clients in Mexico City*, Hampton Press, Cresskill, NJ.
Kress, G.: 2003, *Literacy in the New Media Age*, Routledge, London.
Kress, G. and Street, B.: 2006, 'Multi-modality and literacy practices', in K. Pahl and J. Rowsell (eds.), *Travel notes from the New Literacy Studies: Instances of practice*, Multilingual Matters Ltd, Clevedon, pp. vii–x.
Kress, G. and van Leeuwen, T.: 1996, *Reading Images: The Grammar of Visual Design*, Routledge, London.
Kress, G. and van Leeuwen, T.: 2001, *Multimodal Discourse: The Modes and Media of Contemporary Communication*, Arnold, London.

Kress, G., Jewitt, C., Bourne, J., Franks, A., Hardcastle, J., Jones, J., and Reid, E.: 2005, *English in Urban Classrooms: A multimodal perspective on teaching and learning*, Routledge/Falmer, London, NY.

Ladson-Billings, G.: 1995, 'Towards a theory of culturally relevant pedagogy', *American Educational Research Journal* 32, 465–491.

Lankshear, C. and Knobel, M.: 2003, *New Literacies: Changing Knowledge and Classroom Learning*, Open University Press, Philadelphia.

Larson, J. and Marsh, J.: (forthcoming), *Framing Literacies: Studying and Organizing Literacy Learning*, Sage, NY.

Latour, B.: 1993, *We Have Never Been Modern*, Harvard University Press, Cambridge, MA.

Latour, B.: 1996, 'On interobjectivity: Symposium on the lessons of simian society', *Mind, Culture and Activity*, www.ensmpfr/-latour/Articies/63-interobjectivity.htm, retrieved October 24, 2005.

Leander, K.M.: 2005, April, 'Home/schooling, everywhere: Digital literacies as practices of space-time', paper presented at the annual conference of the American Educational Research Association, Montreal, Canada.

Lewis, C., Enciso, P., and Moje, E.B.: (forthcoming), *New Directions in Sociocultural Research on Literacy*, Lawrence Erlbaum Associates, Mahwah, NJ.

Luke, A.: 2003, 'Literacy and the other: A sociological approach to literacy research and policy in multilingual societies', *Reading Research Quarterly* 38, 132–141.

Luke, A. and Carrington, V.: 2002, 'Globalisation, literacy, curriculum practice', in R. Fisher, G. Brooks, and M. Lewis (eds.), *Raising Standards in Literacy*, Routledge, London, pp. 246–260.

Mahiri, J. (ed.): 2004, *What Kids Don't Learn in School: Literacy in the Lives of Urban Youth*, Peter Lang, NY.

Marsh, J.: 2004, 'The primary canon: A critical review', *British Journal of Educational Studies* 52(3), 249–262.

McCarty, T. (ed.): 2005, *Language, Literacy, and Power in Schooling*, Lawrence Erlbaum, Mahwah, NJ.

Pahl, K. and Rowsell, J.: 2005, *Literacy and Education: Understanding the New Literacy Studies in the Classroom*, Sage, London.

Pahl, K. and Rowsell, J. (eds.): 2006, *Travel Notes from the New Literacy Studies: Case Studies in Practice*, Multilingual Matters Ltd, Clevedon.

Reder, S. and Davila, E.: 2005, 'Context and literacy practices', *Annual Review of Applied Linguistics* 25, 170–187.

Rogers, A.: 2003, *What is the Difference? A New Critique of Adult Learning and Teaching*, National Institute of Adult Continuing Education, Leicester, UK.

Rogers, A. (ed.): 2005, *Urban Literacy: Communication, Identity and Learning in Urban Contexts*, UNESCO, Hamburg, Germany.

Snow, C., Burns, M., and Griffin, P. (eds.): 1998, *Preventing Reading Difficulties in Young Children*, National Academy Press, Washington, DC.

Street, B.: 2003, 'What's "new" in New Literacy Studies? Critical approaches to literacy in theory and practice', *Current Issues in Comparative Education* 5(2), retrieved on May 12, 2003, from http://www.tc.columbia.edu/cice/

Street, B.: 2005a, 'Applying New Literacy Studies to numeracy as social practice', in A. Rogers (ed.), *Urban Literacy: Communication, Identity, and Learning in Development Contexts*, UNESCO, Hamburg, Germany, pp. 87–96.

Street, B.: 2005b, 'The limits of the local—"autonomous" or "disembedding"?', *International Journal of Learning* 10, 2825–2830.

Street, B. (ed.): 2005c, *Literacies Across Educational Contexts: Mediating Learning and Teaching*, Caslon Publishing, Philadelphia.

Street, B. and Street, J.: 1991, 'The schooling of literacy', in D. Barton and R. Ivanic (eds.), *Writing in the Community*, Sage, London, pp. 143–166.

Taylor, D.: 1983, *Family Literacy: Young Children Learning to Read and Write*, Heinemann, Portsmouth, NH.

ARLETTE INGRAM WILLIS

CRITICAL RACE THEORY

INTRODUCTION

Critical race theory (CRT) is the latest iteration of the struggle by people of color in the USA for freedom. It builds upon earlier efforts of political and social activism by César Chavez, Anna Julia (Haywood) Copper, Frederick Douglass, Martin Luther King, Rosa Parks, W. E. B. Du Bois, Sojourner Truth, David Walker, Carter G. Woodson, Malcolm X., and many unsung heroes of all races, but especially those from the US Black Power and Chicano Movements. CRT can be characterized as a modern day response to Walker's (1830) charge that African Americans develop "a spirit of inquiry and investigation respecting our miseries and wretchedness" in this *Republic Land of Liberty* (p. 5, emphasis in the original). Long before CRT emerged, African American scholars and educators (Cooper, 1892; Douglass, 1845; DuBois, 1899, 1903; and Woodson, 1933) critically examined relationships among race, law, and education to reveal the oppression under which African Americans suffered in US society. These scholars offered alternative perspectives of their humanity that challenged the legal system and dominant and racist ideas promoted in science and education. CRT is not limited to individual acts of prejudice; activists and scholars have long believed that it is equally important to address epistemological and ideological racism along with psychological and emotional effects of racism situated in US social and political systems and institutions. A review of the extant literacy research reveals that scholars are using CRT to form a body of literature that, collectively, is in opposition to the traditional, sanctioned, and celebrated research that so often forms the core body of knowledge in the field. To understand the nexus of CRT and literacy, it is imperative to review the genesis, definitions, basic concepts, and tenets of CRT from legal studies, followed by its evolution in educational and literacy research.

B. V. Street and N. H. Hornberger (eds), Encyclopedia of Language and Education,
2nd Edition, Volume 2: Literacy, 15–28.
©*2010 Springer Science+Business Media LLC.*

EARLY DEVELOPMENTS

CRT scholars acknowledge that there is no definitive starting point of CRT. They note that it began in the late 1960s and 1970s, in part as a response to the slow and deliberate enforcement of civil rights legislation; as a response to the fledging critical legal scholarship (CLS) movement that sought to redress civil rights legislation, and, in part the failure of the CLS to address issues of race from the perspective of people of color. Crenshaw, Gotanda, Peller, and Thomas (1995a) describe its evolution in a chain of events, beginning with protests of Harvard Law students over the University's response to Bell's teaching of his Alternative Course in 1981, a course designed to interrogate race and the law. Next, they point to Delgado's article in which he reviewed and critiqued civil rights and antidiscrimination law. Then, after scholars of color began to participate in the Critical Legal Studies (CLS) conferences—established by white male left-leaning legal scholars— they found CLS members did not explicitly address issues of race and discrimination or their intersection with the law. Crenshaw, Gotanda, Peller, and Thomas (1995b) argue that both movements "reject the prevailing orthodoxy that scholarship should be or could be neutral and objective" (p. xiii). The CLS conferences of 1986 and 1987 were turning point years for the genesis of CRT as more scholars of color voiced their concerns over the lack of racial consciousness in the proceedings. Finally, in 1987 at a CLS conference, Crenshaw organized the Critical Race Theory Workshop marking a pivotal point of departure from CLS. It was during this workshop that the name critical race theory emerged as a moniker for the theoretical orientation and movement among the scholars who sought to "reexamine the terms by which race and racism have been negotiated in American consciousness, and to recover and revitalize the radical tradition of race-consciousness among African-Americans and other peoples of color" (Crenshaw, Gotanda, Peller, and Thomas, 1995b, p. xiv). Another meeting outcome was a themed issue of *Harvard Civil Rights—Civil Liberties Law Review* entitled Minority Critiques of the Critical Legal Studies Movement (Delgado and Stefanic, 2000, p. xviii). Thus, the genesis of CRT began in contemporary CLS, and, perhaps unwittingly, takes up the charge of Walker as it demystifies the intersection and complicity of law and racism that are so deeply ingrained in all aspects of US society.

Derrick Bell is recognized as the intellectual founder of CRT. Tate (1997) traces Bell's development from Charles Hamilton Houston's rebuilding of Howard University's Law school, to the hiring of Thurgood Marshall (director-counsel of the NAACP legal defense fund), who subsequently hired Derrick Bell (director of a branch of the NAACP in Pittsburgh). Bell's journey as an opponent of racism helped to inform his thinking about CRT. Other early adherents include John O. Calmore, Kimberlé Williams Crenshaw, Richard Delgado, Alan D. Freeman, Neil Gotando, Angela Harris, Cheryl I. Harris, Charles R. Lawrence, III, Mari Matsuda, and Patricia J. Williams.

MAJOR CONTRIBUTIONS

Crenshaw, Gotanda, Peller, and Thomas (1995a) in their text, *Critical Race Theory: The key writings that formed the movement,* declare that CRT does not draw from a singular doctrine or methodology; instead it adopts an interdisciplinary approach that is informed by Black feminist theory, critical theory, CLS, feminism, liberalism, Marxism/neo-Marxism, poststructuralism, postmodernism, and neopragmatism. According to these editors, CRT scholarship is premised on two foundational ideas:

> The first is to understand how a regime of white supremacy and its subordination of people of color have been created and maintained in America, and in particular, to examine the relationship between that social structure and professed ideals such as the "rule of law" and "equal protection." The second is a desire not merely to understand the vexed bond between law and racial power but to change it (p. xiv).

They posit that race is "'real' in the sense that there is a material dimension and weight to the experience of being 'raced' in American society" (p. xxvi). However, CRT does not rest in a black/white binary; it includes Latino/a, Asian, and Native American groups (Parker and Lynn, 2002). Solórzano and Yosso (2001) suggest that CRT is informed by CSL, Cultural Nationalism, Ethnic and Women's Studies, Internal Colonialism, and Marxist/Neo-Marixism and has inspired Latino/a Critical Studies (LatCrit), Asian American critical studies (AsianCrit), and Native American critical studies. It has spawned other critical studies: feminist race critical studies (FemCrit), queer critical studies, and whiteness studies (WhiteCrit). Latino/as and Asian Americans as cocreators address language rights, ethnicity, national origin discrimination, and immigration. Native American scholars also interrogate the law over land sovereignty (Lawrence, Matsuda, Delgado, and Crenshaw, 1993, p. 6). CRT centers on race, yet acknowledges intersectionality or multiple forms of oppression—class, gender, sexual orientation, nationality, ethnicity, language, and immigration rights— exist and are experienced among people of color.

Descriptions and definitions help illustrate the evolving nature of CRT. Bell (1995) observes that CRT takes a "hard-eyed view of racism as it is and our subordinate role in it . . . the struggle for freedom is, . . . a manifestation of our humanity which survives and grows stronger through resistance to oppression, even if that oppression is never overcome" (p. 308). Lawrence, Matsuda, Delgado, and Crenshaw (1993) write that CRT emerged as part of an effort to "confront and oppose the dominant societal and institutional forces that maintained the structures of racism while professing the goal of dismantling racial discrimination" (p. 3). Calmore (1995) situates CRT within oppositional scholarship while emphasizing that CRT is unique as it "challenges the universality of white experience and judgment as the authoritative standard that binds people of color, and normatively measures, directs, controls, and regulates the terms of proper thought, expression, presentment, and behavior" (p. 318). Additionally, Delgado and Stefanic (2000) posit that the CRT movement

> considers many of the same issues that conventional civil
> rights and ethnic studies discourses take up, but places them
> in a broader perspective that includes economics, history,
> context, group- and self-interest, and even feelings and the
> unconscious (p. 3).

Each of the earlier definitions pertains to the use of CRT in legal studies; however, these definitions, or revised versions, have been extended to the social sciences, including education. For example, Solórzano (1997) defines CRT as "a framework or set of basic perspectives, methods, and pedagogy that seeks to identify, analyze, and transform those structural and cultural aspects of society that maintain the subordination and marginalization of People of Color" (p. 6).

Lawrence, Matsuda, Delgado, and Crenshaw (1993) identify six defining elements that capture basic themes in CRT legal scholarship: (1) CRT recognizes that racism is endemic to American life, (2) CRT expresses skepticism toward dominant legal claims of neutrality, objectivity, color blindness, and meritocracy, (3) CRT challenges ahistoricism and insists on a contextual/historical analysis of the law, (4) CRT insists on recognition of the experiential knowledge of people of color and our communities of origin in analyzing law and society, (5) CRT is interdisciplinary and eclectic, and (6) CRT works toward the end of eliminating racial oppression as part of the broader goal of ending all forms of oppression (p. 6). Their work extends beyond theorizing to working to change society through political activism.

CRT is built on a number of foundational concepts that are important to understand. Drawing on the legal scholarship of three of the key leaders in the field, Bell, Delgado, and Crenshaw, select concepts are described next. Bell's theories include (a) *constitutional contradiction*—an analysis of property rights and human rights as viewed through federal laws and where whiteness is valued as a property, both in terms of identity and privileges; (b) *interest convergence or material determinism*—racial equality is achieved as long as it does not threaten the status of whites; and (c) *price of racial remedies*—the cost, in terms of what whites must give up for racial redress of historic oppression.

Delgado's (1995) review of civil rights scholarship reveals that white scholars (1) exclude the scholarship of minority scholars and focused on one another's work; (2) share a limited ideological and perceptual understanding of the lives of people of color; (3) depend on their limited understandings of the lives of people of color, historically and contemporaneously to situate racial problems and solutions; (4) suggest solutions that failed to account for the past oppressions and did little to ameliorate the present for people of color; and (5) support and sustain notions of white racial superiority (pp. 47–51).

Crenshaw (1995) observes two conflicts in the idea of equality under antidiscrimination law: the expansive view and the restrictive view. The expansive view seeks outcomes from the courts that truly affect the lives of African Americans. By contrast, yet complimentarily, the restrictive view is process oriented, it does not recall past injustices or seek immediate outcomes for all forms of subordination, but places its hope in the future on selective forms that do not impinge on the interests of whites (p. 105). Crenshaw acknowledges that some people may experience oppression from more than one source, race and gender, for example. She labels the site of multiple oppressions, intersectionality: structural, political, and representational. Each form is distinctive: *structural intersectionality* refers to structures within society that help maintain domination; *political intersectionality* focuses on politics that surround domination; *and representational intersectionality* addresses how the dominated are represented (Tate, 1997, p. 231). In the latter form, Crenshaw (1995) addresses the racist discourse that supports notions of color blindness and "Othering" that instills, instantiates, and nourishes the use of stereotypes and myths to describe the alleged inferiority of nonwhites (pp. 112–116).

CRT legal scholars acknowledge that the concept of race is socially constructed and is not a biological or scientific fact while simultaneously understanding that this construct operates as "fact" within the USA. Their goal, in part, is to critique race, racism, and power especially as it is used to support and maintain an ideology of racism within the rule of law. They maintain that racial categories are built on the acceptance of two fundamental untruths: people can be distinguished based on phenotype (as well as physical markers) and Whites are the superior racial group and Whiteness is the norm.

Delgado and Stefanic (2001) explain many of the earlier concepts under slightly different labels: interest convergence (material determinism and racial realism), revisionist history, critique of liberalism, and structural determinism (tools of thought and the dilemma of law reform and the empathic fallacy). In addition, they acknowledge two camps among CRT theorists, the idealists and the realists. Idealists acknowledge that race is a social construct and focus on matters of ideology and discourse (words, mental images, thinking, perceptions) held by individuals as well as sustained by institutions. Realists also acknowledge race as a social construction and the power of words to perpetuate the idea of race and racism; however, they hold that racism is a dominating influence that is sustain through societal, political, and legal structures.

More recent scholarship by Ladson-Billings and Tate (1995) and Tate (1995) has explored these ideas as well as Latina/o scholars, Fernandez (2002), Solórzano and Yosso (2001), and Villenas (1996), to name a few. Likewise, Smith (1999) in her groundbreaking work, *Decolonizing Methodologies: Research and Indigenous Peoples*, presents a guide for thinking about and pursuing research among Indigenous peoples. She observes, however, that the very word "research" is problematic among Indigenous folk in part because their life ways have been so misunderstood and misinterpreted by outsiders. Grande (2000) also adopts an Indigenous perspective that dictates research among indigenous peoples must acknowledge "a cultural orientation, a set of values, a different conceptualization of such things as time, space and subjectivity, different and competing theories of knowledge, highly specialized forms of language, and structures of power" (p. 42). Collectively, these scholars argue that critical theorizing must be disemboweled from Eurocentric perspectives if it is to be useful in education and literacy research. CRT's more explicit interdisciplinary nature continues to evolve and its influence offers scholars alternative epistemological concepts and methods to address the history and contemporary use of privileged paradigms and institutional structures and practices. For example, Pendergast (2002) adopts CRT in her review of the intersection of literacy, race, and federal law. She offers a legal time line to consider these issues using primary source documents to illustrate sociohistorical contexts, legal arguments, and biographies of the major stakeholders. Much like Crenshaw, Gotanda, Peller, and Thomas (1995a), she claims "civil rights ... has been sacrificed for property rights ... and that White identity has been legally recognized as having property value" (p. 208). Further, Pendergast demonstrates how the U.S. Supreme Court adopted a framework that equated Whiteness and literacy as property of Whites. She opines, "the ideologies of literacy supporting the *Brown* decision may have propelled the Court to condemn segregation, but the goal of ensuring equality of education remained elusive and the true character of racial discrimination remained unrecognized" (p. 216). Pendergast concludes that situating the (reoccurring) idea of a national "literacy crisis" is a blind that has help stall the Civil Rights Movement.

PROBLEMS AND DIFFICULTIES

From the onset CRT has been beset with critics that have attacked theorizing about the intersection of the law and race. General themes emerged that include (1) challenges to the use of narratives or storytelling as nonobjective and nongeneralizable, (2) questions about whether "playing the race card" is being too negative, and (3) objections to alleged essentialism and exceptionalism. Similarly, CRT's legitimacy is questioned in education and literacy research because it challenges the basic assumptions that have been used to define and normalize language and literacy as reflective of Eurocentric beliefs and values. CRT threatens to disrupt power and unshackle voices that espouse alternative ideas. To underscore this idea, Brookfield (2003) acknowledges theorizing in education suggests an "unproblematic Eurocentrism .... [that] reflects the racial membership of 'official' knowledge producers in the field" (p. 497). By contrast, CRT exposes how race (as a social construct and lived experience) is central to understanding the deep relationship within privileged paradigms. Darder and Torres (2005) appreciate the role of race, but opine that as race punctuates the CRT literature there is resistance to engage in discourse around race, a resistance that has effectively hampered CRT's use. They suggest that classism is a more powerful determiner of status and by explicitly addressing classism discussions of social justice and equity issues in the USA can be occur. It is important, however, to avoid constructing a hierarchy of oppression and focus, instead, on challenging the basic assumptions that have been deliberately used in education research to shield their role and power to shape how language and literacy are used, understood, and assessed.

There are countless literacy studies that focus on participants of color, from beginning reading to achievement gap differences to transactions with text; however, few scholars have applied CRT theorizing, methods, or analysis. Specific reoccurring themes occur as problematic when race is used as a descriptor and when its social construction and lived realities are not acknowledged or addressed, or deconstructed. First, the language used to describe race centers on color imagery (associated with skin color) and code words that consistently, and unfavorably, identify students of color. Code words typically associated with students of color are: at-risk, lazy, low expectations, ignorant, urban, unmotivated, underachievers, struggling, and low income. By contrast, code words typically associated with white students are: high achievers, high expectations, knowledgeable, suburban, exceptional, industrious, motivated, hardworking, and middle income. Many white literacy researchers claim the words are race-neutral or color blind and merely used to identify students and student performance. CRT deconstructs the discourse of color imagery, code words, and euphemisms, as it situate and clarify the unstated presumptions about people of color that underpin their use.

Second, although literacy scholars have used critical lenses to explore issues of equity and social injustice, few have explicitly adopted a race consciousness. Many literacy researchers have characterized race as a variable, identity, pathology, and cause célébre, but seldom as a framework for research. Morrison (1992) observes that in this sense, race is a metaphor, "a way of referring to and disguising forces, events, classes, and expressions of social decay and economic division far more threatening to the body politic than biological 'race' ever was" (p. 63). Likewise, Grande (2000) notes that race/ethnicity as one form of difference and more fluid, postmodern descriptions of hybridity. She criticizes theorists who "aim to explode the concretized categories of race, class, gender, and sexuality and to claim the intersections the borderlands— as the space to create a new culture—una cultures mestiza—in which the only normative standard is hybridity and all subjects are constructed as inherently transgressive" (p. 47). Such positioning creates a veneer of difference as it resists identification while simultaneously seeking to expose the lives of oppressed or marginalized people whose use of popular culture reflect their race/ethnicity, class, gender, sexual orientation, religion, and geography.

Third, some literacy researchers seek to normalize narratives or storytelling of people of color by foregrounding and retelling the stories of oppression and racism within a Eurocentric frame. Brookfield (2003) characterizes this stance as a "heroic narrative of White alliance-building" (p. 519) that seeks to neutralize the oppression of nonwhites by pointing to similar circumstances undergone by whites. Some literacy researchers, for instance, use an immigrant analogy to suggest that standards, merit, and benchmarks are colorblind, thus the lack of academic accomplishment among students of color is their own failing (while dismissing a history of educational inequality and racist theories and practices).

WORK IN PROGRESS

For decades, educational researchers have embraced critical theory to address inequalities and social justice. Their work is grounded in variations of Marxist theory and cultural studies, inspired by generations of

Frankfurt School scholars, Paulo Freire, Stuart Hall, and others. They seek to expose the ideological and cultural hegemony used by dominant groups to maintain power over others. They believe that explicating the assumptions that have been used to uphold positivism are important before reform and change in education can occur. They do not believe that positivism or empirical science holds the only key to change in education; in fact, they envision change as an outgrowth of more critical conscious awareness and the valuing of all cultures and languages. Further, they reason that social and institutional structures must be dismantled and rebuilt in a more humane manner and where critical theory is translated into praxis. Educational researchers who have adopted CRT have done so because they believe that critical theory has failed to adequately address the historical and present-day contexts of race, racism, and power, in much the same way that CRT legal scholars questioned the intersection of race, racism, and the law. Education scholars that embrace CRT call for race, racism, and power to be squarely addressed, beyond the emphatic fallacy that abounds in education. Their work uses theory(ies), methods, and analyses to comprehend and explain the realities of the lives and experiences of people of color living in racialized societies.

In educational research, CRT is located in theoretical essays, reviews of research, and identity and pedagogical studies. For over a decade, several scholars have adapted CRT as a lens in their work: Ladson-Billings and Tate (1995), Tate (1996, 1997), Solórzano (1997), Solórzano, Ceja, and Yosso (2000), Solórzano and Yosso (2001, 2002), and Parker and Lynn (2002). Tate's (1997) comprehensive review, for example, describes the history and major themes of CRT, draws implications from legal scholarship, and extends the goal of CRT to eliminate all forms of oppression to education (p. 234). He also envisions applications of CRT's themes and methods in his recommendations for education research.

Solórzano, Ceja, and Yosso (2000) stress that CRT in education "simultaneously attempts to foreground race and racism in the research as well as challenge the traditional paradigms, methods, texts, and separate discourse on race, gender, and class by showing how these social constructs intersect to impact on communities of color" (p. 63). Drawing on these concepts, Solórzano and Yosso (2001, 2002) adapted the tenets of CRT for education as follows: "(a) the centrality of race and racism and their intersectionality with other forms of subordination, (b) the challenge to the dominant ideology, (c) the commitment to social justice, (d) the centrality of experiential knowledge, and (e) the transdisciplinary perspective" (p. 63).

Ladson-Billings and Donnor (2005) extend current understandings of CRT to include, more explicitly, the moral and ethical epistemologies espoused and used by scholars of color. They call for researchers to adopt an antiessentialist stance toward a unified or common experience among people of color and within any one racial group and move toward human liberation and activism. Further, they describe the work of a growing number of scholars of color from multiple racial/ethnic groups in the USA whose work centers on race, racism, and power as they resist racial and social injustice. Importantly, they point to how CRT's use of multiple consciousnesses is being embraced globally through the use of post/de/colonial theories that resituate the fight against oppression and the struggle for freedom beyond US borders, by acknowledging that imperialism exists in developing nations and unstable 'hot spots,' where the struggle for freedom continues.

Moreover, Landson-Billings and Donner reveal how CRT clarifies that all researchers speak from their own perspectives (gender, race/ethnicity, class, sexual orientation, religious, and geographical), however scholars of color also "must know the intellectual antecedents of their cultural, ethnic, or racial group. ... for combating the persistent ideology of white supremacy that denigrates the intellectual contributions of others" (p. 292). They also call for the replacement of ideas, i.e., universality, objectivity, generalizability, and empirical, with an engagement in "moral and ethic research and scholarship" (p. 298). They believe that research should address the lived reality of people in a racialized society and seek to eliminate the reproduction of myths, assumptions, and stock stories. They promote CRT as a theoretical position that "ultimately will serve people and lead to human liberation" (p. 291). Finally, they call for educational research that is more openly political and activist.

Solórzano and Yosso (2002) argue CRT methodology is theoretically grounded research that:

> a. foregrounds race and racism in all aspects of the research process; b. challenges the traditional research paradigm, texts, and theories used to explain the experiences of people of color; c. offers a liberatory or transformative solution to racial, gender, and class subordination; d. focuses on the racialized, genderd, and classed experiences of students of color; e. uses the interdisciplinary knowledge base of ethnic studies, women's studies, sociology, history, humanities, and the law to better understand the experiences of students of color. (p. 24)

Literacy scholars have used critical lenses to explore issues of equity and social injustice, but few have explicitly adopted a race consciousness. There are a number of literacy studies that focus on participants of color, from beginning reading to achievement gap differences to transactions with text; however, few scholars have applied CRT theorizing, methods, or analysis. The application of CRT in literacy research encourages a more proactive advocacy role for researchers as they develop under-standings about race, racism, and power that move beyond stereotypical assumptions to understand how race and privilege pervade literacy research from conceptualization to implementation.

A review of the extant literacy research reveals that scholars are using CRT to form a body of literature that, collectively, is in opposition to traditional or mainstream literacy, research. CRT scholars draw from multiple racial/ethnic epistemologies to situate their work (Delgado Bernal, 1998; Duncan, 2002, 2005; Fernandez, 2002; Gonzalez, 2001; Villenas, 1996). Significantly, they ask questions that challenge pre-conceived notions about the beliefs, values, knowledge, and ways of making meaning held by people of color. A CRT framework reveals the importance of literacy in the lives of people of color and how lit-eracy use is multidimensional, multitextual, and multifaceted. This body of research explicates the multiple consciousnesses and multiple literacies that people of color use in their lives, and, most impor-tantly validates that people of color are "holders and creators of knowl-edge" (Delgado Bernal, 2002, p. 108).

Equally important is acknowledging intersectionality in the lives of people of color, which helps to clarify how multidimensional identities are formed and needful for survival within and outside of our commu-nities. For example, Gonzalez (2001) argues in support of a critical raced-gendered epistemology because it permits researchers to "bring together understandings of epistemologies and pedagogies to imagine how race, ethnicity, gender, class, and sexuality are braided with cultural knowledge, practices, spirituality, formal education, and the law" (p. 643). CRT offers original and authentic lenses, detailing lives in which literacy is essential.

A Literacy scholar who has adopted a CRT framework in his research is Duncan, 2002. CRT is not racially limiting as some white scholars also have used CRT in their research (Blackburn, 2003; Pendergast, 2002). Together these scholars also challenge traditional theories of literacy as neutral, objective, and color blind and expose assumptions of white superiority in theories, methods, and analysis. Duncan addresses theoretical, methodological, pedagogical and gender issues; Fisher reveals the literacy connections within the African Di-aspora; Blackburn focuses on intersectionality of race, class, and sexual orientation, and Pendergast tackles the intersection among law, white-ness, and literacy. Duncan (2000) makes a case for the use of transdisci-plinary theories as in his work as his posits that literacy research should include intersectional analyses where racial/ethnic epistemologies are central to understanding and appreciating the culture, language, and meaning making of their participants.

FUTURE DIRECTIONS

To use CRT in literacy research means that we must "re-imagine the role that race—as a structural not just individual problem—has played in our thinking about success and failure. We need to begin to see the relationship between success and community; between failure and the absence of community" (Guinier, 2004). To do less is to continue to privilege an ideology of whiteness in literacy research.

Literacy scholars can envisage CRT's emancipatory and transformative positioning with an emphasis on racial/cultural and experiential knowledge through narratives and voice, a more adequate approach to examine race, racism, and power in literacy research. CRT scholars produce their own narratives that are counterstories to the way culture, lives, and experiences of people of color are depicted. They use autobiography, biography, parables, stories, *testimonio*, and voice and allegory (infusing humour) to expose hidden truths and to explicate and situate race, racism, and power within the experiences of people of color without the need for interlopers, interlocutors, or interpreters of the "Other." Their narratives are exceptionally detailed to help capture the richness of contexts and include revisionist historical information, experiences, and explanations. Scholars also use storytelling to analyze and dispel myths, assumptions, and unfounded beliefs about people of color (Delgado and Stefanic, 2000, p. xvii). They produce stories told from the position of people of color living under racial oppression that contradict or oppose the assumptions and beliefs held by many whites about people of color. Inherent in the narrative forms are voice; that is, the ability of a group to articulate their experience in ways unique to them (Delgado and Stefanic, 2001).

The idea of voice carries with it the notion that individual and group voices of people of color are especially qualified to tell their own stories, without essentializing experiences to all group members. Testifying to the quality of experience does not mean that whites are excluded from research. CRT scholars maintain that some subjects "are often better addressed by minorities" (Delgado and Stefanic, 2001, p. 92). For example, literacy research is dominated by studies that identify participants by race/ethnicity, gender, class, language, and immigrant status. In some cases, white researchers also self-identify by race, gender, or class, although they seldom deconstruct what these markers mean to them and how identities shape their research, their view of the participants, and their findings and recommendations. These white researchers position themselves and their roles as transparent "the ability of whiteness to disguise itself and become invisible" (Delgado and Stefanic, 2001, p. 156), whereas CRT scholars believe that race is visible, tangible, and omnipresent although racism can be overt, dysconscious, or unconscious.

Finally, literacy researchers seek to understand the power of CRT in a more global sense. Some are exploring critical consciousness in African and Asian cosmology and how people draw on these ideas in their language and literature. Others are drawing on the work of Frantz Fanon, replacing the primacy of Freire and Hall, to expose how dominant groups use language and literacy to defend alienation, colonialism, imperialism, isolation, and the oppression of people of color in democratic countries and developing nations.

REFERENCES

Bell, D.: 1995, 'Racial realism', in K. Crenshaw, N. Gotanda, G. Peller, and K. Thomas (eds.), *Critical Race Theory: The Key Writings that Formed the Movement*, New Press, New York.

Blackburn, M.: 2003, 'Exploring literacy performances and power dynamics at The Loft: Queer youth reading the world and the word', *Research in the Teaching of English* 37(4), 467–490.

Brookfield, S.: 2003, 'Racializing the discourse of adult education', *Harvard Educational Review* 73(4), 497–523.

Calmore, J.O.: 1995, 'Critical race theory, Archie Shepp, and fire music: Securing an authentic intellectual life in a multicultural world', in K. Crenshaw, N. Gotanda, G. Peller, and K. Thomas (eds.), *Critical Race Theory: The Key Writings that Formed the Movement*, New Press, New York.

Cooper, A.: 1892, *A Voice from the South*, Aldine Publishing House, Xenia, OH.

Crenshaw, K.: 1995, 'Race, reform and retrenchment', in K. Crenshaw, N. Gotanda, G. Peller, and K. Thomas (eds.), *Critical Race Theory: The Key Writings that Formed the Movement*, New Press, New York.

Crenshaw, K., Gotanda, N., Peller, G., and Thomas, K. (eds.): 1995a, *Critical Race Theory: The Key Writings that Formed the Movement*, New Press, New York.

Crenshaw, K., Gotanda, N., Peller, G., and Thomas, K. (eds.): 1995b, 'Introduction', in K. Crenshaw, N. Gotanda, G. Peller, and K. Thomas (eds.), *Critical Race Theory: The Key Writings that Formed the Movement*, New Press, New York.

Darder, A. and Torres, R.: 2005, *After Race: Racism after Multiculturalism*, New York University Press, New York.

Delgado Bernal, D.: 1998, 'Using a Chicana feminist epistemology in educational research', *Harvard Educational Review* 68, 555–582.

Delgado Bernal, D.: 2002, 'Critical race theory, Latino critical theory, and critical raced-gendered epistemologies: Recognizing students of color as holders and creators of knowledge', *Qualitative Inquiry* 8(1), 105–126.

Delgado, R.: 1995, *Critical Race Theory: The Cutting Edge*, Temple University Press, Philadelphia, PA.

Delgado, R. and Stefanic, J. (eds.): 2000, *Critical Race Theory: The Cutting Edge* (second edition), Temple University Press, Philadelphia, PA.

Delgado, R. and Stefanic, J. (eds.): 2001, *Critical Race Theory: An Introduction*, New York University Press, New York.

Douglass, F.: 1845 *Narrative of the Life of Frederick Douglass, An American Slave Written by Himself*, Penguin, New York.

Du Bois, W.E.B.: 1899, *The Philadelphia Negro*, Ginn & Co., Boston, MA.

28   ARLETTE INGRAM WILLIS

Du Bois, W.E.B.: 1903, *The Souls of Black Folks*, Ginn & Co., New York.
Duncan, G.: 2002, 'Critical race theory and method: Rendering race in urban ethnographic research', *Qualitative Inquiry* 8, 85–104.
Duncan, G.: 2005, 'Critical race ethnography in education: Narrative, inequality and the problem of epistemology', *Race Ethnicity and Education* 8(1), 93–114.
Fernandez, L.: 2002, 'Telling stories about school: Using Critical Race and Latino Critical theories to document Latina/Latino education and resistance', *International Journal of Qualitative Studies in Education* 8(1), 45–65.
Gonzalez, F.: 2001, 'Haciendo que hacer: Cultivating a Mestiza worldview and academic achievement, Braiding cultural knowledge into educational research, policy, and practice', *International Journal of Qualitative Studies in Education* 14(5), 641–656.
Guinier, L.: 2004, *Commencement Address*, University of Illinois at Urbana Champaign, Champaign, IL.
Ladson-Billings, G. and Donnor, J.: 2005, 'The moral activists role of Critical Race Theory scholarship', in N. Denzin and Y. Lincoln (eds.), *The Sage Handbook of Qualitative Research* (third edition), Sage Publications, Thousand Oaks, CA.
Ladson-Billings, G. and Tate, W.: 1995, 'Toward a critical race theory of education', *Teachers College Record* 97, 47–68.
Lawrence, C., Matsuda, M., Delgado, R., and Crenshaw, K.: 1993, 'Introduction', in M. Matsuda, C. Lawrence, R. Delgado, and K. Crenshaw (eds.), *Words that Wound: Critical Race Theory, Assaultive Speech, and the First Amendment*, Westview Press, Boulder, CO.
Morrison, T.: 1992, *Playing in the Dark: Whiteness and the Literary Imagination*, Harvard University Press, Cambridge, MA.
Parker, L. and Lynn, M.: 2002, 'What's race got to do with it? Critical race theory's conflicts with and connections to qualitative research methodology and epistemology', *Qualitative Inquiry* 8(1), 7–22.
Pendergast, C.: 2002, 'The economy of literacy: How the Supreme Court stalled the Civil Rights Movement', *Harvard Educational Review* 72(2), 206–229.
Solórzano, D.: 1997, 'Images and words that wound', *Teacher Education Quarterly* 24, 5–19.
Solórzano, D., Ceja, M., and Yosso, T.: 2000, 'Critical race theory, racial microaggressions, and campus racial climate: The experiences of African American college students', *The Journal of Negro Education* 69(1/2), 60–73.
Solórzano, D. and Yosso, T.: 2001, 'Critical race theory: Counterstorytelling the Chicana and Chicano graduate school experience', *International Journal of Qualitative Studies in Education* 14(4), 471–495.
Solórzano, D., and Yasso, T.: 2002, Critical race methodology: Counterstorytelling as an analytic framework for education research. *Qualidative Inquiry*, 8(1), 23–44.
Tate, W.: 1996, 'Critical race theory', *Review of Research in Education* 22, 201–247.
Tate, W.: 1997, 'Critical race theory and education: History, theory, and implications', *Review of Research in Education* 22, 195–247.
Villenas, S.: 1996, 'The colonizer/colonized Chicana ethnographer: Identity, marginalization, and co-option in the field', *Harvard Educational Review* 66(4), 711–731.
Walker, D.: 1830, *Walker's Appeal, in Four articles; together with a Preamble, to the Coloured Citizens of the World, but in Particular, and Very Expressly, to Those of the United States of American, Written in Boston, State of Massachusetts, September 28, 1829*, Revised and Published by the David Walker, Boston, MA.
Woodson, C.: 1990 (originally published in 1933), *The Mis-Education of the Negro*, Africa World Press, Trenton, NJ.

KWESI KWAA PRAH

LANGUAGE, LITERACY AND KNOWLEDGE PRODUCTION IN AFRICA

INTRODUCTION

This contribution assesses the state of language and literacy studies in Africa. It traces the extent and record of African scripts and debates issues of literacy development in African societies. It poses questions regarding the challenges ahead in literacy enhancement on the continent, and initiates the discussion with an examination of the question of numbers of African languages.

EARLY DEVELOPMENTS

The issue of how many languages exist in Africa, is a complex consideration. Estimates vary very widely. They range from Lord Hailey's figure of 700 to Grimes's figure quoted by UNESCO of "about 2000" (Grimes, 2000; Hailey, 1938, p. 68). Gregersen wrote that, "the nearly 300 million people in Africa speak something over 1000 languages— with only about 40 spoken by more than a million people. Language communities with 1000 or fewer speakers are not rare, and at least 20 languages are reported with fewer than 100 speakers" (Gregersen, 1977, p. 200). Heine notes "the bewildering multiplicity of roughly one thousand languages and several thousands of dialects" (Heine, 1993, p. 1). In *The Languages of Africa* (1970 edition), Greenberg lists 730 languages in his index. The author admitted that, "in the present state of our knowledge, any listing of languages is necessarily unsatisfactory in many respects." Greenberg's listing is inaccurate and displays some of the problems the Center for Advanced Studies of African Society (CASAS) research project is clearing up. For example, dialects of Luo like Shilluk, Anyuak, Acholi, and Lango are listed as separate languages. Bari, Mondari, Fajelu, Kakwa are listed as separate languages when they are in fact simply dialects of the same language. Under Akan, it is suggested that "see individual languages." In the guide to his entry of languages on sectoral maps he explains that,

B. V. Street and N. H. Hornberger (eds), Encyclopedia of Language and Education,
2nd Edition, Volume 2: Literacy, 29–39.
©*2010 Springer Science+Business Media LLC.*

"languages spoken in a number of areas are only entered once on the map." Thus Fulani is only indicated in one of the main West Atlantic areas and not elsewhere. When reference is made to some other language, the number of the language itself is not to be found on any of the maps. The reason for this may be that it is merely a variant name, that the group is too small to be indicated on a map or that they live within the speech area of another people. Whatever the case may be, this way of representation is misleading. Fulani-speakers are to be found in at least 11 countries in the area Dalby calls "fragmentation belt" (an area of extreme linguistic fragmentation), which covers the latitudinal space of the area as far north as the Senegambia basin, to Ethiopia, and down to Northern Tanzania. Fulani is easily one of the largest languages in Africa, spoken by about 50 million people as either first, second or third language; and it named variously as Pulaar, Fulful, Fulfulde, Peul, Tuclour, Fula and Fulani. Greenberg's manner of presentation obscures such important facts about the language and its demographics. These weaknesses have been largely carried into the work of Fivaz and Scott (Fivaz and Scott, 1977).

Mann and Dalby's, *The Thesaurus of African Languages* poses other problems. The authors indicate in their introduction that, "the approach we have adopted is to treat as a 'language' each speech-form whose speakers claim a separate linguistic identity, reserving the term dialect for cases where speakers explicitly acknowledge both a wider and narrower linguistic identity. Linguistic identity is generally manifested in a common name, so that crudely it may be said we have distinguished as many languages as there are names used by communities to refer to their language." (Mann and Dalby, 1987, p. 1) This is unfortunate. A great deal of self-identification in Africa as in many parts of the world is more political than linguistic/cultural in any serious sense. In Africa, many of these identities have been created by a convergence of colonial administrative and missionary activity (particularly with reference in the latter instance to bible translations) (Mann and Dalby, 1987, p. 1).

This confusion of numbers plays into the hands of those who then argue that because there is such a profusion of languages in Africa; since Africa is a Tower of Babel, it is not realistic to envisage the use of African languages as languages of education and development.

What is not easily recognized by many observers is that most of what in the literature, and classificatory schemes, on African languages pass as separate languages in an overwhelming number of cases are actually dialectal variants of "core languages." In other words, most African languages can be regarded as mutually intelligible variants within large clusters (core languages). Indeed, almost all African languages are trans-border languages, and the majority of them cross more than one state border.

MAJOR CONTRIBUTIONS

What the Centre for Advanced Studies on African Society's (CASAS) research has revealed is that over 80–85% of Africans, as first, second and third language-speakers, speak no more than 15 to 17 core languages, based on our clustering on the basis of mutual intelligibility. Africa, for its size is hardly a *Tower of Babel*. If the total population of Black Africa is between 600 and 700 million, (as first, second and third language speakers) the Fula, Pulaar, Peul, Tuculor, Fulful, Fulbe, Fulani cluster alone would account for about 50 million, Hausa and its varieties bring up another 40 to 50 million, Oromo, Igbo, Bambara, Amharic, KiSwahili, Yoruba, the Gbe, would produce another 35–40 million in each instance, the Nguni dialects, the Sotho Tswana, the Akan, the Eastern and the Western inter-lacustrine Bantu (Kitara) languages, Luganda/Lusoga and Luo, Gur, Lingala, Kikongo are between 20 and 30 million per set. Other languages, of much smaller size, but which enjoy preponderance within existing states include, Fang, Nyanja-Cewa, Wolof, Ovambo-Herero, Sango and Somali-Samburu.

Babatunde Fafunwa, basing his viewpoint on David Dalby and UNESCO sources suggests that 120 language clusters have been identified. 85% of the languages are concentrated in the "fragmentation belt." (Fafunwa, 1989, p. 99 & 102) Arguably, the figure for language clusters is actually very much lower. It has been estimated that 75% of the languages in the "fragmentation belt" belong to the two groups of Hamito/Semitic/Afro-Asiatic and the Niger Congo.

Actually, Afro-Asiatic is generic to Hamito/Semitic. In any case the Meinhofian Hamitic theory which suggests that Hamites entered Africa through the Horn area is discredited and enjoys little standing today. Furthermore, whether the Niger-Congo phylum is an offshoot of Proto-Afro-Asiatic or more immediately related to Chadic is evidentially contestable. Fafunwa has reproduced a UNESCO table on, *Languages Used Across National Boundaries* which is rather poor. For example, if Setswana is understood in its narrow sense (that is that it is not a dialectal variant within the Sotho/Tswana cluster but a totally unique language), it features in Namibia, Botswana and South Africa, not two countries as the UNESCO table suggested. In a wider and more significant sense Setswana is part of the wider Sotho-Tswana cluster which includes Lozi in Barotseland. Somali is spoken in five countries but does not appear on the table. Evidence indeed suggests that well over 95% of African languages are spoken across borders.

Another example would be that if Luo is used as a restricted descriptive category it covers parts of three countries (Kenya, Uganda, and Tanzania). In generic usage, in the sense in which it has been used by Crazzolara or Okot Bitek, its coverage will include in geographical scope an area as wide as parts of the Sudan, Ethiopia, Uganda, Kenya, and Tanzania (Crazzolara, 1938). Proximate and mutually intelligible dialects of the Luo language in Eastern Africa for example are sometimes referred to under various designations as Jur (Sudan), Anyuak (Sudan and Ethiopia), Shilluk (Sudan and Ethiopia), Acholi (Sudan and Uganda), Langi (Uganda), Alur (Uganda), Chopadholla (Uganda) and Luo (Uganda, Kenya, Tanzania). Kikuyu, Embu, Meru, Akamba in Kenya are closely related dialects. The Bari-speaking people in the Sudan have been "analytically chopped up" into Mondari, Bari, Nyangbara, Fajelu, Kakwa (Uganda, Sudan, Zaire), and Kuku (Uganda and Sudan). Kipsigi, Nandi, Pokot, Elgeyo Marakwet are not separate languages, but rather dialects of Kalengin. Muerle, Boya, Lopit, Tenet in the Sudan are mutually intelligible. In Ghana, the Akan have been in the anthropological literature referred to as Ashanti, Fanti, Agona, Kwahu, Akim, Akuapim, Nzema, and even sub-units of these like Ahanta, Gomua, Edina etc. The Gbe/Ewe-speaking people can be found in communities all along the West African Coast from Ghana through Togo, Benin and to the Nigerian border area. This cluster which has been orthographically harmonized by the Labo-Gbe Center in Benin and CASAS includes Aja in Badagry/Nigeria, Aja in Benin, Gun in Benin, Mina in Benin, Fon in Benin, Mina and Ewe in Togo, and Ewe in Ghana. In East Africa, the Teso, Kumam, Karamojong, Nyangatom, Dodos, Jie, Turkana, Toposa, Donyiro collectively cover areas in Ethiopia, Kenya, Uganda and the Sudan. The Nguni are found in Tanzania where they closely relate ethno-linguistically to the Nyamwezi, Ngoni, and Konde. They are also located in Malawi. Nyanja in Zambia and Cewa in Malawi are practically the same. In Mozambique, Shangaan/Tsonga/Ronga, are mutually intelligible Nguni variants. But they have phonologically and morphologically grown away from the other languages in the cluster. Nguni in Swaziland is called Swati, Kangwane in northern Natal/Zululand, Zulu in South Africa, Xhosa in South Africa, Ndebele in South Africa and Matabeleland in Zimbabwe. Some classifications even would count as separate languages narrow dialectal sub-forms of Xhosa like Bomvana, Cele Baca, Gcaleka/Ngqika, Hlubi, Mpondo, Mpondomise, Ntlangwini, Tembu and Xesibe. The Sotho-Tswana cluster is to be found as Tswana in Namibia, Tswana in Botswana, Lozi in Barotseland/Zambia, Sotho in Lesotho, and Pedi in South Africa. Again in East Africa, the Interlacustrine Bantu have a high degree of mutual intelligibility. They include the Nyoro, Toro, Haya, Ganda, Ankole, Rwanda. Rendille-Somali and Oromo and Borana are literally closely related pairs. Maasai and Samburu are equally close.

    Heine has identified four key objectives, which motivate the classification of African languages. These are, firstly, the need to bring some order to the multiplicity of African languages (*referential classification*); secondly, a search for origins of these languages (*genetic classification*); thirdly, the inter-linguistic influences between these languages (*areal classification*); and fourthly, the establishment of the structural convergencies and divergencies between African languages (*typological classification*). Heine argues that these different types of classification serve different goals and functions, and that indeed, "non-awareness of the different functions of these classifications may lead to scientifically untenable results." A good example of the pitfalls of this methodological mess is provided by Malcolm Guthrie who "confused two different types of classification by grafting and superimposing a genetic classification on a referential one—with the effect that his reconstruction of Bantu pre-history turned out to be at variance with the historical facts he had intended to describe" (Heine, 1993, p. 1).

WORK IN PROGRESS

The role of language and literacy in contemporary African social life depicts peculiarities which are increasingly unique in the post-colonial world. There is a fairly decisive difference between the languages of the elites and the languages of the broad societal majorities. The elites continue to be social constituencies which utilize erstwhile colonial languages; French, English and Portuguese. The technical instrument required for social performance in the culture of African elites is literacy in the language of the former colonial power. The masses of African countries have little or no facility in these languages. In African societies, the colonial languages are social symbols of power (Brock-Utne and Holmarsdottir, 2003, p. 80). All public business and governmental matters are transacted in these languages, and therefore those that have skills in these languages control all public and government business. These realities are considerably different from the experience of post-colonial Asia.

Indigenous and Colonial Languages and Literacies

About 35 years ago, Gerald Moore made a number of perceptive observations which bear on the considerations here. He wrote that; "In the British West Indies, as successive waves of African, Indian and Chinese immigration spent themselves upon the shore, forgetting in a generation or two the very provinces whence they had come, English in a variety of dialect forms gradually established itself as the unique language of the region. In Asia and Africa it became, at least temporarily, the language of government, of higher education and, more important still, of higher status. In Asia, however, the withdrawal of imperial control revealed how precarious the situation of the language really was. Their volume of literary activity in languages such as Bengali, Tamil, Gujarati, Malay and Urdu, together with the gradual decline of English usage in public life, suggests that ultimately the imperial language may prove as marginal as the English presence itself; whilst in tropical Africa only the recent spread of mass education has offered it the possibility of escape from an equally marginal role." (Moore, 1969, p. xi) In the third of a century, which has passed since these points were made, the role of English in Africa has not gone beyond the narrow elite which is able to use the language with any degree of accomplishment.

By and large, mass literacy education campaigns in Africa have had little impact in effectively spreading the English language. What can however be said is that its role as the linguistic basis for the exercise and the administration of power in former British colonial Africa remains entrenched. Moore added that; ". . . historical experience confirms that a language which remains the property of a small elite cannot provide the basis for a national culture. A recent parallel would be the use of French by polite society in nineteenth century Russia." (Moore, 1969, p. xi) Similarly, Latin could not provide a basis for national cultures in Roman Europe. In contemporary Africa the development of even outlines of national cultures after almost a half-century of post-colonialism continue to be elusive.

Two decades ago, Jack Goody made insightful remarks on this issue. He wrote that; "indeed part of the phenomenon called neo-colonialism has to be seen in terms of this very openness which is associated with the absence of a strong, written tradition that can stand up against the written cultures of the world system." (Goody, 1989, p. 86) Goody's judgement here is persuasive but the additional point has been made that while a written culture has made the resistance against cultural neocolonialism of parts of Asia more successful, what has perhaps been most central in this cultural resilience has been the standing of the world religions of the Near East and Asia proper. Western cultural penetration of the non-western world never successfully undermined the status of the major religions of Asia the way they successfully did in Africa (Prah, 2001, p. 125).

The process of knowledge production in Africa is represented in two histories. There is the indigenous knowledge which precedes the colonial encounter and which has been the result of the age-long transmission of knowledge from generation to generation. The language base of this knowledge in Africa has largely been orally constructed. For this reason as a knowledge depository it irredeemably leaks. Collective memory cannot be held and transferred as integer knowledge with any reliability. With the establishment of western presence and institutions, the processes of knowledge production in Africa were superseded by western modes of knowledge production built into the introduction and use of western languages. This latter form of knowledge production ignored the preceding processes of knowledge production founded on African languages. In effect, two parallel processes for the construction of knowledge were established.

Record of African Scripts

For the most part, until a century ago African societies were preliterate. Literacy based on the Roman alphabet is no more than a century and a half old for the majority of African societies. There are, however, some languages with a long tradition of writing and which employ scripts other than the Roman. The Arabic script has been used to write a number of African languages. Such usage is described as *ajami* in Arabic. They include languages like Swahili, Hausa, Wolof, Fulfulde, Kanuri, and Bambara and others. In all these cases, in more recent times, Roman letters have replaced the Arabic script. The earliest Afrikaans scripts (South Africa) were written as *ajami*. This goes back to the historical record of the early Malay Moslem slaves who were brought into the Western Cape of South Africa from Java by the Dutch colonists. Ethiopic, the old Semitic script from antiquity, is still used to write Geez, Amharic, and Tigrinya, and the Greek alphabet in a revised and adapted form was used for writing Coptic and Nobiin (Old Nubian). Hunwick informs us that; Mansa Musa historically was the best known ruler of the Mali empire. After his return from pilgrimage to Mecca in 1325 he ordered the construction of the Great Mosque of Timbuktu. The construction of the great mosque established Timbuktu's status as an Islamic city, and over the next 200 years Muslim scholars were drawn to it, so that by the mid-fifteenth century Timbuktu had become a major center of Islamic learning under African cultural conditions.

Timbuktu's most celebrated scholar Ahmad Baba (1564–1627) claimed that his library contained 1600 volumes, and that it was the smallest library of any of his family (Hunwick, 2003, p. 2). Libraries supporting the Timbuktu manuscript tradition have for centuries been numerous. There are in Timbuktu alone today some 20 private manuscript libraries and about 100 in the sixth region of Mali (Hunwick, 2003, p. 2). In effect "Arabic was to Muslim Africa what Latin was to medieval Christian Europe (Hunwick, 2003, p. 2).

Over and above all these "imported" scripts, Africa has a few indigenous examples of written forms. Until 1972 when the latin script was adopted by the Siad Barre administration, Somali was unofficially, but popularly rendered in the Osmania script devised by Osman Yusuf

Keenadiid. While it was in form a good part Ethiopic, it had also Arabic and Italian influences.

The Vai script, strictly speaking a syllabary or a catalogue of characters, each of which denotes a syllable rather than a single sound, was created in the 1830s by Momadu Bukele. It remains popular in Liberia, particularly among the Vai, where it is mostly used in informal correspondence. More recently, in the sub-region, Mende (A purely phonetic Mende script from Sierra Leone was devised around 1920 by Kisimi Kamala), Loma, Kpelle and Bassa, have developed related script, which lean on the Vai example. All of these, like the Vai example are syllabaries. An alphabet, Nko was devised by Souleyman Kante in 1949. Till today, it is used very restrictedly and primarily by speakers within the Mandingo, Malinke, Bambara, Dioula, Kasonke cluster, especially in Guinea, Mali and Ivory Coast. A Bambara "Ma-sa-ba" syllabary was devised by Woyo Couloubali in the Kaarta region of Mali in 1930. Between the decade spanning 1920 and 1931, syllabaries had appeared for Mende, Bassa, Loma, Kpelle, Efik-Ibibio. An earlier esoteric alphabet has been in use for about a century among the Efik in southeastern Nigeria. Better known, perhaps, and historically better widely studied is the Bamum script (Shümon) invented and developed under the direction of King Njoya of southern Cameroon. It was originally conceived as a logographic system, and was gradually changed by successive royal edicts first to a syllabary and subsequently to an alphabet (Berry et al. 1970, p. 88). After 1910, his scribes began compiling the chronicle of the Bamum Kingdom. This was finished during the 1920s in the closing years of Njoya's reign (Dugast and Jeffreys, 1950). In sum, specifically in West Africa, over the past century a number of indigenously conceived writing systems have been produced. Most of them have from the start been largely esoteric and invariably religious in inclination. There is also the particularly interesting case of *Oberi Okaime* a language which was created by members of a millenarian sect based in the village of Ikpa in the Itu Division of Calabar Province in 1931. The sect was founded in 1927, but the language emerged in 1931. There is no evidence that the language and script survived beyond the 1930s. None of these African scripts has been effective competition to the colonially introduced Roman alphabet. None seriously moved outside the narrow confines of small exclusivist groups, often semireligious. It is interesting to note that this religious dimension of literacy and scripts is shared by religious communities as historical entities in other parts of the world.

Apart from Ethiopian clericalism, Coptic priesthood and African muslim scholarship, literacy as a sociological phenomenon, in old Africa, never fully emerged. The developers and custodians of the African scripts referred to here like the Efik, Bassa, Vai, Loma and Bamum never formed a composite and coherent priesthood to consolidate, protect and elevate the scripts. This fact may be important in our attempt to understand the absence of literacy in large parts of old Africa.

PROBLEMS AND DIFFICULTIES

When modern literacy came to Africa through the western encounter, the principal agents for its spread were missionaries. Literacy in Africa therefore first made an impact as a way in which the Christian traditions of the west could be transferred to the mind of the African. For this very reason, literacy in Africa introduced by the missionaries was undertaken in African languages, close to the hearts and minds of the people and the first book that was invariably translated was the Bible. Thus literacy for the missionaries was meant in the first instance to serve purely Christian ideals. But rivalries between various Christian church groups and sects were transferred into the forms of orthographies adopted by competing missionary groups. Very frequently rival missionary groups would for the same language, indeed the same dialect translate the Bible using totally different orthographic and spelling systems.

The colonial administrators, especially in the early stage of the establishment and consolidation of colonial rule largely left the tasks of education in the hands of missionaries. The first schools and some of the most prominent schools in Africa today remain missionary schools or schools with distinct Christian affiliation. Slowly as colonial administrations became entrenched, economic, social and political interests move more prominently to the fore in the organization of colonial societies. The administrations were anxious that the products of missionary education could serve the intentions of the colonial administrations. Like Macaulay's intended product which he described in his *Minute on Indian Education, (1835)* for the British Raj, colonialism created "a class who may be interpreters between us and the millions whom we govern; a class of persons, Indian in blood and colour, but English in taste, in opinions, in morals, and in intellect."

Frequently, in the early stages of the introduction of western literacy and education Africans would resist, but with time almost all acquiesced. In British colonial Africa schools like King's College (Budo, Uganda) King's College (Lagos, Nigeria), Achimota College (Achimota, Ghana) quickly acquired reputations for the English literacy proficiency of their pupils. These schools, organized along British public school lines, reproduced in colonial Africa literacy standards in English which permitted pupils to transit from these colonial schools to British universities with relative ease. For as long as colonialism lasted these standards held. Currently in the post-colonial situation from all parts of

Anglophone Africa reports suggest that the literacy skills of students in English are rapidly falling. This is a phenomenon, which is also noticeable in French-based universities in Francophone Africa.

In post-Apartheid South Africa, at university level, poor English communication skills are particularly noticeable amongst African language-speaking students. However, these constraints are by no means exclusive to them. Some lecturers have also pointed out that, the quality of written Afrikaans is also deteriorating. This is happening in a society in which the governmentally engineered supremacy of Afrikaans under Apartheid has over the past ten years been popularly reversed. It is observable that in post-apartheid South Africa, English is fast gaining ground over all the other languages. Although the government on paper has elevated the status to equality of all eleven official languages, in practice there appears to be little use of the African languages for official tasks. In a conversation held with the African National Congress (ANC) parliamentarian Duma Nkosi on the 11 October 2000, he suggested that even in Parliament there are members who battle to express themselves effectively in English. Sometimes the inadequacies of their linguistic expression distort the meaning they wish to convey.

FUTURE DIRECTIONS

Literacy estimates for Africa generally stand at around 50%. But literacy figures for Africa are notoriously unreliable. Apart from the problems of certifiable counting methods, there is the more serious problem of frequently not counting literacy in African languages. Strikingly, literacy in African languages, where it exists, in the absence of literature is tenuous. Literature in African languages continues to be predominantly religious. In many areas, the Bible is the most available text in African languages.

Tanzania is possibly the most successful country in sub-Saharan Africa with regard to literacy in African languages. It is the only country where more newspapers in African languages are sold than English, French or Portuguese newspapers. But even then it is a success story built on one language, Kiswahili. Indeed, on the whole continent newspapers in Kiswahili constitute the overwhelming majority of papers in African languages.

The challenges of democracy and underdevelopment can only be met when Africans begin to work as literate societies in African languages. To do this there is need for the harmonization of mutually intelligible languages so that on the economies of scale the production of literature becomes profitable and cost-wise within reach for the masses. African development must mean the development of literacy in African languages.

REFERENCES

Berry, J.: 1970, 'Language systems and literature', in N.P. John and W.S. Edward (eds.), *The African Experience*, Volume 1, Heinemann Educational Books, London, 88–89.

Brock-Utne, B. and Holmarsdottir, H.B.: 2003, 'Language policies and practices— some preliminary results from a research project in Tanzania and South Africa', in B. Brock-Utne, et al. (ed.), *Language of Instruction in Tanzania and South Africa*, E & D Limited, Dar es Salaam, 80–81.

Crazzolara, J.P.: 1938, *A Study of the Acooli Language. Grammar and Vocabulary, International Institute of African Languages and Cultures*, Oxford University Press, London/New York/Toronto.

Dugast, I. and Jeffreys, M.D.W.: 1950, *L'ecriture des Bamum: Sa naissance, son evolution sa valeur phonetique, son utilization*, Memoires de l'Institut Francais d'Afrique Noire, Centre du Cameroun, Serie: Populations No. 4.

Fafunwa, B.A.: 1989, 'Using national languages in education: A challenge to African educators', in *African Thoughts on the Prospects of Education for All: Selections from Papers Commissioned for the Regional Consultation on Education for All*, (27–30 November), UNESCO/Breda, Dakar, 99 and 102.

Fivaz D. and Scott, P.: 1977, *African Languages: A Genetic and Decimalised Classification for Bibliographic and General Reference*, G.K. Hall, Boston.

Goody, J.: 1986, 1989 edition, *The Logic of Writing and the Organization of Society*, Cambridge University Press, Cambridge, 86.

Gregersen, E.A.: 1977, *Language in Africa. An Introductory Survey*, Gordon and Breach, New York, 200.

Grimes, B.F.: 2000, *Ethnologue: Languages of the World*, Summer Institute of Linguistics, Dallas, Texas.

Hailey, L.: 1938, *An African Survey*, Oxford University Press, Oxford, 68.

Heine, B.: 1993, *Language as a Tool in Reconstructing the African Past*, Raymond Dart Lectures No. 28, University of Witwatersrand, Johannesburg, 1.

Hunwick, J.: 2003, 'The timbuktu manuscript tradition', *Tinabantu: Journal of African National Affairs*, 1, 2, CASAS, Cape Town, 2–3.

Mann, M. and Dalby, D.: 1987, *A Thesaurus of African Languages. A Classified and Annotated Inventory of the Spoken Languages of Africa. With an Appendix on their Written Representation*, Hans Zell, London, 1.

Moore, G.: 1969, *The Chosen Tongue*, Longmans Green and Co. Ltd., London, xi.

Prah, K.K.: 2001, 'Language, literacy, the production and reproduction of knowledge, and the challenge of African development', in D.R. Olson and N. Torrance (eds.), *The Making of Literate Societies*, Blackwell, Oxford, 125–126.

HARVEY J. GRAFF AND JOHN DUFFY

LITERACY MYTHS

INTRODUCTION

Literacy Myth refers to the belief, articulated in educational, civic, religious, and other settings, contemporary and historical, that the acquisition of literacy is a necessary precursor to and invariably results in economic development, democratic practice, cognitive enhancement, and upward social mobility (Graff, 1979, 1987). Despite many unsuccessful attempts to measure it (Inkeles and Smith, 1974), literacy in this formulation has been invested with immeasurable and indeed almost ineffable qualities, purportedly conferring on practitioners a predilection toward social order, an elevated moral sense, and a metaphorical "state of grace" (Scribner, 1984). Such presumptions have a venerable historical lineage and have been expressed, in different forms, from antiquity through the Renaissance and the Reformation, and again throughout the era of the Enlightenment, during which literacy was linked to progress, order, transformation, and control. Associated with these beliefs is the conviction that the benefits ascribed to literacy cannot be attained in other ways, nor can they be attributed to other factors, whether economic, political, cultural, or individual. Rather, literacy stands alone as the independent and critical variable. Taken together, these attitudes constitute what Graff (1979, 1987) has called "the Literacy Myth." Many researchers and commentators have adopted this usage.

Contemporary expressions of the Literacy Myth are evident in cities' sponsorship of book reading, celebrity appeals on behalf of reading campaigns, and promotions by various organizations linking the acquisition of literacy to self-esteem, parenting skills, and social mobility, among others. Individuals are seen to be "at risk," if they fail to master literacy skills presumed to be necessary, although functions and levels of requisite skills continue to shift (Resnick and Resnick, 1977; Brandt, 2001). In stark, indicting versions of the myth, failures to learn to read and write are individual failures. Those who learn to read and write well are considered successful, whereas those who do not develop these skills are seen as less intelligent, lazy, or in some other way deficient (St. Clair and Sadlin, 2004). These and other versions of the Literacy Myth shape public and expert opinions, including policy

B. V. Street and N. H. Hornberger (eds), Encyclopedia of Language and Education, 2nd Edition, Volume 2: Literacy, 41–52.
©2010 Springer Science+Business Media LLC.

makers in elementary and adult education, and those working in development work internationally.

Such attitudes about literacy represent a "myth" because they exist apart from and beyond empirical evidence that might clarify the actual functions, meanings, and effects of reading and writing. Like all myths, the Literacy Myth is not so much a falsehood but an expression of the ideology of those who sanction it and are invested in its outcomes (see, e.g., Goody, 1968, 1986, 1987; Goody and Watt, 1968; Havelock, 1963, 1976, 1986; Olson, 1977, 1994); for contrasting perspectives, see Akinasso, 1981; Collins and Blot, 1995; Graff, 1995a; Graff and Street, 1997). For this reason, the Literacy Myth is powerful and resistant to revision. This chapter examines the scope of the Literacy Myth, considering its varieties, its meanings, and its implications for policy makers in education and other fields who would use literacy in the service of large-scale social and economic transformations.

DEFINITION AND MEASUREMENT ISSUES

Problems inherent in the "literacy myth" begin with confusions over the meanings of the word "literacy" and efforts to measure it. Literacy has been defined in various ways, many offering imprecise and yet nonetheless progressively grander conceptions and expectations of what it means to read and write, and what might follow from that prac- tice. For example, literacy has been defined as in terms of standardized test scores such as the Scholastic Aptitude Test or the Armed Forces Qualifying tests; the completion of a specified grade-levels in school; and a generalized form of knowledge (Pattison, 1984) such as "com- puter literacy," "financial literacy," "civic literacy," neologisms as facile as they are inexact. In other contexts, literacy may be conflated with its desired ends, as when it is represented as "an agent of change," a formulation that confuses relationships of cause and effect.

The vagueness of such definitions allows for conceptions of literacy that go beyond what has been examined empirically, thus investing literacy with the status of myth. Since mythos is grounded in narrative, and since narratives are fundamentally expressions of values, literacy has been contrasted in its mythic form with a series of opposing values that have resulted in reductive dichotomies such as "oral-literate," "literate-pre-literate," "literate-illiterate," and other binaries that carica- ture major social changes. In such hierarchical structures, the "oral," "preliterate," and "illiterate" serve as the marked and subordinate terms, whereas "literate" and "literacy" assume the status of superior terms (Duffy, 2000). Such hierarchies reinforce the presumed benefits of literacy and so contribute to the power of the myth (for detailed examples, see Finnegan, 1973, 1988; Goody, 1986, 1987; Havelock, 1963, 1976, 1986; Ong 1967, 1977, 1982).

We define literacy here not in terms of values, mentalities, generalized knowledge, or decontextualized quantitative measures. Rather, literacy is defined as basic or primary levels of reading and writing and their analogs across different media, activities made possible by a technology or set of techniques for decoding and reproducing printed materials, such as alphabets, syllabaries, pictographs, and other systems, which themselves are created and used in specific historical and material contexts (see Graff, 1987, pp. 3–4). Only by grounding definitions of literacy in specific, qualified, and historical particulars can we avoid conferring on it the status of myth.

EARLY DEVELOPMENTS: HISTORICAL PERSPECTIVES

In contrast with its presumed transformative "consequences," literacy historically has been characterized by tensions, continuities, and contradictions. In classical Greece, where the addition of characters representing vowel sounds to Semitic syllabaries is seen by some as the origin of the first modern alphabet (Gelb, 1963), literacy contributed to the Greek development of philosophy, history, and democracy (Harris, 1989; Havelock, 1963, 1986). Yet literacy in classical Athens was a conservative technology, used to record the cultural memories of an oral civilization in a society based on slavery. Though achievements in the development of popular literacy in fifth-century Rome were substantial, they resulted neither in democratization nor the development of a popular intellectual tradition (Graff, 1987). Neither did the invention of the printing press in fifteenth-century Europe lead to swift or universal changes in prevailing social, political, and economic relationships. These came more slowly.

By the eighteenth and nineteenth centuries in Europe and North America, literacy was seen as a potentially destabilizing force, threatening the established social order. Conservative elites feared that the widespread acquisition of reading and writing skills by the masses—workers, servants, and slaves—would make them unfit for manual labor and unwilling to accept their subordinate status. Education for the popular classes was often discouraged, in fear it might lead to discontent, strife, and rebellion. In some settings, reading and writing instruction was legally withheld, as was the case with slaves in the south USA. Implicit in these views was the suspicion that literacy was a precondition of intellectual, cultural, and social transformation, by which individuals might redefine themselves and challenge existing social conditions.

The reactionary view of literacy was largely trumped in the last decades of the eighteenth century and the first half of the nineteenth century by reformers. These reformers grasped the potential of schooling and literacy as a means for maintaining social control. In their view, education—whether in public or private institutions—was a means through which to instill discipline and prepare the working class for their places in an increasingly urban, industrial society. This meant that literacy lessons in the schools were offered not for their own sake, as a means for promoting intellectual and personal growth, but were instead taught as part of a larger project of instilling generally secular moral values and faith in commercial and industrial capitalism. The destabilizing potential of literacy remained, but it was moderated by education that emphasized discipline, good conduct, and deference to authority. In this way reformers seized on literacy as a central strategy for maintaining social control.

The roots of this perspective are found in religious groups and secular reformers who competed to uplift and save the souls of the poor, and who also competed to influence expanding school systems. Religion, especially but not only Protestantism after the Reformation, was the impetus for learning to read. The Bible served as both the repository of spiritual salvation and an important primer for new readers.

Building on the foundation of the Enlightenment, the second half of the nineteenth century witnessed the emergence of a synthesis of major influences on social thought—idealism, scientism, evolutionism, positivism, materialism, and progressivism—that encouraged belief in the eventual if not inevitable improvement of human beings and society. Literacy was seen to be intrinsic to these advances, a technology through which faith in the progress of civilization and human improvement might be validated. The preferred venue for managing literacy was mass popular education.

This association of literacy with ideology, values, and a stable social order provides a historical basis of the literacy myth.

MAJOR ELEMENTS OF THE MYTH

The Myth of Decline

In contemporary popular discourse, literacy is represented as an unqualified good, a marker of progress, and a metaphorical light making clear the pathway to progress and happiness. The opposing value of "illiteracy," in contrast, is associated with ignorance, incompetence, and darkness. Advertisements run by the National Center for Family Literacy in USA, for example, show an adult and a smiling child accompanied by a text that reads in part: "Because I can read... I can understand... live my life without fear, without shame." Given such sentiments, it is hardly surprising that discussions of literacy would be characterized by persistent fears of its decline. Indeed, much of the contemporary discourse on literacy evokes what John Nerone (1988, Introduction, Communication 11,1 qtd. in Graff, 1995a, xvii), has called "a sense of the apocalypse." In this discourse, the decline of literacy is taken as an omnipresent given and signifies generally the end of individual advancement, social progress, and the health of the democracy. Such associations represent a powerful variant of the Literacy Myth.

The narrative of decline extends beyond literacy to encompass the state of education generally, both higher and lower, as well as the state of society, morality, and economic productivity. In USA, the decline of tests scores in reading assessments is said to represent one "crisis"; the rise in reading "disabilities" another; the movement away from sound reading and writing pedagogy yet another (McQuillan, 1998; see also Graff, 1995a). Where the evidence does not support a decline in literacy rates among the general population, there is a perceived crisis over the kinds of literacy that are or are not practiced—for example, the crisis of declining numbers of people reading "good" literature, said to represent a threat to the ideals of participatory democracy (see, for example, NEA, 2004).

That the myth of decline is largely unsupported by empirical evidence has done little to reduce its potency in contemporary discourse. Rather, the myth is argued by anecdote, often rooted in nostalgia for the past. Moreover, protestations over the decline of literacy are often a prologue for a more sustained argument for a "back to basics" movement in schools. If literacy has declined, it is because schools have strayed from teaching the fundamentals of reading, arithmetic, and other subjects defined, indistinctly, as "the basics." However, as Resnick and Resnick (1977) illustrate, expectations concerning literacy have changed sharply over time, as standards have been applied to large populations that were once applied only to a limited few. It may prove difficult to go back to basics, Resnick and Resnick have written, if "there is no simple path to which we can return" (p. 385).

The myth of decline also neglects the changing modes of communication, and in particular the increasing importance of media that are not wholly reliant on print. Developments in computer technology and the Internet have combined to change the experience of what it means to read, with print becoming but one element in a complex interplay of text, images, graphics, sound, and hyperlinks. The bias toward what Marcia Farr (1993) called "essayist literacy," or formal discursive writing characterized by strict conventions of form, style, tone, both resists and fails to comprehend such changes. Such resistance and failures also have historical antecedents; changes in the technologies of communication have always been accompanied by apprehensions of loss. Plato's notorious distrust of writing was itself a rejection of a technology that threatened the primacy of dialectic in favor of a graphical mode of communication (see, for example, Havelock, 1963).

The myth of decline, then, is an expression of an ideology in which a particular form of literacy is seen to represent a world that is at once stable, ordered, and free of dramatic social change. More than nostalgia for a nonexistent past, the myth of decline articulates a conception of the present and the future, one in which specific forms of literacy practice exemplify an ideological commitment to a status quo that may have already past.

The Myth of the Alphabet

Perhaps the strongest claims concerning literacy have been those attributed to the alphabet, whose invention in classical Greece was said to herald a great leap forward in the progress of human evolution. The "alphabetized word" was said to release human beings from the trance of tribalism and bring about the development of logic, philosophy, history, and democracy. To its proponents, the development of alphabetic literacy brought about profound changes in the very structure of human cognition, as the written word, liberated by its material nature from the "tyranny of the present" (Goody and Watt, 1968), could be objectified, manipulated, preserved, and transmitted across time and distances, leading to the development of abstract thought. Pictographs, hieroglyphs, and other forms of representing speech were seen as prior and inferior to alphabetic literacy, which could more easily represent concepts—justice, law, individualism—and thus engendered the beginnings of philosophical thought.

The bias toward the alphabet resulted in what its proponents called a "great divide" (Goody and Watt, 1968; see also Havelock, 1963, 1976, 1986; Olson, 1994, 1977), with rational, historical, individualistic literate peoples on one side, and "nonlogical," mythical, communal oral peoples on the other. Among other things, such conceptions led to serious misunderstandings of non-Western writing systems, such as those of the Chinese and the Japanese, which were erroneously thought to be inferior to the Western alphabet (Finnegan 1973, 1988; Gough, 1968; Street, 1984, 1995). In the most extreme versions of the myth, the alphabet was seen to represent the beginnings of civilized society.

In the nineteenth century, the myth of the alphabet was an element of the broader narrative of Western history and worked to ratify the educational, moral, and political experiences of colonial Western powers with the cultures of the colonized, especially those that did not practice literacy. To the extent that the alphabet was identified with civilization, its dissemination to nonliterate, nonindustrial, supposedly "primitive" cultures was intrinsic to the larger project and rhetoric of colonial expansion. These attitudes were not confined to colonial contexts but applied, as well, to minority populations in schools, workplaces, and communities, all of which might be "improved" by learning the literacy practices of the dominant group. In this way literacy, and alphabetic literacy in particular, has served as what Finnegan (1994) called the "mythical charter" of the dominant social and political order. The great debates of the past two centuries over reading pedagogy and instructional methods—for example, phonics, phonetics, "look-see" methods, and others—continue to reflect questions about the uses and powers of alphabets. In contemporary debates, they reflected divisions over order and morality as well as pedagogy (Graff, 1979).

WORK IN PROGRESS

Literacy and Economic Development

The assumed link between literacy and economic success is one of the cornerstones of Western modernization theories. Literacy or at least a minimal amount of education is presumed to be necessary and sufficient for overcoming poverty and surmounting limitations rooted in racial, ethnic, gender, and religious differences. Implicit in this formulation is the belief that individual achievement may reduce the effects of social and structural inequalities, and that economic success or failure corresponds at least in part to the quality of personal effort.

On a collective scale, literacy is thought to be a necessary precondition of modernization, a cause and correlate of economic growth, productivity, industrialization, per capita wealth, gross national product, and technological advances, among other advances (Graff, 1979, 1987; Levine 1986). Literacy in this view becomes a commodity to be exported by the developed areas to so-called "developing nations," enabling individuals and nations to participate in the ongoing processes of globalization and partake of their presumed rewards.

Despite such expectations, there is little evidence that increasing or high levels of literacy result directly in major economic advances. Indeed, historical scholarship suggests that in the short run, at least, industrialization may be incidental to literacy development or vice versa, or even work to the detriment of opportunities for schooling. Literacy among the workforce was not a precondition to early industrialization in England and North America, for example. Schofield (1973) found that the literacy rates of textile, metal, and transport workers declined in the late eighteenth century, as these occupations did not require advanced reading and writing skills. Additionally, the demand for child labor disrupted education, as children in the factories had fewer opportunities to attend school. Industrial development may have depended on the inventiveness or innovativeness of a relative few, and thus stimulated their literacy development. It may equally have been disruptive to the lives of many other individuals, their families, their customary work and relationships, and their environments including arrangements for schooling (Furet and Ozouf, 1983; Graff, 1979; Levine, 1980).

It is possible that in nineteenth-century England and elsewhere, to a significant extent, training in literacy was not so much for the purpose of developing skills to promote social, cultural, or economic advancement as it was "training in being trained" (Graff, 1979, p. 230, paraphrasing R. Dore, 1967, *Education in Tokugawa Japan*, Routledge and Kegan Paul, London, p. 292). Schooling and literacy education were the first steps in reordering the values and customs of rural populations entering the Industrial Age, instilling in them the industry, thrift, order, and punctuality required for the successful operation of the factory and a new social order beyond it. Literacy was not primarily or by itself a vehicle for economic advancement, but rather a means of inculcating values and behaviors in the general population that made large-scale economic development possible.

Recent scholarship does not support the assumption that literacy leads directly to economic advancement. Brandt (2001), for example, found that the value of literacy to individuals in the twentieth-century US was influenced by more general social, political, and technological transformations that sometimes elevated the importance of literacy skills but at times undercut or undervalued them. Farmers, teachers, and others in Brandt's study, for example, found that literacy skills learned in the early part of the century were made less valuable or even obsolete by technological, institutional, and economic transformations of the latter part of the century. New forms of literacy training, specific to the needs to changing workplaces and communities, were required to advance or simply maintain one's former status. Literacy, in sum, did not change society. Rather, literacy itself was changed—its forms, uses, and meanings—in response to its environment. Such observations make clear that literacy's and schooling's contribution to economic development merit further detailed study, and that the presumptions of the Literacy Myth demand even more careful qualification.

PROBLEMS AND DIFFICULTIES

Democracy, Literacy, and the Social Order

One of the central tenets of the democratic state is that an educated, informed, and participatory voting public is necessary for the functioning of democracy. In this perspective, one must be able to read and write to understand the issues of the day and think critically about the choices required in a democracy. While that formulation is undoubtedly true, it is also incomplete. It requires the further recognition that literacy and education are necessary but not sufficient conditions of a functioning democracy, which also relies on participation, debate, and a diversity of viewpoints. Although literacy and education can and have been used to stimulate democratic discourse and practices, it is equally true that literacy has been used to foster political repression and maintain inequitable social conditions.

History helps us to understand such tensions. Nineteenth-century schoolbooks stressed the doctrines of order, harmony, and progress, while ignoring or justifying social conflicts and inequities (Graff, 1987, p. 326). Beyond the economic imperatives discussed previously, the purpose of literacy in these contexts was self-consciously conservative, a means for imposing morality, reducing criminality, lessening diversity, and encouraging deference to the established social order, especially in difficult times of change. Literacy was not a means for promoting democracy but rather an instrument for imposing social control. Yet literacy could be and was appropriated by groups and organizations promoting radical social change, for example, among Chartists in nineteenth-century Great Britain and skilled labor organizers more widely. In the shop, meeting hall, and street, oral and written media came together. National literacy campaigns such as those in Cuba and Nicaragua also reflect the dialectical tensions of the literacy myth. Such movements propel literacy workers to action, raise literacy rates significantly, and allow for individual and group development. But literacy remains under the direction of political ideology and doctrine (Arnove and Graff, 1987). Only in the literacy myth does literacy operate as an independent variable.

The functioning of a mature democracy depends on political structures and economic conditions that make participation possible for citizens. Literacy and education are important to the extent that they emphasize critical thinking, open debate, and tolerance for opposing views. Literacy by itself is not a cause for freedom and a guarantee of a working democracy. It is instead one of the many important variables that influences the lives of citizens and their relationship to their governments.

FUTURE DIRECTIONS

Lessons of the Literacy Myth

Myths can be expressions of collective desires, of the many and the few, of their differential agency and power. Perhaps the Literacy Myth expresses a hope that literacy alone is enough to end poverty, elevate human dignity, and ensure a just and democratic world. A less benign reading is that the Literacy Myth is a means through which to obscure the causes of social and economic inequities in Western society at least by attributing them to the literacy or illiteracy of different peoples. In such a reading, literacy is a symptom and a symbol. Either way, the consequences of accepting uncritically the Literacy Myth are continuing to misunderstand the nature of literacy, its development, uses, and potentials to foster or inhibit social and economic development.

To argue that literacy has been accorded the status of myth is not to discount the importance or reading and writing, or to suggest that these are irrelevant in the contemporary world. That is clearly not the case. However, we may contrast the Literacy Myth, and its seamless connections of literacy and individual and collective advancement, with the more complex and often contradictory lessons that are consistent with historical and recent literacy development and practice.

One critical lesson is that literacy is not an independent variable, as in the Myth. It is instead historically founded and grounded, a product of the histories in which it is entangled and interwoven, and which give literacy its meanings. Ignorance of the historical record, in which crucial concepts, notions, arrangements, and expectations about literacy have been fashioned, severely limits understanding. Related to this, second, we must grasp the fundamental complexity of literacy, the extent to which it is a product of the intersection of multiple economic, political, cultural, and other factors. This realization mandates rejecting the simple binaries of "literate–illiterate," "oral–written," and others that have been used to postulate a "great divide." These constructs have been used to sort individuals and cultures in ways that are as damaging as they are conceptually inadequate. The legacies of literacy point instead to connections, relationships, and interactions.

In the Literacy Myth, reading and writing are a universal good and ideologically neutral. However, in a third lesson, the history of literacy and schooling demonstrates that no mode or means of learning is neutral. Literacy is a product of the specific circumstances of its acquisition, practice, and uses, and so reflects the ideologies that guide these. School literacy, in particular, is neither unbiased nor the expression of universal norms of reading and writing; it reflects the structures of authority that govern schools and their societies.

Finally, despite the apparent simplicity of the literacy myth, the historical record points to a much richer and diverse record. It underscores the multiple paths to literacy learning, the extraordinary range of instructors, institutions, and other environments, of beginning "texts," and of the diversity of motivations for learning to read and write. While mass public schooling today presents the most common route for individuals learning to read and write, the diversity of learners, including adult learners, in Europe and North America demands flexible understandings and pedagogies for literacy development. There is no single road to developing literacy. Different societies and cultures have taken different paths toward rising levels of literacy. This suggests that the presumed "consequences" of literacy—individual, economic, and democratic—will always be conditioned by the particulars of time, situation, and the historical moment.

Such reflections offer a more complex narrative than that of the Literacy Myth. They may also point toward new and different ways of understanding, using, and benefiting from the broad and still developing potentials that literacy may offer individuals and societies (Graff, 1995a,b).

REFERENCES

Akinasso, F.N.: 1981, 'The consequences of literacy in pragmatic and theoretical perspectives', *Anthropology and Education Quarterly* 12, 163–200.

Arnove, R. and Graff, H. (eds.): 1987, *National Literacy Campaigns in Historical and Comparative Perspective*, Plenum, NY.

Brandt, D.: 2001, *Literacy in American Lives*. Cambridge University Press, Cambridge.

Collins J. and Blot, R.: 2003, *Literacy and Literacies: Texts, Power, and Identity*, Cambridge University Press, Cambridge.

Duffy, J.: 2000, 'Never hold a pencil: Rhetoric and relations in the concept of 'preliteracy', *Written Communication*, 17.2, 224–257.

Farr, M.: 1993, 'Essayist literacy and other verbal performances', *Written Communication*, 10:1, 4–38.

Finnegan, R.: 1973, 'Literacy versus non-literacy: The great divide', in R. Horton and R. Finnegan (eds.), *Modes of Thought*, Faber and Faber, London.

Finnegan, R.: 1988, *Literacy and Orality*, Blackwell, Oxford.

Finnegan, R.: 1994, 'Literacy as mythical charter', in D. Keller-Cohen (ed.), *Literacy: Interdisciplinary Conversations*, Hampton Press, Creskill, NJ.

Furet, F. and Ozouf, J.: 1983, *Reading and Writing*, Cambridge University Press, Cambridge.

Gelb, I.J.: 1963, *A Study of Writing*, University of Chicago Press, Chicago, IL.

Goody, J.: 1986, *The Logic of Writing and the Organization of Society*, Cambridge University Press, Cambridge.

Goody, J.: 1987, *The Interface Between the Written and the Oral*, Cambridge University Press, Cambridge.

Goody, J. and Watt, I.: 1968, 'The consequences of literacy', in J. Goody (ed.), *Literacy in Traditional Societies*, Cambridge University Press, Cambridge (originally published in 1963).

Gough, K.: 1968, 'Implications of literacy in traditional China and India', in J. Goody (ed.), *Literacy in Traditional Societies*, Cambridge University Press, Cambridge.

Graff, H.J.: 1979, *The Literacy Myth: Literacy and Social Structure in the Nineteenth Century City*, Academic Press, New York and London (Reprinted with a new introduction, Transaction Press, New Brunswick, NJ, 1991.).

Graff, H.J.: 1987, *The Legacies of Literacy: Continuities and Contradictions in Western Culture and Society*, Indiana University Press, Bloomington, IN.

Graff, H.J.: 1995a, *The Labyrinths of Literacy: Reflections on Literacy Past and Present, Revised and Expanded Edition*, University of Pittsburgh Press, Pittsburgh, PA.
Graff, H.J.: 1995b, 'Assessing the history of literacy in the 1990s: Themes and questions', in A. Petrucci and M.G. Blay (eds.), *Escribir y leer en Occidente*, Universitat de Valencia, Valencia, Spain.
Graff, H.J. and Street, B.: 1997, 'A response to Stan Jones, "Ending the Myth of the 'Literacy Myth': A Response to Critiques"', *Literacy Across the Curriculum*, Centre for Literacy, Montreal, 13, 4–6.
Harris, W.V.: 1989, *Ancient Literacy*, Harvard University Press, Cambridge, MA.
Havelock, E.: 1963, *Preface to Plato*, Harvard University Press, Cambridge, MA.
Havelock, E.: 1976, *Origins of Western Literacy*, Ontario Institute for Studies in Education, Toronto.
Havelock, E.: 1986, *The Literate Revolution in Greece and its Cultural Consequences*, Princeton University Press, Princeton, NJ.
Inkeles, A. and Smith, D.: 1974, *Becoming Modern: Individual Change in Six Developing Countries*, Harvard University Press, Cambridge, MA.
Levine, D.: 1980, 'Illiteracy and family life during the first Industrial Revolution', *Journal of Social History*, 14, 25–44.
Levine, K.: 1986, *The Social Context of Literacy*, Routledge and Kegan Paul, London.
McQuillan, J.: 1998, 'Seven myths about literacy in the United States, Practical Assessment, Research and Evaluation', 6(1), retrieved January 9, 2006 from http://PAREonline.net/getvn.asp?v=6andn=1.
National Endowment for the Arts: 2004, *Reading at Risk: A Survey of Literary Reading in America*, Research Division Report #46, June.
Olson, D.R.: 1977, 'From utterance to text: The bias of language in speech and writing', *Harvard Educational Review*, 47(3), 257–281.
Olson, D.R.: 1994, *The World on Paper: The Conceptual and Cognitive Implications of Writing and Reading*, Cambridge University Press, Cambridge.
Ong, W.: 1967, *The Presence of the Word*, Yale University Press, New Haven, CT.
Ong, W.: 1977, *Interface of the Word*, Cornell University Press, Ithaca, NY.
Ong, W.: 1982, *Orality and Literacy*, Methuen, London.
Pattison, R,: 1984, *On Literacy.* Oxford University Press, Oxford.
Resnick, D. and Resnick, L.: 1977, 'The nature of literacy: A historical exploration', *Harvard Educational Review*, 47, 370–385.
Schofield, R.: 1973, 'Dimensions of illiteracy, 1750–1850', *Explorations in Economic History*, 10, 437–454.
Scribner. S.: 1984, 'Literacy in three metaphors', *American Journal of Education*, 93, 6–21.
St. Clair, R. and Sadlin, J.: 2004, 'Incompetence and intrusion: On the metaphorical use of illiteracy in U.S. political discourse', *Adult Basic Education*, 14, 45–59.
Street, B., 1984, *Literacy in Theory and Practice*, Cambridge University Press, Cambridge.
Street, B.: 1995, *Social Literacies: Critical Approaches to Literacy in Development, Ethnography and Education.* Longman, London.

KEVIN M. LEANDER AND CYNTHIA LEWIS

LITERACY AND INTERNET TECHNOLOGIES

INTRODUCTION

A review of research in literacy and Internet technologies, broadly speaking, reveals as much about the current theoretical and ideological paradigms operating in any time period as it does about technology's relationship to literacy. Thus, prior to beginning our discussion, it seems important to bracket our own concerns and investments about literacy and Internet technologies. First, following distinctions regarding information and communication technologies made by Lankshear and Knobel (2003, pp. 72–73), our treatment of technology is particularly invested in interactive and networked computing media, in contrast to stand-alone and noninteractive media. Second, we are chiefly concerned with literacy learning as not merely involving encoding and decoding, but rather, participating in particular sociocultural practices and discourses leading to one's competent handling of texts as an insider. Third, our understanding of relations between literacy and Internet technologies destabilizes conventional understandings of literacy as fundamentally concerned with alphabetic print. While print remains important to practices involving literacy and Internet technologies, print functions increasingly along with other semiotic modalities in order to make meaning, including sound, icons, graphics, and video.

In addition to bracketing literacy–technology relations as networked, as sociocultural, and as multimodal, our discussion is focused on how networked technologies fundamentally change the relationships of literacy to social relations, including one's relations to one's own identity. For example, while purpose and audience have very long histories in rhetoric, assumptions and configurations of purpose and audience are transformed through dynamic use of Internet communication, and purpose and audience may be continuously remixed through chains of distribution and exchange (Kress and Van Leeuwen, 2001). Moreover, social relations, through texts that may have worldwide distribution, are articulated through the local and global in new ways. We describe how such formations are beginning to be practiced and researched within literacy studies, in and out of school contexts, and future directions that such work might take.

B. Street and N. H. Hornberger (eds), Encyclopedia of Language and Education,
2nd Edition, Volume 2: Literacy, 53–70.
©*2010 Springer Science+Business Media LLC.*

EARLY DEVELOPMENTS

The pre-history of the Internet is disputed and multifaceted, as it the relationship of the Internet's pre-history to literacy practices. For instance, if we decide to focus on the development of graphical World Wide Web browsers (e.g., NCSA Mosaic in 1993), which led to the rapid public explosion of Internet activity, then we would bracket out earlier literacy environments opened up by local area networks (LAN's), modems, and the like. Yet the picture is still more complicated than the technological story permits. For instance, an important date noted in on history of MUD's (multiuser dungeons) is the writing of Tolkien's *Lord of the Rings* (1937), a fantasy world that "formed the basis for most early gaming systems" (Burka, 1995). Over 40 years later (1978), the first MUD was developed at Essex University, where the acronym was associated with "Multiple Undergraduate Destroyer" due to its popularity among college students (http://en.wikipedia.org/wiki/MUD.) Thus, a decade and a half before the early web browsers, gamers were engaging in a text-driven world that combined elements of role-playing games with social chat. An extended history of literacy and Internet technologies, as they are related to education, would certainly include early practices in these pre-Internet environments.

Additionally, Minitel was launched in France in 1982 and quickly became a highly successful online service on which customers could make purchases, chat, check stock prices, make train reservations, access databases, and participate in other information and communication practices. As early as 1986, widespread access to Minitel (or Teletel) terminals resulted in several forms of educational practice in homes, schools, and university settings, including homework help lines, databases with model answers to national examination questions, and online registration for university courses (Guihot, 1989).

In the USA, an early paper, "Microcomputer Communication Networks for Education," (Laboratory of Comparative Human Cognition, 1982) describes the use of "non-real time" messaging (p. 32), in which teachers and students could write messages on microcomputers during the day and then send them overnight by telephone lines, saving the high cost and scheduling problems associated with real-time messaging. This group of developers and researchers described a pilot network connecting a classroom in San Diego with a classroom in rural Alaska, using Apple II computers. Early research interests included studying the complexity of discourse structures of multiple threads in online communication, and the problem of the quantity of messages ("electronic junk mail") received in such media. The group expressed the anxiety that unless teachers and students were given means to address such issues that Internet technologies might be abandoned as a learning environment. They also initiated what is likely to be one of the earliest teacher education courses on literacy and ICT (information and communication technology), "Interactive Media for Education," offered at the University of California, San Diego, in the summer of 1982.

A parallel project to the research at UCSD introduced in Alaska in 1983 involved the creation of a computer program called QUILL whose purpose was to help upper elementary students develop as writers (Bruce and Rubin, 1993). Rather than teaching writing skills directly, QUILL contained tools through which teachers and students could create literacy environments in their own classrooms, including an electronic mail program. Bruce and Rubin's (1993) research documents how writing, through an electronic network, created cooperative learning conditions for teachers as well as students as well as particular effects through new, networked constructions of audience and purpose.

Two other areas of early work most relevant to literacy and Internet technologies include studies of reading hypertext and multimedia. Much of this work reflects the cognitive traditions that informed it in the 1980's to early 1990's. In their meta-analysis of hypertext studies from 1988 to 1993, Chen and Rada (1996) considered measures of effectiveness and efficiency for several different cognitive styles, and found a generally small overall effect size. However, Leu (2000) noted that early hypertextual studies contained relatively few multimedia resources than are currently available, and also may not have carefully teased out the interaction of prior knowledge with specific searching and learning tasks (p. 755). From early work on multimedia, we have some evidence that learners with limited prior knowledge tend to learn better with multimedia than with print, as do learners deemed to be "visual" or "auditory" in their learning styles (Kamil et al., 2000, p. 775). Daiute and Morse (1994), reviewing much of the multimedia research, concluded that appropriately combined images and sound might enhance both the comprehension and the production of text. However, Reinking and Chanlin (1994) also review problems with multimedia research, and Lankshear and Knobel (2003, p. 77) note how most multimedia research privileges print rather than studying how learners interpret and create multimodal meanings.

Early research on literacy and technology has been critiqued on a number of levels, and much of this criticism remains of relevance today. A primary critique is of the lack of research, especially in the early years of development. Kamil and Lane (1998) examined 437 research articles appearing in four major journals of reading and writing research during the period of 1990 to 1995 and discovered that only 12 of them were focused on issues of literacy and technology. With a focus on early childhood education, Lankshear and Knobel (2003, p. 64) expanded this type of research review to include journals from

Britain, the USA, and Australia for the years 1996–2002, and note the
"extreme marginalization" within specialist reading and writing journals of research articles on technology and literacy.

MAJOR CONTRIBUTIONS

We have organized our discussion to focus on major contributions in
three categories that are foundational to understanding the changing
nature of literacy in relation to Internet technologies: multimodality,
sociality, and the intersection of the global and local.

Multimodality

Early work on the relationship between technology and literacy tended
to focus on how technology transformed literacy. By way of example,
leading literacy researchers in the influential volume, The *Handbook of
Literacy and Technology: Transformations in a Post-Typgraphic World*
(Reinking et al., 1998), considered the changing nature of literacy in a
digital age. Interested in the shift from print to multimodal representation, the authors nonetheless were careful to underscore continuities as
well. Lemke (1998), for instance, argued that

> All literacy is multimedia literacy: You can never make
> meaning with language alone; there must always be a visual
> or vocal realization of linguistic signs that also carries non-
> linguistic meaning (e.g. tone of voice or style of orthogra-
> phy) (p. 284).

Although literacy has always been multimodal, contemporary literacy
practices rely on an increasingly complex range of modalities. Conceptual
work on technology has considered the relationship between the visual
and linguistic modes, noting the shift to complex images and simpler
texts that contain fewer embedded clauses (Kress, 2003). Communication technologies, which, as Leander (2004) argues, have received less
attention in schools than information technologies, often blur distinctions between speech and writing, depending on aural modalities in
unprecedented ways.

Many scholars have argued that reading and writing practices change
with these changes in textual form and function (Leu, 2000; New London
Group, 1996). They point out that Internet technologies require readers
and writers to make meaning laterally across modes, sampling the
multimodal resources available to them and interpreting an array of
surface features and combinations of texts, genres, and modes. In this
move from page to screen, reading practices associated with print, often
described as linear or deep, can be viewed as *one* way of reading, rather

than *the only* way to be a competent reader (Kress, 2003). Kress and Jewett (2003, p. 16) claim that as the "logic of the image" replaces the "logic of writing," there will be "far-reaching effects on the organization of communication, not just on the screen but also on the page, and on the mode of writing." If this is true, then it follows that the reading and writing instruction common to most classrooms may be inadequate to prepare students for a wide range of reading and writing purposes and practices.

In contemporary youth culture, Mp3 players, such as the iPod, are having a significant impact in shaping multimodal literacy practices. As of 2006, the fifth generation of iPod, with its bundled software, iTunes, can store, transfer, and play most audio, photo, and video files of most popular formats. "Podcasting was coined in 2004 when people combined the words "iPod" with "broadcasting" to refer to the uploading and "posting of audio files online in a way that allows software in a person's computer to detect and download new podcast automatically" (Lenhart, Madden, and Hitlin, 2005)." The rising popularity of podcasting lies in how it enables individuals to distribute their own "radio shows," but it is also being used in various ways, including school's distribution of course recordings as podcasts on iTunes. Flanagan and Calandram suggest that podcast's multimodal affordances make it integrate naturally in auditory-dependent and humanities courses, supports field research, and enables multimodal presentation of student work. By complementing traditional media, podcasting may create different pathways for understanding and learning (Bull, 2005).

Since late 2004, new generation podcasts based on video, or "vodcasts" are joined by an array of online video activity (e.g., video blogs or "vlogs") that signals something of the rapid increase in multimodal production and distribution by everyday users. Youtube.com, founded in 2005, is a "consumer media company" that offers free hosting for videos. With "Broadcast Yourself" as slogan, Youtube is designed to enable simple, fast, and free sharing and viewing of videos online. Among more than 12 million videos uploaded each day, many are personal, original productions, such as home movies, video blogs, and amateur film works. Others, in spite of site policy against copyright infringement, are often short clips from traditional media, including music videos, commercial, news broadcasts, and dubbed parodies of such.

Sociality

New technologies shape and are shaped by social relations and practices. Since they are socially mediated, particular kinds of Internet technologies afford particular types of social relations. In a large-scale study conducted by researchers in the United Kingdom, Livingstone and Bober (2004) investigated uses of the Internet among young people (9–19) in order to find out how the Internet is shaping family life, peer cultures, and learning. Related to Internet communication, these researchers found that a third of the young people found chatting with friends online, more often than not local friends, to be at least as satisfying as talking face-to-face. Distinctions between offline and online worlds fall away as people shift seamlessly from digital to face-to-face contexts (Leander and McKim, 2003). In fact, the maintenance of offline relationships is a documented feature of online communication (Holloway and Valentine, 2003; Lewis and Fabos, 2005; Valentine, Holloway, and Bingham, 2000; Wellman, 2004). Based on a large-scale study of children's access to and use of computers in the home and at school in the South-West of England, Facer (2004) found that the line between home and school uses of Internet is not sharply drawn. For instance, home Internet use involved 'formal' learning with the difference being that young people were often the teachers (instructing parents in computer use, for instance). School Internet use, on the other hand, was, at times, a place for informal learning with Internet technologies serving to fuel social relationships that then were enhanced through Instant Messaging and other Internet technologies taken up at home.

Once a technology becomes commonplace, people tend not to think of it as technological. As Herring (2004) points out, young people with Internet access have come to naturalize particular kinds of Internet technologies, such as text messaging, as an ordinary part of their lives. Bolter and Grusin (2000) use the term "remediate" to describe the process by which new technologies incorporate elements of established technologies. IM incorporates elements of phone exchanges and note passing, for instance, but its status as a "new technology" is already evolving. It is not the computer or the Internet itself that is central to literacy, but the way that these tools of technology shape social relations and practices.

Internet technologies have been found to hold potential for the development of new social linguistic identities and relationships (Alvermann, 2002; Chandler-Olcott and Maher, 2003; Thomas, 2005). In a study of adolescents' uses of Instant Messaging, Lewis and Fabos (2005) found that participants manipulated the tone, voice, word choice and subject matter of their messages to fit their social communication needs. They designed their practice to enhance social relationships and statuses across contexts, circulated texts across buddies, combated unwanted messages, assumed alternative identities, and overcame restrictions to their online communication. These functions revealed that the technological and social affordances of IM gave rise to a performative and multivoiced social subject. Digital technologies, according to some researchers, foster affinity group connections related to common interests and shared norms over common class and race affiliations (Gee, 2002). Others, however, point to the potential for online communication to perpetuate, even exacerbate, inequitable social relations and limiting social roles (Warshauer 2002).

New problems and issues for research on sociality, literacy, and Internet technologies are emerging as new media and technologies rapidly develop, as becomes clear by considering the popularity and complexities of wikis and weblogs. Invented in 1995 by Wart Cunningham, Wikis are a type of digital writing space that allows collaborative revision and editing of texts by multiple users (Leuf and Cunningham, 2001). An exemplary example is Wikipedia, a free content, multilingual, web-based encyclopedia project created volunteers. Wikipedia has become the third most popular information source on the Web (Hafner, 2006). Some argue wikis solicit and store individual's knowledge as a means of "knowledge management" (KMwiki, 2006), others argue that wikis function as a purposeful means of collaboratively discussing or addressing an issue or problem (Ferris and Wilder, 2006). Wikis can be used in the classroom for collaborative writing projects, for example creating reference manuals or glossaries, a class statement or letter to the editor, a WikiBook textbook or handbook on the topic they are studying, or a service learning/inquiry-project report (Barton, 2004).

Weblogs or "blogs," are a type of websites created in web journal format and used by individuals to express opinions, describe experiences, build relationships, and exchange information within digital space. Importantly, the creation and maintenance of blogs demands little in terms of technical knowledge, unlike early web page construction. Blogs are interactive in that each entry links to possible comments from readers, and the page includes links to other online resources. Blogging is considered a powerful digital writing tool that can serve as a useful platform to collect, organize, and share personal writing. Blogs value personal and dialogic expressions that are "spontaneous, subjective, exploratory, and even contradictory" (Anson and Beach, 2005). Two websites that draw on features of blogs and extend them for purposes of social networking are MySpace and Facebook. MySpace is among the most popular English websites, with over 106 million accounts (as of September, 2006) and growing rapidly (wikipedia.org). First created as a campus face book within Harvard University in 2004, Facebook has become highly popular in college, university, and even high school communities. Both MySpace and Facebook afford participants the ability to post texts, photos, links and other media to perform and shape their identities, and also to search for friends and classmates, form and join groups, develop common textual areas, and create social events through internal messaging.

Local and Global Intersections and Tensions

Karaidy's (1999) use of the term "glocal" aptly characterizes how the Internet is a social space where the global and local intersect. To capitalize on this feature of Internet space, projects such as Euro-kids, a partnership among schools across five European countries, uses Internet technologies to enable communication about local citizenship as well as participation in the wider European community (Euro-kids, 2006). Another ambitious project, European Schoolnet, connects learning communities of teachers across the European Union and uses Internet resources to build student awareness of diverse cultures and European citizenship.

As new technologies become integrated in young people's school days and daily lives, creating spaces for communication and identity construction, we need to consider what it means that they are owned and controlled by corporate interests, and have been since 1995 when the Internet became a fully privatized medium (Fabos, 2004). As such, commercial interests are fed by young people's seemingly agentic participation. For example, in a study of an online community for adolescent females, Duncan and Leander (2000) found that while the commercially owned website may have provided a space for girls to display some sense of power and self-definition, its primary purpose was to produce consumer identities and serve commercial interests.

Many chat rooms and bulletin boards, in the guise of enabling young people to create content and speak their minds, are commercially sponsored sites where marketers monitor teens' postings to gather information about popular trends and products. The separation of content from advertising erodes on the Web, targeting teens as a prime market, through chat spaces in which trendy brand-name companies create clubs with 'free membership' that include chat spaces, email newsletters, fashion tips, and so on. Thus, online users become not only *subjects in*, but also the *objects of*, the new global capitalism.

PROBLEMS AND DIFFICULTIES

The "glocalized" space of the Internet presents a particular set of research problems for researchers using ethnographic tools. For researchers who study cultural production in local contexts, the challenge is to figure out how to study online activity from both a local and global perspective, how to study the activity up close using the usual ethnographic tools of participant-observation, interview, video, and local artifacts and also trace this activity as it distributed across sites (Leander and McKim, 2003) and global flows. The "hypersociality" (Ito, 2005, p. 3) and everyday online practices of local peer groups shape and are shaped by "pervasive mass-media ecologies" (2) that flow transnationally. The fact that AOL corners the market for Instant Messaging interfaces, and users must have AOL in order to chat with buddies whose families use AOL, is one example of how transnational flows of capital shape local activity.

Moreover, as Ito (2005) suggests, "the real is being colonized by the virtual" (3) in ways not directly connected to the political economy of the Net. Young people's everyday offline interactions are shaped by their interactions online, and, in turn, reshape their online social worlds. This is true not only in terms of their online conversations, but also in terms of how they market their online personas across sites by carefully crafting profiles that become part of local and global flows. Ethnographers accustomed to site-specific participant-observation need to design new methods to meet the challenges of researching online communities. This is perhaps even more the case as new forms of communication become pervasive that merge the mobile telephone with Internet-related media. Text messaging, for instance, also known as short message service (SMS) and highly popular in Asia and Europe, permits the exchange of concise, text-based messages between mobile phones. Embedded into the pervasive technologies of everyday life and not separated out as a "computing event," text messaging is indicative of the increasing methodological challenges presented for researching literacy as mobile social practice.

Tracing the relationship between the local and the global is an important skill to develop in users as well as researchers. Several British researchers have found that UK-based chat users generally assume that other users are American (see, for instance, Livingstone, 2002). The economic and linguistic dominance of the US presence on the Net makes such assumptions commonplace yet rarely interrogated by US users. Building users' awareness of commercial interests and transnational flows is no easy matter. As a step in this direction, new-media scholars argue for careful, critical readings of Internet sites and texts to uncover the politics of representation and commercial sponsorship. Rather than viewing print as less important than graphical elements to this enterprise, analytic reading of print online will remain important in order for people to thoughtfully examine, critique, and filter extensive amounts of information. However, critical analysis on the screen is different than the page in that it requires skillful intertextual reading, not only across texts but also across genres and modes (Myers et al., 1998).

Teaching strategies for intertextual reading in online environments is important, yet teachers often feel that they lack the knowledge to do so. Literacy that incorporates Internet technologies is generally left up to teachers who themselves have not been trained to read across genres and modes. Moreover, Internet technologies present the additional challenge of interactivity as part of the reading process. Although all reading involves readers interacting with texts, interactive reading is intensified online as a material feature of the reading process. Readers make decisions about text construction and organization through selection of links and modes, among other elements of website design. In so doing, readers can be viewed as participants in the critical processes of production and analysis. On the other hand, website architecture can also seduce readers to take up particular positions and ideologies even as it appears to allow space for readers to 'create' the reading experience. Reconceptualizing reading instruction in ways that address these new forms of critique and participation is a challenge schools have yet to meet.

Writing instruction also needs to change in the wake of Internet technologies. The multimodality and sociality of the technology landscape has resulted in changes in writing processes and identity representations. The writing process for many digital writers does not occur as a set of stages—even recursive ones. Nonetheless, most schools and teacher education programs remain wedded to the stages of the writing process as they were established for pen and paper. Voice is another writing concept that is in flux as researchers and educators begin to understand how it functions in online writing environments. Often presented in schools as something unitary and authentic, voice in digital writing can be purposefully unstable, shifting moment-to-moment for many different audiences. Perhaps students would benefit from learning strategies to negotiate the performance of self in writing online for multiple audiences. Audiences in online writing are rarely the remote academic audiences of school assignments. Communicating more often across space in real-time means that 'remote' audiences become more immediate in online writing. Students need to be prepared to make effective rhetorical choices given such changes. Moreover, because online writing circulates widely, beyond the intended audience of the writer, writers need to consider the possible routes through which their writing may circulate. Finally, writing online is often most effective when it is most conversational. Thus, students may benefit from invitations to practice conversational writing for particular purposes rather than admonishments that conversational writing will cause academic writing skills to deteriorate.

In light of the persistence of the digital divide between low-income and middle-income families, it is important for schools to take up these new challenges related to reading and writing. Neglecting to do so may further advantage the 'haves' at the expense of the 'have nots', who will have fewer opportunities outside of school to practice digital forms of reading and writing. The substantial growth in teen Internet use in recent years suggests a trend that should move those of us in the field of literacy to take seriously the changes that are afoot. It is inevitable that young people will continue to increase the amount and range of their online activities, thus changing their writing practices and processes in ways that schools will increasingly need to address. In the next section, we highlight new studies of young people's digital practices that we believe will have implications for literacy as it relates to Internet technologies in and out of school.

WORK IN PROGRESS

In the summer of 2005, a multidisciplinary conference on digital culture was held in Taiwan, sponsored by the Taipei Institute of Ethnology and Academia. The purpose of the conference was to "place emerging Asian digital cultures in the context of both local cultural traditions and globalization," including how uses of digital technologies are transforming "local experiences, aesthetics, and social formations" (Asian Digital Cultures Conference, 2005). The purposes and discourse of this event, which would have surprised scholars just 5 years ago, is indicative of how quickly diverse fields are moving toward interpreting Internet technologies in relation to social formations and global/local dynamisms. Cultural theorist Arjun Appadurai (1996) uses the metaphor of "scapes" to describe contemporary global movements, including the flows of media (mediascapes), technology (technoscapes), people (ethnoscapes), ideology (ideoscapes) and money (financescapes). In the following consideration of works in progress we feature research that is addressed toward understanding literacy and Internet technologies as related to an increasingly mobile world.

Flows of Learning in and out of School

"Kids' Informal Learning with Digital Media," under the direction of Peter Lyman, Diane Harley (both of UC Berkeley), Mimi Ito (University of Southern California), and Michael Carter (Monterey Institute for Technology and Education) is a major, multisited ethnographic study that involves diverse youth between the ages of 10 and 18 in four physical sites and up to 20 virtual spaces, including online games, web logs, messaging, and online interest groups (http://groups.sims.berkeley.edu/digitalyouth/). While not directly addressed to literacy learning, such work in media studies and education has significant implications for understanding how the social practices of literacy are pivotal to everyday cultural production by youth (Ito, in press). The research considers the gap in engagement between learning in school and online learning online out of school, moving toward the transformation of schooling and software. In related work, Rodney Jones, together with Co-PI David Li, completed in 2005 a 2-year funded study in Hong Kong on the communication and literacy practices of 40 youth, in and out of school. One of Jones' motivations for engaging in the study was to understand why Hong Kong schools seemed so out of step with the wired culture of Hong Kong outside of schools. Broadly, Jones also wanted to give youth an opportunity to reflect on what they were doing online and share their online knowledge and practices with teachers and parents. Currently, as Jones analyzes and reports from his data, he is becoming increasing interested in broader issues, such as the relationships of online and offline practices to time and space (Jones, 2004; Jones, forthcoming).

Flows of Identity and Discourse

The work of Sarah Holloway and Gil Valentine and collaborators in the UK provides an important argument for taking a socially dynamic and connective approach to practice rather than bracketing social spaces such as "home," "school," "online," and "offline," in advance. The researchers reconceive the problem of access to Internet technologies as a problem of identification. Across home and different school settings, Holloway and Valentine (2001) have documented practices of identification with technology by youth, including how they negotiate their technical competence to be more or less visible. Technology emerged as a signifier of social inadequacy for some boys in school, who risked being marked as "geeks" or "homos," while skills in particular computer games, which were acquired at home, carried cultural capital into the school setting. Moreover, while some girls received praise from parents for technical competency at home, they strategically used technical practices sparingly at school to "win social popularity as well as the grudging respect of their peers for their technical skill" (2001, p. 36). Rather then documenting a stable set of meanings and practices "within" contexts, this research traces a complex, dynamically shifting articulation of techno-literacy practices, social spaces, and identity. In another study (Valentine, Holloway, and Bingham, 2002) the researchers analyze how three different schools discursively constituted the Internet as a very different kind of object. These three discourses on Internet technologies included "ICT for all," which included access for the wider community, "ICT as a life skill," and

"ICT in terms of academic achievement" (p. 312). These discourses helped to structure different types of access and surveillance of Internet technologies practices not only within, but also outside of school.

Flows of People and Culture: Immigration and Transnationalism

Eva Lam is developing a program of research investigating how immigrant youth in the USA use digital literacy practices, and the relationships of these practices to their English learning, social networks, and identities (Lam, 2000, 2004). Lam's work is pushing beyond a learning perspective informed by acculturation, prevalent in ESL literature, and moving rather toward a perspective informed by transculturation. She traces how immigrant youth engage in multiple forms of cultural belonging, including online communities that traverse national boundaries and hence cannot be described by a nation-centered discourse or methodology. In a series of case studies, Lam documents how immigrants, segregated within school settings, develop literacy practices online that contribute to their English learning and perspectives on their social futures. For example, code-mixing between English and Romanized Cantonese in a "Hong Kong Chat Room" was considered normative for some students online and was used to index social alignments and cultural assumptions, while such mixing or social alignments were absent in the school context. In the next phase of Lam's work which began in the spring of 2005, she is planning to study language development and modes of literacy participation of 30 immigrant students over the course of a year.

Fanfiction communities are the focus of research conducted by Rebecca Black, another scholar who is interested in the online literacy practices of immigrant youth and English language learners (2005; in press). Black's work examines adolescent English language learners' uses of fanfiction to represent and enhance their cultural and linguistic identities as well as their social and intellectual capital as writers and knowledgeable participants in this form of popular culture. The fanfiction writing produced by these youth draws on school literacy practices as well as deep knowledge of the conventions of fanfiction as a popular genre. In a chapter on feedback in an online fanfiction community (in press), Black gives the example of an "author's note" that prefaced the Internet technologies of a writer whose first language is Japanese., announcing her anxiety about not writing clear English prose. Demonstrating affinity with the writer, and perhaps an insider's knowledge, the feedback of two readers included Japanese terms. Black is completing a book that examines the identity work accomplished for adolescents who are English language learners through their participation in online fanfiction communities.

Creating Zones of Mobility for Underserved Youth

While early research and program development with literacy and Internet technologies has been disproportionately oriented to privileged, white, and middle-class students, an increasing amount of work in progress is beginning to focus on children and youth who are underserved by schooling. Some of this work, under the direction of Theresa Rogers and Andrew Schofield at the University of British Columbia (http://www.newtonliteracies.ca/) is using new multi-media genres, such as digital storytelling, to engage working class and minority youth in meaningful literacy learning. Another recent large-scale project recently underway focuses on helping low-achieving readers develop higher-level comprehension skills demanded by the Internet. This project (http://www.newliteracies.uconn.edu/iesproject/index.html) directed by Don Leu (University of Connecticut) and David Reinking (Clemson University) is developing an adaptation of reciprocal teaching and a series of learning contexts in which students identify problems and then solve them only by locating, evaluating, synthesizing, and communicating information.

FUTURE DIRECTIONS

As research on Internet technologies and literacy continues, and its production level increases, an important future direction for this area of work will be the development of interdisciplinary approaches that benefit from insights from not only literacy studies but also media studies, cultural studies, information science, feminist studies, human and cultural geography, sociology, anthropology, and a host of other areas. Literacy scholars have much to add to conversations in these other areas as well as glean from them. For instance, returning to Appadurai's (1996) "scapes" of modern life, as literacy studies are beginning to take up issues of migration and Internet technologies, the analysis of literacy practices could be enriched through an analysis of flows of economic capital.

Another enduring need for ongoing research involves the development of theoretical and methodological frames that will enable us to understand changing relations of power, changing constructions of identity, and changing uses of literacy. If the meaning of literacy is deictic, or regularly redefined with respect to new technologies (Leu, 2000), then part of what follows from this insight is that studies of individual tools (e.g., wikis, MySpace pages, weblogs), however helpful, must also avoid parochialism and provide theoretical conceptions that contribute to a broader picture of literacy/ICT coproductions. An example of a theoretical insight that might traverse specific tools is the manner in which new literacy practices mediated by Internet technologies are reshaping the experience of time and space. While schooling may often construct literate activity as monochromic (temporally linear, tangible, and divisible), youth often use Internet technologies in ways that treat it as polychromic (fluid, layered, and simultaneous) (Jones, forthcoming). This difference has implications for research as well, challenging researchers' assumptions about a single dominant temporal frame or spatial situation of literate activity.

Further, while the social turn in literacy studies (e.g., Street, 1984) has done much to help us understand literacy as imminently social rather than purely individual, in the area of Internet technologies and literacy we have much to understand concerning how literacy is used to create social effects, or do work in social and cultural worlds. One promising area of study in this vein is work in Internet technologies and political activism, such as taken up by Brian Wilson in Ontario, Canada (Wilson, forthcoming). Little work has been done in media studies, and perhaps less in literacy studies, concerning how youth also organize forms of social critique and activism through online venues. Wilson critiques how youth have been infantilized and apoliticized by the popular media and previous research. In his current work, Wilson traverses online and offline contexts of social action, interpreting how online communications and texts become embedded, interpreted, and realized among youth activist networks.

Another high potential area of investigation concerning how literacy and Internet technologies is used to create social effects is the area of video game research. Video games are fast becoming a pastime of choice among many youth across the globe, involving multimediated experiences in which participants take on new identities, fight battles, go on collaborative virtual missions, take on new textual and visual identities, built art objects, and create new forms of sociality. Gee (2003) has authored a widely read and provocative early work on video games as venues of learning and literacy, drawing on a wide swath of current learning theories to develop 36 learning principles informing video game play as learning activity. Unlike much of contemporary schooling, with its division of knowledge into isolated bits, Gee argues that video games are semiotic domains that one slowly learns and can master. While online game research already has developed its own conferences and publication venues, game research in literacy studies is yet very early in development. Within this area, Constance Steinkueler's (2006) work is developing an analysis of online gaming, discourse, identity, and a host of literacy practices that gamers engage in during gaming and in support of their participation in the discourses and cultures of gaming. Leander and Lovvorn (2006) have developed a comparative analysis of literate practices in online gaming and schooling, drawing on Actor Network Theory in order to trace the circulations in various forms of classroom and game-related literacy practices. What presents a particular challenge in research on gaming is not only that games are rich multimodal environments, but also that that game texts-in-use challenge our ontological separations of texts from objects, bodies, and identities.

REFERENCES

Alvermann, D.E. (ed.): 2002, *Adolescents and Literacies in a Digital World*, Peter Lang, New York.

Appadurai, A.: 1996, *Modernity at Large: Cultural Dimensions of Globalization*, University of Minnesota Press, Minneapolis.

Asian Digital Cultures Conference. Accessed May 24, 2006, at http://www.sinica.edu.tw/ioe/chinese/r2711/050728-29/origin.htm.

Black, R.W.: 2005, 'Access and affiliation: The literacy and composition practices of English language learners in an online fanfiction community', *Journal of Adolescent & Adult Literacy* 49(2), 118–128.

Black, R.W.: 2007, 'Digital design: English language learners and reader feedback in online fanfiction', in M. Knobel and C. Lankshear (eds.), *A New Literacies Sampler*, Peter Lang, New York, 116–136.

Bolter, J. and Grusin, R.: 2000, *Remediation: Understanding New Media*, MIT Press, Cambridge, MA.

Bruce, B.C. and Rubin, A.: 1993, *Electronic Quills: A Situated Evaluation of Using Computers for Writing in Classrooms*, Lawrence Erlbaum, Hillsdale, NJ.

Bull, G.: 2005, 'Podcasting and the long tail', *Learning & Leading with Technology* 33(3), 24–26.

Burka, L.P.: 1995, The MUDline. Accessed October 30, 2006 at http://www.linnaean.org/~lpb/muddex/mudline.html.

Chandler-Olcott, K. and Mahar, D.: 2003, '"Tech-savviness" meets multiliteracies: Exploring adolescent girls' technology-mediated literacy practices', *Reading Research Quarterly* 38, 356–385.

Chen, C. and Rada, R.: 1996, 'Interacting with hypertext: A meta analysis of experimental studies', *Human-Computer Interaction* 11, 125–156.

Cohen, M. and Riel, M.: 1989, 'The effect of distant audiences on students' writing', *American Educational Research Journal* 26, 143–159.

Daiute, C. and Morse, F.: 1994, 'Access to knowledge and expression: Multimedia writing tools for students with diverse needs and strengths', *Journal of Special Education Technology* 12, 221–256.

Duncan B. and Leander, K.: 2000, November, Girls just wanna have fun: Literacy, consumerism, and paradoxes of position on gurl.com, Reading Online, 4. Accessed May 24, 2006, at *http://www.readingonline.org/electronic/elec_index.asp?HREF=/electronic/duncan/index.html*.

Euro-Kids Comenius project. Accessed October 28, 2006, at http://www.euro-kids.org/index.html

European Schoolnet. Accessed October 28, 2006, at http://www.eun.org/portal/index.htm

Fabos, B.: 2004, *Wrong turn! Education and Commercialism on the Information Superhighway*, Teachers College Press, New York.

Facer, K.: 2004, 'Different worlds? A comparison of young people's home and school ICT use', *Journal of Computer Assisted Learning* 20, 440–455.

Flanagan, B.C.: 2005, 'Podcasting in the classroom', *Learning & Leading with Technology* 33(3), 20–24.

Gee, J.P.: 2002, 'Millennials and Bobos, Blue's Clues and Sesame Street: A story for our Times', in D.E. Alvermann (ed.), *Adolescents and Literacies in a Digital World*, Peter Lang, New York.

Gee, J.: 2003, *What Video Games Have to Teach us about Learning and Literacy*, Palgrave Macmillan, New York.

Guihot, P.: 1989, 'Using Teletel for learning', in R. Mason and A. Kaye (eds.), *Mindweave: Communication, Computers and Distance Education*, Pergamon Press, Oxford, 192–195.

Herring, S.: 2004, 'Slouching toward the ordinary', *New Media and Society* 6, 26–36.

Holloway, S. and Valentine, G.: 2001, "It's only as stupid as you are': Children's and adults' negotiation of Internet technologies competence at home and at school', *Social and Cultural Geography* 2(1), 25–42.

Ito, M.: 2005, Technologies of childhood imagination: Yugioh, media mixes, and everyday cultural production, Accessed May 24, 2006, at http://www.itofisher.com/mito/archives/000074.html

Jones, R.: 2004, 'The problem of context in computer mediated communication', in P. LeVine and R. Scollon (eds.), *Discourse and Technology: Multimodal Discourse Analysis*, Georgetown University Press, Washington, DC.

Jones, R.: forthcoming. 'Sites of engagement as sites of attention: Time, space and culture in electronic discourse', in S. Norris and R. Jones (eds.), *Discourse in Action: Introducing Mediated Discourse Analysis*, Routledge, London.

Karaidy, M.M.: 1999, 'The global, the local, and the hybrid: A native ethnography of Glocalization', *Critical Studies in Mass Communication* 16, 454–467.

Kress, G.: 2003, *Literacy in the New Media Age*, Routledge, New York.

Kress, G. and Van Leeuwen, T.: 2001, *Multimodal Discourse: The Modes and Media of Contemporary Communication*, Edward Arnold, London.

Kress, G. and Jewitt, C.: 2003, 'Introduction', in C. Jewitt and G. Kress (eds.), *Multimodal Literacy: New Literacies and Digital Epistemologies* Volume 4, Peter Lang, New York.

Laboratory of Comparative Human Cognition: 1982, 'Microcomputer communication networks for education', *The Quarterly Newsletter of the Laboratory of Comparative Human Cognition* 4, 32–34.

Lam, W.S.E.: 2000, 'Second language literacy and the design of the self: A case study of a teenager writing on the Internet', *TESOL Quarterly* 34, 457–483.

Lam, W.S.E.: 2004, 'Second language socialization in a bilingual chat room', *Language Learning and Technology* 8(3), 44–65.

Lankshear, C. and Knobel, M.: 2003, 'New technologies in early childhood research: A review of research', *Journal of Early Childhood Literacy* 3(1), 59–82.

Leander, K.M.: 2004, 'Home/schooling, everywhere: Digital literacies as practices of space-time', paper presented at the annual meeting of the American Educational Research Association, San Diego, CA.

Leander, K.M. and McKim, K.: 2003, 'Tracing the everyday "sitings" of adolescents on the Internet: A strategic adaptation of ethnography across online and offline spaces', *Education, Communication, & Information* 3, 211–240.

Leander, K.M. and Lovvorn, J.: 2006, 'Literacy networks: Following the circulation of texts, bodies, and objects in the schooling and online gaming of one youth', *Cognition & Instruction*, 24(3), 291–340.

Leask, M. and Younie, S.: 2001, 'The European Schoolnet. An online European community for teachers? A valuable professional resource?', *Teacher Development* 5, 157–175.

Lemke, J.L.: 1998, 'Metamedia literacy: Transforming meanings and media', in D. Reinking, M.C. McKenna, L.D. Labbo, and R.D. Kieffer (eds.), *Literacy and technology: Transformations in a Post-Typographic World*, Lawrence Erlbaum, Mahwah, NJ.

Lenhart, A., Madden, M., and Hitlin, P.: 2005, *Teens and Technology: Youth are Leading the Transition to a Fully Wired and Mobile Nation*, Pew Internet & American Life Project, Washington, DC.

Leu, D.J.: 2000, 'Literacy and technology: Deictic consequences for literacy education in an information age', in M. Kamil, P.B. Mosenthal, P.D. Pearson, and R. Barr (eds.), *Handbook of Reading Research* (Volume III), Erlbaum, Mahwah, NJ.

Lewis, C. and Fabos, B.: 2005, 'Instant messaging, literacies, and social identities', *Reading Research Quarterly* 40, 470–501.

Livingstone, S.: 2002, *Young People and New Media, Sage*, London.

Myers, J., Hammett, R., and McKillop, A.M.: 1998, 'Opportunities for critical literacy and pedagogy in student-authored hypermedia', in D. Reinking, M.C. McKenna, L.D. Labbo, and R.D. Kieffer (eds.), *Handbook of Literacy and Technology: Transformations in a post-typographic world*, Erlbaum, Mahwah, NJ.

New London Group: 1996, 'A pedagogy of multiliteracies: Designing social futures', *Harvard Educational Review* 66, 60–92.

Reinking, D. and Chanlin, L.J.: 1994, 'Graphic aids in electronic texts', *Reading Research and Instruction* 33, 207–232.

Reinking, D., McKenna, M.C., Labbo, L.D., and Kieffer, R.D. (eds.): 1998, *Handbook of Literacy and Technology: Transformations in a Post-Typographic World*, Erlbaum, Mahwah, NJ.

Riel, M.: 1990, 'Telecommunications: A tool for reconnecting kids with society', *Interactive learning environments* 1, 255–263.

Steinkuehler, C.A.: 2006, 'Massively multiplayer online videogaming as participation in a Discourse', *Mind, Culture, & Activity* 13(1), 38–52.

Street, B.V.: 1984, *Literacy in Theory and Practice*, Cambridge University Press, Cambridge, UK.

Thomas, A.: 2005, 'Children online: Learning in a virtual community of practice', *E- Learning* 2, 27–38.

Valentine, G., Holloway, S.L., and Bingham, N.: 2000, 'Transforming cyberspace: Children's interventions in the new public sphere', in S.L. Holloway and G. Valentine (eds.), *Children's Geographies: Playing, Living, Learning*, Routledge, New York.

Warshauer, M.: 2002, 'Languages.com: The Internet and linguistic pluralism', in I. Snyder (ed.), *Silicon Literacies*, Routledge, New York, NY.

Wilson, B.: forthcoming, 'Ethnography, the Internet and youth culture: Strategies for examining social resistance and "online-offline" relationships', *Canadian Journal of Education*.

Wellman, B.: 2004, 'The three stages of Internet studies: Ten, five and zero years ago', *New Media and Society* 6, 123–129.

JIM CUMMINS

BICS AND CALP: EMPIRICAL AND THEORETICAL
STATUS OF THE DISTINCTION

INTRODUCTION

The distinction between *basic interpersonal communicative skills* (BICS) and *cognitive academic language proficiency* (CALP) was introduced by Cummins (1979, 1981a) in order to draw educators' attention to the timelines and challenges that second language learners encounter as they attempt to catch up to their peers in academic aspects of the school language. BICS refers to conversational fluency in a language while CALP refers to students' ability to understand and express, in both oral and written modes, concepts and ideas that are relevant to success in school. The terms conversational fluency and academic language proficiency are used interchangeably with BICS and CALP in the remainder of this chapter.

Initially, I describe the origins, rationale, and evolution of the distinction together with its empirical foundations. I then discuss its relationship to similar theoretical constructs that have been proposed in different contexts and for different purposes. Finally, I analyze and respond to critiques of the distinction and discuss the relationship of the distinction to the emerging field of New Literacy studies (e.g. Barton, 1994; Street, 1995).

EARLY DEVELOPMENTS

Skutnabb-Kangas and Toukomaa (1976) initially brought attention to the fact that Finnish immigrant children in Sweden often appeared to educators to be fluent in both Finnish and Swedish but still showed levels of verbal academic performance in both languages considerably below grade/age expectations. The BICS/CALP distinction highlighted a similar reality and formalized the difference between conversational fluency and academic language proficiency as conceptually distinct components of the construct of "language proficiency." Because this was a conceptual distinction rather than an overall theory of "language proficiency" there was never any suggestion that these were the only important or relevant components of that construct.

The initial theoretical intent of the BICS/CALP distinction was to qualify Oller's (1979) claim that all individual differences in language

B. Street and N. H. Hornberger (eds), Encyclopedia of Language and Education,
2nd Edition, Volume 2: Literacy, 71–83.
©2010 Springer Science+Business Media LLC.

proficiency could be accounted for by just one underlying factor, which he termed *global language proficiency*. Oller synthesized a considerable amount of data showing strong correlations between performance on cloze tests of reading, standardized reading tests, and measures of oral verbal ability (e.g. vocabulary measures). Cummins (1979), however, argued that it is problematic to incorporate all aspects of language use or performance into just one dimension of general or global language proficiency. For example, if we take two monolingual English-speaking siblings, a 12-year old child and a 6-year old, there are enormous differences in these children's ability to read and write English and in the depth and breadth of their vocabulary knowledge, but minimal differences in their phonology or basic fluency. The 6-year old can understand virtually everything that is likely to be said to her in everyday social contexts and she can use language very effectively in these contexts, just as the 12-year old can. In other words, some aspects of children's first language development (e.g. phonology) reach a plateau relatively early whereas other aspects (e.g. vocabulary knowledge) continue to develop throughout our lifetimes. Thus, these very different aspects of proficiency cannot be considered to reflect just one unitary proficiency dimension.

CALP or academic language proficiency develops through social interaction from birth but becomes differentiated from BICS after the early stages of schooling to reflect primarily the language that children acquire in school and which they need to use effectively if they are to progress successfully through the grades. The notion of CALP is specific to the social context of schooling, hence the term "academic." Academic language proficiency can thus be defined as "the extent to which an individual has access to and command of the oral and written academic registers of schooling" (Cummins, 2000, p. 67).

The relevance of the BICS/CALP distinction for bilingual students' academic development was reinforced by two research studies (Cummins, 1980, 1981b) showing that educators and policy-makers frequently conflated conversational and academic dimensions of English language proficiency and that this conflation contributed significantly to the creation of academic difficulties for students who were learning English as an additional language (EAL).

The first study (Cummins, 1980, 1984) involved an analysis of more than 400 teacher referral forms and psychological assessments carried out on EAL students in a large Canadian school system. The teacher referral forms and psychological assessment reports showed that teachers and psychologists often assumed that children had overcome all difficulties with English when they could converse easily in the language. Yet these children frequently performed poorly on English academic tasks within the classroom (hence the referral for assessment) as well as on the verbal scales of the cognitive ability test administered as part of the psychological assessment. Many students were designated as having language or communication disabilities despite the fact that they had been in Canada for a relatively short amount of time (e.g. 1–3 years). Thus, the conflation of second language (L2) conversational fluency with L2 academic proficiency contributed directly to the inappropriate placement of bilingual students in special education programs.

The need to distinguish between conversational fluency and academic aspects of L2 performance was further highlighted by the reanalysis of language performance data from the Toronto Board of Education (Cummins, 1981b). These data showed that there was a gap of several years, on average, between the attainment of peer-appropriate fluency in English and the attainment of grade norms in academic aspects of English. Conversational aspects of proficiency reached peer-appropriate levels usually within about two years of exposure to English but a period of 5–7 years was required, on average, for immigrant students to approach grade norms in academic aspects of English (e.g. vocabulary knowledge).

The differential time periods required to attain peer-appropriate L2 conversational fluency as compared to meeting grade expectations in academic language proficiency have been corroborated in many research studies carried out during the past 30 years in Canada (Klesmer, 1994), Europe (Snow and Hoefnagel-Hohle, 1978), Israel (Shohamy, Levine, Spolsky, Kere-Levy, Inbar, Shemesh, 2002), and the United States (Hakuta, Butler and Witt, 2002; Thomas and Collier, 2002).

The following example from the psychological assessment study (Cummins, 1980, 1984) illustrates how these implicit assumptions about the nature of language proficiency can directly affect the academic trajectories and life chances of bilingual students:

> PR (289). PR was referred in first grade by the school principal who noted that "PR is experiencing considerable difficulty with grade one work. An intellectual assessment would help her teacher to set realistic learning expectations for her and might provide some clues as to remedial assistance that might be offered."

No mention was made of the fact that the child was learning English as a second language; this only emerged when the child was referred by the second grade teacher in the following year. Thus, the psychologist does not consider this as a possible factor in accounting for the discrepancy between a verbal IQ of 64 and a performance (nonverbal) IQ of 108. The assessment report read as follows:

> Although overall ability level appears to be within the low average range, note the significant difference between verbal and nonverbal scores .... It would appear that PR's development has not progressed at a normal rate and

consequently she is, and will continue to experience much difficulty in school. Teacher's expectations at this time should be set
accordingly.

What is interesting in this example is that the child's English communicative skills are presumably sufficiently well developed that the psychologist (and possibly the teacher) is not alerted to the child's EAL
background. This leads the psychologist to infer from her low verbal
IQ score that "her development has not progressed at a normal rate"
and to advise the teacher to set low academic expectations for the child
since she "will continue to experience much difficulty in school."

During the 1980s and 1990s in the United States exactly the same
misconception about the nature of language proficiency underlay the
frequent early exit of bilingual students from English-as-a-second language (ESL) or bilingual programs into mainstream English-only programs on the basis of the fact that they had "acquired English." Many of
these students experienced academic difficulties within the mainstream
class because no supports were in place to assist them to understand
instruction and continue their development of English academic skills.

The relevance of the BICS/CALP distinction is illustrated in Vincent's
(1996) ethnographic study of second generation Salvadorean students in
Washington DC. Vincent points out that the children in her study began
school in an English-speaking environment and "within their first two or
three years attained conversational ability in English that teachers would
regard as native-like" (p. 195). She suggests, however, that this fluency
is largely deceptive:

> The children seem to have much greater English proficiency
> than they actually do because their spoken English has no
> accent and they are able to converse on a few everyday, fre-
> quently discussed subjects. Academic language is frequently
> lacking. Teachers actually spend very little time talking with
> individual children and tend to interpret a small sample of
> speech as evidence of full English proficiency. (p. 195)

BICS/CALP made no claim to be anything more than a conceptual
distinction. It provided a way of (i) naming and talking about the classroom realities that Vincent (1996) discusses and (ii) highlighting the
discriminatory assessment and instructional practices experienced by
many bilingual students.

EVOLUTION OF THE THEORETICAL CONSTRUCTS

The initial BICS/CALP distinction was elaborated into two intersecting continua (Cummins, 1981a) that highlighted the range of cognitive demands and contextual support involved in particular language
tasks or activities (context-embedded/context-reduced, cognitively

undemanding/cognitively demanding). Internal and external dimensions of context were distinguished to reflect the fact that "context" is constituted both by what we bring to a task (e.g., our prior knowledge, interests, and motivation) and the range of suports that may be incorporated in the task itself (e.g., visual supports such as graphic organizers). This "quadrants" framework stimulated discussion of the instructional environment required to enable EAL students to catch up academically as quickly as possible. Specifically, it was argued that effective instruction for EAL students should focus primarily on context-embedded and cognitively demanding tasks. It was also recognized, however, that these dimensions cannot be specified in absolute terms because what is "context-embedded" or "cognitively demanding" for one learner may not be so for another as a result of differences in internal attributes such as prior knowledge or interest (Coelho, 2004; Cummins, 1981a).

The BICS/CALP distinction was maintained within this elaboration and related to the theoretical distinctions of several other theorists (e.g. Bruner's [1975] communicative and analytic competence, Donaldson's [1978] embedded and disembedded language, and Olson's [1977] utterance and text). The terms used by different investigators have varied but the essential distinction refers to the extent to which the meaning being communicated is strongly supported by contextual or interpersonal cues (such as gestures, facial expressions, and intonation present in face-to-face interaction) or supported primarily by linguistic cues. The term "context-reduced" was used rather than "decontextualized" in recognition of the fact that all language and literacy practices are contextualized; however, the range of supports to meaning in many academic contexts (e.g., textbook reading) is reduced in comparison to the contextual support available in face-to-face contexts.

In later accounts of the framework (Cummins, 2000, 2001) the distinction between conversational fluency and academic language proficiency was related to the work of several other theorists. For example, Gibbons' (1991) distinction between *playground language* and *classroom language* highlighted in a particularly clear manner the linguistic challenges of classroom language demands. She notes that playground language includes the language which "enables children to make friends, join in games and take part in a variety of day-to-day activities that develop and maintain social contacts" (p. 3). She points out that this language typically occurs in face-to-face situations and is highly dependent on the physical and visual context, and on gesture and body language. However, classroom language is very different from playground language:

> The playground situation does not normally offer children the opportunity to use such language as: *if we increase the angle by 5 degrees, we could cut the circumference into equal parts.*

Nor does it normally require the language associated with the higher order thinking skills, such as hypothesizing, evaluating, inferring, generalizing, predicting or classifying. Yet these are the language functions which are related to learning and the development of cognition; they occur in all areas of the curriculum, and without them a child's potential in academic areas cannot be realized (1991, p. 3).

The research of Biber (1986) and Corson (1995) also provides evidence of the linguistic reality of the distinction. Corson highlighted the enormous lexical differences between typical conversational interactions in English as compared to academic or literacy-related uses of English. The high-frequency everyday lexicon of English conversation derives predominantly from Anglo-Saxon sources while the relatively lower frequency academic vocabulary is primarily Graeco-Latin in origin (see also Coxhead, 2000).

Similarly, Biber's (1986) factor analysis of more than one million words of English speech and written text from a wide variety of genres revealed underlying dimensions very consistent with the distinction between conversational and academic aspects of language proficiency. For example, when factor scores were calculated for the different text types on each factor, telephone and face-to-face conversation were at opposite extremes from official documents and academic prose on Textual Dimensions 1 and 2 (Interactive vs. Edited Text, and Abstract vs. Situated Content).

Conversational and academic language registers were also related to Gee's (1990) distinction between *primary* and *secondary* discourses (Cummins, 2001). Primary discourses are acquired through face-to-face interactions in the home and represent the language of initial socialization. Secondary discourses are acquired in social institutions beyond the family (e.g. school, business, religious, and cultural contexts) and involve acquisition of specialized vocabulary and functions of language appropriate to those settings. Secondary discourses can be oral or written and are equally central to the social life of nonliterate and literate cultures. Examples of secondary discourse common in many nonliterate cultures are the conventions of story-telling or the language of marriage or burial rituals which are passed down through oral tradition from one generation to the next. Within this conception, academic language proficiency represents an individual's access to and command of the specialized vocabulary and functions of language that are characteristic of the social institution of schooling. The secondary discourses of schooling are no different in principle than the secondary discourse of other spheres of human endeavor—for example, avid amateur gardeners and professional horticulturalists have acquired vocabulary related to plants and flowers far beyond the knowledge of those not involved in this sphere of activity. What makes acquisition of the secondary discourses associated with schooling so crucial, however, is that the life chances of individuals are directly determined by the degree of expertise they acquire in understanding and using this language.

Other ways in which the original BICS/CALP distinction has evolved include:

- The addition of *discrete language skills* as a component of language proficiency that is distinct from both conversational fluency and academic language proficiency (Cummins, 2001). Discrete language skills involve the learning of rule-governed aspects of language (including phonology, grammar, and spelling) where acquisition of the general case permits generalization to other instances governed by that particular rule. Discrete language skills can sometimes be learned in virtual isolation from the development of academic language proficiency as illustrated in the fact that some students who can "read" English fluently may have only a very limited understanding of the words they can decode (see Cummins, Brown, and Sayers, 2007, for an analysis of discrete language skills in relation to current debates on the teaching of reading in the USA).
- The embedding of the BICS/CALP distinction within a broader framework of academic development in culturally and linguistically diverse contexts that specifies the role of societal power relations in framing teacher–student interactions and determining the social organization of schooling (Cummins, 1986, 2001). Teacher–student interactions are seen as a process of negotiating identities, reflecting to varying degrees coercive or collaborative relations of power in the wider society. This socialization process within the school determines the extent to which students will engage academically and gain access to the academic registers of schooling.

CONTRIBUTIONS OF THE BICS/CALP DISTINCTION TO POLICY AND PRACTICE

Since its initial articulation, the distinction between BICS and CALP has influenced both policy and practice related to the instruction and assessment of second language learners. It has been invoked, for example, in policy discussions related to:

- The amount and duration of funding necessary to support students who are learning English as an additional language;
- The kinds of instructional support that EAL students need at different stages of their acquisition of conversational and academic English;

- The inclusion of EAL students in nationally mandated high-stakes testing; for example, should EAL students be exempt from taking high-stakes tests and, if so, for how long—1, 2, 3, 4, or 5 years after arrival in the host country?
- The extent to which psychological testing of EAL students for diagnostic purposes through their L2 is valid and ethically defensible.

The distinction is discussed in numerous books that aim to equip educators with the understanding and skills required to teach and assess linguistically diverse students (e.g. Cline and Frederickson, 1996, in the United Kingdom; Coelho, 2004, in Canada; Diaz-Rico and Weed, 2002, in the USA) and has been invoked to interpret data from a range of sociolinguistic and educational contexts (e.g. Broome's [2004] research on reading English in multilingual South African schools).

CRITIQUES OF THE BICS/CALP DISTINCTION

The BICS/CALP distinction has also been critiqued by numerous scholars who see it as oversimplified (e.g. Scarcella, 2003; Valdés, 2004), reflective of an "autonomous" rather than an "ideological" notion of literacy (Wiley, 1996), an artifact of "test-wiseness" (Edelsky et al., 1983; Martin-Jones and Romaine, 1986) and a "deficit theory" that attributes bilingual students' academic difficulties to their "low CALP" (e.g. Edelsky, 1990; Edelsky et al., 1983; MacSwan, 2000).

In response to these critiques, Cummins and Swain (1983) and Cummins (2000) pointed out that the construct of academic language proficiency does not in any way depend on test scores to support either its construct validity or relevance to education. This is illustrated in Vincent's (1996) ethnographic study and Biber's (1986) research on the English lexicon discussed above. Furthermore, the BICS/CALP distinction has been integrated since 1986 with a detailed sociopolitical analysis of how schools construct academic failure among subordinated groups. The framework documents educational approaches that challenge this pattern of coercive power relations and promote the generation of power and the development of academic expertise in interactions between educators and students (Cummins, 2001; Cummins, Brown, and Sayers, 2007).

The broader issues in this debate go beyond the specific interpretations of the distinction between conversational fluency and academic language proficiency. They concern the nature of theoretical constructs and their intersection with research, policy and practice. Theories must be consistent with the empirical data to have any claim to validity. However, any set of theoretical constructs represents only one of potentially many ways of organizing or viewing the data. Theories frame phenomena and provide interpretations of empirical data within particular contexts and for particular purposes. However, no theory is "valid" or "true" in any absolute sense. A theory represents a way of viewing phenomena that may be relevant and useful in varying degrees depending on its purpose, how well it communicates with its intended audience, and the consequences for practice of following through on its implications (its "consequential validity"). The generation of knowledge (theory) is always dialogical and just as oral and written language is meaningless outside of a human communicative and interpretive context, so too theoretical constructs assume meaning only within specific dialogical contexts. (Cummins, 2000).

Thus, the BICS/CALP distinction was initially formulated to address certain theoretical issues (e.g. whether "language proficiency" could legitimately be viewed as a unitary construct, as Oller [1979] proposed) and to interpret empirical data related to the time periods required for immigrant students to catch up academically. It spoke directly to prejudicial policies and practices that were denying students access to equitable and effective learning opportunities.

Much of the criticism of the distinction derives from taking the constructs out of their original dialogical or discursive context and arguing that they are not useful or appropriate in a very different dialogical context. This can be illustrated in Scarcella's (2003) critique. She argues that the dichotomous conceptualization of language incorporated in the BICS/CALP distinction "is not useful for understanding the complexities of academic English or the multiple variables affecting its development" (p. 5). Both BICS and CALP are more complex than a binary distinction implies. She points out that some aspects of BICS are acquired late and some aspects of CALP are acquired early. Furthermore, some variables such as phonemic awareness (sensitivity to sounds in spoken words) are related to the development of both BICS and CALP (e.g. in helping readers to access difficult academic words). She concludes that the distinction is "of limited practical value, since it fails to operationalize tasks and therefore does not generate tasks that teachers can use to help develop their students' academic English .... the BICS/CALP perspective does not provide teachers with sufficient information about academic English to help their students acquire it" (p. 6).

Scarcella goes on to elaborate a detailed framework for conceptualizing academic language and generating academic tasks that is certainly far more useful and appropriate for this purpose than the notion of CALP. What she fails to acknowledge, however, is that the BICS/CALP distinction was not formulated as a tool to generate academic tasks. It addresses a very different set of theoretical, policy, and classroom instructional issues. Scarcella's critique is analogous to rejecting an apple because it is not an orange.

Related to Scarcella's critique are concerns (Valdés, 2004; Wiley, 2006) that the conversational fluency/academic language proficiency

distinction reflects an "autonomous" view of language and literacy that
is incompatible with the perspective of New Literacies theorists that
language and literacy represent social and cultural practices that are
embedded in a context of historical and current power relations (e.g.
Barton, 1994; Street, 1995). As expressed by Valdés (2004, p. 115):

> The view that there are multiple literacies rather than a single
> literacy, that these literacies depend on the context of the
> situation, the activity itself, the interactions between partici-
> pants, and the knowledge and experiences that these various
> participants bring to these interactions is distant from the
> view held by most L2 educators who still embrace a techno-
> cratic notion of literacy and emphasise the development of
> decontextualised skills.

There is nothing in the BICS/CALP distinction that is inconsistent with
this perspective on language and literacy practices. It makes no claim to
focus on any context other than that of the school. Furthermore, the
pedagogical practices that have been articulated to support the development of academic expertise (CALP) are far from the decontextualized
drills appropriately castigated by numerous researchers and educators.
They include a focus on critical literacy and critical language awareness together with enabling EAL and bilingual students to generate
new knowledge, create literature and art, and act on social realities, all
of which directly address issues of identity negotiation and societal
power relations (Cummins, 2001; Cummins, Brown, and Sayers, 2007).

One can accept the perspective that literacies are multiple, contextually specific, and constantly evolving (as I do) while at the same time
arguing that in certain discursive contexts it is useful to distinguish
between conversational fluency and academic language proficiency.
To illustrate, the fact that the concept of "European" can be broken down
into an almost infinite array of national, regional, and social identities
does not invalidate the more general descriptor of "European." In some
discursive contexts and for some purposes it is legitimate and useful to
describe an individual or a group as "European" despite the fact that it
greatly oversimplifies the complex reality of "Europeanness." Similarly,
in certain discursive contexts and for certain purposes it is legitimate
and useful to talk about conversational fluency and academic language
proficiency despite the fact that these constructs incorporate multiple
levels of complexity.

Clearly, theorists operating from a New Literacies perspective have
contributed important insights into the nature and functions of literacy.
However, this does not mean that a New Literacies perspective is the
best or only way to address all questions of literacy development. For
example, highlighting the social and contextually specific dimensions
of cognition does not invalidate a research focus on what may be

happening inside the heads of individuals as they perform cognitive or linguistic tasks. There are many important questions and research studies associated with first and second language literacy development that owe little to New Literacy Studies but have played a central role in policy discussions related to equity in education. Research studies on how long it typically takes EAL students to catch up to grade norms in English academic proficiency have, within the context of the research, focused on literacy as an autonomous skill measured by standardized tests but have nevertheless contributed in substantial ways to promoting equity in schooling for bilingual students.

FUTURE DIRECTIONS

The BICS/CALP distinction was not proposed as an overall theory of language proficiency but as a very specific conceptual distinction that has important implications for policy and practice. It has drawn attention to specific ways in which educators' assumptions about the nature of language proficiency and the development of L2 proficiency have prejudiced the academic development of bilingual students. However, the distinction is likely to remain controversial, reflecting the fact that there is no cross-disciplinary consensus regarding the nature of language proficiency and its relationship to academic development.

The most productive direction to orient further research on this topic, and one that can be supported by all scholars, is to focus on creating instructional and learning environments that maximize the language and literacy development of socially marginalized students. Because academic language is found primarily in written texts, extensive engaged reading is likely to be a crucial component of an effective learning environment (Guthrie, 2003). Opportunities for collaborative learning and talk about text are also extremely important in helping students internalize and more fully comprehend the academic language they find in their extensive reading of text.

Writing for authentic purposes is also crucial because when bilingual students write about issues that matter to them they not only consolidate aspects of the academic language they have been reading, they also express their identities through language and (hopefully) receive feedback from teachers and others that will affirm and further develop their expression of self (Cummins, Brown, and Sayers, 2007). Deeper understanding of the nature of academic language and its relationship both to conversational fluency and other forms of literacy will emerge from teachers, students, and researchers working together in instructional contexts collaboratively pushing (and documenting) the boundaries of language and literacy exploration.

REFERENCES

Barton, D.: 1994, *Literacy: An Introduction to the Ecology of Written Language*, Blackwell, Oxford.

Biber, D.: 1986, 'Spoken and written textual dimensions in English: Resolving the contradictory findings', *Language* 62, 384–414.

Broome, Y.: 2004, 'Reading English in multilingual South African primary schools', *International Journal of Bilingual Education and Bilingualism* 7, 506–528.

Bruner, J.S.: 1975, 'Language as an instrument of thought', in A. Davies (ed.), *Problems of Language and Learning*, Heinemann, London, 61–88.

Cline, T. and Frederickson, N. (eds.): 1996, *Curriculum Related Assessment, Cummins and Bilingual Children*, Multilingual Matters, Clevedon, England.

Coelho, E.: 2004, *Adding English: A Guide to Teaching in Multilingual Classrooms*, Pippin Publishing, Toronto.

Corson, D.: 1997, 'The learning and use of academic English words', *Language Learning* 47, 671–718.

Coxhead, A.: 2000, 'A new academic word list', *TESOL Quarterly* 34(2), 213–238.

Cummins, J.: 1979, 'Cognitive/academic language proficiency, linguistic interdependence, the optimum age question and some other matters', *Working Papers on Bilingualism* 19, 121–129.

Cummins, J.: 1980, 'Psychological assessment of immigrant children: Logic or intuition?', *Journal of Multilingual and Multicultural Development* 1, 97–111.

Cummins, J.: 1981a, 'The role of primary language development in promoting educational success for language minority students', in California State Department of Education (ed.), *Schooling and Language Minority Students: A Theoretical Framework*, Evaluation, Dissemination and Assessment Center California State University, Los Angeles.

Cummins, J.: 1981b, 'Age on arrival and immigrant second language learning in Canada: A reassessment', *Applied Linguistics* 1, 132–149.

Cummins, J.: 1984, *Bilingualism and Special Education: Issues in Assessment and Pedagogy*, Multilingual Matters, Clevedon, England.

Cummins, J.: 2000, *Language, Power and Pedagogy: Bilingual Children in the Crossfire*, Multilingual Matters, Clevedon, England.

Cummins, J.: 2001, *Negotiating Identities: Education for Empowerment in a Diverse Society* (second edition), California Association for Bilingual Education, Los Angeles.

Cummins, J., Brown, K., and Sayers, D.: 2007, *Literacy, Technology, and Diversity: Teaching for Success in Changing Times*, Allyn & Bacon, Boston.

Cummins, J. and Swain, M.: 1983, 'Analysis-by-rhetoric: Reading the text or the reader's own projections?', A reply to Edelsky et al. *Applied Linguistics* 4, 23–41.

Diaz-Rico, L.T. and Weed, K.Z.: 2002, *The Crosscultural, Language, and Academic Development Handbook: A Complete K-12 Reference Guide* (second edition), Allyn & Bacon, Boston.

Donaldson, M.: 1978, *Children's Minds*, Collins, Glasgow.

Edelsky, C.: 1990, 'With literacy and justice for all: Rethinking the social in language and education', The Falmer Press, London.

Edelsky, C., Hudelson, S., Flores, B., Barkin, F., Altweger, B., and Jilbert, K.: 1983, 'Semilingualism and language deficit', *Applied Linguistics* 4, 1–22.

Gee, J.P.: 1990, *Social Linguistics and Literacies: Ideologies in Discourses*, Falmer Press, New York.

Guthrie, J.T.: 2004, 'Teaching for literacy engagement', *Journal of Literacy Research* 36, 1–30.

Hakuta, K., Butler, Y.G., and Witt, D.: 2000, *How Long Does It Take English Learners to Attain Proficiency?*, University of California Linguistic Minority Research Institute, Santa Barbara.

Klesmer, H.: 1994, 'Assessment and teacher perceptions of ESL student achievement', *English Quarterly* 26(3), 8–11.

MacSwan, J.: 2000, 'The threshold hypothesis, semilingualism, and other contributions to a deficit view of linguistic minorities', *Hispanic Journal of Behavioral Sciences* 22(1), 3–45.

Martin-Jones, M. and Romaine, S.: 1986, 'Semilingualism: A half-baked theory of communicative competence', *Applied Linguistics* 7, 26–38.

Oller, J.: 1979, *Language Tests at School: A Pragmatic Approach*, Longman, London.

Olson, D.R.: 1977, From utterance to text: The bias of language in speech and writing. *Harvard Educational Review* 47, 257–281.

Scarcella, R.: 2003, *Academic English: A conceptual framework*, The University of California Linguistic Minority Research Institute Technical Report, Santa Barbara, 2003-1.

Skutnabb-Kangas, T. and Toukomaa, P.: 1976, *Teaching Migrant Children's Mother Tongue and Learning the Language of the Host Country in the Context of the Socio-Cultural Situation of the Migrant Family*, The Finnish National Commission for UNESCO, Helsinki.

Shohamy, E., Levine, T., Spolsky, B., Kere-Levy, M., Inbar, O., and Shemesh, M.: 2002, *The academic achievements of immigrant children from the former USSR and Ethiopia*. Report (in Hebrew) submitted to the Ministry of Education, Israel.

Snow, C.E. and Hoefnagel-Hohle, M.: 1978, 'The critical period for language acquisition: Evidence from second language learning', *Child Development* 49, 1114–1128.

Street, B.: 1995, *Social Literacies: Critical Approaches to Literacy in Development, Ethnography and Education*, Longman, London.

Thomas, W.P. and Collier, V.P.: 2002, *A National Study of School Effectiveness for Language Minority Students' Long-Term Academic Achievement*, Center for Research on Education, Diversity and Excellence, University of California-Santa Cruz, Santa Cruz, CA, http//www.crede.ucsc.edu.

Valdés, G.: 2004, 'Between support and marginalization: The development of academic language in linguistic minority children', *International Journal of Bilingual Education and Bilingualism* 7, 102–132.

Vincent, C.: 1996, *Singing to a Star: The School Meanings of Second Generation Salvadorean Students*, Doctoral dissertation, George Mason University, Fairfax, VA.

Wiley, T.G.: 1996, *Literacy and Language Diversity in the United States*, Center for Applied Linguistics and Delta Systems, Washington, DC.

JOHN EDWARDS

READING: ATTITUDES, INTERESTS, PRACTICES

INTRODUCTION

The social psychology, or sociology, of reading remains a relatively
small part of a vast literature largely concerned with skills acquisition
and development. This is curious for two reasons. First, it is obvious
that both teachers and researchers do not want merely to facilitate
reading ability—they hope to form and maintain reading habits. Second,
there are regular laments—as perennial as grumblings over the inadequacies of the younger generation—about low levels of reading, poor
attitudes, lack of enthusiasm and so on. Indeed, surveys often suggest
a gulf between reading ability and reading practices; in many contemporary societies, the essential problem seems to be *aliteracy* rather than
illiteracy (see later). On both counts, then, questions of what people
read, how much they read, and the purposes and effects of their reading
surely assume central importance.

Attention to the social psychology of reading is even more timely in
a post-modern era that has reinterpreted the roles of author and reader.
Nell (1988) touched upon the 'new criticism' underpinned by a relativ-
ism that suggests that the book is essentially created by the reader
(Tinker, 1965), that a book is 'a relationship, an axis of innumerable
relationships' (Borges, 1964, p. 13), that 'the reader makes literature'
(Fish, 1980, p. 11). The degree to which this criticism has taken hold
in academe is indicated by even more modern attempts to reclaim
ground for the 'common reader', to re-establish the centrality of the
aesthetic qualities of (fiction) reading, to cast aside those professional
'isms' that have turned reading into a job requiring doctoral qualifica-
tions (see Bloom, 2000; Edmundson, 2004).[1]

---

[1] Both the 'professionalisation' of literature, and arguments against it, have quite a
long history. The teaching of English literature, for example, was generally resisted by
the academy until the mid-nineteenth century (later still in Oxford and Cambridge)—
on the grounds that it was of insufficient depth, but also because of apprehensions
about the baleful influence of 'experts'. On the other hand, as early as 1927, Forster
heaved a regretful sigh that 'the novel tells a story ... I wish that it was not so'. The
story 'runs like a backbone—or may I say a tape-worm' supporting other 'finer
growths' (p. 45). Here we have the disdain for the obvious—and the obviously
appealing—that has so distressed the 'common reader' ever since; see also the Leavis
influence, later.

B. V. Street and N. H. Hornberger (eds), Encyclopedia of Language and Education,
2nd Edition, Volume 2: Literacy, 85–93.
©2010 Springer Science+Business Media LLC.

The book itself has also been defended in recent years, in the face of challenges from the electronic media, and arguments for a digitised and book-less chiliasm (see Negroponte, 1995). Thus, for example, Birkerts (1994) defended the more traditional pleasures and values of the text. Of course, words on computer screens, like words in books, are *read*—but it is fair to say that the act of reading, constant for many centuries, is undergoing considerable change, and the essence of this change is social and psychological. (It is interesting to note here that the pervasiveness of the 'e-book' has turned out to be less than complete: see the commentaries by Max, 1994, 2000.)

Although the proportion of illiterate people has been in steady decline for some time, an increase in absolute numbers means that one-third of the world's population can still neither read nor write. In 'developed' societies, however, the problem of illiteracy *tout court* is less significant than that of so-called 'functional literacy', some socially meaningful ability that goes beyond elementary skills (see Oxenham, 1980). Several surveys have suggested that, in Europe and North America, as much as a quarter of the population may have difficulty with mundane but important tasks like understanding road signs or product-warning labels (Creative Research Group, 1987; Edwards, 1991; Kozol, 1985; OECD, 2000).

In many modern societies, *aliteracy* (Maeroff, 1982; Neuman, 1986) is as much an issue as functional literacy. It is certainly more compelling in a social-psychological sense, because the question here is why some of those who *can* read *don't* read. The term may be new but the phenomenon (as implied earlier) is old, and if television is the modern villain of the piece, other distractions once came readily to hand (Edwards, 1981). It is true, of course, that many of the commentators here have had particularly snobbish axes to grind—thus, when Queenie Leavis observed (in 1932) that 'the reading capacity of the general public ... has never been so low as at the present time' (p. 231), she was reflecting the higher Leavisite criticism. The real problem for such self-appointed arbiters is not that people don't read; it's that they don't read anything worthwhile. This attitude can still be detected, wherever debate rages over issues of reading 'quality', and there is a double psychological import here: on the one hand, such *de haut en bas* attitudes are, in themselves, worthy of analysis; on the other, questions of reading 'quality', of whether *all* reading should be encouraged, of whether early tastes for 'popular' literature can be expected to refine themselves over time, and so on—these are real enough matters.

EARLY DEVELOPMENTS

Some early work has been unjustifiably neglected—possibly because the area has yet to achieve much theoretical coherence. Waples and

Tyler (1931), for example, made a fairly comprehensive examination of topics of reading interest, and a subsequent publication (Waples, Berelson and Bradshaw, 1940) dealt with the complexity of adult reading responses. The authors also advocated the use of the case-study method to probe more deeply into reading practices, habits and attitudes, and this was taken up by Strang (1942). Leavis's very personal study (1932) has already been referred to; when it first appeared, it evoked a large critical response. Interested in developments in fiction and its readership since the eighteenth century, Leavis proceeded with what she termed an 'anthropological' method. Few would describe it that way today, but Leavis did conduct a survey of sorts, as well as examining library and bookshop choices (see also Rose, 2001). A more systematic, if drier, approach is that of Link and Hopf (1946), who considered who reads, what kinds of books are read, what competitors for readers' attention exist, and how (and why) people go about choosing their books. Beyond these—and beyond the highly personal commentaries of literary critics and authors—some of the most useful early insights are to be found in general treatments of the intellectual and leisure habits of the 'masses' [Hoggart's work (1957, 1995) immediately comes to mind, but the later overview by Rose (2001) is particularly recommended].

MAJOR CONTRIBUTIONS AND WORK IN PROGRESS

In the late 1970s, Greaney and his associates began to pay rather more systematic attention to the social aspects of reading. Greaney (1980), for example, found that the amount and type of leisure reading were related to such variables as basic ability, sex, socioeconomic status, family size and primary-school type (see also Greaney and Hegarty, 1987). Greaney and Neuman (1990) also investigated the functions of reading, in a study of children in more than a dozen countries: utility, enjoyment and escape were the three recurring motivations, and it was found that girls rated the second factor more positively than did boys (sex differences, particularly in the early years, are a consistent finding in the literature). The survey work of Anderson and his colleagues (Anderson, Hiebert, Scott and Wilkinson, 1985), particularly that dealing with children's reading habits vis-a-vis other leisure-time activities (see also Anderson, Wilson and Fielding, 1988), draws upon the investigations by Greaney and others, and suggests low levels of leisure reading. In terms of intervention, Neuman (1999) has adapted the 'book flood' idea (see Ingham, 1981) from primary schools in England to day-care centres in the USA. The concept is straightforward—make a large number of books available to economically disadvantaged children—and the results encouraging. (The advantages of what Neuman calls the 'physical proximity' of books, coupled with appropriate adult support and guidance, are borne out in most reading surveys—and well-understood by all enlightened parents.)

Nell's (1988) interesting investigation of 'ludic' (i.e., pleasure) reading has been reasonably criticised for its psychoanalytic bent and its methodological difficulties while, at the same time, praised as establishing a base from which further study of ludic reading might proceed (see Venezky, 1990). Nell's most important contribution is his documentation of 'escapist' reading (reading 'fever', as one respondent put it): in one of the families he studied, the father claimed to read 30 books a month, the mother read 25 and the two daughters, 18 and 28.

Large-scale survey work has also continued. In 1993, the Roehampton Institute in London launched the pilot phase of a survey of 8,000 British children's reading habits: a report on the pilot project (involving 320 children) was published in 1994 (Children's Literature Research Centre), and the full report appeared in 1996. Among the important findings: boys read less than girls (particularly as they get older), patterns of reading interests (boys like adventure stories more than romances; girls prefer animal stories to science fiction) are remarkably resilient, and it is much too simplistic to blame television and computer games for depressed levels of reading (indeed, the study endorses earlier suggestions that 'voluntary readers tend to be active in other pursuits' [p. 116]—and these can include television viewing). Hall and Coles' (1999) survey of about 8,000 English 10- to 14-year-olds—in some ways an updating of earlier investigations by Whitehead, Capey, Maddren and Wellings (1974, 1977)—also illustrated the relationships between family socioeconomic status and reading, between pleasure reading and television viewing (while those who read most watch least, some of the 'heaviest' readers are also avid viewers), and between gender and reading (girls read more than boys, have more positive feelings about reading and enjoy their reading more). Broadly similar results were reported by McKenna, Kear and Ellsworth (1995) in their study of more than 18,000 American primary-school children. Worrying age and gender gaps in reading were also revealed in a province-wide survey in Ontario: at the third-grade level, 69% of boys and 83% of girls said they enjoyed reading; by the sixth grade, these proportions had decreased to 55% and 71%, respectively (EQAO, 1999).

Some of the most recent findings illustrate the continuing difficulties in assessing reading habits. In its dourly-titled *Reading at Risk* (2004), the (American) National Endowment for the Arts reported that book reading had declined over the previous twenty years, and that this decline was sharpest for 'literary reading'—the report speaks of 'imminent cultural crisis' and a 'rising tide of mediocrity', arguing that 'at the current rate of loss, literary reading as a leisure activity will virtually disappear in half a century' (p. xiii). The word 'literary' is key here, since the NEA survey only concerned itself with fiction, plays and poetry (not counting, that is to say, the apparently growing taste for non-fiction); as well, no weighting was made for 'quality' (see also Bauerlein, 2005). A Canadian government-commissioned report found that the amount spent on books (in 2001) was exceeded only by that on newspapers and cinemas; however, the average annual outlay was less than $200—not very much for, say, a family of four and when a new book can easily cost $40—and fewer than half of all Canadian households bought any books at all (Hill Strategies, 2005). Another Canadian survey (Créatec, 2005) has recently found that—although the ratio of reading to television viewing is about 1:5—almost 90% of adults reported themselves as regular readers. A perceptive commentator (Taylor, 2005) asked how one could reconcile this percentage with the fact (noted earlier) that one in four people lack full functional literacy—and two main points suggest themselves, one substantive, the other methodological. First, there is again the matter of 'quality'. This is not simply a question of trying to argue that Charles Dickens should count while Danielle Steel should not; Taylor notes, for instance, that comics and joke books can qualify as reading material. Second, most surveys depend upon self-reported data and, in many instances, the 'interview' is a matter of a brief telephone call. These two issues are, in fact, common across survey findings.

There are relatively few investigations that have combined large respondent numbers with detailed assessment instruments. Some recent work in Nova Scotia, however, falls into this category. (Simple statistics on gross levels of magazine, newspaper and book reading have shown that Nova Scotia is a good reflection of the larger Canadian picture—which, in turn, is broadly similar to that in other 'developed' countries: see e.g. Ekos, 1991.) In a pilot survey of university students and teachers, Walker (1990) found that, overall, reading for pleasure was not a generally favoured leisure activity, and that material read was largely of a 'light' or ephemeral nature. There was a small group of very active, or 'core', readers, and significant sex differences emerged with regard to both the quantity and the type of reading done. Walker also reported that the presence of books at home, being read to as a child, and parental value placed upon reading *per se* were important determinants of reading habits.

The more comprehensive follow-up study (Edwards, 1999) involved some 875 students (from the upper grades in both primary and secondary schools), 1,700 parents and 625 teachers. The questionnaires administered to these three groups, while not exactly the same, were designed to produce complementary and interlocking information; the questions asked reflected a close reading of the existing literature. Teachers and parents were asked for information about their own reading habits and attitudes and, as well, to give us their perceptions of children's reading practices. The information elicited on the questionnaires dealt with demographic factors (age, sex, family size, income level and occupation), with overall school achievement patterns and subject preferences, and with focussed probing of reading ability, attitudes and practices (involving such variables as time spent reading, quantity and type of material read, factors influencing reading choices, home and school encouragement of reading, home reading practices, reading related to other leisure-time pursuits and so on). Beyond categorical and scaled responses, qualitative data were also elicited (e.g. lists of favourite books, magazines and authors). Allowing for multiple-section questions, each respondent answered well over 100 queries.

I will touch here upon some of the findings from the children's survey. It is of course impossible to delve at all deeply into them, but they do broadly confirm trends noted earlier. Thus, for instance, girls report greater ability and more favourable attitudes towards reading than do boys—and they do more of it. Primary-school children apparently enjoy reading more than do those in secondary school, and the amount of reading decreases with age. As to type of leisure reading: girls prefer biographical and 'romance' fiction, as well as books about travel and animals; boys say they like to read adventure, sports and science-fiction books. Across the board, there is more television viewing than reading (as much as three hours daily at the lower grade level), but girls say that they watch less than the boys, and they are as twice as likely to prefer reading to television. When we asked children to rank-order their preferences for ten common leisure habits, their answers suggested four categories: the most favoured activity was simply being with friends, then came music, movies and television, sports and hobbies comprised a third grouping—*and* reading appeared in fourth and final position. Books and television were more popular among the younger children; and, again, girls were more likely than boys to prefer reading.

FUTURE DIRECTIONS

Despite a reasonable amount of data, and despite some very robust findings—having to do with age, gender, attitudes, and amount and type of reading—we are still largely at descriptive levels. There is much of interest that we have learned about reading in the electronic age, and there have also been occasional attempts at stimulating the reading habit. We still require, however, theoretical perspectives to unite and augment existing data, to treat such matters as the underlying factors influencing reading motivation and development, the rewards and consequences of reading, and the establishment and maintenance of leisure-time activities.[2] It is readily apparent that a coherent and comprehensive social psychology of reading is a very large undertaking—necessitating, for example, hitherto untried marriages of the 'technical' and the sociological literature.

Along the way, as it were, useful work can be done under a large number of headings. One example is the longstanding concern about reading 'quality', a current manifestation of which involves teenagers' preferences for horror stories—the 'most popular genre for adolescents' according to the Roehampton survey (Children's Literature Research Centre, 1996, p. 210; see also Hall and Coles, 1999). The consumption of such material predictably attracts a variety of opinion. In some schools, teachers use these juvenile shockers on the grounds that, after all, they are of obvious interest and (it is hoped) will lead to 'better' things. The general assumption seems to be that almost any reading is better than nothing. Others, however, strongly disagree, arguing that reading books produced to a formula—endlessly recycled plots peopled by wooden stereotypes ['flat' characters, as Forster (1927) styled them]—only induces the sort of non-progressive escapism that Nell (1988) has discussed at length. Another aspect of current debates about 'quality' that cries out for further analysis is the resurgent interest in banning some books altogether; a group in Virginia (Parents Against Bad Books in Schools) would have removed from study such authors as Atwood, Doctorow, Eco and Morrison (see the pabbis.com website). A third contemporary avenue into the sociology of reading is provided by another resurgent phenomenon: the book club. Freeman (2005) provides a brief overview—from the mid-nineteenth century to Oprah—and Hartley (2001) raises some interesting questions: why, for example, are women more attracted to such groups than are men? And finally here, I suggest that larger issues of print versus screen, of shelf versus computer, constitute an increasingly important part of the contextualisation of reading (see Schonfeld, 2003, for an illuminating account of the rapid growth of electronic information storage; see also Arms, 2000—and, for the most sustained and highly charged defence of the paper media, Baker, 2001).

However, we approach the matter, any meaningful social psychology of reading should concern itself primarily with aliteracy: why don't some readers read? Valpy (2001) has recently reported what we already

---

[2] We might consider following the lead of Hall and Coles (1999) a little more closely. They asked children how *they* accounted for gender differences in reading. Girls, it was reported, are more mature and sensitive than boys, they are not as physically active, they have more patience; boys see reading as 'sissy' or 'square', they can't sit still long enough to read, reading is neither 'cool' nor 'tough', and so on. In effect, these children were constructing a theory that related socialisation in general to reading in particular.

knew: questions of reading motivation, attitudes and practices have been relatively ignored, largely because of current emphases upon achievement, testing and assessment. Thus, 'there is much more interest in whether children can read than in whether they do'. It is apparent that an area that pays vastly more attention to the development of skills than to their application is neglecting ends for means.

REFERENCES

Anderson, R., Wilson, P., and Fielding, L.: 1988, 'Growth in reading and how children spend their time outside of school', *Reading Research Quarterly* 23, 285–303.

Anderson, R., Hiebert, E., Scott, J., and Wilkinson, I.: 1985, *Becoming a Nation of Readers*, National Institute of Education, Washington.

Arms, W.: 2000, *Digital Libraries*, MIT Press, Boston.

Baker, N.: 2001, *Double Fold: Libraries and the Assault on Paper*, Random House, New York.

Bauerlein, M. (ed.): 2005, *Reading at Risk: A Forum*, Association of Literary Scholars and Critics, Boston.

Birkerts, S.: 1994, *The Gutenberg Elegies: The Fate of Reading in an Electronic Age*, Ballantine, New York.

Bloom, H.: 2000, *How to Read and Why*, Scribners, New York.

Borges, J.L.: 1964, *Labyrinths*, New Directions, New York.

Children's Literature Research Centre (Roehampton Institute): 1994, *Contemporary Juvenile Reading Habits*, British Library, London.

Children's Literature Research Centre (Roehampton Institute): 1996, *Young People's Reading at the End of the Century,* Roehampton Institute, London.

Créatec: 2005, *Reading and Buying Books for Pleasure*, Créatec, Montreal.

Creative Research Group: 1987, *Literacy in Canada,* CRG, Toronto.

Edmundson, M.: 2004, *Why Read?*, Bloomsbury, New York.

Education Quality and Accountability Office (EQAO): 1999, *Ontario Provincial Report on Achievement*, EQAO, Toronto.

Edwards, J. (ed.): 1981, *The Social Psychology of Reading*, Institute of Modern Languages, Silver Spring MD.

Edwards, J.: 1991, 'Literacy and education in contexts of cultural and linguistic heterogeneity', *Canadian Modern Language Review* 47, 933–949.

Edwards, J.: 1999, *Reading in Nova Scotia*, unpublished paper, St Francis Xavier University, Antigonish (Nova Scotia).

Ekos Research Associates: 1991, *Reading in Canada*, Ekos Research Associates, Ottawa.

Fish, S.: 1980, *Is There a Text in This Class?*, Harvard University Press, Cambridge.

Forster, E.M.: 1927, *Aspects of the Novel*, Edward Arnold, London.

Freeman, S.: 2005, 'End of discussion', *American Scholar* 74(1), 138–142.

Gibson, E. and Levin, H.: 1975, *The Psychology of Reading*, MIT Press, Cambridge.

Greaney, V.: 1980, 'Factors related to amount and type of leisure time reading', *Reading Research Quarterly* 15, 337–357.

Greaney, V. and Hegarty, M.: 1987, 'Correlates of leisure-time reading', *Journal of Research in Reading* 10, 3–20.

Greaney, V. and Neuman, S.: 1990, 'The functions of reading: A cross-cultural perspective', *Reading Research Quarterly* 25, 172–195.

Hall, C. and Coles, M.: 1999, *Children's Reading Choices*, Routledge, London.

Hartley, J.: 2001, *Reading Groups*, Oxford University Press, Oxford.

Hill Strategies: 2005, *Who Buys Books in Canada?*, Hill Strategies, Hamilton (Ontario).

Hoggart, R.: 1957, *The Uses of Literacy*, Chatto & Windus, London.

Hoggart, R.: 1995, *The Way We Live Now*, Chatto & Windus, London.

Ingham, J.: 1981, *Books and Reading Development*, Heinemann, London.

Kozol, J.: 1985, *Illiterate America*, Doubleday, New York.

Leavis, Q.D.: 1965 (1932), *Fiction and the Reading Public*, Chatto & Windus, London.

Link, H. and Hopf, H.: 1946, *People and Books: A Study of Reading and Book-Buying Habits*, Book Manufacturers' Institute, New York.

Maeroff, G.: 1982, 'Dismay over those who shun reading', *New York Times*, 28 September.

Max, D.T.: 1994, 'The end of the book?', *Atlantic Monthly*, September, 61–71.

Max, D.T.: 2000, 'The electronic book', *American Scholar* 69(3), 17–28.

McKenna, M., Kear, D., and Ellsworth, R.: 1995, 'Children's attitudes toward reading: A national survey', *Reading Research Quarterly* 30, 934–956.

National Endowment for the Arts (NEA): 2004, *Reading at Risk*, NEA, Washington.

Negroponte, N.: 1995, *Being Digital*, Knopf, New York.

Nell, V.: 1988, *Lost in a Book: The Psychology of Reading for Pleasure*, Yale University Press, New Haven.

Neuman, S.: 1986, 'The home environment and fifth-grade students' leisure reading', *Elementary School Journal* 3, 335–343.

Neuman, S.: 1999, 'Books make a difference: A study of access to literacy', *Reading Research Quarterly* 34, 286–311.

Organisation for Economic Co-Operation and Development (OECD): 2000, *Literacy in the Information Age: Final Report of the International Adult Literacy Survey*, OECD, Paris.

Oxenham, J.: 1980, *Literacy: Writing, Reading and Social Organisation*, Routledge & Kegan Paul, London.

Rose, J.: 2001, *The Intellectual Life of the British Working Classes*, Princeton University Press, New Haven.

Schonfeld, R.: 2003, *JSTOR: A History*, Princeton University Press, Princeton.

Steiner, G.: 1975, *After Babel*, Oxford University Press, Oxford.

Strang, R.: 1942, *Exploration in Reading Patterns*, University of Chicago Press, Chicago.

Taylor, K.: 2005, 'Reading: Even joke books count', *Globe & Mail* (Toronto), 29 June.

Tinker, M.: 1965, *Bases for Effective Reading*, University of Minnesota Press, Minneapolis.

Valpy, M.: 2001, 'Can read, won't read', *Globe & Mail* (Toronto), 9 June.

Venezky, R.: 1990, 'Review of *Lost in a Book* (Nell)', *American Journal of Psychology* 103, 136–141.

Walker, S.: 1990, 'A survey of reading habits and attitudes in a university population' (unpublished report), Psychology Department, St Francis Xavier University.

Waples, D. and Tyler, R.: 1931, *What People Want to Read About*, University of Chicago Press, Chicago.

Waples, D., Berelson, B., and Bradshaw, F.: 1940, *What Reading Does to People*, University of Chicago Press, Chicago.

Whitehead, F., Capey, A., and Maddren, W.: 1974, *Children's Reading Habits*, Evans/Methuen, London.

Whitehead, F., Capey, A., Maddren, W., and Wellings, A.: 1977, *Children and Their Books*, Macmillan, London.

GEMMA MOSS

GENDER AND LITERACY

INTRODUCTION

This article reviews the ways in which gender and literacy have been linked in educational contexts, and the different patterns of intervention this has led to. In particular it will highlight the switch in the literature from a focus on the formation of (girls') gendered identities to a focus on (boys') gendered patterns of attainment within the literacy curriculum. The emergence of boys' underachievement in literacy as a policy problem will be linked to the current dominance of performance-management cultures within governments, and the accompanying processes of large-scale education reform which they have led to around the globe. Often such interventions are designed with the aim of securing maximum homogeneity in outcomes from education. This provides a new context in which to consider the range of social explanations for inequalities in educational performance, their currency, and the challenges this new more managerial landscape in education poses for a feminist politics.

FEMINISM, GENDER AND LITERACY

Historically feminist work on gender and literacy can be grouped under two main headings. On the one hand there is a well established tradition of feminist textual analysis that focuses on text content, and examines the meanings texts hold for their readers or writers (Ang, 1985; Moss, 1989; Radway, 1984). This work has largely arisen out of a broader feminist concern for the social construction of gendered identities and has followed a similar trajectory from a primary interest in the ideological constraints which produce femininity to an understanding of girls' appropriation and reworking of a range of cultural resources for a wider and often more oppositional set of purposes (Hey, 1997; Williamson, 1981/1982). The judgements made are about the value of the text and the contribution the text makes to the formation of gendered identities (Cherland, 1994; Christian-Smith, 1993; Gilbert and Taylor, 1991).

   This kind of attention to the relationship between gender and literacy attracted most interest through the seventies and eighties. One of the most hotly contested issues within the literature during that time was whether genres which were strongly associated with female readers,

B. V. Street and N. H. Hornberger (eds), Encyclopedia of Language and Education,
2nd Edition, Volume 2: Literacy, 95–105.
©2010 Springer Science+Business Media LLC.

such as the romance and soap operas, should be condemned as part of the ideological apparatus which constrained women's sphere of action. Or whether they pointed to contradictions in the ideological construction of femininity which their readers could potentially exploit (Moss, 1989). Radway's study of women romance readers provides a good example of the tensions within this literature as these issues increasingly sought resolution through direct study of the texts' readers as well as of the text itself (Radway, 1984).

By contrast the second and, until recently, much smaller strand of work has focused more closely on literacy learning. Using ethnographic perspectives this work has tracked how literacy has come to stand for a social good which enables full and meaningful participation in the broader society as well as access to the world of work. This literature has considered both the acquisition and distribution of the competencies associated with the literacy curriculum in this light and has used this emphasis to draw attention to gender inequalities in patterns of illiteracy. Early work in this area explored women's unequal access to education and the promise of literacy it brought with it (Horsman, 1991; Rockhill, 1993). The work centred on marginalised social groups such as adult women who were the target of basic skills courses or women or girls in the developing world who had been denied equal opportunities to learn to read or write. Much of the literature drew attention to the social constraints which shaped women's lives and in the process restricted their participation in education (Mace, 1998). This became part of the backdrop to the study of illiteracy more generally (see Robinson-Pant, Women, Literacy and Development: Overview, Volume 2).

Although these two strands of work were in many ways quite distinct, nevertheless they shared a common concern for social justice, and were grounded in a feminist analysis of the difficulties both women and girls face in a world shaped often in disregard of, if not positively against, their own interests. From this point of view they are complementary approaches in a longer campaign designed to bring about greater gender equality. There were some notable successes. The persistent attack on sexism in children's books did lead publishers to review and modify their output. Whilst literacy campaigns in the developing world increasingly recognised the importance of reaching women and girls as well as boys and men and resources were retargeted accordingly. Despite this, many of the structural inequalities which relegated women to second place economically and socially remain in place. Although the precise focus of debate in these two areas has shifted over time, neither literature considered that gender equality had been achieved by the point in the mid-nineties when the discourse over gender and literacy suddenly began to change.

GENDER AND LITERACY AS A POLICY PROBLEM: SHOULD BOYS DO BETTER?

By the mid-nineties, gender differences in performance in the school literacy curriculum had begun to attract a new kind of attention. Whether in official reports based on outcomes from the education system, in media coverage of the same data, or in the academic literature, boys' underachievement in literacy began to surface as a strong topic in its own right (Barrs and Pidgeon, 1993; Gilbert and Gilbert, 1998; Millard, 1997; Ofsted, 1993; QCA, 1998; Rowan et al., 2002). In the UK, the government's school inspection agency, Ofsted, summed up the available evidence in the following trenchant terms:

> Boys do not do as well as girls in English in schools. There are contrasts in performance and attitudes towards the subject. The majority of pupils who experience difficulty in learning to read and write are boys. Boys' results in public examinations at 16 are not as good as girls', and many more girls than boys continue to study English beyond 16. (Ofsted, 1993 p. 2 quoted in Millard, 1997, p. 15)

Yet the curious thing about this summary is that it actually reports a state of affairs that had been known for a long while. The picture is entirely consistent with the evidence for literacy attainment available for at least the previous fifty years within the UK school system. On this basis, boys' test scores were adjusted up in the 11+exam that was used to determine entry to grammar schools in order to even out the gender balance of those going forward from the higher end of the ability spectrum (Millard, 1997). Elsewhere, the advantage girls have over boys in standardised reading tests had been sufficiently well established for long enough for many such tests to adjust girls' scores downwards as a matter of routine (Barrs, 1993). The difference in the nineteen nineties is therefore not the evidence itself but rather its salience at this time and the changed conditions which make it capable of being read in new ways.

Feminist commentators account for why boys' performance has emerged as such a high profile problem within education discourse in different ways (Epstein et al., 1998; Foster, Kimmel and Skelton, 2001; Rowan et al., 2002). Certainly boys' underachievement in literacy acquired a new resonance from the broader educational picture which had begun to show substantial improvements in girls' attainment in a range of subjects, such as Maths and Science, where traditionally they had lagged far behind boys (Arnot et al., 1999). For some feminists this sudden focus on boys' comparative failure in the education system looked like evidence of an anti-feminist backlash which would be used to rebuild boys' competitive advantage (Epstein et al., 1998;

Foster, Kimmel and Skelton, 2001; Hallman, 2000). The media discourse which accompanied the initial reporting of the data certainly justified this response, as commentators were able to demonstrate using headlines or articles which had appeared in the US, in Australia and in the UK at that time, all of which presented boys' failures as a direct corollary of girls' success (Cohen, 1998, p. 19; Gilbert and Gilbert, 1998, p. 4–5; Mahoney, 1998, p. 46; Rowan et al., 2002, p. 15). By contrast, many feminists treated the data with caution, and argued instead for the need to pay much closer attention to how gendered attainment was intersected by both ethnicity and social class. Not all boys were doing badly, just as not all girls were doing well (Epstein et al., 1998).

But feminists also began to generate an alternative explanation for this sudden turn of affairs. The increased prominence given to boys' educational underachievement can be construed less as evidence of a straightforward strengthening of patriarchal values than as a new twist in a more complex relationship between education and the economy (Arnot et al., 1999; Mahoney, 1998). From this perspective, what marks out the nineteen nineties are changes in the economy, the rise of new managerialism and the increasing economisation of social life that happens as a response to the pressures of a globalisation (Kenway and Kelly, 1994). Governments increasingly expect education to demonstrate its value in economic terms. They export to education the kinds of systems for tracking production used in the commercial sector, and the tools of quality control associated with this (Morley and Rassool, 1999). In this context, children's performance in examinations increasingly counts as output data.

As new technologies make tracking and managing such data on a large scale easier so governments increasingly put in place more extensive testing regimes which can generate more detailed information about pupil progress. This has happened worldwide. As one example, in the UK, the introduction of a National Curriculum in 1988 was accompanied by the introduction of mandatory testing at 7, 11 and 14. These assessment points have now been supplemented by further optional tests in English and Maths for the intervening year groups which are administered annually. The wide-scale use of performance data in the education system produces the conditions in which boys' relative underachievement in literacy becomes much more publicly visible.

It has been in the interests of many governments to both collect and then make such data public as part of a broader discussion over the value of public services. They want to know and to demonstrate how well the education system is doing, as part of their contract with the voters. Being able to demonstrate that the system is working well operates as a means of winning consent for continuing support for a publicly funded system of education. Equally, publicising apparent failures applies more pressure to that system to improve and deliver better value for the money spent. A new dynamic is put in place. Boys' underachievement in literacy gains its charge from this context.

Of course, any anomalies that surface in the performance data can be used to steer education policy, not just differences in girls' and boys' attainment. In the UK performance differences between schools and between LEAs (school districts) have exerted most influence on the direction of policy as a whole. In this sense social class trumps gender. Nevertheless, as successive governments have taken increasing control over the content of the literacy curriculum in England, a series of official publications have continued to flag up the discrepancies in boys' and girls' attainment in both reading and writing and to suggest ways in which schools might address this issue (Ofsted, 2003; DfES, 2003; QCA, 1998). Yet gender and literacy in this context is contained by a broader discourse of improving educational performance in which the school and its effective delivery of the curriculum take centre stage, rather than the feminist goal of achieving greater gender equity. As an indication of this, the most recent materials designed to support boys' writing and issued to English schools by the Primary National Strategy, the body charged with improving performance in primary schools, took as their main topics talk for writing; visual texts; purpose and audience; and feedback on learning. The advice they offer underwrites a particular view of what constitutes good literacy pedagogy, and is premised on the value of carefully structured and explicit support for writing. In important respects it is gender neutral. Indeed, this is in line with government policy-making in education which eschews advocating strategies that might benefit boys at the expense of girls for the simple reason that this would not help put results up across the board (Ofsted, 2003). That would not fit with a managerialist impulse which insists on greater homogeneity of outcomes. In this new policy context, the kind of affirmative action that was put in place in response to the same kind of data fifty years before seems unimaginable.

SUCCESS AND FAILURE IN THE LITERACY CURRICULUM: REWORKING FEMINIST IDEAS IN A NEW CONTEXT

As unskilled manufacturing jobs have moved abroad, many governments have committed to building a high-skill, knowledge-based economy at home. This aspiration has brought with it changed assumptions about the levels and spread of achievement in reading and writing required in the workforce. Demands for an improvement in boys' performance in the literacy curriculum happen within this context (Mahoney, 1998).

The aim of fixing performance outcomes increasingly acts as the backdrop to the discussion of gender and literacy. Yet it is not yet clear what the best solutions to the problems demonstrated in the data might be. Review of the available data show that when girls are not prevented from enrolling or regularly attending school, then as a group they achieve higher scores in reading and writing than boys. The pattern is consistent across many countries (OECD, 2003). Yet by no means all girls do better than all boys. Rather the distribution patterns for attainment vary between the genders, with boys' demonstrating a far longer tail of underachievement.

In exploring the data, feminists have looked for possible explanations which make sense in a context where girls' competitive edge in the literacy curriculum does not always lead on to better educational achievement overall or better employment prospects in the wider society. This kind of disconnection has to be taken into account. As a first step, this has often meant returning to earlier understandings about the causes of girls' educational disadvantage and assessing whether and how they might apply to boys. This is not a simple matter of translation (Gilbert and Gilbert, 1998, p. 21). By and large the most common assumption is that boys' underachievement in literacy is created by a dissonance between aspects of masculinity and aspects of schooling. There is less consensus over precisely which aspects of masculinity or schooling matter most in this respect. This leads to different proposed solutions to fixing literacy attainment. In each case the potential impact on girls is weighed as carefully as the consequences for boys. The following examples from the literature represent three different ways of addressing these issues.

Fixing the Content of the Literacy Curriculum

Elaine Millard's *Differently Literate* examines the differences between boys' and girls' interests in reading and writing and their respective fit with the content of the literacy curriculum in the secondary school (1997). Her work draws on studies of genre preferences. She proposes that the prominence given to specific kinds of narrative fiction and the emphasis on character and personal response in the study of literature in the secondary school present difficulties for boys because they do not match with their interests. She comments:

> (boys') favoured genres are less in harmony with the English curriculum and the choices made for them in class by their teachers. The largest contrast is between boys' interest in action and adventure and girls' preference for emotion and relationships. (Millard, 1997, p. 75)

In her view, the fact that the curriculum lines up with girls' not boys' existing interests matters because it reduces boys' full participation

within the literacy curriculum. Many of them switch off reading. Outside school, boys unlike girls commit their time to other pursuits. They
associate reading at home with female members of the household. If
they have interests in reading then they rarely share them with their
peers. Overall this means that they gain less familiarity with the structures of written language. They are less adept at dealing with the kinds
of tasks the literacy curriculum sets them. The picture Millard paints is
of girls and boys acting as relatively self-contained communities of
practice each constructed on gendered terrain. Rather than continue to
allow one group's interests to dominate over the other's, her solution
is to try to rebalance the English curriculum so that it embraces a wider
range of reading material, non-fiction as well as fiction, and a greater
range of media texts. She argues that such an expansion in the range
of texts taught would extend girls' repertoire with beneficial outcomes
for them too whilst 'draw(ing) boys in to the classroom community of
story book readers and writers' (ibid, p. 180).

Fixing Boys (and Girls Too)

Rowan et al's *Boys, Literacies and Schooling* occupies rather different
territory (2002). It draws more closely on feminist post-structuralist
work on the formation of gendered identities. The authors are more cir-
cumspect about polarising gendered interests, pointing out that there
are different ways of doing masculinity and femininity, and that consequently there may be as many differences within as well as between
these two categories. One of their case studies sets out to challenge
the easy supposition that boys will show a keen interest in new technologies, and will be relatively skilful in this domain whilst girls will not
(ibid, p. 137). They argue that this supposition does not provide a sufficient basis for re-engaging boys with the literacy curriculum. Instead
of seeking to identify and then incorporate boys' existing interests into
the curriculum as a way of improving literacy attainment, they set their
sights on the transformation of gendered assumptions about what and
who both boys and girls can be. This means working with and against
the grain of teachers' and pupil's expectations about their own and
others' place within the curriculum. They describe this as a 'transformative project' which seeks to re-make gender identities.

> If we keep looking inwards to this same set of characteristics in
> order to come up with a solution to the "problems" produced by
> traditional discourses around masculinity, we run the risk of
> reproducing rather than critiquing those discourses that produce
> the problem. From a transformative perspective we need . . . . to
> be able to imagine the new: new possibilities, new masculinities,
> new ways of being and performing as a 'boy' (ibid, p. 71).

They consider that the English curriculum is a good place for this kind of political project to unfurl because of the relative fluidity of the subject domain and its ability to incorporate new kinds of texts and practices that can help develop new kinds of stories. The English curriculum is already under pressure in this way precisely because of the emergence of new technologies. They consider that the practical interventions that they document act as templates for explorations of the dominant mindsets on gender and on literacy pedagogy rather than as specific recipes for reform. There are no hard and fast answers here, rather attempts to get things right. By placing the transformation of gender identities at the heart of their work they hope that they can begin to re-gear the curriculum towards a more equitable and expansive future.

Fixing Literacy Pedagogy

By contrast, Judith Solsken's *Literacy, Gender and Work* focuses on the social interactions that surround learning how to read and write (1993), rather than with the construction of gender identities per se. She draws primarily on literacy as social practice perspectives to demonstrate that in both home and school literacy learning can be variously construed as self-directed play or adult-sponsored work, a distinction which she maps onto Bernstein's categories of visible and invisible pedagogies (ibid, p. 60, see also Bourne, Official Pedagogic Discourses and the Construction of Learners' Identities, Volume 3). She argues that these contradictory orientations to the process of becoming a reader or writer present children with a series of dilemmas which they then have to resolve. The way they respond influences their development as readers and writers in school and at home:

> Both Luke and Jack seemed to define literacy as a particular
> kind of work in the sense that it was an activity required and
> overseen by adults, rather than one engaged in for their own
> purposes or pleasure. ... While Luke played a mischievous
> 'bad boy' role in resisting most literacy activities (except those
> he defined as play), Jack played a 'good boy' role by treating
> literacy activities as chores to be completed (ibid, p. 36).

For Solsken, the positions children adopt in relation to literacy interact with their understanding of gender relations in the home. Solsken argues that this in part happens because more women than men shoulder the burden of preparing children for the work of learning literacy at school and find themselves responsible for ensuring a successful outcome to that process. The high stakes involved in making a smooth and success-ful entry into the literacy curriculum provide part of the backdrop against which children negotiate over what literacy means for them and the position they will adopt as literacy learners. Solsken concludes that gender does not of itself determine whether children will align themselves with play-based or work-based pedagogies. Rather gender identities interact with and coalesce around children's experience of literacy learning. The consequences of the positions they adopt develop over time and in relation to the pedagogic culture of the classroom. Gender matters in this context.

Gemma Moss has followed up this focus on literacy and gender in a study of the literacy events which make up the school curriculum for pupils aged 7–10 (Moss, 1999). She has highlighted the particular salience that teachers' judgements of their pupils' proficiency at reading has in classrooms. The ways in which children are seated in class, the kinds of books they are expected to read, and the choices they are allowed to exercise over their reading both construct and make visible the categories of 'able' and 'poor' readers. More than any other group, boys labelled 'poor readers' show the most consistent preference for non-fiction texts. The precise texts they choose are visually rich but with a print size normally associated with adult not children's texts. Moss argues that these design characteristics enable this group to act as experts whether they have read the text or not, thus allowing them to escape others judgements about their proficiency as readers (Moss, 1999). She suggests that boys' genre preferences are created in response to not ahead of the literacy curriculum and the hierarchy of readers it constructs. Girls and boys labelled 'poor readers' react differently to this designation. Girls are more willing to accept that label and work within it, but may underestimate what they can do. Boys are more inclined to resist. This leads to different profiles of underachievement, which require different remedies.

CURRENT PROBLEMS AND FUTURE DIRECTIONS

Can the approaches outlined in brief above address the distribution problem within the performance data, namely why different proportions of boys and girls struggle to do well within the literacy curriculum whilst others sail through? Are they specific enough about which boys (and girls) struggle most? Does it make sense to try and search for these latter categories, so that their problems can be fixed? Solsken's work certainly suggests that outside of the context of the curriculum this may be an elusive quest. That the problem does not lie so much with a certain kind of boy (or girl) who stands apart from the content of the literacy curriculum, as with the demands that the literacy curriculum places on all children. Her work re-orientates debate away from consideration of the literacy curriculum as the place where gendered tastes are arbitrated and gender identities made to an examination of the conflicting modes of social control such a curriculum instantiates.

This turn in analysis from what the curriculum says directly about gender to how the curriculum orders its knowledge base and regulates knowers is in line with Bernstein's theory of pedagogic discourse (Bernstein, 1996). It may well be that this is the best direction in which to turn at a time when education itself is being re-shaped and made accountable for what it does in new ways, and when gender politics struggles to find a place in a managerialist culture.

REFERENCES

Ang, I.: 1985, *Watching Dallas: Soap Opera and the Melodramatic Imagination*, Methuen, London.
Arnot, M., David, M., and Weiner, G.: 1999, *Closing the Gender Gap*, Polity Press, London.
Barrs, M.: 1993, 'Introduction: Reading the difference,' in M. Barrs and S. Pidgeon (eds.), *Reading the Difference*, CLPE, London.
Barrs, M. and Pidgeon, S. (eds.): 1993, *Reading the Difference*, CLPE, London.
Bernstein, B.: 1996, *Pedagogy, Symbolic Control and Identity*, Taylor and Francis, London.
Cherland, M.R.: 1994, *Private Practices: Girls Reading Fiction and Constructing Identity*, Taylor & Francis, London.
Christian-Smith, L. (ed.): 1993, *Texts of Desire: Essays on Fiction, Femininity and Schooling*, The Falmer Press, Sussex.
Cohen, M.: 1998, 'A habit of healthy idleness: Boys' underachievement in historical perspective,' in D. Epstein et al. (eds.): *Failing Boys? Issues in Gender and Achievement*, Open University Press, Buckingham.
Epstein, D. et al. (eds.): 1998, *Failing Boys? Issues in Gender and Achievement*, Open University Press, Buckingham.
Foster, V., Kimmel, M., and Skelton, C.: 2001. 'Setting the scene' in W. Martino and B. Meyenn (eds.), *Teaching Boys: Issues of Masculinity in Schools*, Open University Press, Buckingham.
Gilbert, R. and Gilbert, P.: 1998, *Masculinity Goes to School*, Routledge, London.
Gilbert, P. and Taylor, S.: 1991, *Fashioning the Feminine*, Allen and Unwin, Sydney.
Hallman, D.M.: 2000, '"If We're So Smart, ...": A Response to Trevor Gambell and Darryl Hunter,' in *Canadian Journal of Education* 25, 1, 62–67
Hey, V.: 1997, *The Company She Keeps: An Ethnography of Girls' Friendship*, Open University Press, Buckingham.
Horsman, J.: 1991, 'The problem of illiteracy and the promise of literacy,' in Mary Hamilton et al. (eds.): *Worlds of Literacy*, Multilingual Matters, Clevedon, Avon.
Kenway, J. and Kelly, P.: 1999, *Economising Education: The Post-Fordist Directions*, Deakin University, Geelong.
Mace, J.: 1998, *Playing with Time: Mothers and the Meaning of Literacy*, UCL Press, London.
Mahoney, P.: 1998, 'Girls will be girls and boys will be first' in D. Epstein et al. (eds.): *Failing Boys? Issues in Gender and Achievement*, Open University Press, Buckingham.
Millard, E.: 1997, *Differently Literate*, Falmer Press, London.
Morley, L. and Rassool, N.: 1999, *School Effectiveness: Fracturing the Discourse*, Falmer, London.
Moss, G.: 1989, *Un/Popular Fictions*, Virago, London.
Moss, G.: 1999, 'Texts in context: Mapping out the gender differentiation of the reading curriculum,' *Pedagogy, Culture and Society* 7(3), 507–522.

OECD: 2003, *Programme for International Student Assessment*, Organisation for Economic Development and Co-operation. Available at url: http://www.oecd.org/pages/0,2966,en_32252351_32236173_1_1_1_1_1,00.html

Ofsted: 1993, *Boys and English*, DfES, London.

Ofsted: 2003, English: Improving boys' writing at Key Stages 2 and 3. Ofsted subject conference report series 2002/03. E-publication.

QCA: 1998, *Can Do Better: Raising boys' achievement in English*, HMSO, London.

Radway, J.: 1984, *Reading the Romance*, University of North Carolina Press, Chapel Hill, North Carolina.

Rockhill, K.: 1993, 'Gender, language and the politics of literacy' in B. Street (ed.), *Cross-Cultural Approaches to Literacy*, Cambridge University Press, Cambridge.

Rowan, L. et al. 2002, *Boys, Literacies and Schooling*, Open University Press, Buckingham.

Solsken, J.: 1993, *Literacy, Gender and Work in Families and in School*, Ablex, Norwood, NJ.

Williamson, J.: 1981/2, 'How does girl number twenty understand ideology?', in *Screen Education* 40, 80–87.

PETER FREEBODY

CRITICAL LITERACY EDUCATION: ON LIVING WITH "INNOCENT LANGUAGE"

INTRODUCTION

Attacks on the basic rights of the people are invariably couched in innocent language.

Nelson Mandela, to the Constitutional Court of
South Africa, 1995.

The starting point for critical literacy education is this: Societies strive toward convergence in the interpretive practices of their members— toward the production of a culture. Socialization entails, among other things, using language as if its relation to material and social realities were innocent and natural—transparently determinable, fixed, singular, and portable (Siegel and Fernandez, 2000). Controlling interpretation, securing both the fact of its determinacy and its particular contents, is thus an ongoing political project, profoundly connecting the individual to public interests. A core concern of critical literacy education is inter- rupting and naming that project, finding principled, teachable ways of affording a productive ideological appreciation of social organization, human conduct, and language. Appreciating the potentially multiple ways in which language can be used to understand, act in and on, and appraise the world calls for explicit educational effort, and afford- ing these ways constitutes a core component of any mature form of acculturation into literate society. Such an education effort, however, is always contentious in contemporary, schooled societies, because the organizational features that perform the regulatory functions of schooling militate against the "ability to think 'critically' in the sense of understanding how systems and institutions inter-relate to help and harm people" (Gee, 2001, p. 2).

EARLY DEVELOPMENTS

Janks (2000) has identified four interrelated lines of work in critical lit- eracy education, focusing on (i) the role of literacy education in ana- lyses of cultural and political domination, (ii) access to powerful ways

B. V. Street and N. H. Hornberger (eds), Encyclopedia of Language and Education, 2nd Edition, Volume 2: Literacy, 107–118.
©2010 Springer Science+Business Media LLC.

of knowing and communicating, (iii) understanding the significance of linguistic, dialectical and cultural diversity, and (iv) learning the role of literate communication in the design of personal and social futures. These preoccupations have evolved in distinctive ways in various disciplinary and professional sites. Advocates and practitioners have included writers, teachers, and policy makers in universities, colleges, and schools, grouped generally under the banners of social, linguistic, humanities, and cultural studies. Active as well have been policy makers, curriculum developers, and evaluators in education-oriented civil-service units.

The key realization at the core of the distinctive problem of literacy is not new:

> *You might suppose that [written words] understand what they are saying, but if you want to know something and you ask them a question, they simply give you the same answer over and over again ... nobler by far is the serious pursuit of the dialectician.* (Socrates in Phaedrus, Sections 275e–277a, Plato, 360 BCE)

Several millennia later, Smith (1999) made the problem of the implacability of written language, in contrast to the coordinated agency afforded by interaction, a centerpiece of a feminist analysis of contemporary conditions:

> *For the reader ... the text pursues its remorseless way, unresponsive to the impassioned marginal notes, the exclamation points, the question marks ... It scripts her part in the conversation, ... she has no choice* (1999, pp. 146–147) ... *The practice of ruling involves the ongoing representation of the local actualities of our worlds in the standardized general forms of knowledge that enter them into the relations of ruling. It involves the construction of the world as texts, whether on paper or in computer, and the creation of a world in texts as a site of action. Forms of consciousness are created that are properties of organization or discourse rather than of individual subjects.* (Smith, 1987, pp. 2–3)

Although the term *critical literacy education* mobilizes different forms of advocacy and practice around these ideas on different sites, it has a specific provenance dating from the 1960s. The originator of the term, and of an orientation to its role in understanding and practicing teaching, was Paulo Freire. Freire was a politically active adult educator who worked with Brazilian peasant farmers whom he characterized as living in structures, including interpretive structures, that made them not marginal to society but rather embedded in it as beings for others (1970, p. 55). His aims (see Freire and Macedo, 1987) were to have his students/coworkers:

1. able to make critical readings of the social practices and relations, and the institutional and governmental procedures that are made possible and sustained by certain literacy practices;
2. see how texts are socially situated, intelligible only via an understanding of their sources, purposes, and interests, the conditions that make them possible and materially available; and
3. have a critical perspective on literacy as an educational phenomenon, a market commodity, a talisman of modernity, and a source of both liberation and oppression.

Connecting with the lines of work related to of Freire were developing ideas about critical pedagogy (e.g., Bernstein, 1971; Bourdieu, 1974; Bowles and Gintis, 1976; Giroux, 1981). These theoreticians were examining the socio-economic and cultural reproductionist functions of schooling, and pointing to the particular role of literacy materials and interpretive practices in the prosecution of those functions.

Much of this early work has been criticized for, essentially, being itself too determinate in its interpretation of the reading and writing conditions of people and the role of literacy in clarifying and challenging those conditions, specifically, for ignoring (i) socio-political dimensions other than class, (ii) the new industrial and pop-cultural conditions in the midst of which young people live, and (iii) the postmodern, postcolonial features of contemporary experience. These themes inform discussion in the following sections.

MAJOR CONTRIBUTIONS AND WORK IN PROGRESS

The expression *critical literacy education* points to a loose affiliation among theories, research methods, practices, and dispositions. It is convenient for the purpose at hand, if not entirely inclusive, to cluster contributions under the headings of anthropological, sociological, linguistic, and pedagogical traditions. These distinctions are, of course, blurred and constantly traversed partly because any given educational practitioner may draw on ideas and methods from among these and other traditions. Each orientation has a distinct view of what constitutes the critical aspects of critical literacy education, and each deploys different forms of data, analysis, and argument to support that view.

Anthropological contributions have used observational, cross-cultural, and documentary methods to expand on two key ideas about literacy: first is a theoretical focus on understanding literacy as coordinated and shared sets of practices and events (Street, 1984). That is, literacy activities, as they are conducted and learned formally and informally, are taken to be primordially social activities, best understood in terms of the qualities of various literacy events and practices, and the relationships among them. A *literacy event* is taken to be "any occasion in which a piece of writing is integral to the nature of the participants' interactions and their interpretive processes" (Heath, 1982, p. 23). These events provide the social experiential bases for the development of *literacy practices*—ways of using written language that people display routinely, including commonly shared ideas, literacy's part in relationships and identities, and the ideological assumptions that underlie those ideas (Street, 2001). This emphasis on interactional qualities stands in direct opposition to cognitivists' focus on individuals' strategies for reading and writing, psychometricians' focus on measurable abilities of reading and writing, and those linguistic accounts that attend largely to the clause- and text-level grammatical demands of text management and production.

A second key motivation of anthropological approaches is to document literacy activities in homes, schools, and workplaces. One aim is to highlight the diversity of literacy activities among subcultural groups. The documentations generally show school-based literacy events and practices to be restricted in contrast with those found in homes and workplaces (e.g., the collection edited by Anderson, Kendrick, Rogers, and Smythe, 2005, esp. chapters by Gregory, and Prinsloo and Stein). But they also show that certain patterns of literacy events and practices are consequential in that they can act systematically to exclude people of certain cultural and economic backgrounds from access to the practices that make up literacy work in schools and elsewhere (Freebody, Forrest, and Gunn, 2001; Purcell-Gates, 1995). The argument is that it is a failure to realize or act on this diversity that makes for the durability of uneven access to and facility with important literacy practices.

Anthropological orientations point to the need to reconstitute schooling in general and literacy education in particular in light of postmono-conditions: the diversity and hybridity of cultures and languages in most school settings and workplaces in the world, of the socio-economic and socio-political formations and life trajectories facing young people, and of the ways of knowing that have conventionally been over-written by colonized forms of education (e.g., Cope and Kalantzis, 2000). Such reconstitutions range from pedagogies that restore marginalized language and experience to a legitimate place in school literacy learning, to those approaches that are more specifically directed at the use of literacy education for explorations of gender, race, or other socio-political dimensions through reading and writing practices (e.g., Lewis, 2001).

While anthropologists of literacy generally favor neither explicit ideological critiques of social structures that privilege certain interest groups, nor the explicit recommendation of normative pedagogical strategies, they offer nonetheless bases in theory and research for the mounting of a diversity-based critique of the unproductively narrow ideologies and repertoires of practice through which much contemporary schooling does ideologically reproductionist work (e.g., Gregory and Williams, 1998). Barton (1994, p. 218), for instance, in concluding a major study of community literacy, made a case for the centrality of socio-economic, gender, and racial inequality in an understanding of these patterns of connection:

> Ultimately Literacy reflects inequalities in society: inequalities of power, inequalities in the distribution of wealth, and inequalities in access to education. ... Literacy can only be fully understood in the context of these social relations.

But the distinctive contribution of anthropologists of literacy resides in their attention to documenting the details of how these patterns arise and are conveyed, valued, and devalued. They begin with the everyday empirics of how people do things with texts, day in, day out, and with how much of this remains unrecognized or misrecognized in the settings of modern public institutions (as many of the chapters in this volume illustrate, see especially Robinson-Pant, Women, Literacy and Development: Overview, Volume 2; Kalman, Literacies in Latin America, Volume 2; Richardson, African American Literacies, Volume 2).

While anthropologists may arrive at such understandings about the macro-structures that build and are built by social order, it is the phenomenon of social order itself that constitutes the starting puzzle for sociologists. For our purposes, that means developing critical understandings of the social orders that sustain certain types of literacy education, and, simultaneously, of the ways in which certain types of literacy education sustain social orders.

Sociological approaches to critical literacy education have their roots in critical theories, mostly Marxian or poststructuralist, and have developed to address questions from within sociology and political economy concerning schooling as a social, cultural, economic, and political formation. These have included the critique that the features of schooling correspond at a number of levels (system, individual institution, individual classroom) to the occupational systems in a society, and that, conversely, school systems actively reproduce the material distribution evident in that occupational system. Literacy education is also taken to play a key role in schools' ability to shape social structures via the targeted distribution of the varying life chances and trajectories of groups and individuals by selectively providing the skills and cultural capital that legitimate the material orders of society (Bourdieu, 1991), culturally and economically reproductive processes by which material and cultural gifts are systematically mistaken for academic or intellectual gifts.

Sociological accounts that inform critical literacy education also point specifically to all the machineries of remediation, policy, and curriculum development that support them, and inquire into the ways in which this ensemble of ideas and practices actively sustain the interests of ruling groups in a society. The argument is that these ideas and practices do not just passively maintain a *status quo*, but actively and persistently divert, disrupt, and militate against the distributive and meritocratic rhetorics of contemporary educational policy. Conventional forms of literacy education do this partly by attaching young members of a society to textual forms of social organization: That is, it is argued that literate societies, radically unlike others, recruit textual print and digital materials, relying upon specific forms of reading and writing among their members, to continually reestablish relations of ruling (Smith, 1987). So passive, compliant, or dehistoricized forms of the human disciplines and paradigms that inform education (psychology, developmentalism, constructivism) actively conjure particular ontologies that appear to crystallize ruling interests, through discourses about: children as literate citizen-learners (see A. Luke, 1988), and competent, functioning citizen-workers (see, e.g., Gee, Hull, and Lankshear, 1996; Lankshear, 1987).

With respect to educational practice, these accounts have provided pedagogies that build on the critical pedagogy movement more generally and upon understandings about the particular role of literacy education in transmitting and legitimating the cultures and interests of dominant groups. Specifically, these accounts include critiques of:

- the masculinism of contemporary pedagogical practices, including some forms of critical pedagogy as conventionally understood (e.g., Luke and Gore, 1992);
- the failure of most pedagogical treatments of race-based issues to make visible the enduring white privilege that under-writes much multicultural and pluralism-based approaches to teaching, curriculum, and assessment (e.g., Allen, 2004, for an account of critical race theory); and
- the systematic production of strong correlations between family affluence and literacy learning, and the significance of powerful pedagogies in reshaping that relationship (e.g., Comber and Simpson, 2001).

Applied linguists with an interest in the critical literacy education program, most prominently those drawing on Halliday (1985) and his colleagues, have contributed a variety of analytic means, generally collected under the title critical discourse analysis, to form the bases of pedagogic approaches to texts. A central contributor has been Fairclough (1989, 2003), who has argued that semiotic resources such as language are caught up in the production of social life because they provide us with ways of (i) representing reality, (ii) providing modalities for acting and relating socially, and (iii) building social, communal, and individual identities (see Wallace, 2003, for classroom applications). Cultures build and transmit flexible, recognizable, and durable ways of representing (which Fairclough termed discourses), (inter)acting (genres), and being (styles). With respect to education, Fairclough has described the how elements of one socially situated practice (e.g., the conduct of professional history) are selectively recruited into another (e.g., doing History in and for school). This process of recruitment, or appropriation, involves the reshaping of how reality is represented, dealt with, and embedded in and as part of institutionalized teacher–student relations; the argument is that an understanding of literacy in school must begin with an analysis of these appropriation processes.

Applied linguists have contributed to the critical analysis of texts made without verbal content or with ensembles of different semiotic contents (e.g., Lemke, 1998). The argument has been that it is increasingly the case that language is no longer central or even significant to many print- and digital-based meaning events in educational settings. Important here is the distinction Lemke drew between typological (meaning by kind) and topological (meaning by degree). Different semiotic resources are differentially good at, or organized around, one or the other of these types of meaning:

Language, as a typologically oriented semiotic resource, is unsurpassed as a tool for the formulation of difference and relationship, for the making of categorical distinctions. It is much poorer ... [in its] resources for formulating degree, quantity, gradation, continuous change, continuous co-variation, non-integer ratios, varying proportionality, complex topological relations of relative nearness or connectedness, or nonlinear relationships and dynamical emergence. (Lemke, 1998, pp. 87, 92, insert added)

Thus, the distinction is made between writing, which materializes activity, causation, and agency in the world, and other semiotic activities such as drawing or graphing, which materialize the states stasis, correlation, and co-incidence (Kress, 2001). The critique of contemporary schooling that motivates these analyses is clear: the epistemologies and logics of these semiotic systems are different (the materiality of images is space; the materiality of language is time and causality) and thus they lead to different ways of knowing about and interacting with knowledge. The danger is that schools remain artificially isolated from the cultural and communicational transitions currently underway from fixed book-words to digitally manipulable screen-images as dominant meaning-making systems.

In contrast to the emphasis, found especially in most sociological approaches on the effects of the consumption of official school texts, applied linguists have emphasized the transformative effects of the production of texts by students (Martin, 1999). This focus offers one possible productive positive thesis—"how the different strands of work in language and social justice can be brought together to emphasise power as productive" (Janks, 2000, p. 184)—for critical literacy education: the remaking of knowledge. This brings with it an appreciation of the restrictiveness of conventional assessments in educational settings. Learning, the argument goes (e.g., Kress, 2001, 2003), is not primarily an acquisitional activity or the traces of developmental tracks. It entails students' developing ways of demonstrating sequences of principled changes in their material capacities and, significantly, showing how those capacities have changed their understanding of the world and how to act in and upon it.

Arising from their critical perspectives on literacy education, anthropologists, sociologists, and applied linguists have provided, or at least implied, a range of distinctive transformations for educational policy, pedagogy, assessment, and curriculum, all aimed generally at productive and responsible appreciations of the noninnocent relation between language and reality. One major set of implications concerns the assessment of literacy capabilities in schools: one outcome of the effortful preoccupation displayed by some institutions with measuring *how much* basic technical proficiency in script recognition and production that individuals or groups possess has been to draw attention away from the considering the particularities of *how* people are acculturated and apprenticed into literacy, and the moral, civic, and ideological implications of those particularities. The kinds of transformed practices recommended by critical literacy educators involve not just ways of challenging the assumptions and effects of school texts by teaching the technical procedures for making these visible; they involve as well ways of understanding more broadly the consequences of different forms of literacy education for the naturalizing, interrupting, or challenging of system in social organization and human conduct; they offer researchers, teachers, and learners ways of reflecting on their own understandings of equity, social justice, and critical transformation as potentially the products of power and ruling interests, and on practical regimens for re-writing and re-directing those understandings.

PROBLEMS AND DIFFICULTIES

Problems encountered in the affiliations that constitute the domain of critical literacy education are of two kinds: problems facing critical theories generally and their particular expressions in different disciplines, and tussles between these disciplines for the ownership of the essence of the critical literacy education project.

In the first case, three central challenges face the critical project. The first concerns the unclear relationships among socio-political formations (such as class, gender, and race), strategies of governance (such as educational policies and practices), and the prosecution of particular social and economic interests via these strategies. Accounts of critical literacy education often offer tenuous connections between these constructs, and one practical consequence of this is that researchers, teachers, and policy makers interested in advocating or practicing critical literacy pedagogies are vulnerable to challenges of subjectivity or bias. Such practices need to be based in a firm theorization that locates critical literacy in a collection of skills, understandings, and dispositions urgently needed by students to face the contemporary and future vocational, civic, and domestic experiences lying in wait for them.

Second is the question of which approach to language and semiotic analysis best inform a critical literacy education program. This discussion notwithstanding, the disciplines of anthropology, sociology and applied linguistics are, of course, no less driven by conceptual and methodological divisions than any other site of academic or professional practice.

Practitioners of the various disciples that inform critical literacy education disagree primordially on what the critically literate teacher and learner look like. Anthropologists object to the preemptively normative practices that emanate from sociological and most linguistic accounts; sociologists object to the absence of a theorization of power in anthropological and most linguistic accounts; applied linguists object to the lack of ideological agency attributed to learners in sociological versions of critical literacy education, and to the lack of appreciation or use of durable ideological formations as explanatory devices in anthropology.

These difficulties are not trivial or, worse still, merely academic: They present significant problems to teachers, educational policy makers, and curriculum developers. They make available too many options, the most comfortable of which amount to versions of reader response theory with its teeth showing, a conservative resort to critical or higher-order thinking that personalizes and authenticates the very interpretive determinacy against which the project originally set itself. In this way, the life cycle of an educationally transformational project can be seen to repeat itself: emergence, enthusiasm, orthodoxy, institutional recruitment, and residualization as yesterday's product.

FUTURE DIRECTIONS

Texts are integral to the operation of many everyday settings, such as people's contractual, civic commitments and their dealings with government and other public institutions; because of that, along with everyday practical work, texts are used simultaneously to organize social relations, and, thereby, are put to ideological, moral, and political work. Further, texts do not just accompany or comment on social organization: They materially constitute relations of power, embody those relations, and can naturalize or legitimate them, just as surely as they can adapt, challenge, or refashion them. They can, therefore, be systematically analyzed to show the structure and consequences of the work they are put to in embodying, reproducing, inflecting, adapting, or challenging prevalent and dominant practices and assumptions about social life. To conduct this work in schools is to foreground contestation, and the discomfort, disruption and criticism that this can attract call for principles that are both intellectually and pedagogically defensible. If critical literacy education is to have a reputable and enduring future, then more work will center on the need to develop and empirically examine the consequences of such principles.

The tensions and polarities traversing the study and application of critical literacy education include:

- text-in-and-of-context (how should students be shown that texts are both the products and elements of their context of interpretation?);
- language-in-and-for-society (a form of the "access paradox: how can the powerful interpretive and productive textual resources be made available to students without over-writing the students" own local forms of representation, interaction and knowledge?);
- the possibility of a dissenting mainstream in school and as a resource for understanding literacy for school (can dissenting literate practices emanate only from demographically, socio-economically marginal groups, from linguistic and cultural hybridities/minorities—beings for others—and what is the *educational* place of, for example, white, middle-class males in mobilizing the critical literacy project?);
- critical literacy curriculums (pedagogies, assessments, materials; what can be sustained in the face of schooling that is increasingly accountable via test scores?);
- how can studies of literacy in *educational* settings go beyond both humanist progressivism and a liberal acknowledgement of diversity? and

- how can theoretical and empirical work offer a justification for critical literacy education that goes beyond the marketplace's needs for proactive workers and the enhanced literacy performance of critical thinkers, readers, and writers?

There is a positive thesis at the heart of critical literacy pedagogies, methodologies, and practices: interpreting and producing texts is a way of rendering experience more understandable, of transforming experience through the productive application of epistemological, ideological, and textual resources, thereby revisiting and reunderstanding experience though active work on articulating the stuff of experience and on rearticulating the experience of others. This project includes articulating how to build alternative paths for self- and social development, an attitude toward one's self as in and of history, and usable, against-the-grain ways of knowing, feeling, and interacting, actively informed by, rather than silently determined by, the socio-economic histories of victories and defeats that have produced that self.

REFERENCES

Allen, R.L.: 2004, 'Whiteness and critical pedagogy', *Educational Philosophy and Theory* 36, 121–136.

Anderson, J., Kendrick, M., Rogers, T., and Smythe, S. (eds.): 2005, *Portraits of Literacy Across Families, Communities and Schools: Intersections and Tensions*, Lawrence Erlbaum Associates, Mahwah, NJ.

Barton, D.: 1994, *Literacy: An Introduction to the Ecology of Written Language*, Blackwell, Oxford.

Bernstein, B.: 1971, *Class, Codes and Control, Volume 1: Theoretical Studies Toward a Sociology of Education*, Routledge and Kegan Paul, London.

Bourdieu, P.: 1974, 'The school as a conservative force: scholastic and cultural inequalities', in J. Eggleston (ed.), *Contemporary Research in the Sociology of Education*, Methuen, London, pp. 32–46.

Bourdieu, P.: 1991, *Language and Symbolic Power*, Polity Press, Cambridge.

Bowles, S. and Gintis, H.: 1976, *Schooling in Capitalist America*, Routledge and Kegan Paul, London.

Comber, B. and Simpson, A. (eds.): 2001, *Negotiating Critical Literacies in Classrooms*, Lawrence Erlbaum, Mahwah, NJ.

Cope, B. and Kalantzis, M. (eds.): 2000, *Multiliteracies: Literacy Learning and the Design of Social Futures*, Routledge, London, NY.

Fairclough, N.: 1989, *Language and Power*, Longman, London.

Fairclough, N.: 2003, *Analysing Discourse: Textual Analysis for Social Research*, Routledge, London.

Freebody, P., Forrest, T., and Gunn, S.: 2001, 'Accounting and silencing in interviews: Smooth running through the 'problem of schooling the disadvantaged', in P. Freebody, S. Muspratt, and B. Dwyer (eds.), *Difference, Silence, and Textual Practice: Studies in Critical Literacy*, Hampton Press, Cresskill, NJ, pp. 119–151.

Freire, P.: 1970, *Pedagogy of the Oppressed*, Seabury, New York.

Freire, P. and Macedo, D.P.: 1987, *Literacy: Reading the Word and the World*, Bergin & Garvey, South Hadley, MA.

Gee, J.P.: 2001, 'Critical literacy as critical discourse analysis', in J. Harste and P.D. Pearson (eds.), *Book of Readings on Critical Perspectives on Literacy: Possibilities and Practices*, International Reading Association, New Orleans, LA.

Gee, J.P., Hull, G., and Lankshear, C.: 1996, *The New Work Order: Behind the Language of the New Capitalism*, Westview Press, Boulder, CO.

Giroux, H.: 1981, *Ideology, Culture, and the Process of Schooling*, Falmer Press, London.

Gregory, E. and Williams, A.: 1998, 'Family literacy history and children's learning strategies at home and at school', in G. Walford and A. Massey (eds.), *Studies in Educational Ethnography: Children Learning in Context*, JAI Press, Greenwich, CT, pp. 1–46.

Halliday, M.A.K.: 1985, *Spoken and Written Language*, Deakin University Press, Victoria.

Heath, S.B.: 1982, 'Protean shapes in literacy events: Ever-shifting oral and literate traditions', in D. Tannen (ed.), *Spoken and Written Language: Exploring Orality and Literacy*, Ablex, Norwood, NJ, pp. 91–117.

Janks, H.: 2000, 'Domination, access, diversity and design: A synthesis for critical literacy education', *Educational Review* 52, 175–186.

Kress, G.: 2001, *Multimodal Discourse*, Edward Arnold, London.

Kress, G.: 2003, *Literacy in the new media age*, Routledge, London.

Lankshear, C. (with Lawler, M.): 1987, *Literacy, Schooling and Revolution*, Falmer Press, London.

Lemke, J.L.: 1998, 'Multiplying meaning: Visual and verbal semiotics in scientific text', in J.R. Martin and R. Veel (eds.), *Reading Science: Critical and Functional Perspectives on Discourses of Science*, Routledge, London, pp. 87–113.

Lewis, C.: 2001, *Literary Practices as Social Acts: Power, Status, and Cultural Norms in the Classroom*, Lawrence Erlbaum, Mahwah, NJ.

Luke, A.: 1988, *Literacy, Textbooks and Ideology: Post-War Literacy and the Mythology of Dick and Jane*, Falmer Press, London.

Luke, C. and Gore, J. (eds.): 1992, *Feminisms and Critical Pedagogy*, Routledge, NY.

Mandela, N.:1995, *Speech at the inauguration of the South African Constitutional Court*, Johannesburg, http://www.concourt.gov.za/text/court/mandela_speech.html, retrieved May, 2006.

Martin, J.R.: 1999, 'Mentoring semiogenesis: 'genre-based' literacy pedagogy', in F. Christie (ed.), *Pedagogy and the Shaping of Consciousness: Linguistic and Social Processes*, Cassell, London, pp. 123–155.

Plato (360 BCE, trans. B. Jowett): *Phaedrus*, retrieved April 30, 2006, from http://ccat.sas.upenn.edu/jod/texts/phaedrus.html

Purcell-Gates, V.: 1995, *Other People's Words: The Cycle of Illiteracy*, Harvard University Press, Cambridge, MA.

Siegel, M. and Fernandez, S.: 2000, 'Critical approaches', in M. Kamil, R. Barr, P.D. Pearson, and P. Mosenthal (eds.), *Handbook of Reading Research (Vol. 3)*, Erlbaum, Mahwah, NJ, pp. 141–152.

Smith, D.: 1987, *The Everyday World as Problematic*, University of Toronto Press, Toronto.

Street, B.V.: 1984, *Literacy in Theory and Practice*, Cambridge University Press, Cambridge.

Street, B.V.: 2001, 'Literacy events and literacy practices in multilingual literacies: comparative perspectives on research and practice', in M. Martin-Jones and K. Jones (eds.), *Multilingual Literacies: Reading and Writing Different Worlds*, John Benjamin, Amsterdam, pp. 17–29.

Wallace, C.: 2003, *Critical Reading in Language Education*, Palgrave Macmillan, Basingstoke, UK.

VINITI VAISH

BILITERACY AND GLOBALIZATION

INTRODUCTION

The confluence of biliteracy and globalization is somewhat uncharted water. What text types and practices does one find at the lifeworlds of this confluence and what implications do they have for the bilingual classroom? Who are the main players at this meeting place of texts (as in biliteracy) and processes (as in globalization): markets, policy-makers, teacher practitioners or finally the consumers and producers of languages? What does a biliterate text in our globalizing world look like both inside and outside the classroom? This chapter explores some of the answers to these questions.

The fields of biliteracy and globalization are highly specialized within their broader disciplines. Hornberger (Continua of Biliteracy, Volume 9) has provided an updated review on the field of biliteracy, which goes back to the 1970s. Thus, this chapter will not repeat what Hornberger has already provided for us, instead it will concentrate more on the nexus of biliteracy and globalization. The data herein come from the two countries where I conduct research—India and Singapore. Research in the former, which is ongoing since 1999, is an ethnographic analysis of a Hindi–English dual medium government school (Rajkiya Sarvo-daya Kanya Vidyalaya), which follows the three language formula (TLF), India's language in education policy. In the case of Singapore, data come from the Sociolinguistic Survey of Singapore (SSS, 2006), a project undertaken by the Centre for Research in Pedagogy and Practice.

EARLY DEVELOPMENTS

Globalization

The literature on globalization can be considered to be somewhat bounded by two massive trilogies: Wallerstein's (1974, 1980, 1989) *World Systems Analysis* and Castells' (1996/2000, 1997/2004, 1998/ 2000) *The Information Age*. Both sets of work are brilliant in their analyses of the ways the globe is networked into congeries of empires, corporations, communities and pan national organizations. However, Wallerstein's Marxist perspective is now dated due to the demise of

B. V. Street and N. H. Hornberger (eds), Encyclopedia of Language and Education,
2nd Edition, Volume 2: Literacy, 119–130.
©2010 *Springer Science+Business Media LLC.*

communism as an enduring political alternative. Though Castells' early writings are Marxist, his later work is more applicable to the world in which we live today. The shortcoming of his trilogy is that the work does not make India a major focus as it does China, thus excluding not only a globalizing country of 1 billion people but also one of the dominant cultures of our world.

Globalization has been defined somewhat differently by economists (Bhagwati, 2004), sociologists (Castells, 1996/2000, 1997/2004, 1998/2000) and anthropologists (Appadurai, 1996) but they all agree on the high level of connectivity in this phenomenon between nations, corporations and individuals. Pieterse, the cultural anthropologist, gives a definition that encompasses many of these views. He writes that globalization 'is an objective, empirical process of increasing economic and political connectivity, a subjective process unfolding in consciousness as the collective awareness of growing global interconnectedness, and a host of specific globalizing projects that seek to shape global conditions' (Pieterse, 2004, pp. 16–17). As a phenomenon, Friedman (2005) points out that globalization is not new; in fact it is a process that started around 1492 and has manifested itself in three phases so far. In the first phase, 1492–1800, globalization was about imperial forces acquiring colonies by brute force; the second phase, 1800–2000, saw the rise of multinationals and the early version of the World Wide Web; and finally, since 2000, globalization is about individuals participating in the global economy leading to what Friedman calls a 'flat world' or level playing field.

Biliteracy and Related Terminology

Hornberger (Continua of Biliteracy, Volume 9) points out that in the 1970s the word 'biliteracy' carried connotations of fluency or mastery in the reading and writing of two or more languages. Her own definition of biliteracy, on which this chapter is based, is 'any and all instances in which communication occurs in two (or more) languages in or around writing' (Hornberger, 2003, p. 35). This definition includes varying levels of competencies, text types (traditional and multimodal) and verbal and symbolic communication. It thus encompasses biliteracy as exhibited in the lifeworld of the bilingual, and not as confined only to the classroom through school-related texts. Hornberger's model is a way of analyzing what is taught (content of biliteracy), in which languages it is taught (media of biliteracy), where it is taught (contexts of biliteracy) and what is the outcome of the teaching (development of biliteracy). The nestedness of these four sets of continua emphasize that for optimal biliterate development the learner should be allowed to access as many points on the continua as possible.

Related terms that have currency today are multimodal literacy (Kress, 2003), which is literacy based on the affordances of a web page, gesture, sound and other semiotic symbols including script, new literacies that one finds in cyberspace or workplace (Lankshear and Knobel, 2003) and finally multiliteracies (Cope and Kalantzis, 2000). None of these terms is about multiple languages and scripts as directly as is the term 'biliteracy', though all these terms are based on linguistic and cultural diversity. The term that comes closest in meaning to biliteracy is 'multilingual literacies' used by Martin-Jones and Jones (2000). Recently Pahl (2006) has edited a book that ethnographically links New Literacy Studies to multimodality in an age of globalization. However, the multimodality inherent in the diverse scripts and languages in which a bilingual has competence is not the major focus of this otherwise excellent volume.

MAJOR CONTRIBUTIONS

The themes that emerge from the field of biliteracy and globalization are changing media of instruction in national school systems, new literacies required in the workplace, the threatened linguistic ecology of the globe and finally biliterate textual practices influenced by the Internet. Each of these will be briefly described in this section. Let me begin with changing media of instruction and new literacies. Block and Cameron (2002, p. 5) point out that 'globalization changes the conditions under which language learning takes place' by commodifying languages and creating new literacies required by the workplace that schools are expected to teach. This is definitely true of India. TLF, which offered English as a second language only in secondary schools, is being transformed by globalization because the urban disadvantaged are demanding earlier access to the linguistic capital of English. This demand is linked to new sectors of the economy which are opening up since India started globalizing in 1991, like the mushrooming of call centres all over New Delhi. Consequently, government schools have initiated dual-medium programmes, which offer English as one of the media of instruction along with Hindi from nursery itself.

The spread of global English is perceived as threatening the linguistic diversity of the globe. Using the metaphor of biodiversity Skutnabb-Kangas (2003, p. 34) argues that not only can the world's linguistic diversity be documented in the same way as biodiversity there is also a correlation and even causal connection between the two. She writes that 'Maintenance of diversities . . . is one end of the continuum where ecocide and linguistic genocide are at the other end'. Skutnabb-Kangas' main point through these arguments is to raise awareness about language endangerment of small languages from the threat of big killer languages, like English. In a similar vein, Phillipson (1992, 2006) sees globalization, Americanization and Englishization as part of one process. He finds that English has retained its hold in former colonies and that it remains a divisive tool with which socio-economic strata are separated into the haves and have-nots. This view has been critiqued by Canagarajah (1999) who shows how English has been appropriated in Sri Lanka and Vaish (2005) who finds an agentive demand for and use of English in India.

Contesting the well-known view that globalization homogenizes languages is the not so well-known literature documenting the rise of non-English languages due to globalization. Dor's (2004, p. 98) thesis is that 'the forces of globalization do not have a vested interest in the global spread of English. They have a short-term interest in penetrating local markets through local languages and a long-term interest in turning these languages into commodified tools of communication'. He predicts that the Internet 'is going to be a predominantly non-English-language medium'. In 2004, there were 280 million English users and no less than 657 million non-English users and this gap is widening in favour of the latter. A similar view is expressed by Indrajit Banerjee, Secretary-General of the Asian Media Information and Communication Centre (AMIC), who comments:

> One would think that globalization in Asia would mean going English but that's not the case ... The diasporic market means you can have international newspapers, international TV and radio channels which are completely based on local languages. This is what I call the globalization of the local (p. 29).

In keeping with Dor's view, Warschauer (2002) and Warschauer, El, Ghada and Zohry (2002) point out that though in the Internet's history and design English and Romanized languages are privileged, this is changing due to the increasing online usage of languages like Arabic. For instance, the website of CNNArabic.com is a biliterate text that uses both Roman and Arabic scripts. Interestingly it is also a multimodal text because it has photos, videos and sound. Also in informal e-mails, colloquial Arabic is extensively used in the Roman script—a type of biliterate text that is becoming very common on the Internet.

This is also found in data from India where Hindi–English bilinguals use similar biliteracy practices to communicate. The following e-mail, which was sent to me by one of the young students in my study in India, is a case in point. Here the sender uses Romanized Hindi (bolded) and English to communicate:

Hi Mam
Main Bahut Khus Hua Apki E-Mail **Pakar**
(I was very happy to receive your e-mail)
& Thanks for my reply.

Finally, English is not the only language to claim a global status. Goh (2000) stakes a similar claim for Mandarin saying that like English it is used in inner, outer and expanding circles. Goh's claim is based on the increasing economic power of the inner circle (China) and the increasing number of Mandarin learners in the outer circle.

Goh also points to the rising use of Mandarin on the Internet through sites like the Chinese Google and Chinese Wikipedia. Thus, the emergence of languages like Arabic and Mandarin in cyberspace and the mingling of scripts with diverse languages in informal communication point to new biliterate practices that are yet to be explored in depth.

WORK IN PROGRESS

Broadly speaking, work in biliteracy tends to fall into two discrete domains—either the research is in the classroom or on the linguistic landscape of a site. A project of the former type is 'Signs of Difference: How Children Learn to Write in Different Script Systems' undertaken by the Institute of Education in the UK (Kenner, 2004; Kenner and Kress, 2003). This was a year-long study of 6-year-olds in London learning Chinese, Arabic and Spanish along with English. The methodology involved asking the case study children to teach their peers how to write Chinese, Arabic and Spanish using their own work. They found that in this biscriptal experience each script is a different 'mode' and the child organizes the Chinese and the Arabic scripts in terms of spatiality and directionality.

A recent issue of the *International Journal of Multilingualism* has focused on the concept of 'linguistic landscape'. An illustration of such research is Cenoz and Gorter (2006) who compare 975 signs on two streets in the Netherlands and Spain, respectively, on the basis of type of sign, number and names of languages on the sign, order of languages, type of font and whether the sign represents top-down language policy or bottom-up language use. Such literature perceives biliteracy as semiotic texts, which are not just found in the classroom, but also in the lifeworld of advertising, newspapers, comics, television, movies and other textual practices that influence school-going children.

In similar studies both Bhatia and Ritchie (2004) and Ladousa (2002) write about Hindi–English advertising in India. Bhatia and Ritchie (2004, p. 513) hypothesize: 'The economic forces of globalization together with the rise of global media have set the stage for a dramatic, exponential rise in global bilingualism,' thus challenging Phillipson's idea of English language hegemony. Ladousa's data come from the city of Banaras where she finds that the English-only advertisements in the Roman script signal a global language of the centre, whereas the Hindi ones in the Devanagari script index either a powerless periphery or an emerging Hindu–Hindi power that resists the linguistic colonization of English.

The literature on linguistic landscape does not use the term 'biliteracy' preferring 'bilingualism' as a catch all that accommodates speech and text. However, changes in the linguistic ecology of the globalizing world and medium of instruction demand a closer look at biliteracy so as to define it in terms of specific texts and practices as well as enrich existing theory. Vaish (forthcoming) suggests that biliterate texts can be categorized as traditionally biliterate or hybrid. A biliterate text is an artefact, for instance a road sign, piece of writing in the classroom, an advertisement on the street or graffiti and finally an English textbook that has been glossed and annotated in Hindi, in which there is written or symbolic (as in an image) evidence of two or more languages or cultures. A hybrid text is a subset of biliterate texts in that it has an aesthetic, creative nature, is usually not grammatically acceptable and is popular in sites like advertising and public culture. Specifically a hybrid text represents symbolically or through a comingling of scripts, what a bilingual does through code switching. While the former may be accommodated inside the bilingual classroom the latter is proscribed.

Figure 1 may be considered a biliterate text. It is a page from the English textbook of a girl in grade 10 of the dual-medium Rajkiya Sarvodaya Kanya Vidyalaya in New Delhi.

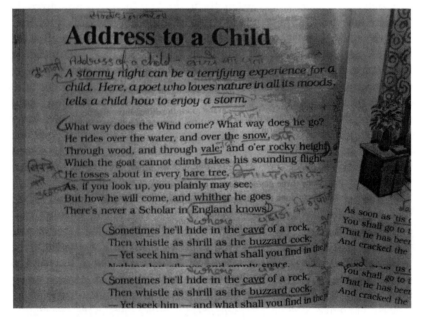

Figure 1 A biliterate text.

This poem by William Wordsworth appears in the English textbook for class 10, which is used in the government school system in India. The student to whom this textbook belongs has underlined all the words she has found difficult and written their meanings in Hindi. For instance:

Bare tree: बिना पत्ते का पेड़

Cave: पहाड़ों की गुफ़ा

In some cases, the student has made annotations in English; for instance she has written 'address of a child' and glossed this phrase in Hindi as बच्चे का पता so as to make a distinction between the two meanings of the noun 'address'.

The teachers in the Rajkiya Sarvodaya Kanya Vidyalaya actively encourage the creation of biliterate annotations in the texts because they use L1 as a resource in the classroom. One of them, Mrs Shobhana Gulati, explained to me (Field notes, October 16, 2005) that the Devanagari script is a great way to teach pronunciation in English. This is because Devanagari is a phonetic script and the words are pronounced exactly the way they are written. There are no silent letters or two pronunciations of a single letter like /s/ and /k/ for the letter 'c'. Thus if there are difficult pronunciations in the English lesson she makes the children write the exact pronunciation of the English word in Devanagari.

On the other hand the advertisement under Hindu–Muslim is a hybrid text (see Figure 2).

The first word under Hindu–Muslim is in Sanskrit: शुभमंगलम्, which means 'blessed marriage'. The main text under 'Sorry Sir, We don't have non-quality proposals' reads:

जो लाखों प्रपोजल्स की बात करते हैं वे आपको obsolete व settled या e-mail वाले पते व फोन रहित proposals की भीड़ में ढकेल देते हैं.. We show you the 'Quality Proposals' then constantly work for you. हम उनकी तरह 'member ID' देकर अलग नहीं हट जाते हैं । निर्णय आपको करना ह । Prof. and Personalised.

(Those who talk of lakhs (this is 1,000,000 in India) of proposals give you obsolete or settled or e-mail addresses and push you in the crowd of non-phone number proposals. We show you the 'Quality Proposals' then constantly work for you. Like them we don't just give a 'member ID' and move away. The decision is yours. Professional and personalized)

This advertisement mixes languages and scripts with dazzling flexibility. The pragmatic force of this advertisement is that it is written very much like a Hindi–English bilingual would speak. Such biliterate and hybrid texts are becoming increasingly common in the lifeworld of a bilingual as the world globalizes.

Figure 2 A hybrid text.

PROBLEMS AND DIFFICULTIES

One of the main problems in this field is what implications these new texts and practices have for the bilingual classroom. In countries like Singapore, the mother tongue classroom, where children are taught Tamil, Malay and Mandarin according to their ethnic group, is an enunciative space where the use of English is proscribed. There are even mother tongue classes where children are fined if they use English. In such a classroom, where even code switching is not encouraged, the nested nature of the variables on the *Continua of Biliteracy* are not acknowledged leading to biliterate development which is not optimal.

However, data from SSS (2006) show that the children are creating such texts on their own. This project is a large-scale survey of 1,000 10-year-olds linked to 24 follow-up studies. One of the girls in the follow-up studies who is biliterate in Cantonese, Mandarin and English enjoys the Dreamworks movie *Chicken Little* with Mandarin subtitles. The screen of this movie, not possible to replicate on paper, is a fine illustration of a multimodal biliterate text situated in a culturally globalizing world. Figure 3 is a biliterate page from the language log of this Chinese girl in which she has used both Mandarin and English to show her TV-watching practices.

Globalization has created hybrid textual forms that are proscribed in the bilingual classroom. However, these are the texts that children encounter in their multilingual lifeworlds. The challenge is for teacher education in the field of bilingualism to include an understanding of

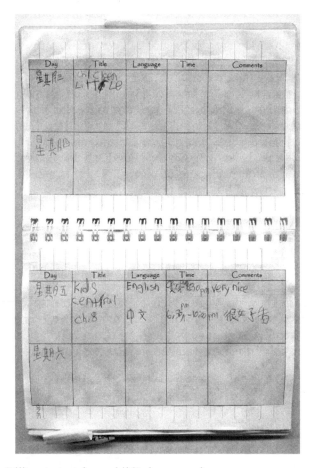

Figure 3 Biliterate text from child's language log.

these changing textual practices and use them as a resource in the class-room. Hornberger and Vaish (2006) show, through a comparison of bilingual classrooms in India, Singapore and South Africa, how teach-ers use linguistic resources that the children bring to the classroom to teach the language of power. For instance, in the classroom in India the teacher uses Hindi to explain to the student that 7 times 2 is not 13, though the medium and textbook of instruction for Mathematics is English.

FUTURE DIRECTIONS

Globalization has created new workplaces, like the call centre, where biliterate skills, especially 'English-knowing bilingualism', a term orig-inally used by Kachru (1982), are critical. In call centres in New Delhi though the computer screen is in English, the agent working on it might seek clarification of something on the screen in Hindi and English. There is an emergent literature on bilingualism (Roy, 2003) and iden-tity (Shome, 2006) in the worksite of call centres. Roy discusses issues of linguistic racism where employees are punished for incorrect accents as what they are selling is a service packaged in a particular kind of lan-guage. Shome's article on identity is linked to Castells' idea about globalization, though she herself does not make this link, creating an opposition between the Net and the Self. By the Net, Castells means a networked society that has replaced traditional social structures of family and human behaviour. On the other hand, the Self refers to reaf-firming identity in a landscape of change. There is a need to explore issues of identity and biliteracy practices.

The field of biliteracy would also benefit from research projects, which backward map from the workplace what biliterate skills are valu-able in a globalizing economy. Are schools in multilingual countries able to provide these skills? For instance, in Singapore's bilingual education policy Mandarin has both an instrumental value, in that it can promote business with China and a symbolic value in maintaining Chineseness. How do young Singaporeans make use of biliteracy in the workplace? Do they value what the nation's bilingual policy has given them? A host of such questions about biliteracy and globali-zation are waiting to be researched in our changing communicational landscape.

REFERENCES

Appadurai, A.: 1996, *Modernity at Large: Cultural Dimensions of Globalization*, Uni-versity of Minnesota Press, Minneapolis.
Banerjee, I.: 2005, 'Why Asia's local-language media will grow and grow: Globaliza-tion of the local', by Felix soh. *Straits Times, The* September, p. 29.

Bhagwati, J.: 2004, in *Defense of Globalization*, Oxford University Press, Oxford.

Bhatia, T.K. and Ritchie, W.C.: 2004, 'Bilingualism in the global media and advertising', in Bhatia and Ritchie (eds.), *The Handbook of Bilingualism*, Blackwell Publishing, Oxford.

Block, D. and Cameron, D. (ed.): 2002, *Globalization and Language Teaching*, Routledge, London.

Canagarajah, A.S.: 1999, *Resisting Linguistic Imperialism in English Teaching*, Oxford University Press, Oxford.

Castells, M.: 1996/2000, 'The rise of the network society', *The Information Age: Economy, Society and Culture*, Volume I (second edition), Blackwell Publishers, Oxford.

Castells, M.: 1997/2004, 'The power of identity', *The Information Age: Economy, Society and Culture*, Volume II (second edition), Blackwell Publishers, Oxford.

Castells, M.: 1998/2000, 'The end of the millennium', *The Information Age: Economy, Society and Culture*, Volume III (second edition), Blackwell Publishers, Oxford.

Cenoz, J. and Gorter, D.: 2006, 'Linguistic landscape and minority languages', *International Journal of Multilingualism* 3, 67–80.

Cope, B. and Kalantzis, M.: 2000, *Multiliteracies: Literacy Learning and the Design of Social Futures*, Routledge, London.

Dor, D.: 2004, 'From Englishization to imposed multilingualism: Globalization, the Internet, and the political economy of the linguistic code', *Public Culture* 16, 97–118.

Friedman, T.: 2005, *The World is Flat: A Brief History of the Globalized World in the 21st Century*, Allan Lane, London.

Goh, Y.S.: 2000, 'The rise of global Mandarin: Opportunities and challenges', in H.W. Kam and C. Ward (eds.), *Language in the Global Context: Implications for the Language Classroom*, REL, Singapore.

Hornberger, N.H. (ed.): 2003, *Continua of Biliteracy: An Ecological Framework for Educational Policy, Research, and Practice in Multilingual Settings*, Multilingual Matters, Clevedon.

Hornberger, N.H. and Vaish, V.: 2006, 'Multilingual language policy and school linguistic practice: Globalization and educational equity in South Africa, India and Singapore', *Paper presented at Sociolinguistics Symposium 16, July 5–8, 2006*, Ireland, Limerick.

Kachru, B.R.: 1982, *The Other Tongue: English Across Cultures*, University of Illinois Press, Urbana, IL.

Kenner, C.: 2004, *Becoming Biliterate: Young Children Learning Different Writing Systems*, Trentham Books, UK.

Kenner, C. and Kress, G.: 2003, 'The multisemiotic resources of biliterate children', *Journal of Early Childhood Literacy* Volume 3, 179–202.

Kress, G.: 2003, *Literacy in the New Media Age*, Routledge, London.

Ladousa, C.: 2002, 'Advertising in the periphery: Languages and schools in a North Indian city', *Language in Society* 31, 213–242.

Lankshear, C. and Knobel, M.: 2003, *New Literacies: Changing Knowledge and Classroom Learning*, Open University Press, Philadelphia.

Martin-Jones, M. and Jones, K. (eds.): 2000, *Multilingual Literacies: Reading and Writing in Different Worlds*, John Benjamins, Philadelphia.

Pahl, K. (ed.): 2006, *Travel Notes from the New Literacy Studies: Instances of Practice*, Multilingual Matters, Clevedon.

Phillipson, R.: 1992, *Linguistic Imperialism*, Oxford University Press, Oxford.

Phillpson, R.: 2006, 'Language policy and linguistic imperialism: An introduction to language policy: Theory and method', in T. Ricento (ed.), Blackwell Publishing, London.

Pieterse, J.N.: 2004, *Globalization & Culture: Global Melange*, Rowman & Littlefield Publishers Inc, New York.

Roy, S.: 2003, 'Bilingaulism and standardization in a Canadian call centre: Challenges for a linguistic minority community: Language socialization in bilingual and multilingual societies', in R. Bayley and S.R. Schecter (eds.), *Language Socialization in Bilingual and Multilingual Societies*, Multilingual Matters, Clevedon.

Shome, R.: 2006, 'Thinking through the diaspora: Call centres, India and the new politics of hybridity', *International Journal of Cultural Studies* 9, 105–124.

Soh, F.: 2005, 'Why Asia's local-language media will grow and grow: Globalization of the local', in *The Straits Times*, p. 29.

Skutnabb-Kangas, T.: 2003, 'Linguistic diversity and biodiversity: The threat from killer languages', in C. Mair (ed.), *The Politics of English as a World Language: New Horizons in Postcolonial Cultural Studies*, Rodopi, Amsterdam.

Vaish, V.: 2005, 'A peripherist view of English as a language of decolonization in post-colonial India', *Language Policy* 4, 187–206.

Vaish, V (forthcoming), *Biliteracy and Globalization: English Language Education in India*, Multilingual Matters, Clevedon.

Wallerstein, I.: 1974, *The Modern World-System 1: Capitalist Agriculture and the Origins of the European World-Economy in the Sixteenth Century*, Harcourt Brace Jovanovich Publishers, San Diego.

Wallerstein, I.: 1980, *The Modern World-System 11: Mercantilism and the Consolidation of the European World-Economy, 1600–1750*, Harcourt Brace Jovanovich Publishers, New York.

Wallerstein, I.: 1989, *The Modern World-System III: The Second Era of Great Expansion of the Capitalist World-Economy, 1730–1840*, Harcourt Brace Jovanovich Publishers, San Diego.

Warschauer, M.: 2002, 'Languages.com: The Internet and linguistic purism', in I. Snyder (ed.), *Silicon Literacies: Communication, Innovation and Education in the Electronic Age*, Routledge, London.

Warschauer, M., El S., Ghada, R., and Zohry, A.: 2002, 'Language choice online: Globalization and identity in Egypt', *Journal of Computer Mediated Communication-JCMC* 7(4), retrieved January 2006.

Section 2

Literacies and Social Institutions

ALAN ROGERS

INFORMAL LEARNING AND LITERACY

INTRODUCTION

Interest in informal learning has been strong for many years, but it has rarely been applied to the learning of literacy by adults which is usually seen as a formal learning process. This paper first reviews some of the developments in our understanding of informal learning, discusses some new findings from research into adult literacy learning in developing societies and suggests some applications of this to literacy learning programmes in the future.

EARLY DEVELOPMENTS AND MAJOR CONTRIBUTIONS IN INFORMAL LEARNING

Although there has been discussion of informal learning for many years (e.g. Archambault, 1974; Dewey, 1933; see also Lucas, 1983), it has played a minor role compared with studies of formal learning (see e.g. Davies, 1971). However, there has been a significant rise in interest in informal learning in the last few years (Bjornavold, 2000; Carter, 1997; Colardyn and Bjornavold, 2004; Livingstone, 2001; Marsick and Watkins, 1990; Richardson and Wolfe, 2001). The recent discourse of lifelong learning/education has encouraged wider recognition that learning goes on 'outside formal educational establishments' (Straka, 2004, p. 3)—that it is lifewide as well as lifelong. Many writers, especially those concerned with workplace learning and self-directed learning through new technologies (Rose, 2004), are exploring 'notions of learning in everyday life and how everyday strategies of learning can be taken into educational settings' (see Papen, 2005, p. 140; Hager, 2001; Imel, 2003; Visser, 2001).

It is however an area with many different definitions, often contested, and there is no space here to explore the many dimensions of this debate (Coffield, 2000; Colley, Hodgkinson and Malcolm, 2003; Eraut, 2000; McGivney, 1999).

Most however would agree that learning is a natural activity which continues at all times. Learning is the way in which the experience of the external is internalised and utilised for growth, a way of drawing from the natural and human environment the sustenance for living. Much of it is making sense (meaning) of experience and using that

B. Street and N. H. Hornberger (eds), Encyclopedia of Language and Education,
2nd Edition, Volume 2: Literacy, 133–144.
©2010 Springer Science+Business Media LLC.

for dealing with new experiences. Part of it is the building up of funds of cultural knowledge (Moll, Amanti, Neff and Gonzalez, 1992). A good deal of learning is intentional, planned and directed, but most learning from infancy until the end of life is unplanned, unintended and often unconscious, learning through tasks or play/imagination or social engagement; and this kind of learning results in tacit or implicit (unrecognised and unacknowledged) knowledge, understandings, skills and attitudes (Polyani, 1966; see Reber, 1993). As with literacy, there are learning events and learning practices; and there are throughout life 'learning episodes'(Rogers, 2002, pp. 120–125)—incidents when individuals decide and engage in more systematic learning for specific purposes, using all the perceived resources which their nature and the society within which they are situated provide. There is thus a continuum ranging from what I have called elsewhere (Rogers, 2003) 'task-conscious learning' (where learning is not conscious but takes place while engaged in some activity and where achievements are measured not in terms of learning but of task fulfilment) and 'learningconscious learning' (where learning is intended and conscious and achievements are measured in terms of learning).

The use of the word 'informal' to describe these natural learning processes has created the demand to search for 'formal' learning, and the creation in the 1960s of the term 'non-formal' to represent hybrid forms of learning (Rogers, 2004) has reinforced this search. A further distinction is sometimes made between 'informal learning' and 'incidental learning' (Enslin, Pendlebury and Tjattas, 2001; see Rogers, 2003, pp. 14–15). One way of representing these distinctions is through the analysis of the exercise of power and control: thus 'incidental learning' is sometimes seen as that learning which takes place without anyone being in control, 'informal learning' as that learning which the learner controls, 'non-formal learning' as that learning where control is shared between learner and a 'teacher' (learning support agent), and 'formal learning' as that learning which is controlled by the learning opportunity provider.

Rather than see incidental, informal, non-formal and formal learning as categories, it would seem more satisfactory to view these as positions on a continuum; there are many shades of learning between these positions. Such distinctions are tied up with contemporary value systems. Despite the fact that 'the majority of human learning does not occur in formal contexts' (Eraut, 2000, p. 12), modern Western societies tend to value formal learning above informal. The emphasis on formal learning (education) however can lead to the ignoring, demeaning or even denial of the existence of informal learning. Recent surveys (e.g. NIACE,1996) have shown that many people, when asked, would assert that they have done no learning since leaving school—identifying 'learning' with formal learning in educational establishments and ignoring all the learning they have done through their work, their families, their social interactions, their build up of capital, property and skills, etc. And this has implications for identities—both those ascribed by others and self-ascribed: 'If we simply picture learning as something that happens in the classroom, then we can see many . . . literacy learners as poor learners. If we see it [learning] as bound up in social activity we see something different' (Fowler and Mace, 2005, p. 31; see Lave and Holland, 2001).

Nevertheless, some distinction may be drawn between the various positions on the continuum. A useful example of this distinction can be seen in language learning (Krashen, 1982). The first language is learned through what Krashen calls 'acquisition learning', through the *use* of language without any structure, learning through tasks of communication and through play with sounds, experimentation, learning through errors with social scaffolding for reinforcement and correction until the cultural means of communication are more or less mastered. It is a process that has no 'formal' end. On the other hand, a later language is usually learned through more carefully structured, time-bound and controlled processes, through sequenced teaching-learning materials and designed practice, with pre-determined goals and measures of achievement. These two approaches can be taken to represent the distinction between informal learning and formal learning. Formal learning is seen as governed by rules outside of the learner. Informal learning is unplanned, non-linear, applied, contextualised and therefore limited (it ceases when the learner perceives that the task is completed rather than when the teacher determines). Informal learning involves 'ways of social and psychological functioning which explicitly differ from practices to be seen in formal educational environments' (Llorente and Coben, 2003; see Rogers, 2003, pp. 14–43 for a discussion of the two kinds of learning).

'Informal learning' (the natural learning process) then takes place in the home, in the community, at work (Garrick, 1998; Marsick and Watkins, 1990) and leisure (Enslin, Pendlebury and Tjattas, 2001, p. 62), in engagement with social movements (Foley, 1999; Mayo, 2005; Welton,1993), in all of life's experiences. It needs to be distinguished from informal education, which implies intention and planned and assisted learning. Informal education is usually seen as self-directed and self-controlled learning (Boekaerts, 1999; Imel, 2003; Smith, 2002). (Apprenticeships which some writers identify with informal learning is often put by others among the 'non-formal' learning strategies; indeed, there is much confusion between informal and non-formal learning programmes which may be seen as programmes which combine elements of both contextualisation and learner control on the one hand and standardisation and teaching agency control on the other; see Jeffs and Smith, 1990; Rogers, 2004).

One of the important elements of informal learning is analogous learning. Much meaning-making and problem solving relies on the identification of analogies, the application of what has already been learned elsewhere (formally and informally) to new situations. As we engage in new learning, so the fund of prior experiential learning, including tacit knowledge (Polyani 1966; Reber 1993) which may be called upon or reconstructed to enable analogous learning, increases.

Thus the natural learning which we all do, far from being unimportant, is in fact the foundation of all new learning and all education (planned and assisted learning). It is like breathing which is also a natural process relating the individual to the environment which she/he inhabits, and which is also usually unconscious but at times a conscious process, capable of improvement (e.g. for singing, swimming, sports etc). Despite this continual learning process, because much of it is unconscious, the learner may feel ignorant, incompetent and lacking in confidence; and the recognition of this learning is often the first stage of assisting someone with their intended and planned learning.

It would however be a mistake to assume that informal learning is the same across all sectors of life; and what is needed is an investigation into the ethnography of learning in relation to different areas. This paper seeks to examine one such area, informal learning and literacy[1].

WORK IN PROGRESS IN INFORMAL LEARNING AND LITERACY

The current application of the concepts of informal (natural) learning to literacy seems to lie in three main fields: the perceptions of literacy, the acquisition of literacy skills, and the practice of literacy. Such understandings will affect the ways in which formal literacy learning can be assisted.

Perceptions of Literacy

It can be argued that in today's world, there is no person (except perhaps some very young children) who has never directly or indirectly come across written forms of communication in some context or other. Even in so-called less developed society contexts, literacy practices lie embedded within many daily life activities—shopping and the market,

---

[1] Recent studies of the ethnography of numeracy suggest that this important area is a field which needs specialist treatment (see Street, Rogers and Dave, 2006) and it has been omitted from this article.

farming or other livelihoods, community relationships, the family (e.g. a calendar) etc. Both formal and informal literacy practices are an essential part of the social practices of health care, policing, religion, politics as well as schooling. There are displayed texts in most environments—in shops on packets, in street signs, advertisements, notices and graffiti on walls etc, although the frequency of such texts within the overall literacy environment (GMR, 2005, pp. 207–213; see Doronila, 1996) will vary. Such literacy material is often concentrated at certain points in most living contexts (post offices, clinics, police stations, churches, schools, shops, etc.) and not in other places, and from this, literate and non-literate alike will learn (informally) where literacy is appropriate and where it is not, to whom literacy belongs and to whom it does not belong, who is excluded, which kinds of literacy practices belong to which contexts and kinds of people. Informal learning teaches each of us our place in the society we inhabit.

Thus, although some people encounter writing fairly frequently and others more rarely, for all, 'literacy' in some form or other has entered their experience. And this calls for meaning-making—the establishment of a relationship between the experience and the sense of self. That is, literacy in today's world helps to create identities. So that everyone has built up some picture of literacy, what it means, and its practices in relation to themselves. For some, it may be a sense that such practices belong to other persons (communities of practice of the educated, the religious, the professionals, the rich etc.), that literacy is 'not for me', that it is out of their reach, beyond their capabilities or status. This informal learning is not confined to the so-called 'illiterate'. It applies also to those educated and literate persons who nevertheless feel excluded from certain communities of practice—those for example who find it difficult to handle computer manuals, insurance documents and technical papers or other languages and scripts. Perceptions of literacy include or exclude people from certain literacy practices.

But in fact the so-called illiterate are not in practice excluded from engaging in literacy practices. They will engage in these literacy practices, sometimes unconsciously, sometimes more consciously. Some of this engagement will be through mediation, getting someone to help them (Kalman, 1999; Mace, 2002); or they will find their own way of coping with literacy communications, 'develop their own strategies to make meaning from [and engage in] literacies that extend beyond their current abilities to process written language' (Ewing, 2003: cited in Papen, 2005, p. 139).

This is important, for (as we shall see) some of these persons have developed some form of literacy which neither they nor the society they inhabit recognise as 'literacy'. Thus, they will describe themselves as 'illiterate' even when engaged in some form of literacy practices. And in relation to the formal schooled literacies which form the content of most literacy learning programmes for both children and adults, they will continue to feel ignorant, incompetent and unconfident.

The Acquisition of Literacy Skills

Just as with language communication skills, so with literacy communication skills, there are two more or less distinct ways of learning—through informal acquisition learning (task-conscious learning) or through formal learning (learning-conscious learning).

Recent studies have shown that 'adults who ... are regarded as having serious literacy deficiencies are in fact not only involved in numerous literacy and numeracy events throughout their lives, but may possess a range of informally acquired literacy and numeracy skills' (Papen, 2005, p. 131); they have acquired these without going through primary school or adult literacy class. Investigations of the ways in which such skills have been developed have revealed that they come through engagement in some activity or other. The Vai learned their script 'outside of school' (Scribner and Cole, 1981) as do other language groups where the local language is not used in school (Aikman, 1999 etc.). Similarly, a car mechanic develops knowledge of reading and writing texts related to that trade; a tailoress keeps a notebook of her clients' measurements and requirements; a carpenter possesses a wall full of material cut out from catalogues and scribbles on them names and dates of work to be completed; a shopkeeper writes the names of customers, goods, prices and credit extended on his hand each day for someone else to write up more formally in the evening—all of them at the same time protesting that they are 'uneducated, illiterate' because they cannot read a newspaper (Rogers and Uddin, 2005; see Uddin, 2006). This is not confined to so-called 'developing societies': in more industrialised societies, hotel staff can cope with the informal texts of their particular hotel but not with discursive texts (Rogers, Hunter and Uddin, 2007; Rose, 2004); a restaurant waiter learns through 'looking over people's shoulders at the menu' (Fowler and Mace, 2005, p. 101). Much of this informal learning has been unconscious but a good deal comes from the adult learner seeking out personal assistance, from relatives, friends and work colleagues, from community members and religious leaders, even informally from the formal teacher of literacy at meetings held outside of the class sessions (Uddin, 2006). And much of what has been learned is not perceived as 'literacy'. What is and what is not literacy has thus been learned from the context: 'He did not really view what he did in his daily life as using literacy; to his mind, literacy meant learning, and learning took place in a classroom' (Fowler and Mace, 2005, p. 32).

Study of the processes involved in such informal learning of literacy shows that they are not linear, starting with simple words and moving to more complex words; rather they move from the known to the unknown. Informal literacy learning is always purposeful, associated with existing or changing identities, seeking identity confirmation, joining in a community of practice (Barton and Tusting 2005; Lave and Wenger 1991). Rather than learning literacy leading to change, it is change which leads to learning literacy. Such informal learning is always applied in a particular context, but it is almost always limited to that context and the activity in which it is embedded. In some cases, it may lead on to the development of further more discursive schooled literacies, but in other cases it does not (Uddin, 2006).

The Practice of Literacy

It is often assumed that a person, once having acquired a pre-set 'level' of literacy skills through formal (schooled) means—completing the literacy textbook, for example,—can apply those skills to any text, that literacy learning has ceased. But every new text form which is encountered calls for new learning. Again much of this is unconscious informal learning—new ways of writing and new formats of reading. Some people are conscious of this fact—like the adult literacy class member in Nepal who said that she could now read the literacy primer (textbook) but not read anything else like a newspaper or health booklet (field notes of author 1993). Learning to read a newspaper in columns and following the text from page to page; learning to fill in a bank or driving licence form; learning the format of poetry, of hymns and religious texts, of letter writing, of bills and invoices and of price lists; learning to distinguish the meaning of advertisements, the writing of formal papers and academic literacies (Mahiri, 2004)—all this calls for further learning. And almost all of this learning is informal. Who taught young people how to write text messages on their mobile phones? How do most people learn to send e-mails? Some formal instruction in computers is available, but even here, most of the learning each day is informal learning. 'In everyday life we not only use literacy ... but we also learn new literacies' (Papen, 2005, p. 140). Meeting and coping with new genres requires further learning: 'The processes of informal learning through which we learn to deal with unfamiliar types of texts, learn to adapt our style of writing to the requirements of new technologies, or learn to navigate the literacy environment of unfamiliar institutional settings' (Papen, 2005, p. 24) are often unconscious or semi-conscious. Making meaning and transmitting meaning are constantly being learned and relearned, most of this informally although formal courses are sometimes available. The view that primer literacy learning will equip the learner for the universal use of literacy is simply false.

FUTURE DIRECTIONS: INFORMAL LEARNING AND THE FORMAL LEARNING OF LITERACY

The recognition of the informal learning of literacy (both perceptions and skills) and of the need for continued learning of literacy practices has important implications for the design and implementation of literacy learning programmes for both children and adults. Four main areas call for attention but more work needs to be done on this interaction between informal and formal learning (see Fowler and Mace, 2005; Larson and Marsh, 2005; Pahl and Rowsell, 2005; Papen, 2005).

First, the learned belief systems about literacy and the self will affect the motivation and confidence of the potential literacy learner. Simply casting him/herself as a learner of literacy is itself a major step calling for emotional investment and determination, and is not lightly to be brushed aside with an emphasis on deficits. The view that 'literacy is not for people like me' is often strong—in the case of children, because of an over-emphasis on age-related learning and stereotyping by adults, in the case of adults through years of experience. Non-literate adults are members of a number of over-lapping communities of practice in which literacy practices may be relatively weak or confined to a small number of members of those communities; and perceptions of 'literacy' developed through informal learning over many years often leads to a sense of exclusion from such practices (Barton and Tusting, 2005).

Thus with adults it is important to try to bring the unconscious informal learning of many years into consciousness. As with the Assessment of Prior Experiential Learning (APEL), one needs to recognise and give value to the informal learning acquired through adult life and build on it to make progress in further learning (Weil and McGill, 1989); so with literacy, it is important to give recognition and value to the informal learning about literacy, both the perceptions of literacy which help to create the learner's identity, and the strategies which have been built up. This is increasingly being recognised in formal education where home-school linkages are being closely studied. In some cases, this will involve the recognition of the informal literacy skills which have been acquired to enable non-literate persons to engage in their own literacy practices, which the potential literacy learners bring with them, not to ignore or 'correct' these, not to compartmentalise them but to help all (teacher and learners alike) to give them value and to build on them. Such background understandings need to be developed by the teacher through ethnographic-style research (Street, Rogers and Dave, 2006).

Secondly, there is much informal learning going on even *within* formal literacy learning groups or classes. The scaffolding of learning by teaching agents (Greenfield 1984) brings with it many implications which literacy learners are not slow to recognise and internalise—who is important and who is not; what kinds of literacy are acceptable and what are not, what one can and cannot write or read (the notes some children send round the class under the desks are often forbidden rather than built upon; see Camitta, 1993). Many textbooks contain hidden messages—that poverty, for example, is the fault of the poor who need to change to become prosperous; that sickness can be avoided by hygiene; that gender inequalities can be remedied without the change of male dominance; etc. A climate is built up in a classroom and the literacy learners are being asked to engage with that; and such participation 'shapes not only what we do but also who we are and how we interpret what we do' (Wenger, 1998, p. 4). But unfortunately the literacy classroom is often an inappropriate context for learning, hierarchical and dictatorial. 'Learning to be literate is [or should be] like learning to be an artisan in a guild, to play an instrument in an ensemble, like acquiring a craft within a community whose art and forms of life are dynamic, rather than robotic acquisition and automatization of core skills' (Luke, 2005, p. xi). Learning literacy through apprenticeship may be a more appropriate model for both child and adult than formal schooling (Overwien, 2005; Collins, Brown and Newman, 1989).

Thirdly, the fact that informal learning of literacy continues after the initial learning period indicates that a 'single-injection' model of adult literacy learning programmes will always be ineffective. Learning literacy skills is not a simple matter of a short course (3 years, 2 years, 9 months or even, as in Pakistan, 3 months) which will transmute the 'illiterate' into the 'literate'. Learning to read a primer (textbook) may lay the foundation for learning to read a newspaper but it does not necessarily mean that everyone who completes an adult literacy learning programme will be confident enough to go on to read a newspaper or magazine or to write other forms of texts.

Fourthly, the methods by which the informal learning of literacy has been developing throughout the life of the adult and the methods by which the child is learning their first language and learning about texts could with profit be used in the literacy class: 'the everyday strategies of learning can be taken into educational settings' (Papen, 2005, p. 140). The need to bring the everyday literacy practices of the learners—whether children or adults—into every planned learning programme has been emphasised several times (Cole and Scribner, 1974; Lave, 1988; Rogoff and Lave, 1984). This is as true of literacy learning as of other learning activities. And this means that a one-size-fits-all literacy learning programme can never be successful: each literacy learning group needs its own learning programme based on the informal literacy learning of the learners.

Task-related learning; cyclic rather than linear learning (the progression from simple to complex, while useful in some circumstances, can be ignored when engaged in task-related learning, for the task provides the parameters of the learning); collaborative learning rather than individual; real literacy activities and texts drawn from the literacy learners themselves rather than imposed from outside (Rogers, 1999); critical reflection on both the literacy learning tasks and the contents of the teaching-learning materials; changed relationships of the teacher and learners where the teacher becomes a literacy mediator and scaffolder/mentor rather than instructor – these are some of the implications of informal literacy learning for formal literacy learning.

REFERENCES

Aikman, S.: 1999, *Intercultural Education and Literacy: An Ethnographic Study of Indigenous Knowledge and Learning in the Peruvian Amazon*, Benjamins, Amsterdam.

Archambault, R.D. (ed.): 1974, *John Dewey on Education: Selected Writings*, Chicago University Press, Chicago.

Aspin, D., Chapman, J., Hatton, M., and Sawano, Y. (eds.): 2001, *International Handbook of Lifelong Learning*, Kluwer, London.

Barton, D. and Tusting, K.: 2005, *Beyond Communities of Practice, Language, Power and Social Context*, Cambridge University Press, Cambridge.

Bjornavold, J.: 2000, *Making Learning Visible*, CEDEFOP, Thessaloniki.

Boekaerts, M.: 1999, 'Self-regulated learning: Where we are today', *International Journal of Educational Research* 31: 445–458.

Camitta, M.: 1993, 'Vernacular writing: Varieties of literacy among Philadelphia high school students', in Street, B.V. (ed.), *Cross-cultural Approaches to Literacy*, Cambridge University Press, Cambridge, 228–246.

Carter, C.: 1997, *Recognising the Value of Informal Learning*, Learning from Experience Trust, Chelmsford.

Coffield, F. (ed.): 2000, *The Necessity of Informal Learning*, Policy Press, Bristol.

Colardyn, D. and Bjornavold, J.: 2004, 'Validation of formal, non-formal and informal learning: Policy and practices in EU member states', *European Journal of Education* 39(1): 69–89.

Cole, M. and Scribner, S.: 1974, *Culture and Thought*, Wiley, New York.

Colley, H., Hodgkinson, P., and Malcolm, J.: 2003, *Informality and Formality in Learning: a Report for the Learning and Skills Research Centre*, University of Leeds, Leeds, http://www.LSRC.ac.uk accessed 13 January 2006

Collins, A., Brown, J.S., and Newman, S.E.: 1989, 'Cognitive apprenticeship: Teaching the crafts of reading, writing and mathematics', in Resnick (ed.), L.B. *Knowing, Learning and Instruction*, Erlbaum, Hillsdale, 453–494.

Collins, J. and Blot, R.K.: 2003, *Literacy and Literacies: Texts, Power and Identity*, Cambridge University Press, Cambridge.

Davies, I.K.: 1971, *The Management of Learning*, McGraw-Hill, London.

Dewey, J.: 1933, *How We Think: A Restatement of the Relation of Reflective Thinking to the Educative Process*, Heath, Boston, MA.

Doronila, M.L.C.: 1996, *Landscapes of Literacy: An Ethnographic Study of Functional Literacy in Marginal Communities*, UIE, Hamburg.

Enslin, P., Pendlebury, S., and Tjattas, M.: 2001, 'Political inclusion, democratic empowerment and lifelong learning', in Aspin et al., 61–78.

Eraut, M.: 2000, 'Non-formal learning, implicit learning and tacit knowledge in professional work', in Coffield (ed.), 12–31.

Ewing, G.: 2003, 'The New Literacy Studies: A point of contact between literacy research and literacy work', *Literacies* 1: 15–21.

Foley, G.: 1999, *Learning in Social Action: A Contribution to Understanding Informal Education*, Zed Books, London.

Fowler, E. and Mace, J. (ed.): 2005, *Outside the Classroom: Researching Literacy with Adult Learners*, NIACE, Leicester.

Garrick, J.: 1998, *Informal Learning in the Workplace: Unmasking Human Resource Development*, Routledge, London.

GMR: 2005, *Literacy for Life: EFA Global Monitoring Report*, UNESCO, Paris.

Greenfield, P.: 1984, 'Theory of teacher in the learning activities of everyday life', in Rogoff and Lave (eds.).

Hager, P.: 2001, 'Lifelong learning and the contribution of informal learning', in Aspin et al. (eds.), 79–92.

Imel, S.: 2003, *Informal Adult Learning and the Internet: Trends and Issues: Alert 50 Columbus*, ERIC, Ohio.

Jeffs, T. and Smith, M.: 1990, *Using Informal Education*, Open University Press, Milton Keynes.

Kalman J.: 1999, *Writing on the Plaza: The Mediated Literacy Practice Among Scribes and Clients in Mexico City*, Hampton Press, Cresskill, New Jersey.

Krashen, S.D.: 1982, *Principles and Practice in Second Language Acquisition*, Pergamon, Oxford.

Larson, J. and Marsh, J.: 2005, *Making Literacy Real: Theories and Practices for Learning and Teaching*, Sage, London.

Lave, J.: 1988, *Cognition in Practice: Mind, Maths and Culture in Everyday Life*, Cambridge University Press, Cambridge.

Lave, J. and Holland, D. (eds.): 2001, *History in Person: Enduring struggles. Contentious Practice, Intimate Identities*, School of American Research Press, New Mexico.

Lave, J. and Wenger, E.: 1991, *Situated Learning: Legitimate Peripheral Participation*, Cambridge University Press, Cambridge.

Livingstone, D.W.: 2001, *Adults' Informal Learning: Definitions, Findings, Gaps and Future Research*, http://www.nall.ca accessed 12 January 2006

Llorente, J.C. and Coben, D.: 2003, 'Reconstituting our understanding of the relationship between knowledge and power in analysis of the education of adults: Sociocognitive and political dimensions', *Compare* 33(1): 101–113.

Lucas, A.M.: 1983, 'Scientific literacy and informal learning', *Studies in Science Education* 10: 1–36.

Luke, A.: 2005, 'Foreword', in Pahl and Rowsell (eds.), x–xiv.

Mace J.: 2002, *The Give and Take of Writing: Scribes, Literacy and Everyday Life*, NIACE, Leicester.

Mahiri, J. (ed.): 2004, *What the Kids Don't Learn in School: Literacy in the Lives of Urban Youth*, Peter Lang, New York.

Marsick, V.J. and Watkins, K.E.: 1990, *Informal and Incidental Learning in the Workplace*, Routledge, London.

Mayo, M.: 2005, *Global Citizens: Social Movements and the Challenge of Globalization*, Zed Books, London.

McGivney, V.: 1999, *Informal Learning in the Community*, NIACE, Leicester.

Moll, L., Amanti, C., Neff, D., and Gonzalez, N.: 1992, 'Funds of knowledge for teaching: Using a qualitative approach to connect homes and classrooms', *Theory into Practice* 31.2: 3–9.

NIACE: 1996, *Headline Findings on Lifelong Learning from the NIACE/Gallup Survey*, NIACE, Leicester.

Overwien, B.: 2005, 'Informal learning and the role of social movements', in Singh M. (ed.), *Meeting Basic Learning Needs in the Informal Sector*, Springer, Heidelberg.

Pahl, K. and Rowsell, J.: 2005, *Literacy and Education: Understanding the New Literacy Studies in the Classroom*, Paul Chapman, London.

Papen, U.: 2005, *Adult Literacy as Social Practice: More than Skills*, Routledge, London.

Polyani, M.: 1966, *The Tacit Dimension*, Doubleday, New York.

Reber, A.: 1993, *Implicit Learning and Tacit Knowledge*, Oxford University Press, New York.

Richardson, L.D. and Wolfe, M. (eds.): 2001, *Principles and Practice of Informal Education: Learning Through Life*, Routledge Falmer, London.

Rogers, A.: 1999, 'Improving the quality of adult literacy programmes in developing countries: The 'real literacies' approach', *International Journal of Educational Development* 19: 219–234.

Rogers, A.: 2002, *Teaching Adults (third edition)*, Open University Press, Buckingham.

Rogers, A.: 2003, *What is the Difference? A New Critique to Adult Learning and Teaching*, NIACE, Leicester.

Rogers, A.: 2004, *Non-Formal Education: Flexible Schooling or Participatory Education*, University of Hong Kong/Kluwer, Hong Kong/ Dordrecht.

Rogers, A. and Uddin, A. Md.: 2005, 'Adults learning literacy: Adult learning theory and the provision of literacy classes in the context of developing societies', in Street, B.V. (ed.), *Literacy Across Educational Contexts*, Caslon, Philadelphia, 235–260.

Rogers, A. with Hunter, J. and Uddin, A. Md.: 2007, Adult Learning and Literacy Learning for Livelihoods: Some International Perspectives, *Development in Practice* 17.1:137–146.

Rogoff, B. and Lave, J. (eds.): 1984, *Everyday Cognition: Its Development in Social Context*, Harvard University Press, Cambridge, MA.

Rose, M.: 2004, *The Mind at Work: Valuing the Intelligence of the American Worker*, Viking Books, New York.

Scribner, S. and Cole, M.: 1981, *The Psychology of Literacy*, Harvard University Press, Cambridge, MA.

Smith, M.K.: 2002, *Informal and Non-Formal Education, Colonialism and Development*, www.infed.org accessed 10 January 2006.

Straka, G.A.: 2004, Informal Learning: Concepts, Antagonisms and Questions, www.itb.uni-bremen.de accessed 2 January 2006.

Street, B.V., Rogers, A., and Dave, B.: 2006, 'Adult teachers as researchers: Ethnographic approaches to numeracy and literacy as social practices in South Asia, *Convergence* 39(1): 31–44.

Street, B.V, Baker, D., and Tomlin, A.: 2005, *Navigating Numeracies: Home/School Numeracy Practices*, Springer, Heidelberg.

Uddin, A. Md.: 2006, *Perceptions, Motivations, Learning and Uses of Literacies in Relation to Livelihoods: A Case Study of Two Bangladeshi Villages*, Unpublished PhD thesis, University of Nottingham.

Visser, J.: 2001, 'Integrity, completeness and comprehensiveness of the learning environment: Meeting the basic learning needs of all throughout life', in Aspin et al., 473–500.

Weil, S.W. and McGill, I.: 1989, *Making Sense of Experiential Learning: Diversity in Theory and Practice*, Open University Press, Buckingham.

Welton, M.: 1993, 'Social revolutionary learning: The new social movements as learning sites', *Adult Education Quarterly* 43(3): 152–164.

Wenger, E.: 1998, *Communities of Practice: Learning, Meaning and Identity*, Cambridge University Press, Cambridge.

SECOND LANGUAGE ACADEMIC LITERACIES: CONVERGING UNDERSTANDINGS

INTRODUCTION

Increasingly schools and universities in many parts of the world are expected to serve ethnically and linguistically diverse students. Scholarly discussions on language and literacy education have, however, tended to maintain either a first language or a second language stance in some mutually insulating way. This intellectual divide was perhaps fostered by the educational and intellectual climate that prevailed in an earlier historical period. In the past 30 years or so, however, public educational institutions have been made progressively more conscious of the need and the obligation to serve diverse student populations under the aegis of marketization of education provision for international students, and/or social integration for all students, irrespective of their language backgrounds. It is recognized that many linguistic minority students find the use of their second language for academic purposes problematic (Cummins, 2000; Leung and Safford, 2005; Mohan, Leung and Davison, 2001; Scarcella, 2003). The ability to communicate informally for social purposes in a second language, even at high levels of lexico-grammatical accuracy and pragmatic familiarity, does not automatically translate into effective academic use, particularly in relation to reading and writing. A good deal of discussion in second language curriculum and pedagogy is focussed on this 'problem'. In this discussion, my main focus is on the use of second language in academic discourse (with particular reference to written discourse) because it highlights a profound conceptual issue in the prevailing notions of second language competence. I explore this not just as a teaching issue, but also as a conceptual and research issue.

In this chapter, I use the terms 'second language pedagogy' and 'academic literacy' in a broad sense and refer to relevant teaching and curriculum literature covering a range of educational settings (e.g. school, college and work-based programmes) and students (e.g. school-aged and adult).[1] Perhaps it would be useful to point out that there are

---

[1] Traditionally in the English-speaking education systems, the term 'English as a second language' (ESL) is often used to refer to a context of use and/or learning where English is the medium of communication for at least some public or government

B. V. Street and N. H. Hornberger (eds), Encyclopedia of Language and Education, 2nd Edition, Volume 2: Literacy, 145–161.
© *2010 Springer Science+Business Media LLC.*

some discipline-specific ways in which the terms 'language' and 'literacy/literacies' are interpreted. In the second language literature the term 'language' has tended to be used as a general catch-all label to include the development and use of language for listening, speaking, reading and writing (the so-called four basic skills); the second language lexico-grammar system and (often generalized) pragmatic rules of use form the basis of most curricular specifications. Concerns for 'literacy' development tend to be subsumed under the banner of reading and writing; specialist branches of English as a second language teaching such as English for Academic Purposes (EAP) often prioritize reading and writing. In the field of academic literacies, language use is assumed to be part of students' lived experience and the use of the lexico-grammar of 'language' itself is seen in relation to observed socio-cultural and pragmatic conventions in discourse. A basic familiarity with lexico-grammar is generally assumed to be in place, irrespective of students' first or second language background. There is relative little explicit discussion on the different trajectories in first and second language developments and the impact these may have on literacy development (see Davison, 1996 for a further discussion). The plural form 'literacies' is preferred by some writers (Lea, 2004; Street, 2003, 2005) and it will be used in this discussion where appropriate to signal the existence of a literature which acknowledges the multiple ways language and other semiotic means are used for meaning-making in academic contexts. Although the second language in this discussion is English, the conceptual issues raised are not necessarily language specific.

MAJOR CONTRIBUTIONS: SECOND LANGUAGE IN COMMUNICATION

A, if not *the*, major influence on English as second language teaching (ELT) in the past three decades has been the advent of the concept of communicative competence, which in turn has spawned a broad set of theoretically linked principles and classroom practices now commonly known as Communicative Language Teaching (CLT). The concept of

---

functions (e.g. English in Singapore and India, and for some minority language communities in countries such as the USA and the UK); and the term 'English as a foreign language' (EFL) is used where English is not used/learned for public communication. English as an additional language (EAL) is sometimes used to refer to contexts in which English is used by ethnolinguistic minority students, e.g. Polish-mother tongue children in school in England. Recent developments in the use of English in different contexts have made these terms increasingly difficult to apply. For instance, the use of English as a preferred common language of communication in European political and business organizations have blurred the traditional distinctions. In this article, author uses 'second language' as a general label to signal a contra-distinction to first language.

communicative competence, built on Hymes' work on ethnography of communication (1972, 1977), was elaborated and recontextualized for second language pedagogy by Canale and Swain in a series of papers (Canale 1983, 1984; Canale and Swain, 1980a, b). An essential tenet of CLT is that second language learning and teaching should be concerned with both rules of grammar (all aspects of lexico-grammar for speech and writing) and social rules of use. Historically this represented an intellectual move away from an earlier tendency to treat grammar as the main focus in second language pedagogy. Teachers and curriculum designers are expected to take both formal linguistic properties and context of use into account. For instance, Yalden (1983, pp. 86–87) suggests that the designer of a communicative curriculum has to attend to the following:

1. ... the *purposes* for which the learners wish to acquire the target language
2. some idea of the *setting* in which they will want to use the target language ...
3. the socially defined *role* the learner will assume in the target language, as well as their interlocutors ...
4. the communicative *events* in which the learners will participate ... [emphasis in original]

This approach to building up a picture of communication needs quite clearly draws on Hymes' discussion on components of speech (1977, 1994). The purposes, settings, roles and events were, at least in principle, established by carrying out student needs surveys. This empirically oriented approach to the drawing up of learning content is generally accepted in all areas of CLT. The curriculum designer is meant to use this kind of contextual information to identify socio-culturally and pragmatically appropriate language for learning. So particular grammatical forms for requests such as 'would you ...', 'could you ...' and 'will you ...' will be selected according to students' projected purposes and contexts of use. Likewise, students are inducted into a range of different text types such as formal reports, informal accounts and study notes in accordance with the identified needs. This socio-culturally alert approach is applicable to every aspect of curriculum development. Furthermore, CLT eschews formal didactics and it is in favour of hands-on classroom activities. In other words, the CLT classroom is where students are encouraged to engage in the actual use of the language through purposeful participatory communication activities such as role play and simulated games. This combination of socio-culturally sensitive curriculum development and activity-oriented classroom pedagogy has held sway in popular course books and teacher training manuals (Brown, 2001; McDonough and Shaw, 2003; Morrow, 1981). For instance, Brown's (2001, p. 43) characterization of CLT includes the following:

- a focus on 'the components (grammatical, discourse, functional, sociolinguistic and strategic) of communicative competence';
- the use of language teaching techniques and student tasks 'to engage learners in the pragmatic, authentic, functional use of language for meaningful purposes';
- the positioning of the teacher as 'a facilitator and guide ... Students are therefore encouraged to construct meaning through genuine linguistic interaction with others'.

In an authoritative account of the nature of English for Academic Purposes (EAP), an expanding specialist branch of ELT traditionally associated with higher education, Hyland and Hamp Lyons (2002, p. 2) state that

> English for Academic Purposes refers to language research and instruction that focuses on the specific communicative needs and practices of particular groups in academic contexts. It means grounding instruction in an understanding of the cognitive, social and linguistic demands of specific academic disciplines. This takes practitioners beyond preparing learners for study in English to developing new kinds of literacy: equipping students with communicative skills to participate in particular academic and cultural contexts.

In general, CLT attempts to approximate conditions of 'real communication' in the classroom. The extent to which this commitment to an empirically grounded approach can be seen in pedagogic practice will be discussed in the next section.

Perhaps it should be pointed out that CLT is not the only influential theoretical framework in second language education. In a psychocognitively oriented body of work directly concerned with the second language development of linguistic minority school students, Cummins (1984, 1992, 1996, 2000) also takes communication in context as a point of departure. He proposes that language proficiency in a curriculum context can be seen in terms of basic interpersonal communicative skills (BICS) and cognitive/academic language proficiency (CALP). BICS is understood to mean 'the manifestation of language proficiency in everyday communicative contexts'; CALP is conceptualized as 'manipulation of language in decontextualized academic situations' (Cummins, 1992, p. 17). BICS is generally held to occur in situations where the meanings communicated are broadly familiar to the participants and/or the immediate context or action provides supportive clues for understanding; social greetings and ordering food in a student canteen are examples of context-supported BICS. A science class teacher-led discussion on the production advantages and environmental problems of the use of pesticides in farming, without any supporting print, sound, visual or video materials, can be regarded as an example of context-impoverished and cognitively demanding CALP. These two conceptual categories do not yield precise linguistic descriptions, nor do they map on to any specific area of the curriculum directly. But they can be used to estimate the language complexity and cognitive demands of a variety of communicative situations in school. Teachers can, with this analytical insight, help students acquire proficiency in spoken and written academic language by judiciously increasing or reducing contextual support and cognitive demand as their needs change and develop in different areas of the curriculum. This framework has been particularly influential in education systems where second language students are mainstreamed without a dedicated second language curriculum (e.g. England). There are other second language pedagogic frameworks such as the Cognitive Academic Language Leaning Approach (CALLA) (Chamot and O'Malley, 1992) and the Topic Approach (Evans, 1986). Focus and scope preclude a full account of all of them here. Suffice it to say that in one way or another, these frameworks tend to be built on the assumption that active communicative use is fundamental to the development of academic English. (For a further discussion, see Leung, 2005.)

PROBLEMS AND DIFFICULTIES: PEDAGOGIZING ACADEMIC COMMUNICATION IN SECOND LANGUAGE

It would seem that the literature on second language pedagogy in general has in place developed conceptual frameworks for assisting second language students in navigating and developing the complex ways in which language is used in academic settings, particularly in terms of writing. However, it is also the case that the use of language for academic purposes remains a major challenge for many second language students. The existence of a specialist literature and research tradition (e.g. EAP), and language centres or similar units designed to support second language academic language proficiency in English-speaking universities across the globe readily bears witness to this widespread 'problem' (see Gee, 2004; Scarcella, 2003; Schleppegrell and Colombi, 2002, for further discussion). Scarcella (2003, p. 1), for instance, illustrates the issues vividly by citing an email request for information written by a second language student to a professor in an American university:

> How do you do? ... I am a student currently on the freshman level. I am going to be attend Biology 5C next

year ... Although my major is in Social Science, I am consider to have Biology as my second major. I am currently attending Professor Campbell lecture. He suggested to me that maybe I should seek around to for research projects ... He suggest that maybe I should contact you to see would it be possible for you to provide me with some information. As I have understand that you are currently conducting a research on the subject of plasma, and I would like to know more about it, that is, if I am not costing any convenience. Thank you very much, and have a good day.

This student did not succeed in getting the desired assistance from the biology professor who commented on this text to a colleague thus: 'Syntax, spelling, whew!' (loc.cit.). Over and above the grammatical infelicities, this message is uncomfortable as a piece of formal student–teacher communication in a number of ways—the informal opening and closing, the possibly unwarranted assumption that a first-year student might be granted access to work-in-progress research, the lack of specificity in terms of the type of information requested and so on. These are instances of agentive meaning-making that are at odds with conventionalized assumptions informing institutional student–teacher relations and the associated communication practices. So a legitimate question at this point is: would it be possible for the kinds of social rule flouting (as seen by the professor) displayed in the email text shown above to be addressed by CLT? The answer is potentially yes but a good deal of further conceptual and theoretical work would have to be done first.

Despite its ethnography-inspired conceptual origin, CLT practice has not generally privileged the type of information and data discussed by Hymes, i.e. how communication is performed and what patterns of meaning-making and meaning-taking occur in specific contexts (although see Belcher, 2006, for an exception). Curriculum developers tend to be concerned with determining students' projected communication purposes and contexts, e.g. learning English as a school subject or learning to use English in an English-speaking work environment. The general idea here is that once the students' purposes and contexts of use are established—by means of needs surveys, in-course discussions, analyses of model texts and student language performance (e.g. written texts) and scrutiny of academic programme requirements—curriculum designers can draw on their knowledge of language teaching/learning (i.e. theory and practical know-how) and 'typical' language use (i.e. the 'what' and the 'how') to specify the teaching content with respect to the various parts of the overall competence to be taught (Hutchinson and Waters, 1987; Nunan, 1988). The language learning content is thus built on idealized typifications of what abstracted 'competent' native speakers may say and do in projected contexts.[2] In ELT textbooks it is not unusual to find advice such as this:

> Today's way of conducting business is informal so that's what we should aim for in our business writing too – a friendly, conversational style. We should use short words and simple expression, short sentences and paragraphs ... (Cunningham, Moor and Carr, 2003, p. 34)

In a not too dissimilar way, Scarcella (2003, p. 9), drawing on her observations that school teachers tend to work with strong assumptions about the sort of language children should use on the one hand, and that they (school teachers) often do not actively help children develop this language repertoire on the other, argues that university students (particularly second language students) need to learn to use academic English:

> Academic English is a variety or a register of English used in professional books and characterized by the specific linguistic features associated with academic disciplines. The term 'register' refers to a constellation of linguistic features that are used in a particular situational context ... Academic English tasks include reading abstracts, getting down the key ideas from lectures, and writing critiques, summaries ... It includes a wide range of genres ... I define genre as a discourse type having 'identifiable formal properties, identifiable purposes, and a complete structure ...

On the strength of this perception (and description), Scarcella goes on to provide an account of the components of academic English in terms of phonology, lexis, grammar, sociolinguistic and discourse conventions. At a general level, this kind of expert advice sounds very convincing and helpful. But the extent to which such advice is of any use to the hapless university student whose email was negatively judged is open to question.

This approach privileges the expert knowledge and intuition of the curriculum designer and the teacher. I have argued elsewhere that the pedagogizing of communicative competence in this way has put the original ethnographical interest in communication practices through an epistemic transformation, which reifies real-life language practices. The consequence is that the so-called student needs analysis and assessment now function as a clutch mechanism linking a more or less recognized range of student language needs (e.g. a student writer in Business Studies) to sets of typified options of how language is used in projected language use situations. (For further discussion, see

---

[2] Perhaps it ought to be pointed out that in ELT curriculum discussions the 'competent' speaker is often tacitly assumed to be a native speaker (although see Jenkins, 2000, 2002, 2006; Prodromou, 2005).

Canagarajah, 2002; Dubin, 1989; Finney, 2002; Leung, 2005). This reification represents a somewhat ironic turn in the development of CLT whose pedagogic principles and practices are validated largely by a claim that they enjoy close correspondence to 'real' language use by 'competent' native speakers. As Wolfson (1990, p. 3) points out, native speakers are not good at describing their own rules of language use with any degree of accuracy:

> ... speakers do have strong and well-formed ideas about what they *should* say, but this is not at all the same as knowing what they *do* say. Speech norms, or community ideals concerning appropriate speech behaviour, is not at all the same as actual speech use which is the behaviour itself ... native speaker intuitions are very limited and do not provide a valid basis upon which to build a description of the actual patterns that exist in the day to day speech of community members.

One might add that English language teachers, including native speaking ones, often cannot claim direct knowledge of the community- and discipline-based language norms and practices of their students' subject disciplines. It is improbable that any language teacher can claim first-hand knowledge and expertise in the language practices of a full range of academic disciplines that stretches from Accounting to Zoology. Relying on generalized teacher professional knowledge and intuition to specify what second language students need to learn in terms of academic language (and literacies) in specific contexts is at best a hit-or-miss affair. One would need a more close-up view.

WORK IN PROGRESS: COMMUNICATION IN ACADEMIC LITERACIES

All this is not meant to suggest that CLT is inescapably locked into an exercise of unsafe expert description and prescription. The epistemological and theoretical foundations of CLT have provided intellectual spaces for a concern for the dynamics of lived experiences at a local level, even though this strand of enquiry has not always found its way into the popular textbooks. For instance, in a theoretical discussion on language-in-culture and culture-in-language in second language curriculum development Candlin (1989, p. 6) argues that there is a 'need for teaching and learning of language-in-culture to move beyond the descriptive ...' and '... to focus on ... [the] ways of organizing our world in language ... [and] to explore how speakers and hearers (and writers and readers) categorize and interpret their own experience, how they process information and structure their reference' (op.cit.: 8). This foregrounding of the dynamic meaning-making process argues for a focus on the always emergent ways of using language; it acknowledges individual teacher and student volition and agency in language teaching and learning activities which existing target community-based speech norms and practices (however defined) can shape but cannot completely pre-determine. (See Berwick, 1989, and Brindley, 1989, for further discussion in the formative period of CLT in the 1980s.)

The conceptual argument for attending to actual participants' own perceived needs is not just a point of epistemological refinement. At a practice level, Uvin (1996, p. 43) shows the value of this conceptual approach when he, as a language course designer, shadowed a group of ethnic Chinese health workers in their work place in Boston in an attempt to verify their English language needs. He made these observations:

> I had addressed only the work-related needs of learners [in the course design], and my perception of those needs had guided my initial decision making about what to include and leave out. I learned quickly, however, that learners wanted more than just the language to perform their jobs. As many of the learners in the programs were recent arrivals, they had language needs that went beyond the workplace and so demonstrated resistance, inconsistent attendance being the major one. I had also failed to accommodate the affective, social, cultural, cognitive, and metacognitive needs that learners expressed . . .

These observations signalled the need for an emic perspective on students' assessment of their communication needs and learning priorities.

For CLT in general not to be constitutionally closed off to an orientation anchored in 'live' real settings (as opposed to 'abstracted' real contexts), it would seem that ethnographic sensitivities and sensibilities need to be foregrounded and be made more prominent both in theory and in practice. This general requirement also holds in the particular case of second language academic English. Belcher's (2006) reflexive account of English for Specific Purposes (ESP), another branch of ELT generally associated with teaching adults or university students, notes that there have been attempts to encourage students to understand that academic language use is not just about following fixed rules, and that it is important to see how different texts work in different contexts. Indeed both ESP and EAP appear to be adopting a more ethnographic outlook (Belcher, 2006; Hyland and Hamp-Lyons, 2002). At this juncture it would be useful to look at some examples of research in another field of research, academic literacy, which have focused on aspects of participant practices.

One way of getting closer to what is said and how language is used in academic activities is to investigate how participants, teachers and students, engage with one another. Lillis (1999, 2001) looks into the ways in which the content selection of the academic essay, a predominant format for organizing and presenting knowledge, is played out in a British university setting. In one of the case studies presented by Lillis, a student, Nadia, wanted to make use of what she learned from a previous course in her essay on 'Working class children are underachieving in schools. How much of this may be attributed to perceived language deficiencies?' (Lillis, 1999, p. 134). This is the opening section of Nadia's draft essay:

> Throughout this essay I will be focusing on the types of underachievers. Firstly the working class bilinguals and the misleading intelligence tests, of which bilingual children are expected to do. Secondly the working class monolinguals which are underachieving. Thirdly I will seek information on how much of this may be attributed to perceived language deficiencies. (Loc.cit.)

And this is the tutor's comment:

> Your beginning section moves away from essay title. Need to organize your thoughts more carefully and adhere to the essay title more clearly. (Loc.cit.)

In a subsequent seminar discussion, it became clear to Nadia that her tutor did not consider the case of bilingual children an appropriate issue for the essay. Nadia reported the exchange in this way:

> She didn't like it *one bit* . . . She said not all bilingual kids are working class . . . (Loc.cit.; original emphasis)

The tutor's view on what constituted legitimate content for discussion appeared to be firmly fixed in advance. But it was not communicated in the essay title. This particular instance is indicative of the difficulties students may have in understanding what is expected of them. The 'essay' is in fact a very complex package of established ways of argumentation, culturally sanctioned principles for content selection, subject or discipline-informed ways of using language, text format and prose. Given the generally limited amount of direct contact between students and staff, much of this staff-engendered complexity is not immediately obvious to students. Lea and Street (1998, p. 161) studied the experiences of 47 students and 23 staff members in 3 disciplinary areas (humanities, social sciences and natural sciences) in two universities in England and report that

> As students switch between . . . disciplines [e.g. physics and anthropology], course units, modules and tutors different assumptions about the nature of academic knowledge and

learning, are being brought to bear, often implicitly on the specific writing requirements of their assignments ... it is frequently very difficult for students to 'read off' from any such context what might be the specific academic writing requirement of that context.

Woodward-Kron (2005) finds that on a teacher education course, particularly in the advanced stages of the degree programme, the exposition genre (texts presenting a sequenced argument in favour of a judgement) appeared to be more valued than the discussion genre (texts examining different sides of an issue and making an informed recommendation) by faculty. Creme and Lea (1997, p. 15) describe academic knowledge and uses of language in higher education metaphorically as '... a foreign country, far away from you and your familiar setting ...' where there is a 'gap between what you came with and a different way of thinking and speaking'. The volumes of published guidance books on how to write essays and dissertations would testify to the complexity involved. Worse, this complexity is not fixed and static. The conventions and practices are subject to interpretation by tutors. Lillis (1999, p. 143) observes that '[t]he socio-discursive space which is inhabited by student-writers and tutors ... is predominantly monologic: it is the tutor's voice which predominates ...'; and there is evidence that tutor expectations and requirements vary within and across different disciplines (Lea and Street, 1998). Yet in a good deal of discussion on uses of language for academic purposes 'there is denial of real participants, that is, actual tutors and student-writers with their particular understandings and interests ...' (Lillis, 1999, p. 143). In other words, there is an assumption that local and particular academic language practices are part of a universal order of things. All of this can be seen as a form of what Lillis calls the 'practice of mystery', particularly from a student's point of view. This particular instance shows the importance of going beyond formal descriptions of what students are expected to do with language for academic purposes.

FUTURE DIRECTIONS

Our knowledge of academic conventions and practices in specific contexts cannot be complete without knowing something about how students understand and respond to the demands placed on them, how they make use of prevailing conventions and models, and how they insert their own selves in the use of English for academic purposes. Ivanič (1997) offers an analytical framework of indices of self and identity in student writing, which can be extended to examine spoken language discourse, that taps into the different aspects of what one might call 'authorial space'. Three inter-related authorial selves are of particular interest to this discussion[3]:

- Autobiographic self—'[t]his is the identity which people bring with them to any act of writing' (op. cit.: 24). This aspect of self is not fixed; it is continuously developing as part of a person's life history and their perception of their life experience. This aspect of self surfaces when an aspect of a person's past experience is used or invoked in an effort to respond to a task.
- Discourse self—This aspect of the self is 'constructed through the discourse characteristics of a text, which relate to values, beliefs and power relations in the social context in which they were written' (loc.cit.). Different text types carry different kinds of authorial presences. Laboratory notes may convey greater technical authorial presence than an informal account of an experiment.
- Self as author—this is concerned with the extent to which students see and explicitly insert something of themselves in their writing. In academic writing this aspect of self is particularly significant because 'writers differ considerably in how they claim authority as the source of the content of the text, and how far they establish an authorial presence in their writing.' (op.cit.: 26; also see Hyland, 2001).

The kind/s and the amount/s of authorial space that are allowed, or disallowed, in academic language use can be seen as detection indicators of Lillis' 'practice of mystery'. For instance, Nadia's use of her previous learning (autobiographic self) was clearly not welcome; not much authorial space was afforded in this aspect of the written assignment. Using this analytic framework to investigate how student texts are evaluated can begin to help identify relevant directions for further enquiries. I will use a piece of writing by a student to illustrate the potentials.

In England university applicants are required to include a 'personal statement' in their applications. This statement plays an important role in an applicant's claim to a university offer of a place, especially when there are many more or less equally qualified candidates. And yet there does not appear to be any system-wide shared evaluation criteria as to what constitutes a 'good' personal statement beyond generalities such as 'showing the right qualities for being a university student'. Individual admission tutors in effect operate their own evaluation criteria, although there is an assumption that they share a broad set of common expectations. The mock 'personal statement' below was written by a 17-year-old second language student, Naseem, who attended an

---

[3] There is a fourth aspect of self in Ivanic's (1997) discussion. For reasons of focus and scope, this aspect—possibilities for self-hood—is not discussed here.

academic language development course to improve his use of English for academic purposes.[4]

> *I want to study a degree in Computer Science because I am interested in the role that computers play in society now and in the future. Now-a-days each and every organisation uses IT. Currently I am studying ICT, Mathematics, Physics and Urdu which I hope will help me to be successful in Computer Science degree. Apart from studying I also have some experience of fixing computer hardware wiring problems. What I find most interesting about the computer is that it is helping humans in many aspects of life. Where will computers go in the next 15 or 20 years? What will be the reaction of humans to the increasing use of them? My ambition is to be a computer engineer either in relation to hardware problems, software problems or both. Perhaps I will be able to be involved in solving hardware design difficulties or in devising better software solutions in the areas of databases or spreadsheets ...*

When this statement, alongside other student statements, was presented to a university admission tutor it triggered, *inter alia*, the following comment:

> *... I am ... a bit wary of kind of massive, banal, generalisations ... OK this person is saying 'where will computers go in the next 15–20 years?... What I find most interesting about the computer is that it is helping humans in many aspects of life' my reaction to both of those comments is ... big deal ... you know ... say something a bit more precise about you and why you want to do this course and what is it about computers which interests you in a more specific sense ...*

This admission tutor's comment is clearly related to the presentation of self and the kind/s of information associated it. More specifically, it suggests that in this case the tutor was looking for the author's unique reasons for wanting to study computing, i.e. a stronger presence of the autobiographic self, not a pre-fabricated student profile composed of 'banal' statements on the importance of computers culled from what might be regarded as platitudes. Naseem's chosen presentation of himself is also reflected by the kind of presence of the discourse self in the text. The 'public good' discourse (e.g. '... *helping humans* ...')

---

[4] This academic language development course was part of a community outreach programme run by a university in London. It provided non-fee-paying specialist language literacy tuition for linguistic minority 16/17-year-olds from local schools to enhance their chances of achieving high grades in their matriculation examinations.

extolling the virtues of (depersonalized) contribution to society was, in this case, not highly rated by the tutor. The somewhat depersonalized 'public good' discourse self did not provide sufficient authorial personal presence (despite the presence of self as author expressions such as 'My ambition is ...' and '... I will be able to ...' which are propositionally oriented towards technical problems). The tutor's negative evaluation of these statements also indicates that certain kinds of information are preferred. It would also be reasonable to suggest that in this case more self-declarative (self as author) statements indicating personal goals and plans would be welcome (e.g. I would like to make use of my knowledge in mathematics ...).

This informal account of a tutor's response to a short piece of student writing shows that the three authorial selves in Ivanič's framework can be used not only to analyse student interpretation of and responses to academic tasks, but also to investigate tutors' expectations and requirements. Perhaps it ought to be said that this admission tutor's evaluation criteria, and that of Nadia's tutor seen earlier, are not just random instances of local decision-making; they also represent an interpreted version of institutional or discipline-based requirements. In this sense the focus on the local is connected to wider linguistic and social expectations at work (see Brandt and Clinton, 2002, for a wider discussion on this point). Earlier in this discussion, it was noted that conceptually CLT has a strong interest in empirically-based accounts of actual language use in context, but it has tended to rely on expert description and prescription for social and pragmatic rules of use. It is argued here that by using the three authorial selves as analytic devices, it is possible to regard actual instances of student language use, in speech and/or writing, as a site of investigation into what meaning students have taken from an academic task and how they have responded to it, and what tutors require by their tasks and what they expect from their students. Seen in this light, the three authorial selves are not just about aspects of a speaker/writer's past experience and current personal disposition that are allowed or disallowed in academic tasks. The particular kind and the amount of authorial presence sanctioned by the tutor are also simultaneously about the kind and the amount of substantive content (disciplined-related and/or discursive) that are required, as the tutors' response to Nadia's and Naseem's work clearly demonstrate. Conceptually the authorial selves are useful detection devices capable of revealing a whole host of tutor-, discipline- and context-specific requirements concerned with substantive subject content, in addition to genre and style selection.

This chapter has focused on a particular conceptual issue in second language academic language research and pedagogy: the need to pay attention to how language is actually used in academic settings. A good deal of the recent discussion on second language curriculum has tended to specify teaching content in terms of inventories of needs built on surveys and expert knowledge. This approach has produced the basis of a socio-culturally sensitive approach to enumerating the linguistic elements for teaching. But the actual (language and other forms of semiotically mediated) meaning making and meaning taking in specific academic settings remain a 'mystery', as Lillis puts it. It is suggested here that some of the research approaches in the field of academic literacy studies which directly engage with academic practices can be helpful in reducing the ontological abstractness at the heart of the prevailing communicative approaches. For second language students, who are grappling with the 'mystery of practice' in academic settings, to understand how things are expected to be done through language discourse, they would need to have a sense of the expectations or criteria of judgment at work. The Hymsian origins of the communicative turn in second language pedagogy are theoretically compatible with, indeed built on, an ethnographically oriented needs assessment. Drawing on Ivanič's (1997) analytic framework, the three authorial selves can be developed as 'local' indices of (a) students' actual use of language discourse, and tutor (*qua* rater) criteria for discipline-based content selection, and genre and pragmatic preferences, and (b) the extent of fit between the two. The emphasis on 'local' signals an epistemic insistence on taking account of the actual ways in which students and tutors do things with language in context. The ethnographic lacuna in CLT can, in principle, be filled with empirical investigations of texts and practices.

REFERENCES

Belcher, D.D.: 2006, 'English for Specific Purposes: teaching to perceived needs and imagined futures in worlds of work, study and everyday life', *TESOL Quarterly* 40(1), 133–156.

Berwick, R.: 1989, 'Needs assessment in language programming: from theory to practice', in R.K. Johnson (ed.), *The Second Language Curriculum*, Cambridge University Press, Cambridge, 48–62.

Brandt, D. and Clinton, K.: 2002, 'Limits of the local: expanding perspectives on literacy as a social practice', *Journal of Literacy Research* 34, 337–356.

Brindley, G.: 1989, 'The role of needs analysis in adult ESL programme design', in R.K. Johnson (ed.), *The Second Language Curriculum*, Cambridge University Press, Cambridge, 63–78.

Brown, H.G.: 2001, *Teaching by Principles: An Interactive Approach to Language Pedagogy* (second edition), Pearson Education, White Plains, NY.

Canagarajah, S.: 2002, 'Multilingual writers and the academic community: towards a critical relationship', *Journal of English for Academic Purposes* 1(1), 29–44.

Canale, M.: 1983, 'From communicative competence to language pedagogy', in J. Richards and J. Schmidt (eds.), *Language and Communication*, Longman, London, 2–27.

Canale, M.: 1984, 'A communicative approach to language proficiency assessment in a minority setting', in C. Rivera (ed.), *Communicative Competence Approaches to Language Proficiency Assessment: Research and Application.* Multilingual Matters, Clevedon, 107–122.

Canale, M. and Swain, M.: 1980a, 'Theoretical bases of communicative approaches to second language teaching and testing', *Applied Linguistics* 1(1), 1–47.

Canale, M. and Swain, M.: 1980b, *A Domain Description for Core FSL: Communication Skills*, Ministry of Education, Ontario.

Candlin, C.N.: 1989, 'Language, culture and curriculum', in T.F. McNamara and C.N. Candlin (eds.), *Language Learning and Curriculum*, NCELTR, Sydney, 1–24.

Creme, P. and Lea, M.R.: 1997, *Writing at University: A Guide for Students*, Open University Press, Buckingham.

Cummins, J.: 1984, *Bilingualism and Special Education: Issues in Assessment and Pedagogy*, Multilingual Matters Ltd, Clevedon, Avon.

Cummins, J.: 1992, 'Language proficiency, bilingualism, and academic achievement', in P.A. Richard-Amato and M.A. Snow (eds.), *The Multicultural Classroom: Readings for Content-Area Teachers*, Longman, New York, 16–26.

Cummins, J.: 1996, *Negotiating Identities: Education for Empowerment in a Diverse Society*, California Association of Bilingual Education, Ontario.

Cummins, J.: 2000, *Language, Power and Pedagogy: Bilingual Children in the Cross-fire*, Multilingual Matters, Clevedon.

Cunningham, S., Moor, P., and Carr, J.C.: 2003, *Cutting Edge*, Longman, Harlow, Essex.

Davison, C.: 1996, 'The multiple meanings of 'literacy' in the TESOL and adult literacy professions: problems of perspective?', *Prospect* 11(2), 47–57.

Dubin, F.: 1989, 'Situating literacy within traditions of communicative competence', *Applied Linguistics* 10(2), 171–181.

Finney, D.: 2002, 'The ELT curriculum: a flexible model for a changing world', in J.C. Richards and W.A. Renandya (eds.), *Methodology in Language Teaching: An Anthology of Current Practice.* Cambridge University Press, Cambridge, 69–79.

Gee, J.P.: 2004, 'Learning language as a matter of learning social languages within discourses', in M.R. Hawkins (ed.), *Language Learning and Teacher Education: A Sociocultural Approach*, Multilingual Matters, Clevedon, 13–31.

Hutchinson, T. and Waters, A.: 1987, *English for Specific Purposes: A Learning-Centred Approach*, Cambridge University Press, Cambridge.

Hyland, K. 2001, 'Humble servants of the discipline? Self-mention in research articles', *English for Specific Purposes* 20, 207–226.

Hyland, K. and Hamp-Lyons, L.: 2002, 'EAP: issues and directions', *Journal of English for Academic Purposes* 1(1), 1–12.

Hymes, D.: 1972, 'On communicative competence', in J.B. Pride and J. Holmes (eds.), *Sociolinguistics*, Penguin, London,

Hymes, D.: 1977, *Foundations in Sociolinguistics: An Ethnographic Approach*, Tavistock Publications, London.

Hymes, D.: 1994, 'Towards ethnographies of communication (edited version)', in J. Maybin (ed.), *Language and Literacy in Social Practice*, Multilingual Matters in association with Open University, Clevedon, 11–22.

Ivanič, R.: 1997, *Writing and Identity: The Discoursal Construction of Identity in Academic Writing*, John Benjamins Publishing Company, Amsterdam.

Jenkins, J.: 2000, *The Phonology of English as an International Language: New Models, New Norms New Goals*, Oxford University Press, Oxford.

Jenkins, J.: 2002, 'A sociolinguistically based, empirically researched pronunciation syllabus for English as an International Language', *Applied Linguistics* 23(1), 83–103.

Jenkins, J.: 2006, 'Current perspectives on teaching World Englishes and English as a lingua franca', *TESOL Quarterly* 40(1), 157–181.

Lea, M.R. 2004, 'Academic literacies: a pedagogy for course design', *Studies in Higher Education* 29(6), 739–756.

Lea, M.R. and Street, B.V.: 1998, 'Student writing in higher education: an academic literacies approach', *Studies in Higher Education* 23(2), 157–172.

Leung, C. 2005, 'Convivial communication: recontextualizing communicative competence', *International Journal of Applied Linguistics* 15(2), 119–144.

Leung, C. and Safford, K.: 2005, 'Non-traditional students in higher education: EAL and literacies', in B. Street (ed.), *Literacies across educational contexts*, Caslon Publishers, Philadelphia, 303–324.

Lillis, T.M.: 1999, 'Whose common sense? Essayist literacy and the institutional practice of mystery', in C. Jones, J. Turner, and B. Street (eds.), *Student Writing in University: Cultural and Epsitemological Issues*, John Benjamins, Amsterdam, 127–147.

Lillis, T.M.: 2001, *Student Writing: Access, Regulation, Desire*, Routledge, London.

McDonough, J., and Shaw, C.: 2003, *Materials and Methods in ELT: A Teacher's Guide* (second edition), Blackwell, Oxford.

Mohan, B., Leung, C., and Davison, C. (eds.).: 2001, *English as a Second Language in the Mainstream: Teaching, Learning, and Identity*, Longman, London.

Morrow, K.: 1981, 'Principles of communicative methodology', in K. Johnson and K. Morrow (eds.), *Communication in the Classroom*, Longman, Harlow, Essex, 59–66.

Nunan, D.: 1988, *The Learner-Centred Curriculum: A Study in Second Language Teaching*, Cambridge University Press, Cambridge.

Prodromou, L.: 2005, *You See; It's Sort of Tricky for the L2-user: The Puzzle of Idiomaticity in English as a Lingua Franca*, Unpublished PhD, Nottingham University, Nottingham.

Scarcella, R.: 2003, *Academic English: A Conceptual Framework*, University of California, Irvine.

Schleppegrell, M.J. and Colombi, M.C. (eds.): 2002, *Developing Advanced Literacy in First and Second Languages: Meaning with Power*, Lawrence Erlbaum Associates, Publishers, Mahwah, NJ.

Street, B.: 2003, 'What's "new" in New Literacy Studies? Critical approaches to literacy in theory and practice', *Current Issues in Comparative Education* 5(2), 1–14.

Street, B.: 2005, 'Introduction: new literacy studies and literacies across educational contexts', in B.V. Street (ed.), *Literacies Across Educational Contexts: Mediating Learning and Teaching*, Caslon Publishing, Philadelphia, 1–21.

Uvin, J.: 1996, 'Designing workplace ESOL courses for Chinese health-care workers at a Boston nursing home', in K. Graves (ed.), *Teachers as Course Developers*, Cambridge Univeristy Press, Cambridge, 39–62.

Wolfson, N.: 1990, 'Intercultural communication and the analysis of conversation', *Working Papers in Educational Linguistics* 6(2), 1–19.

Woodward-Kron, R.: 2005, 'The role of genre and embedded genres in tertiary students' writing', *Prospect* 20(3), 24–41.

Yalden, J.: 1983, *The Communicative Syllabus: Evolution, Design and Implementation*, Pergamon press, Oxford.

VIVIAN GADSDEN

FAMILY LITERACY

INTRODUCTION

There is little doubt that family literacy has emerged as an increasingly dominant area of language and literacy research over the past 30 years. Any search for studies on family literacy would yield countless citations in which researchers and practitioners outline a range of activities—from parent-child book reading programs to family learning in home, school, and community settings. However, as a formal area of inquiry in language and literacy research, family literacy has a relatively recent history. A tension that has persisted in the field centers on disjunctures between research that emphasizes multiple literacies, sociocultural contexts, and social change in understanding families' learning and the policy push for instructional programming for parents and children that assumes universality of interests, needs, and backgrounds of learners. This tension is linked to family literacy's historical focus on low-income and minority families and to ideological and theoretical perspectives that have drawn heavily upon deficit models. Using selected works representing broad areas of inquiry in family literacy, this review focuses on the ways that the debates in the field have been shaped and on problems and possibilities for the field in (re)constructing its identity within current and emerging discourses of language and literacy theory, research, and practice.

EARLY DEVELOPMENTS

The concept and accompanying research and practice in family literacy can be traced to three different, though overlapping, themes: parent–child literacy, in which the nature of parent–child interactions is examined and the implications for children's school achievement are studied; home literacy practices, in which families' ways of communicating with each other are investigated; and intergenerational literacy which initially focused on the transmission of literacy practices in two generations but has come to denote the pathways and patterns of literacy learning and practices in families over time and multiple generations.

Although family literacy's roots are in the USA, family literacy is cited often in international discussions. In these discussions, family literacy definitions vary, based on factors unique to a particular country: e.g., the country's history of commitment to literacy education for men

B. V. Street and N. H. Hornberger (eds), Encyclopedia of Language and Education, 2nd Edition, Volume 2: Literacy, 163–177.
©2010 Springer Science+Business Media LLC.

and women, the placement of literacy within political hierarchies, the availability of funding, the severity of poverty and social need within the population, access to schooling for boys versus girls, geographic constraints, and diversity among family structures and cultures. A common definition used in the USA and the UK describes family literacy as "encompassing a wide variety of programs that promote the involvement of both parents and their children in literacy enhancing practices and activities" (Ponzetti and Bodine, 1993, p. 106). Attached to this apparently innocuous definition is a more purposeful and arguably problematic intent: "to improve the literacy of educationally disadvantaged parents and children, based on the assumption that parents are their child's first and most influential teachers" (p. 106).

It is the simplicity of this definition and the universalism implicit in its description of children and families that contribute to family literacy's status as a contested area of study. On the one hand, the field has struggled to situate itself in broad conceptualizations and critical discourses of literacy. For example, a series of rich ethnographic studies from the 1980s to present, described later in this chapter, pointed to multifaceted and complex relationships within home, school, and community contexts. These contexts were thought to influence how children and adults engage in formal literacy instruction, draw upon diverse linguistic and cultural practices to communicate within and across different settings, and make meaning of literacy. On the other hand, some would argue that the field has not moved far enough outside of autonomous models (Street, 1984), in which literacy as a technique is applied across all social and cultural contexts with uniformity, to embrace more expansive models (e.g., critical literacy or new literacy studies) (Barton and Hamilton, 1998; Street, 1997, 2001).

Family literacy programs date from the mid-1980s, however, research on parent–child literacy as it relates to current-day discussions began in the 1960s and 1970s in the USA, during a time of social upheaval when the issues of educational access, equity, and quality were at the center of public discussions and when reading researchers were being asked to explain the poor school achievement of minority children from low-income homes. Many of the studies focused on the influence of verbal language—that is, nonstandard dialects such as black or African-American Vernacular English (AAVE)—on children's reading development, specifically the reading of poor, urban minority children. In many of these studies, reading problems were attributed to "deficits" in the linguistic and literacy experiences of children resulting from their "disadvantaged" families and low-income communities (e.g., Deutsch, 1965) while other studies (e.g., Baratz, 1969; Labov, 1968, 1972) proposed a "difference" theory, in which AAVE was viewed simply as one dialect among many spoken dialects and was examined to determine whether (or the degree to which) it interfered with reading development (see also the early work of Durkin, 1966). Still others (e.g., Goodman and Buck, 1973) argued that the reading failure of African-American children was largely due to their teachers' problematic attitudes about their dialect.

Two broad types of responses emerged from the field. One focused on the sociolinguistic, cultural, and contextual factors that influenced children's literacy. It challenged existing cognitive frameworks used to teach reading and to study children's oral and textual literacies and urged a more critical analysis of how language and literacy learning occurs within and across diverse settings. The second reversed a trend from the 1960s, during which time parents' and families' low literacy, among other characteristics, was described as the major problem facing children in low-income homes (Coleman, 1966; Moynihan, 1965). Policymakers were encouraged to invest directly in children's school experiences, particularly their early learning, as a way to change the attitudes, beliefs, and practices of these families in subsequent generations. One successful program that emerged was Head Start, which included a parent involvement component. In the new programs, teachers and schools, representing the public sphere, were taking on the full responsibility of shaping the next generation of learners, with relatively little attention to integrating home and family practices.

Hence, the second response shifted this role and responsibility, identified in the 1960s and 1970s as the purview of schools, back to parents and the preparation of parents to use school-like practices with their children. Children's literacy achievement in school was seen as inextricable from parents' capacity to engage in school-like interactions and communications with their children. Although there has been little research that shows a causal relationship between reading to young children and their textual language knowledge, book reading routines, in which middle-class families were found to engage, were highlighted as a significant divide between poor and middle-class children. This view—that poor and undereducated parents are restricted in their ability to promote their children's literacy—did not account for those children whose parents could not read but who, nonetheless, achieved in school (Schieffelin and Cochran-Smith, 1984).

From the mid-1970s to the 1980s, literacy itself took on a much broader definition, embracing more than reading and writing and extending to problem-solving and ways of engaging and functioning in the world through culturally grounded and context-specific practices and skills. However, at one and the same time, the fledgling field of family literacy was advancing competing purposes: i.e., opening up discussions about the ways in which learners representing diverse cultural, ethnic, and class backgrounds approached, used, and valued literacy while creating an educational policy and practice context that shifted the responsibility of children's literacy performance in schools to parents—in other words, from the public to the private (Tett and Crowther, 1998).

As questions about the meanings of literacy were being raised and the privileging of linear and school-based literacies was being challenged, family literacy emerged as a research-based concept, with the publication of Denny Taylor's seminal work (1983), *Family Literacy: Young Children Learning to Read and Write* changing the text and context of discussions about children and parents learning. Her work provided insights into the processes of literacy learning within diverse homes and into ethnography as a viable approach to unearthing the range and diversity of patterns in households. Focused on six middle-class white families and their children, all of whom were successfully learning to read, the study's findings questioned accepted ways of thinking about who succeeds in formal literacy learning and the contexts for their success, the practices that contribute to learners' success, the ways that children and families construct acts and processes of literacy learning, and the inherent danger of limited perspectives on teaching and learning literacy.

A second critical work, Heath's (1983) *Ways with Words*, also raised questions about the (dis)continuity of literacy practices from home to school and the (bi)directionality of learning between these two contexts. Based in a Black working class community, a white working class community, and a white middle-class community in the Piedmont Carolinas, the study found that the practices of the middle-class families and the school matched, but that the practices of both the white working class and Black working class families did not match the schools' practices. Moreover, there were differences in the practices of the white and black working class communities, demonstrating the multidimensionality of class within and across different groups. Heath found that teachers expected all children to enter school with the same home experiences and predispositions to engage in school literacy activities as those of middle-class children; teachers were unable to use the knowledge, literacy practices, and the cultural experiences of the children sitting before them to create engaging and open spaces for dialogue and meaning-making for and with them.

In these works, both Taylor and Heath demonstrated the role of race, class, and family cultural practices in constructing classrooms as sites that engage all students for learning; they uncovered some of the dissonance created by cultural and home differences when students' experiences are not familiar to or valued in the school setting. Their studies and subsequent work by others in the 1980s, including Teale and Sulzby's (1986) study on emergent literacy, began to revise some of the deficit perspective and to argue for a more in-depth analysis of the relationship between home interactions and children's academic achievement. Several other studies focused on specific issues that helped to frame the theoretical and research context for the field.

For example, Taylor and Dorsey-Gaines' (1988) study examined the literacy contexts of poor, inner-city African-American families, determining that these homes were steeped in rich practices and traditions with oral and written texts. In another study on children's narrative processes that demonstrates the disconnectedness of home, culture, and teacher pedagogies and classroom practice, Michaels (1981) posited that teachers understood the topic centeredness of white children's stories and responded positively but did not understand the underlying structure of black children's topic associative stories. A few years later, Gee (1989) argued that the topic associative stories were more linguistically complex in the literary structures. Delgado-Gaitan's (1987) work on the continuity between home and school for immigrant children and families pointed to the linguistic diversity and integration of oral and written texts in the daily lives of Mexican-American families. Auerbach (1989) in a review of ethnographic research on poor and language minority families concluded that rather than being literacy impoverished, the homes of linguistic minority students were typically literacy-rich, with parents and families who held high expectations for the possibilities that literacy would create for their children.

These widely acclaimed works attested to the richness of cultural and social contexts and urged a critical examination of children's and parents' experiences in them to build responsive pedagogy. However, policymakers often interpreted the findings of these and other studies to be evidence that poor and minority families were caught in a web of low aspirations, restricted to limited facility with oral and textual literacies, destined for school failure, and by extension were a drain of public resources. Without assuming responsibility for the inequity of access to quality schooling and limited economic resources available to these families, policy efforts were directed at building programs that would give parents the necessary knowledge, awareness, beliefs, and attitudes to support their children.

To make the point, these efforts drew from educational and psychological studies which have historically used mothers' education as the best predictor of children's school achievement. In other words, children's whose mothers had low formal literacies were seen as putting their children at risk for school failure. Adult literacy efforts were increasing as well, reinforcing this point by highlighting the persistence of low literacy within low-income and minority communities. Family literacy was seen as one alternative to stem the tide of low literacy and came to be driven by policymakers' interpretations of the need, with relatively little literacy research to inform the interpretations.

By 1990, several programs were being established in response to the national call. The Kenan Model developed by the National Center for Family Literacy became the most widely known of the programs created. In addition, other curricular models were created: e.g., the Edwards' Parents as Partners program (1995) the Missouri Parents as Teachers program (Winter and Rouse, 1990), and the Home Instruction Program for Preschool Youngsters (HIPPY). In addition, parent–child reading curricula and on-site programs were being developed (e.g., Handel and Goldsmith, 1989; Nickse, Speicher, and Burchek, 1988). These and other programs drew selectively from research, with most reinforcing policy expectations informed by deficit models and others building upon some combination of approaches.

PROBLEMS AND DIFFICULTIES

Well into the 1990s, family literacy was dominated by models that assumed deficits in the cognitive and social experiences of children and their families. Some researchers (e.g., Klassen-Endrizzi, 2000; Strickland, 1995; Taylor, 1997) argued that programs' emphasis on eradicating the problem of low literacy within poor families was too narrow and misdirected, not focusing enough on how different families use cultural knowledge to promote literacy. Thus, a mismatch often existed between family literacy research that focused on the processes of learning (Bloome and Willett, 1991; Gadsden, 1998; Moll and Greenberg, 1990; Moll, Andrade, and Gonzalez, 1997) and family literacy programs that emphasized the products of learning. Family literacy, unlike most other areas of research and practice, was building on selected evidence and had not begun to explore the options and possibilities for constructing an integrative framework that responded to the issues of culture, race, and difference among children and families as well as the (dis)continuities between home and school.

THE SEARCH FOR AN IDENTITY

From the 1990s to present, family literacy's focus on parent–child interactions, home practices, and intergenerational literacy has led to increased ethnographic and other empirical research on children and families shifts—varying in type, nature, and intensity—in programs and the degree to which programs build on research. However, as a field, family literacy still seeks an identity within discourses in the larger field of literacy (Gadsden, 2004). Particularly interesting and controversial have been the increased governmental demands for rigorous randomized studies that stress learning outcomes without also addressing the pathways to those outcomes. For example, Lonigan (2004), decrying the absence of well-designed experimental research, suggests the need for higher-level assessment of children's early learning in family literacy programs. More recent emphasis on evidence-based approaches reinforces Lonigan's position. While such sentiments are valid, they do not completely or accurately capture the complexities of studying the problems of program aimed at reducing them. As evaluations of Even Start suggest (e.g., St. Pierre and Layzer, 1999), findings on the effectiveness of family literacy programs are mixed, at best, for children and/or parents (most programs do not focus on other family members). Arguments are being made for better measures and measurement, but comparatively less emphasis has been placed on practice constructing conceptual frameworks, epistemologies, and appropriate pedagogies developed around the interactions and intersections between home and school.

A related strand of research examines the intersection between family and culture and the ways in which culture is embedded in the practices of individual family members who are learning literacy in programs. Most of these studies use cultural frames of reference to examine family literacy and acknowledge their importance in accessing and engaging families, as well as determining what learners know, what they want to know, and what they are wiling to invest. For example, in her 1995 volume, Purcell-Gates documents parent-child literacy within a low-income, White, Appalachian family. The protagonists in her account, Jenny and her son, Donny, manipulated literacy and personal events in relationship to the cultural markers that were influenced by their social class, geography, family folklore, and families' values around learning, schooling, and societel options. In one of the few studies that focuses specially on culture, Bhola (1996) proposes a model of family literacy in which the family is at the center of the model. The family is located in a network of mutual relationships with multiple institutions such as schools and workplaces.

Gadsden's (1998) concept, family cultures, draws upon life-course family development and intergenerationality in families and provides a framework for thinking about the ways culture is examined within family functioning and literacy learning and for charting the ways in which families develop their own cultures as a subset of larger and complex cultural traditions, beliefs, histories, and folklore. In addition, Rogers' (2003) examines the complexity of family literacy practices within a low-income African-American family, focusing on issues of power and identity, as the mother in the study seeks to negotiate the school experiences of her daughter, and on the discursive practices and traditions in the family.

To organize assumptions, goals, and practices in the field, Auerbach (1995, 1997) identified three models—intervention/prevention, multiple literacies, and social change—that still hold currency. The intervention/ prevention approach is consistent with historical efforts to eradicate low literacy among poor, undereducated parents, through a series of programs and approaches designed to replace home practices with school-like approaches. The approach speaks to the power of school literacies and the poverty of home and community literacies. As she suggests, and I agree, family literacy programs of all types claim to embrace sociocultural approaches to teaching. However, the evidence is limited in the actual practices.

Curricula that reflect familial and community interests and that integrate cultural artifacts would be a first step, and some programs have achieved this entry point. However, curricula that promote inter-changes around the uses of knowledge, perceptions of the world, and engagements in critical dialogue around questions of opportunities to learn (real and perceived barriers), social inequities, discrimination, justice, and the role of schooling may be seen as inappropriate for basic instruction in programs, are often uncomfortable topics for practi-tioners who have not been prepared to examine these issues, or are seen as incompatible as policy and program mandates. In a chapter in Wasik's (2004) *Handbook of Family Literacy*, Gadsden suggests that the understanding of culture, family cultures, and the inextricability of culture and literacy are under-discussed and poorly interpreted in most programmatic efforts and daily instruction.

The multiple literacies approach takes up this sociocultural perspec-tive in a particular way by examining the much-discussed mismatch between the expectations and practices of school-based literacy learn-ing and the home practices of children who are not achieving in school. Supporters of a multiple literacies model "see the solution as investigat-ing and validating students' multiple literacies and cultural resources in order to inform schooling" (Auerbach, 1997, p. 157), using a range of approaches—from utilizing community resources and cultural artifacts in the classroom (Madigan, 1995; Paratore, Melzi, and Krol-Sinclair, 1999); to engaging parents as co-constructors of the research and inquiry process (Gadsden, 1998; Shockley, Michalove, and Allen, 1995; Voss, 1996); to learning about family histories and experiences as a precursor to teaching (Gadsden, 1998; Weinstein-Shr, 1995); to immersing teachers in the home contexts of parents (Gonzalez, Moll, and Amanti, 2005).

A third approach, social change, is focused on multiple literacies but also highlights the role of power hierarchies in sustaining political and social structures that alienate rather than engage learners and their cultural histories. Failure to attend to these imbalances of power reinscribes inequity and inequality. For example, in a series of texts during the 1990s (*From the Child's Point of View*; *Learning Denied*; *Toxic Literacies*; and *Many Families, Many Literacies*), Taylor discusses the need for structural change in the social and political hierarchies that govern institutions and work against the inclusion of historically marginalized groups. The responsibility for change is placed back in the arms of the public, while recognizing the role that private spheres (such as families and communities) can play in effecting such change. Other perspectives suggest that parents and other family members should be involved in the planning and strategizing of programs, increasing opportunities for them to identify, grapple with, and respond to pressing social problems affecting them, the education of their children, and the goals of their families and communities.

Auerbach's categories while useful are not discrete, and studies that appear to fit under one model may well have components that fall under others, particularly multiple literacies and social change. Within the past few years, a few studies in progress attempt to build curricula that integrate knowledge from home to influence curricula. This work is emerging and is still inexact in its analyses of appropriate approaches or interpretations of results. Where and how this work will be situated over time is unclear, but it will require a new construction away from intervention to represent the collaborative and partnership focus of many existing and energy efforts work and the integration of a multiple literacies framework, leading to social change.

PROBLEMS AND DIFFICULTIES

There are several neglected issues in the study of family literacy programs. The subtle disconnects between socially and grounded theoretical frameworks for family literacy research and the practices of family literacy programs persist. Lee's (2005) analysis of students' use of AAVE provides a useful frame of reference to situate the inherent contradictions and difficulties in family literacy and to connect the problems of research, practice, and policy. She notes that the complex issues involved in understanding how students' discursive practices in their families and communities are taken up to support learning to read and write are still under-studied. Particularly poignant, she argues is that "the problem may not be so much the limitations of language use in the families of children from low-income backgrounds who speak vernacular dialects [but] ... with the ability of the research community and teachers to recognize what in these language practices may be generative for literacy learning" (p. 251).

FUTURE DIRECTIONS

The future of family literacy lies largely in its ability to reconceptualize its goals, given societal changes around who constitutes a family, who family members are, the divide of poor and wealthy in schools, and the nature of learning in out-of-school contexts—all necessary contributors to understanding the cultural and social dimensions of learning and the contexts in which it occurs. In addition to the current streams of work, several other areas of inquiry hold promise for the future.

- *A more in-depth focus on and analysis of culture.* Despite regular references to culture, the field still examines it in relatively narrow terms, often categorizing by ethnicity or race. With a grasp of theoretical context and possibilities, programs could engage participants in intellectually inviting discussions about traditions, beliefs, and practices; people who share a common culture; or the complexity of changes that occur among traditions, beliefs, and practices over time. Such classrooms would take an inquiry approach (Cochran-Smith and Lytle, 2001) and would consider culture as being more than national heritage (e.g., Korean or American) they would try to address the ways in culture forms as part of an individuals ethnic, racial, or national identity as well as their other identities (e.g., poor or gay) that are formed out of a shared perspective, life circumstances, or societal response and institutional barriers and that challenge reliance on "one size fits all" instructional packages (see Blackburn, 2005; Osterling, 2001; Quintero, 1999; Whitehouse and Colvin, 2001).
- *Focused attention on gender and the roles ascribed to a gendered identity for girls and boys as well as women and men.* The emergence of women's issues in adult and family literacy has provoked questions about gender more broadly. These questions are informed by other socially significant features of identity, including the large numbers of poor women in programs and the persistence of racial discrimination experienced by adult learners (men and women) who are ethnic minorities (Gowen and Bartlett, 1997; Horsman, 1990; Stromquist, 1999). A similarly growing body of work examines the issues of men, mostly as fathers (Gadsden, 2003; Ortiz, Stile, and Brown, 1999).
- *Examination of different types of learning environments with different forms of participation and linguistic and literacy repertoires* (Gutierrez, 2005). In such cases, the intersections of identity and learning are a part of the classroom discourse. In addition to the traditional home environments, the field might begin to explore uses of technology and digital modalities in building on the knowledge of families and to teach and study families.

- *Deepened efforts to examine immigrant and language minority families.* The recent US governmental responses to immigrants and the public attention to second language makes the present and immediate future important times to examine these critical issues. Work by Suárez-Orozco, Suárez-Orozco, and Qin-Hilliard (2005) and others have initiated discussions that draw upon interdisciplinary knowledge to identify the border crossings of these families.
- *Research that addresses two fundamental questions.* Who are the families, and how do they describe literacy within their own family trajectories? Researchers might ask (or continue to ask in some cases) what learners negotiate in their learning across contexts, how the process of learning and negotiation by the learner can be understood better as an intergenerational activity, and how this process can be utilized effectively as a model or tool for studying intergenerational literacy.

Families in literacy programs differ in race, cultural traditions, ethnic heritage, religion, gender, class, and life experiences. However, they also differ in the literacies that they bring to the program, the ways in which they learn literacy, the purposes and everyday uses they have or will have for literacy, the value they assign to literacy as well as the reasons they assign it, and the family cultures that they bring to the literacy learning experience. Research and practice are still left with the challenge of building upon this knowledge while aiming to create new frameworks that capture the breadth of possibilities in family literacy and allows us to understand the particular ways that deverse families and the learners in them engage in literate acts and are engaged in different social contexts.

REFERENCES

Auerbach, E.: 1989, 'Toward a socio-contextual approach to family literacy', *Harvard Educational Review* 59, 165–181.

Auerbach, E.: 1995, 'Deconstructing the discourse of strengths in family literacy', *Journal of Reading Behavior* 27, 643–661.

Auerbach, E.: 1997, 'Family literacy', in V. Edwards and D. Corson (eds.), *Encyclopedia of Language and Education: Vol. 2. Literacy*, Springer Press, London, 153–161.

Baratz, J.C.: 1969, 'Teaching reading in an urban school system', in J.C. Baratz and C. Shuy (eds.), *Teaching Black Children to Read*, Center for Applied Linguistics, Washington, DC, 92–116.

Barton, D. and Hamilton, M.: 1998, *Local Literacies: Reading and Writing in One Community*, Routledge, New York.

Barton, D., Hamilton, M., and Ivanic, R. (eds.).: 2000, *Situated Literacies: Reading and Writing in Context*, Routledge, New York.

Bhola, H.S.: 1996, 'Family, literacy, development and culture: Interconnections, reconstructions', *Convergence* 29, 34–45.

Blackburn, M.V.: 2005, 'Disrupting dichotomies for social change: A review of, critique of, and complement to current educational literacy scholarship on gender', *Research in the Teaching of English* 39(4), 398–416.

Bloome, D. and Willett, J.: 1991, 'Toward a micropolitics of classroom interaction', in J. Blase (ed.), *The Politics of Life in Schools: Power, Conflict, and Cooperation*, Sage Publications, Newbury Park, CA, 207–236.

Cochran-Smith, M. and Lytle, S.: 2001, 'Beyond Certainty: Taking an inquiry stance on Practice' in A. Lierberman and L. Miller (eds.), *Teachers caught in the Action: Professional Development and Action*, Teachers College Press, New York, 45–60.

Coleman, J.S.: 1966, *Equality of Educational Opportunity*, Government Printing Office, Washington, DC.

DeBruin-Parecki, A. and Krol-Sinclair, B. (eds.): 2004, *Family Literacy: From Theory to Practice*, International Reading Association, Newark, DE.

Delgado-Gaitan, C.: 1987, 'Mexican adult literacy: New directions for immigrants', in S.R. Goldman and H.T. Trueba (eds.), *Becoming Literate in English as a Second Language: Cognition and Literacy*, Ablex Publishing, Westport, CT, 9–32.

Delgado-Gaitan, C.: 1991, 'Involving parents in the schools: A process of empowerment', *American Journal of Education* 100, 20–46.

Delgado-Gaitan, C.: 1994a, *Empowerment in Carpinteria: A Five-Year Study of Family, School, and Community Relationships*. Center for Research on Effective Schooling for Disadvantaged Families, Baltimore, MD. (ERIC Document Reproduction Services No. ED375228).

Delgado-Gaitan, C.: 1994b, 'Socializing young children in Mexican-American families: An intergenerational perspective', in P.M. Greenfield and R.R. Cocking (eds.), *Cross-Cultural Roots of Minority Child Development*, Lawrence Erlbaum Associates, Inc., Hillsdale, NJ, 55–86.

Duran, R.P., Duran, J., Perry-Romero, D., and Sanchez, E.: 2001, 'Latino immigrant parents and children learning and publishing together in an after school setting', *Journal of Education for Students Placed at Risk* 6(1–2), 95–113.

Durkin, D.: 1966, *Teaching Young Children to Read*, Allyn & Bacon, Boston.

Gadsden, V.L.: 1995, 'Representations of literacy: Parents' images in two cultural communities', in L. Morrow (ed.), *Family Literacy Connections in Schools and Communities*, International Reading Association, Newark, NJ, 287–303.

Gadsden, V.L.: 1998, 'Family culture and literacy learning', in F. Lehr, J. Osborn, and P.D. Pearson (eds.), *Learning to Read*, Garland, New York, 32–50.

Gadsden, V.L.: 2002, 'Family literacy: Issues in research and research-informed practice', *Annual Review of Adult Learning and Literacy*, Jossey-Bass, Thousand Oaks, CA.

Gadsden, V.L.: 2003, 'Expanding the concept of "family" in family literacy: Integrating a focus on fathers', in A. DeBruin-Parecki and B. Krol-Sinclair (eds.), *Family Literacy: From Theory to Practice*. International Reading Association, Newark, DE, 86–125.

Gadsden, V.L.: 2004, 'Family literacy and culture', in B.H. Wasik (ed.), *Handbook of Family Literacy*, Lawrence Erlbaum Associates, Inc., Mahwah, NJ, 401–424.

Gadsden, V.L.: in press, 'The adult learner in family literacy: Gender and its intersections with role and context', in Belzer and H. Beder (eds.), *Defining and Improving Quality in Adult Basic Education: Issues and Challenges*, Lawrence Erlbaum Associates, Inc., Mahwah, NJ.

Gadsden, V.L., Ray, A., Jacobs, C.Y., and Gwak, S.: 2006, 'Parents' expectations of their children's early literacy', in R.T. Jimenez and V.O. Pang (eds.), *Race, Ethnicity, and Education: Language, Literacy, and Schooling*, Praeger, New York, 201–216.

Gee, J.P.: 1889, 'The narrativation of experience in the oral style', *Journal of Education* 17(1), 75–96.

Goldenberg, C. and Gallimore, R.: 1991, 'Local knowledge, research knowledge, and educational change: A case study of early Spanish reading improvement', *Educational Researcher* 20, 2–14.

Gonzalez, N. and Moll, L.C.: 2002, 'Cruzando el puente: Harnessing funds of knowledge in the Puente project', *Journal of Educational Policy* 16(4), 623–641.

Gonzalez, N., Moll, L.C., and Amanti, C.: 2005, *Funds of Knowledge: Theorizing Practices in Households and Classrooms.* Lawrence Erlbaum Associates, Inc., Mahwah, NJ.

Goodman K. and Buck, C.: 1973, 'Dialect barriers to reading comprehension revisited', *Reading Teacher* 27, 6–12.

Gowen, S.G. and Bartlett, C.: 1997, 'Friends in the kitchen: Lessons from survivors', in G. Hull (ed.), *Changing Work, Changing Workers, Critical Perspectives on Language, Literacy, and Skills*, State University Press, New York, 131–158.

Gutierrez, K.D.: 2005, 'The persistence of inequality: English-language learners', in J. Flood and P. Anders (eds.), *Literacy Development of Students in Urban Schools: Research and Policy*, International Reading Association, Newark, DE, 288–304.

Handel, R.D. and Goldsmith, E.: 1989, 'Children's literature and adult literacy: Empowerment through intergenerational learning', *Lifelong Learning* 12, 24–27.

Heath, S.B.: 1983, *Ways with Words*, Cambridge University Press, Cambridge.

Horsman, J.: 1990, *Something in Mind Besides the Everyday*, Women's Press, Toronto, Canada.

Kao, G. and Tienda, M.: 1995, 'Optimism and achievement: The educational performance of immigrant youth', *Social Science Quarterly* 76, 1–19.

Klassen-Endrizzi, C.: 2000, 'Exploring our literacy beliefs with families', *Language Arts* 78(1), 62–69.

Labov, W.: 1968, *A Study of Non-Standard English of Negro and Puerto Rican Speakers in New York City, Volume 1: Phonological and Grammatical Analysis.* Office of Education, Bureau of Research, Washington, DC.

Labov, W.: 1972, *Language in the Inner City: Studies in the Black English Vernacular*, University of Pennsylvania Press, Philadelphia, PA.

Lee, C.D.: 2005, 'Culture and language: Bidialectical issues in literacy', in J. Flood and P. Anders (eds.), *Literacy Development of Students in Urban Schools: Research and Policy*, International Reading Association, Newark, DE, 241–274.

Lonigan, C.J.: 2004, 'Emergent literacy skills and family literacy', in B.H. Wasik (ed.), *Handbook of Family Literacy*, Lawrence Erlbaum Associates, Inc., Mahwah, NJ, 57–82.

Madigan, D.: 1995, 'Shared lives and shared stories: Exploring critical literacy connections among family members', in L. Morrow (ed.), *Family Literacy Connections in Schools and Communities*, International Reading Association, Newark, DE, 269–286.

Michaels, S.: 1981, '"Sharing time": Children's narrative styles and differential access to literacy', *Language in Society* 10, 423–442.

Moll, L.C. and Greenberg, J.B.: 1990, 'Creating zones of possibilities: Combining social contexts for instruction', in L.C. Moll (ed.), *Vygotsky and Education: Instructional Implications and Applications of Sociohistorical Psychology*, Cambridge University Press, New York, 319–348.

Moll, L., Andrade, R., and Gonzalez, N.: 1997, *Rethinking Culture, Community, and Schooling: Implications for the Education of Bilingual Students, Improving Schooling for Language-Minority Children: A Research Agenda.* National Academies Press, Washington, DC.

Moynihan, D.P.: 1965, *The Negro Family: The Case for National Action*, Department of Labor, Office of Policy, Planning, and Research, Washington, DC.

Nickse, R., Speicher, A., and Burchek, P.: 1988, 'An intergenerational adult literacy project: A family intervention/prevention model', *Journal of Reading* 31, 634–642.

Orellana, M.F.: 1995, 'Literacy as a gendered social practice: Tasks, texts, talk, and take-up', *Reading Research Quarterly* 30(4), 678–708.

Ortiz, R., Stile, S., and Brown, C.: 1999, 'Early literacy activities of fathers: Reading and writing with young children', *Young Children* 65(5), 16–18.

176   VIVIAN GADSDEN

Osterling, J.P.: 2001, 'Waking the sleeping giant: Engaging and capitalizing on the sociocultural strengths of the Latino community', *Bilingual Research Journal* 25(1–2), 59–88.
Paratore, J.R., Melzi, G., and Krol-Sinclair, B.: 1999, *What Should We Expect of Family Literacy? Experiences of Latino Children Whose Parents Participate in an Intergenerational Literacy Project*, International Reading Association, Newark, DE.
Ponzetti, J. and Bodine, W.: 1993, 'Family literacy and parent education', *Adult Basic Education* 3, 104–108.
Purcell-Gates, V.: 1995, *Other People's Words: The Cycle of Low Literacy.* Harvard University Press, Cambridge, MA.
Purcell-Gates, V.: 2000, 'Family literacy', in M.L. Kamil, P.D. Pearson, and Barr, (eds.), *Handbook of Reading Research*, Volume 3, Lawrence Erlbaum Associates, Mahwah, NJ, 853–888.
Purcell-Gates, V.: 2004, 'Family literacy as the site for emerging knowledge of written language', in B.H. Wasik (ed.), *Handbook of Family Literacy*, Lawrence Erlbaum Associates, Inc., Mahwah, NJ, 101–116.
Quintero, E.: 1999, 'The new faces of Head Start: Learning from culturally diverse families', *Early Education & Development* 10(4), 475–497.
Rodriguez-Brown, F.V.: 2004, 'Family literacy in English language learning communities: Issues related to program development, implementation, and practice' in A. DeBruin-Parecki and B. Krol-Sinclair (eds.), *Family Literacy: From Theory to Practice*, International Reading Association, Newark, DE, 126–146.
Rogers, R.: 2003, *A Critical Discourse Analysis of Family Literacy Practices: Power In and Out of Print*, Lawrence Erlbaum Associates, Mahwah, NJ.
Schieffelin, B.B. and Cochran-Smith, M.: 1984, 'Learning to read culturally: Literacy before schooling', in H. Goelman, A.A. Oberg, and F. Smith, *Awakening to Literacy: The University of Victoria Symposium on Children's Response to a Literate Environment: Literacy Before Schooling*, Heinemann Educational Books, Exeter, UK, 3–23.
Shockley, B., Michalove, B., and Allen, J.: 1995, *Engaging Families, Connecting Home and School Literacy Communities*, Greenwood-Heinemann, Portsmouth, NH.
Sticht, T.G., and McDonald, B.: 1989, *Making the Nation Smarter: The Intergenerational Transfer of Literacy*, Institute of Adult Literacy, San Deigo, CA.
Street, B.: 1984, *Literacy in Theory and Practice*, Cambridge University Press, Cambridge.
Street, B.: 1997, 'Social Literacies', in V. Edwards and D. Corson (eds.), *Encyclopedia of Language and Education: Vol. 2. Literacy*, Springer Press, London, 133–141.
Street, B.V.: 2001. *Literacy and Development: Ethnographic Perspectives*, Routledge, New York.
Strickland, D.K.: 1995, *Literacy, Not Labels: Celebrating Students' Strengths through Whole Language*, Heinemann, Portsmouth, NH.
St. Pierre, R.G., and Layzer, J.I.: 1999, 'Using home visits for multiple purposes: The Comprehensive Child Development Program', *Future of Children* 9, 134–151.
Stromquist, N.: 1999, *What Poverty Does to Girls' Education: The Intersection of Class, Gender, and Ethnicity in Latin America*, paper presented at the Oxford International Conference on Education and Development, Oxford, England.
Suarez-Orozco, M.: 2001, 'Globalization, immigration, and education: The research agenda', *Harvard Educational Review* 71(3), 345–365.
Suárez-Orozco, M., Suárez-Orozco, C., and Qin-Hilliard, D.: 2005, 'Series introduction: Theoretical perspectives', in M. Suárez-Orozco, C. Suárez-Orozco, and D. Qin-Hilliard (eds.), *Interdisciplinary Perspectives on the New Immigration: Theoretical Perspectives.* Routledge, New York, ix–xiv.
Taylor, D.: 1983, *Family Literacy: Young Children Learning to Read and Write*, Heinemann, Portsmouth, NH.

Taylor, D.: 1990, *Learning Denied*, Heinemann, Portsmouth, NH.

Taylor, D.: 1993, *From the Child's Point of View*, Heinemann, Portsmouth, NH.

Taylor, D. (ed.): 1997, *Many Families, Many Literacies: An International Declaration of Principles*, Heinemann, Portsmouth, NH.

Taylor, D. and Dorsey-Gaines, C.: 1988, *Growing up Literate: Learning from Inner-City Families*, Greenwood-Heinemann, Portsmouth, NH.

Tett, L. and Crowther, J.: 1998, 'Families at a disadvantage: Class, culture and literacies', *British Educational Research Journal* 24(4), 449–460.

Voss, M.: 1996, *Hidden Literacies: Children Learning at Home and at School*, Greenwood-Heinemann, Portsmouth, NH.

Wasik, B.H. (ed.): 2004, *Handbook of Family Literacy.* Lawrence Erlbaum Associates, Inc., Mahwah, NJ.

Weinstein-Shr, G.: 1995, 'Learning from uprooted families', in G. Weinstein-Shr and E. Quintero (eds.), *Immigrant Learners and Their Families: Literacy to Connect Generations*, Center for Applied Linguistics & Delta Systems, Inc., McHenry, IL, 113–133.

Whitehouse, M. and Colvin, C.: 2001, '"Reading" families: Deficit discourse and family literacy', *Theory Into Practice* 40(3), 212–219.

Winter, M. and Rouse, J.: 1990, 'Fostering intergenerational literacy: The Missouri parents as teachers program', *The Reading Teacher* 43, 382–386.

ANNA ROBINSON-PANT

WOMEN, LITERACY AND DEVELOPMENT: OVERVIEW

INTRODUCTION

The belief that women's literacy is the key to development has informed government and international aid agency policy and programmes around the world. In the poorest countries, the gap between male and female literacy rates has led policy makers to focus on increasing women's as opposed to men's access to literacy, through programmes designed particularly around women's reproductive role. Researchers have been concerned to find statistical evidence that there are the positive connections between female literacy rates and health indicators such as decreased child mortality and fertility rates.

The assumption that illiterate women cannot participate fully in development programmes has led to literacy classes being set up as the entry point to health, nutrition, income generation, community forestry and family planning interventions. This objective has often influenced the curriculum: many women's literacy programmes adopt a functional literacy approach, linking literacy learning with vocational skills training, health education and 'awareness raising' about social issues such as alcoholism. Partly because of the importance of these non-literacy programme elements, there is a tendency to use the term 'literacy' synonymously with 'adult women's basic education'. For instance, evaluation reports on the benefits of women's literacy frequently emphasise the social aspects of confidence building, group solidarity, improved health practices and community action, as compared with reading and writing outcomes.

EARLY DEVELOPMENTS

The WID (Women In Development) approach of the early 1970s promoted the idea that women needed literacy skills to catch up with men and become equal partners in development. The research agenda was influenced by the 'efficiency' policy approach (Moser, 1993) to women's development at that time, which stressed the economic benefits of educating women and girls. Women's literacy rates were found to be inversely related to fertility rates (Cochrane, 1979) and child mortality rates (Caldwell, 1979). The book of King and Hill's (1993) book,

B. V. Street and N. H. Hornberger (eds), Encyclopedia of Language and Education, 2nd Edition, Volume 2: Literacy, 179–190.
©*2010 Springer Science+Business Media LLC.*

Women's Education in Developing Countries: Barriers, Benefits and Policies, was a major landmark in bringing together these statistical studies on these health linkages, as well as on the links between literacy and income and employment (see Schultz on 'Returns to Women's Education', ibid.).

This body of research shared the starting point that literate women had different characteristics and behaved in different ways from illiterate women (LeVine, LeVine, Richman, Uribe, Correa, and Miller, 1991), perpetuating a stereotype of the 'blind' illiterate woman to be found in many policy documents (see Robinson-Pant, 2004). The statistical evidence appeared to support Summer's (foreword in King and Hill, 1993) proposition that the 'vicious cycle' of poverty could be transformed into a 'virtuous' cycle through increasing women's access to education. Although these statistical correlations were often used to justify the need for adult women's education, many studies had failed to disaggregate between those adult women who had learnt to read and write in school, as compared with those who had learnt as adults. As Bown (1990) pointed out, the female adult literacy rates were actually a composite measure of the impact of girls' schooling as well as adult education programmes. Bown's (1990) report *Preparing the Future: Women, Literacy and Development* was one of the first attempts to distinguish between the impact on women of learning in an adult literacy class, as compared to school.

The policy objective of integrating women into development through literacy meant that planners were concerned with overcoming the barriers that prevented women from attending adult literacy programmes. Ballara (1991) and Lind (1990) identified the obstacles to women attending classes as structural (around location, timing and lack of childcare facilities) as well as social barriers, such as male teachers, limited mobility and lack of support from other family members. The factors preventing women's participation in literacy courses could also be seen in similar terms to the reasons for girls not enrolling in schools. These were related to women's low status in society and the lack of priority afforded by communities and families to educating women. Many of the early literacy programmes included an 'awareness' component on the importance of women's education. This was, however, expressed in terms of the value of literacy in making women better wives and mothers, reflecting the fact that the literacy curricula focused almost exclusively on women's reproductive role and that development policy took a 'welfare' approach towards women. Literacy primers often overlooked women's significant productive role outside the home, in agriculture for instance, depicting instead a stereotype of women as primarily active in the kitchen and looking after children (Bhasin, 1984, Dighe, 1995).

The early work in women's literacy was greatly influenced by research that attempted to measure the impact of women's literacy on development. The main aim was to enhance adult women's access to education through tackling the structural and the cultural barriers to participation, rather than to look at the quality and the relevance of literacy programmes to their lives more broadly.

MAJOR CONTRIBUTIONS

The shift to the Gender and Development (GAD) approach in the 1980s meant that the impact of literacy programmes was no longer measured only in relation to women. Men were also brought into the picture. In research on the links between women's literacy and fertility rates, Basu (1999) looked at a third variable—marriage—and analysed how educated women's choice of partner influenced the couple's decisions about family planning. This was partly due to the growing understanding that the linkages between girls' schooling (as well as women's literacy) were in fact more complex than those previously believed. Bledsoe et al.'s (1999) *Critical Perspectives on Schooling and Fertility in the Third World* moved the debate on from identifying linkages, to look at the reasons why there might be statistical correlations between education and fertility. Similarly, studies of the impact of adult literacy programmes on health outcomes suggested the need for a more holistic approach to research and evaluation (Robinson-Pant, 2001b).

The feminist debate that informed the GAD approach brought a new critical perspective on literacy. Freire's 'conscientisation' approach to literacy was extended to include not just awareness of class oppression, but also to make women more aware of their subordinate position in relation to men. Stromquist (1997) suggested that Freirean literacy programmes can enable women to develop 'the ability to think critically' about their situations. Using a feminist framework of analysis, researchers began to identify patriarchal structures that prevented women from participating fully in literacy programmes. Rockhill's (1993) research on the gendering of literacy practices in immigrant communities in Los Angeles gave insight into the ways in which women's literacy classes could appear to threaten men's identities. In particular, through 'deconstructing the homogeneous woman' (Mohanty, 1991), feminist writers drew attention to women's multiple identities and the diversity of women attending literacy classes. A 'one size fits all' approach to literacy programming (such as had been promoted through functional literacy and literacy campaigns) failed to respond to the differing needs of young unmarried girls and older married women. Case studies have revealed how literacy programmes can be shaped by and meet the needs of specific groups of women, such as low caste communities (Khandekar, 2004).

The policy objective for promoting women's literacy is now being discussed in terms of literacy as a human right, influencing the kind of research questions asked. From researching 'How can women's contribution to development be enhanced through literacy?' (the efficiency approach discussed earlier), studies have adopted an empowerment approach, asking 'What does empowerment mean to individual women in this literacy class?' (Robinson-Pant, 2004). The influence of the New Literacy Studies, with its more ethnographic approach to actual uses and meanings of literacy (cf. Papen, 2005; Street, 2001) has meant a move away from the notion of 'literacy' as a technical fix (for instance, as the variable that makes the difference between adopting family planning or not) to a concern with researching what literacy means in the lives of the women participants. The symbolic value of literacy for women has emerged—that a woman may want to learn to read and write to feel 'educated' like her brothers (Flores-Moreno, 2004). Ethnographic studies of literacy programmes have found contradictions between the instrumental objectives of the policy makers and the objectives of women who attend literacy classes (Betts, 2004; Robinson-Pant, 2001a). Case studies of individual women (Egbo, 2000; Kalman, 1999; Kell, 1996) have countered the notion of the 'illiterate woman' being ignorant and needing to be literate before having a voice in the community. This ethnographic body of research has given more insight into the gendered nature of literacy practices in everyday life (see Zubair's (2001) work in Pakistan on women's personal literacy practices such as diary writing) and how literacy programmes can build on these in the classroom.

While adult literacy teaching in many countries is still dominated by the functional literacy approach, many programmes have responded to the reasons why women want to learn to read and write. Legal literacy programmes have become increasingly popular—aiming to provide women with information about their legal rights in relation to issues such as marriage, dowry and land ownership (D'Souza, 2003). Similarly, literacy programmes have recognised that many women wish to learn to read religious texts, rather than development information. Mainstream literacy and development approaches, such as REFLECT, have attempted to address unequal gender relations by facilitating discussion, for instance, about different gender workloads through mixed groups of men and women constructing a PRA seasonal calendar (see Attwood, Castle and Smythe, 2004, p. 148).

On the other hand, many women welcome single-sex literacy classes as an unusual space where they can discuss issues of concern with other women. To overcome the difficulties of attending literacy classes on a nightly basis, some programmes have established residential literacy camps for women (cf. Nirantar in India). Here the women are able to study more intensively and build up close relationships with the other participants and trainers, without the burden of domestic work that they would have at home. 'Each one teach one' approaches (where women are taught on an individual basis at home) have also proved useful for communities where women have limited mobility to go out and attend a class.

The feminist perspective on women's literacy has raised the question about how far literacy programmes challenge women's traditional roles. Stromquist (1990) suggested that women are encouraged to adapt within the patriarchal education system, rather than transforming those structures. On a micro level, there have been many examples of literacy programmes that aim to counter gender stereotypes. This has involved supporting non-conventional occupations for women—such as the Banda project in India (Nirantar, 1997) where women are trained as hand-pump mechanics and produced a newsletter to share ideas among other women mechanics.

In the context of women's literacy programmes, there is a growing recognition that promoting literacy instruction only in participants' mother tongue could be seen to promote gender inequality. For instance, literacy trainers in the HIL literacy programme in Nepal (Robinson-Pant, 2001a) responded to women's request to learn to read and write in English and Nepali rather than their mother tongue (Newari language). The women saw that their brothers and husbands had learnt to read in a second language at school and wanted to challenge the local assumption that women could only learn to read their mother tongue. Language choices about the medium of instruction within literacy programmes can be related to issues of power and status, rather than seen only in terms of educational effectiveness (see Volume 3). As the recent *EFA Global Monitoring Report* notes: 'the use of mother tongues is pedagogically sound but must offer a smooth transition to learning opportunities in regional and official languages' (UNESCO, 2005, p. 17).

WORK IN PROGRESS

Feminist and 'ideological' approaches to literacy, informed by the New Literacy Studies, have continued to influence the kind of research undertaken in the field of women's literacy and development (cf. Kalman, 2005; Kell, 1996; Robinson-Pant, 2004). In particular, researchers have challenged the dominant policy discourse on literacy and development through exploring women's own discourses on literacy. Chopra's work in India (2004) shows how so-called 'illiterate' women can 'speak back' to the dominant discourse through their narratives. Research like this has contributed a critical dimension to concepts that were treated as unproblematic in the early literature, such as 'motivation', 'drop out', 'empowerment' and even 'literacy'. For instance, women's motivation can be seen in terms of the tension between the dominant and local discourses around literacy and development.

Through her stance that 'literacy is a feminist issue', Horsman (1996, p. 65) expanded the earlier debates about the 'barriers' to women's participation and the reasons for 'drop-out'. Her research in Canada has revealed how women's experience of violence often contributes to early failure in learning and makes it difficult for them to remain in literacy programmes. Horsman (2006) suggests that educators need to 'break the silence' about violence as a barrier to learning.

The research focus on literacy practices in everyday life as well as within the classroom has enabled planners to develop literacy approaches that build on people's existing literacy practices (see Real Literacies and Community Literacies Approaches, e.g., Rogers, 2002). In the context of women's literacy, this has encouraged policy makers to make a distinction between education and literacy, rather than using the terms synonymously (see Oxenham, 2003 and World Bank, 2001 on Adult Basic Education and Literacy).

Though ethnographic research has revealed how literacy practices are gendered, there is surprisingly little evidence in the policy arena of large-scale literacy programmes adopting a gendered perspective. Many of the key policy documents are concerned with women's literacy, but there is noticeably little attention to the ways in which the literacy curriculum may support or challenge traditional gender relations and gender stereotyped roles. Rogers (2006) and Rao and Robinson-Pant (2006) note the lack of gender awareness and engagement with a gender equality discourse in the fields of lifelong learning and indigenous adult education, respectively. Though literacy programmes for indigenous adult communities have been successful in addressing the oppression of minority indigenous groups, there has been little recognition of the differing experiences and needs of indigenous women as compared with men (see case studies from south and south-east Asia in Rao and Robinson-Pant, 2006). Similarly, though concepts like 'empowerment' have been problematised in the academic research literature, much aid agency-sponsored research has continued to adopt quantitative approaches to measuring the impact of women's literacy programmes on empowerment and health practices (see Burchfield, Hua, Iturry and Rocha, 2002a,b).

The growing recognition of a 'rights perspective' on women's literacy has turned attention to how women's literacy is connected to citizenship. Stromquist (2006) discusses a more holistic (and less instrumental) approach to citizenship within literacy programmes in which women can learn new forms of leadership to tackle gender discrimination in access to land, credit, capital and legal structures. For literacy to challenge gender relations, she argues that 'women's rights need to be embedded in a visible and conscious political project' (ibid.).

Seeing women's empowerment in terms of gender relations has meant that men too have been brought into the picture. Lind (2006) argues that more attention should be given to encouraging men as well as women to attend adult basic education classes. Taking a wider perspective on 'gender equality' than simply increasing women's access to education, Lind suggests that projects need to deal with issues around male roles and masculinities. This contrasts with the earlier approaches to women's literacy (and Lind's own early seminal work) that focused exclusively on the skills and attributes that women needed to gain through literacy to 'catch up' with men.

The recently published Education for All Global Monitoring Report, *Literacy for Life*, stresses that 'women's literacy is of crucial importance in addressing gender inequality' (UNESCO, 2005, p. 19). Although the report does not take a gendered perspective on literacy in terms of the analysis of policy objectives and programme approaches, it argues strongly that literacy has to be better resourced if the EFA goals are to be achieved. However, by continuing to emphasise the importance of child literacy alongside adult literacy, the report reinforces the tendency to conflate issues around girls' schooling with women's literacy.

PROBLEMS AND DIFFICULTIES

A major problem in the area of women, literacy and development is the continued focus on girls' education at the expense of adult women's—particularly in terms of the allocation of resources. In policy-focused research, this is reflected in the continued failure by many education ministries to disaggregate between girls' and women's literacy rates. Given the under-resourcing of adult education (only 1% of the education budget in many countries, UNESCO, 2005, p. 17) and the fact that classes consist overwhelmingly of women, literacy tends to be seen as a second-class educational option as compared with formal education. This reinforces women's subordinate role in society since the better-resourced schooling becomes associated with boys and men. Partly due to the lack of funding, most literacy programmes depend on volunteer part-time facilitators and community contributions for materials and class facilities. Many facilitators are women, and the lack of career structure within literacy programmes—notably those with a campaign approach that move from district to district—make it difficult for facilitators to develop their teaching skills, particularly women who, compared with men, often lack mobility to teach in another area. Just as the classes are seen as a second-rate education, the career of literacy facilitator is often regarded as suitable for women because it is low-paid and part-time. In many cases, the poor quality of education offered in literacy classes and the lack of linkages with the formal sector contributes to high dropout rates, perpetuating the idea that women are unable to learn effectively.

As noted earlier women-only programmes have been demonstrated to have many advantages, such as providing a safe environment for women to speak freely and develop their confidence. However, the fact that a programme is staffed by women may impose its own constraints: women's limited mobility and lack of access to quality education means that few experienced and well-qualified female facilitators are available. In addition, the local women available to teach often promote gender-stereotyped activities such as sewing and kitchen gardening as part of functional literacy programmes, since they themselves lack experience of non-conventional occupational skills. The question of how to tackle gender bias in materials and primers is also problematic. As Stromquist (1997) observed in her research of women's literacy programmes in Brazil, the women wanted to learn to read women's magazines that promoted images of subordinate women in traditional domestic roles, a point also explored by Rockhill (1993). If programmes are to adopt a participatory approach to curriculum design, there is a tension around how to develop materials that promote an idealised image of gender relations, yet build on women's existing literacy practices.

The potential of women's literacy classes to strengthen group activities, such as social action and income generation activities, has long been recognised. However, research insights into the differences between women as a group (their differing experiences according to age, family situation, language, ethnic and caste group) has also pointed to the importance of recognising diversity within literacy classes. The problem is that 'we [researchers, educators] are concerned about *diversity* in literacies, in women's interests, in locales and methods of literacy learning, while policy makers with costs in mind, are concerned about *uniformity*' (Bown, 2004, p. 248). This issue is not of course unique to women, but has particular relevance, as literacy programmes are targeted mainly at women. There is still a tendency for policy makers and planners to generalise about the needs of the 'homogeneous woman' and to neglect to take their multiple roles into account in planning.

FUTURE DEVELOPMENTS

The traditional paradigm of women's literacy still dominates policy and planning debates. However, the slow movement towards a rights perspective on literacy and growing popularity of qualitative research approaches within this area suggest that a gendered perspective on literacy and development may be more evident in the future. As Aikman and Unterhalter (2005, p. 5) discuss, the future challenge is how to 'switch the focus of the debate from parity of access to quality, equality and equity'. As literacy has been often been seen in terms of increasing adult women's access to education, there has been less attention to the questions about what kind of education is provided, whether these programmes are as well-resourced and have the same status in society as the educational programmes that men participate in. Advocacy work on girls' education and the stronger role of women's organisations in promoting gender equality within education should lead to a more radical approach to promoting adult women's rights through literacy in future. Similarly, the current focus on improving the quality of formal education may impact on the non-formal sector too, with particular relevance for women.

In future, the 'ideological' approach to researching literacy may raise new questions for policy makers about the assumed linkages between women, literacy and development. For instance, a gendered perspective on debates about language policy (cf. Volume 1, Language Policy and Political Issues in Education) raises the question—what are the implications for women of learning to read in their mother tongue as compared with an official language? In terms of class structures and approaches that promote literacy in the community, we can ask: What do women (as compared with men) lose and gain by no longer meeting as a group to learn literacy? How far does the structure of a literacy class provide a socially acceptable (in the eyes of their husbands) reason for women to meet and talk together? The challenge at the present is for researchers to translate ethnographic findings from in-depth local studies into questions that policy makers can begin to address.

The more holistic approach to adult education in general has drawn attention to the importance of supportive development and employment policies. In the field of women, literacy and development, there has been long recognition of the need for improved access to services such as credit, health-care facilities and agricultural extension, if women are to be able to use the knowledge and skills learnt in literacy courses. As well as the need to explore the links between women's literacy and the economy, there is an increasing interest in how societal discourses shape literacy and development programmes. As Aikman and Unterhalter (2005, p. 4) comment, 'gender equality in education cannot be separated as a goal from gender equality in society as a whole'. This account of the early and main developments has shown how gender relations in society influence not only the curriculum and the structure of literacy classes, but also the resourcing and the status of women's literacy programmes.

REFERENCES

Aikman, S. and Unterhalter, E.: 2005, *Beyond Access: Transforming Policy and Practice for Gender Equality in Education*, Oxfam Publications, Oxford.

Attwood, G., Castle, J., and Smythe, S.: 2004, '"Women are lions in dresses": negotiating gender relations in REFLECT learning circles in Lesotho', in A. Robinson-Pant (ed.), *Women, Literacy and Development: Alternative Perspectives*, Routledge, London.

Ballara, M.: 1991, *Women and Literacy*, Zed Books Ltd., London.

Basu, A.: 1999, 'Women's education, marriage and fertility in South Asia: Do men really not matter?' in C. Bledsoe, J.B. Casterline, J.A. Johnson-Kuhn, and J.G. Haaga (eds.), *Critical Perspectives on Schooling and Fertility in the Developing World*, National Academy Press, Washington, DC.

Betts, J.: 2004, 'Creating the gender text: Literacy and discourse in rural El Salvador', in A. Robinson-Pant (ed.), *Women, Literacy and Development: Alternative Perspectives*, Routledge, London.

Bhasin, K.: 1984, 'The how and why of literacy for women: Some thoughts in the Indian context', *Convergence* 17, 4.

Bledsoe, C., Casterline, J.B., Johnson-Kuhn, J.A., and Haaga, J.G. (eds.): 1999, *Critical Perspectives on Schooling and Fertility in the Developing World*, National Academy Press, Washington, DC.

Bown, L.: 1990, *Preparing the Future: Women, Literacy and Development*, Action Aid Development Report No. 4, Action Aid, London.

Bown, L.: 2004, 'Afterword: Reading ethnographic research in a policy context', in A. Robinson-Pant (ed.), *Women, Literacy and Development: Alternative Perspectives*, Routledge, London.

Burchfield, S., Hua, H., Iturry, T., and Rocha, V.: 2002a, *A longitudinal study of the effect of integrated literacy and basic education programs on the participation of women in social and economic development in Bolivia*, USAID/World Education Inc. (September 2002).

Burchfield, S., Hua, H., Baral, D., and Rocha, V.: 2002b, *A longitudinal study of the effect of integrated literacy and basic education programs on women's participation in social and economic development in Nepal*, USAID/World Education Inc. (December 2002).

Caldwell, J.C.: 1979, 'Education as a factor in mortality decline', *Population Studies* 33, 395–413.

Chopra, P.: 2004, 'Distorted mirrors: (de) centring images of the "illiterate Indian village woman" through ethnographic research narratives', in A. Robinson-Pant (ed.), *Women, Literacy and Development: Alternative Perspectives*, Routledge, London.

Cochrane, S.H.: 1979, *Fertility and Education: What do We Really Know?*, John Hopkins University Press, Baltimore, MD.

D'Souza, N.: 2003, *Empowerment and Action: Laya's Work in Tribal Education*, ASPBAE Case Study Series on Indigenous Adult Education, ASPBAE, Mumbai.

Dighe, A.: 1995, 'Deconstructing literacy primers', *Economic and Political Weekly*, July 1, 1995, 1229–1561.

Egbo, B.: 2000, *Gender, Literacy and Life Chances in Sub-Saharan Africa*, Multilingual Matters, Clevedon.

Flores-Moreno, C.: 2004, "Out of school, now in the group': Family politics and women's il/literacy in the outskirts of Mexico City', in A. Robinson-Pant (ed.), *Women, Literacy and Development: Alternative Perspectives*, Routledge, London.

Horsman, J.: 1996, 'Thinking about women and literacy: Support and challenge', in C. Medel-Anonuevo (ed.), *Women, Education and Empowerment: Pathways Towards Autonomy*, UNESCO Institute for Education, Hamburg.

Horsman, J.: 2006, 'Moving beyond "stupid": Taking account of the impact of violence on women's learning', *International Journal of Educational Development* Vol. 26/2, 177–188.

Kalman, J.: 1999, *Writing on the Plaza: Mediated Literacy Practices Among Scribes and Clients in Mexico City*, New Jersey Press, Creskill, NJ.

Kalman, J.: 2005, *Discovering Literacy: Access Routes to Written Culture for a Group of Women in Mexico*, UNESCO, Hamburg.

Kell, C.: 1996, 'Literacy practices in an informal settlement in the Cape Peninsula', in M. Prinsloo, and M. Breier (eds.), *The Social Uses of Literacy: Theory and Practice in Contemporary South Africa*, John Benjamins and SACHED Books, Amsterdam and Johannesburg.

Khandekar, S.: 2004, 'Literacy brought us to the forefront: Literacy and empowering processes for Dalit community women in a Mumbai slum', in A. Robinson-Pant (ed.), *Women, Literacy and Development: Alternative Perspectives*, Routledge, London.

King, E.H. and Hill, M.A.: 1993, *Women's Education in Developing Countries: Barriers, Benefits and Policies*, Published for the World Bank by The John Hopkins University Press, London and Baltimore.

LeVine, R., LeVine, S.E., Richman, A., Uribe, F., Correa, C., and Miller, P.M.: 1991, 'Women's schooling and child care in the demographic transition: A Mexican case study', *Population and Development Review* 17/3, 459–496.

Lind, A.: 1990, *Mobilising Women for Literacy*, International Bureau of Education, UNESCO, Paris.

Lind, A.: 2006, 'Reflections on mainstreaming gender equality in adult basic education programmes', *International Journal of Educational Development* Vol. 26/2, 166–176.

Mohanty, C.: 1991, 'Under Western eyes: Feminist scholarship and colonial discourses' in Mohanty, Russo, and Torres (eds.), *Third World Women and the Politics of Feminism*, Indiana University Press, USA.

Moser, C.: 1993, *Gender Planning and Development: Theory, Practice and Training*, Routledge, London.

Nirantar: 1997, 'Innovating for change: Women's education for empowerment. An analysis of the Mahila Samakhya Program in Banda district (India)', in W. Mauch and U. Papen (eds.) *Making a Difference: Innovations in Adult Education*, UNESCO Institute for Education, Hamburg.

Oxenham, J.: 2003, *Review of World Bank Operations in Support of Adult Basic Education with Literacy in Indonesia, Ghana, Bangladesh, Senegal and Cote d'Ivoire 1977–2002*, Human Development Education Network, The World Bank, Washington, DC. First draft March 2003,

Papen, U.: 2005, *Adult Literacy as Social Practice; more than skills*, Routledge, London.

Rao, N. and Robinson-Pant, A.: 2006, 'Adult education and indigenous people: addressing gender in policy and practice', *International Journal of Educational Development* Vol. 26/2, 209–223.

Robinson-Pant, A.: 2001a, *Why Eat Green Cucumber At the Time of Dying? Exploring the Link Between Women's Literacy and Development in Nepal*, UNESCO Institute for Education, Hamburg.

Robinson-Pant, A.: 2001b, 'Women's literacy and health: Can an ethnographic researcher find the links?', in B.V. Street (ed.), *Literacy and Development: Ethnographic Perspectives*, Routledge, London.

Robinson-Pant, A.: 2004, 'The "illiterate woman": Changing approaches to researching women's literacy', in A. Robinson-Pant (ed.), *Women, Literacy and Development: Alternative Perspectives*, Routledge, London.

Rockhill, K.: 1993, 'Gender, language and the politics of literacy', in B.V. Street (ed.), *Cross-cultural Approaches to Literacy*, Cambridge University Press, Cambridge.

Rogers, A.: 2002, *Teaching Adults*, Open University Press, Milton Keynes.

Rogers, A.: 2006, 'Lifelong learning and the absence of gender', *International Journal of Educational Development* Vol. 26/2, 189–208.

Street, B. (ed.): 2001, *Literacy and Development: Ethnographic Perspectives*, Routledge, London.

Stromquist, N.: 1990, 'Women and illiteracy: The interplay of gender subordination and poverty', *Comparative Education Review* 34(1), 95–111.

Stromquist, N.: 1997, *Literacy for Citizenship: Gender and Grassroots Dynamics in Brazil*, State University of New York Press, Albany.

Stromquist, N.: 2006, 'Women's rights to adult education as a means to citizenship', *International Journal of Educational Development*, Vol. 26/2, 140–152.

UNESCO: 2005, *Literacy for Life,* EFA, Global Monitoring Report 2006, UNESCO, Paris.

The World Bank: 2001, *Engaging With Adults: The Case for Increased Support to Adult Basic Education in Sub-Saharan Africa*, Africa Region Human Development Working Papers Series, The World Bank, Washington, DC.

Zubair, S.: 2001, 'Literacies, gender and power in rural Pakistan', in B.V. Street (ed.), *Literacy and Development: Ethnographic Perspectives*, Routledge, London.

ROSHAN CHITRAKAR AND BRYAN MADDOX

A COMMUNITY LITERACY PROJECT: NEPAL

INTRODUCTION

The concept of community literacy is based on the idea that local meanings and uses of literacy should inform the design and implementation of adult literacy programmes and that literacy programmes should respond and be flexible to people's expressed needs. The *Community Literacy Project* in Nepal was informed by the socio-cultural model of literacy developed within the 'New Literacy Studies' (Street, 1995) and was funded by the UK Department for International Development (DFID).[1] The New Literacy Studies is informed by socio-linguistic and ethnographic studies of literacy. Rather than viewing literacy as an autonomous 'skill' these approaches view literacy and literacies as a diverse social practice embedded in local contexts, institutions and practices (Collins and Blot, 2003; Street, 1993). This perspective assumes that literacy programmes can provide a public space for the articulation and debate over local 'situated' meanings of literacy and provide practical mechanisms to help people to learn and use literacy in real life situations. The paper discusses some of the tensions between the articulation of 'local' meanings of literacy within the wider national and international discourses of development and some of the creative responses that emerged.

GOING LOCAL

The Community Literacy Project responds to the expressed literacy and numeracy needs of local groups and communities. The approach is flexible, and allows people to learn literacy and numeracy that is directly linked to their daily life and livelihoods 'Community Literacies' newsletter, Issue 7, July 2002.

---

[1] The Community Literacy Project ran between February 1997 and September 2003. It was initially managed by the Centre for British Teachers (CfBT), and then by World Education Nepal (WEN). Project staff changed during the course of the project. The views expressed in this paper are those of the authors.

B. V. Street and N. H. Hornberger (eds), Encyclopedia of Language and Education, 2nd Edition, Volume 2: Literacy, 191–205.

One of the strongest claims of the New Literacy Studies has been that there is both a democratic and pragmatic rationale for localising our understandings of how literacy is learned and used (Collins and Blot, 2003). In recognising the existence of 'literacies', and the multiple ways in which written media is used and made meaningful, we can avoid imposing dominant models of literacy that are unwanted, or that lack local relevance and utility. Localised perspectives offer the opportunity to engage with dominant literacy practices, or to develop vernacular skills and practices. In the Nepali context this is particularly challenging, not only because of extensive cultural and linguistic diversity, but also because of the ways in which discourses on literacy (and education in general) are framed by nationalist and development concerns (Ahearn, 2001; Robinson-Pant, 2001; Rogers, 1999). In such a context, it is not always clear that local aspirations can be articulated. The 'gift' of development aid normally comes wrapped in nationalist and donor-inspired conditionalities and is accessed and expressed through an unyielding and omnipresent developmentalist discourse (Pigg, 1992). In this case, such politics were also complicated by the intellectual agenda of the project, influenced as it was by a radically new perspective on literacy which was often perceived as being alien to Nepal. This presented some significant challenges to the project which had explicitly wanted to localise provision and to 'empower' local communities.

CHANGING LITERACIES

The concept of localised provision was influenced by wider processes of change occurring within Nepal during that time and by broader changes in development discourse and priorities. The national context was in the process of rapid social change, as democratic parties, civil society organisations and left wing Maoist revolutionary forces attempted to replace the elitist, caste-based polity and ideology with a more inclusive and radical politics (Mainali, 2005). These processes involved a radical democratisation of communication media including literacy practices, as silent majorities claimed a voice in these processes of change (Holland, 1995; Maddox, 2001). These changes included more decentralised and democratic access to radio broadcasting and TV and the promotion of language policy and practice in education, media and governance that recognised linguistic diversity within the country (Maddox, 2003).[2]

---

[2] Nepal is one of the most linguistically diverse countries in the world, with 127 spoken languages, and many major language groups.

Local Literacies: Wall Newspapers

The Community Literacy Project supported local community organisations in Nepal to produce regular community newspapers. The
'wall newspapers' (literally, local newspapers stuck to a notice-
board or wall) were hand written by community groups. They discussed a range of community issues, information on resources and
politics as well as cultural activities. The wall-newspapers were written in multiple languages and scripts reflecting the high linguistic
diversity in Nepal. The newspapers challenged the hierarchical
modes of media being produced in and for the local communities.
Non-literate community members were able to 'write' for the wall-
newspapers with the support of scribes.

Figure 1 Women in an eastern hill village reading a community wall
newspaper.

These new forms of communicative politics challenged the discriminatory forms of literacy practice and the lack of transparency often

practiced by government institutions in a country where according to 2001 census data 56% of adults cannot read and write (Ministry Education and Sports, 2002) and where case-based ideologies of social hierarchy remain pervasive.

In addition to these shifting cultural politics, the donor priorities and expectations also changed, from an initial concern with localised community development, to a rhetoric of 'livelihoods' and 'poverty reduction'. These changes in national and international politics and priorities provided an important backdrop for understanding the work of the project and influenced and gave it shape, as it tried to 'localise' and operationalise the concept of community literacy.

This paper describes some of the main activities of the project, the mechanisms and processes it developed for localising literacy activities and the way in which it developed from small-scale pilot activities in a few communities, to a large-scale programme covering ten districts of Nepal, with some 70,000 beneficiaries and 139 partner organisations.

LITERACY, COMMUNICATION AND ACCESS TO INFORMATION

The *Community Literacy Project* developed through three distinct stages, which we can retrospectively describe as those of exploration, consolidation and expansion. The first exploratory and experimental stage, involved in-depth participatory and ethnographic research in a few communities in the east of Nepal. Working with local partner organisations, lengthy 'baseline studies' and initial pilot programmes were conducted using a combination of ethnographic research and action-research methodology. Many of the initial activities of the project had a broader remit than many conventional literacy programmes, and many were not considered as 'literacy' at all. This entailed activities to support people in literacy use, communication and access to information in applied in-situ social activities such as in saving and credit groups, health promotion, community broadcasting, community forestry and community newspapers.

In these activities the focus was often on informal literacy support rather than formal literacy instruction. In fact formal instruction was often avoided, as it distracted attention from the applied nature of the activities and people's tasks and goals. As the project consolidated its approach it developed a distinctive ethos and approach. The project literature promoted an approach based on the idea that '*literacy is something that is used and learned in the community, rather than just being the activity of the literacy class, and communication and access to information can be enhanced through oral, visual and literacy based practices*' ('Community Literacies', 2001).

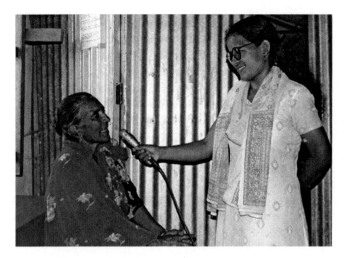

Figure 2 A woman being interviewed during a live broadcast on the community 'audio tower' (Audio broadcast via loud speaker), Dhankuta district.

This approach to literacy was, however, not widely accepted within Nepal, and the project faced significant criticism from a number of areas in early evaluation reports. The criticism centred on the failure of the project to promote and support formal literacy instruction and the limited geographical coverage of the project activities. The unconventional approach adopted by the project clashed with the conventional model of literacy instruction.

MANAGING DIVERSITY

Following this criticism the project consolidated its activities, and prepared to deliver them on a wider scale. The second stage of the project can be described as consolidation, and involved learning from the initial phase, and developing and testing the project's approach, methods and products. The project invested heavily in developing its human resources (and those of partner organisations) and the strong and very committed team became the mainstay of the work. The project prioritised three clear areas of activity:

i. *literacy support (scribing, mentoring, mediation) to help people to access and engage with necessary literacy texts and practices;*

ii. *tailor-made packages of literacy and numeracy instruction based on specific sets of literacy tasks; and*

iii. *training packages of 'communication audit' to help institutions to review and modify their communication (and literacy) texts and practices to make them more inclusive and suitable for non-literate groups and those who speak minority languages.* (Source: 'Community Literacies' newsletter).

The process of project consolidation also involved a shift from lengthy processes of action-research, to more clearly structured and goal driven activities. These activities included training packages of literacy support—for example in legal literacy and scribing for literacy mediators and materials for 'tailor-made' literacy teaching and learning materials based on people's uses of literacy in particular social and economic activities (such as in vegetable production and marketing, saving and credit activities). These activities, which had been developed in the exploratory phase of the project, were developed for delivery on a large-scale, but with mechanisms for adapting them for local variations in content, language and script and for different geographical and cultural locations. Local language and multi-lingual formats were developed. In a radical move, partner organisations were trained in the principles of community literacy and encouraged to innovate and adapt materials kept on CD, to suit the expressed needs of local communities. In that way local variations in language, script and literacy use could be accommodated.

SCRIBES AND LEGAL LITERACY

One of the most popular activities of the project involved training local people in legal literacy and in scribing (or literacy mediation). This activity which was developed in a direct response to a community based request, was not focused on 'making people literate' but in helping people to access and manage the many necessary formal literacy tasks involved in encounters with government bureaucracy. These literacy tasks included applications for citizenship, registration of births, deaths and marriage, women's property and inheritance rights, police cases and so on. The governance-related literacy texts that were used for public communication or notification of important official announcement were too complex and virtually inaccessible even to literate people, let alone partially literate and non literate people. It was in such a context that the locals acknowledged the significance of the project trained literacy scribes, not only for literacy support but also to become familiar with the relevant official documents. Many of these local scribes were young women who spoke local languages, and this helped to address the gender and linguistic imbalances and inequalities in many of these official uses of literacy. The training of scribes was complimented by the production of easy-to-read booklets on legal rights describing the associated forms and literacy requirements of the activities. Scribes were also used to help people

Figure 3 Tailor made literacy materials based on literacy and numeracy tasks in vegetable production and marketing.

Figure 4 Learning and using literacy. Women using the 'tailor-made' literacy and numeracy materials on vegetable production and marketing.

to access written information and engage with literacy tasks in community forestry management and public health. Although these activities had a local focus, and were responsive to local languages, the texts and practices that they engaged with had a more national orientation and significance.

TAILOR-MADE MATERIALS

The *Community Literacy Project* was initially weary of promoting formal teaching and learning activities and materials, viewing them as insufficiently flexible and lacking a focus on in-situ application of literacy in daily life. It became clear though, that while literacy mediation activities were often sufficient for occasional interaction with formal institutions and access to complex legal or technical texts, other activities were better suited to more conventional literacy instruction. These activities were often the 'vernacular' practices that people required in their daily lives.

In response to requests for literacy training related to vegetable production and marketing and credit and saving activities, the project involved several communities in a process of action research where they identified literacy texts and practices and developed dedicated sets of teaching and learning materials. These materials were not generic in nature. Instead they focused specifically on the skills and tasks required for those activities. At the same time, the materials provided a foundation of literacy skills and practices that people could develop. For example, the vocabulary for vegetable production (names of vegetables, numeracy associated with calculation, record-keeping, weighing and measuring) provided applied instruction including familiar vocabulary, the alphabet and basic numeracy. This literacy instruction materials can be viewed as an outcome of the donor's agenda of 'literacy and livelihoods' (Chitrakar, Maddox and Shrestha, 2002; DFID, 2000) and as such, are quite different to the literacy activities in scribing and governance (discussed above).

In the 'tailor-made' materials, the focus was on the direct application of literacy learning in daily activities. The materials were developed in local languages and multi-lingual formats in response to the requests of different communities (see Figure 3). The materials (and visual diagrams and pictures) were stored on personal computer and CD, and so they could easily be modified to suit variations in language and dialect, different types of literacy practice and cultural variation. Teaching and learning activities were conducted in special classes and mentoring and support was provided in the classes and during in-situ application of the learning. These materials provided the opportunity for non-literate people to quickly learn and apply literacy and numeracy in their daily lives, and different sets of materials were developed to suit levels of ability. The course of instruction was only 3 or 4 months (much shorter than many conventional literacy programmes), as the literacy learning (initial literacy) and application of learning (post-literacy) aspects were fused. Within 3 or 4 months people were able to intensively practice and develop their skills on a daily basis. At the same time, what was very striking about the materials was that they tended to avoid the narrative literary form of conventional materials. The materials focused on the basic literacy and numeracy tasks and vocabulary (with the emphasis on peoples application and sustained use of literacy, e.g., as expressed by the learners themselves,[3] being able to read and/or write minutes of group meetings, constitutions of forest users' groups, legal documents, etc.), rather than jumping rapidly to the narrative text and development messages that are often contained in literacy primers.

GOING NATIONAL

In the final phase of the project the activities were scaled up to ten districts of Nepal involving some 70,000 beneficiaries. This was achieved through some standardisation of the approach and by training of partner organisations in the principles and practice of community literacy. The project produced sets of training materials on each of its activities, focusing on training of scribes in legal literacy and in the use and production of 'tailor-made' literacy materials. This standardisation of the approach and rapid expansion of the programme came with some risks. To try to ensure continued responsiveness and flexibility the programme developed a participatory monitoring and evaluation system and trained local partners in participatory needs assessment and baselines studies and in how to adjust literacy materials to the expressed needs of different communities.

Promoting Community Literacy Scribes

The need to promote the development of community literacy scribes was first expressed by an elected Chairman of a rural VDC (Village Development Committee[4]) within a district from east Nepal. The

---

[3] One of the striking examples had been the folksongs that a women's savings group composed in Bardiya district, which included verses of their joyous feeling of being able to fill-up bank vouchers, write and read group minutes and the very songs they composed.
[4] There are almost 4000 Village Development Committees in Nepal, each of which oversees the governance and development activities of the 9 wards. A ward is the smallest political unit comprising of about 300 households.

severity of illiteracy in local communities, even among the elected heads and members of the executive boards at the most local political entity known as ward, posed a serious challenge for the VDC to realise the spirit of local self governance act and decentralisation (Chhetri, 2003). The local administration could not handle the officially required means of communication i.e., in writing while providing services to its people and also to report to the higher authorities. Therefore, the VDC Chairman came up with the idea that the local people with basic ability to read and write could be mobilised as the literacy mediators if they were to be trained in procedures of the local governance and the use of the official documents. The VDC and CLP worked collaboratively to organise such training programme and promote the concept of community literacy scribes. Many local people, mostly women who had left school after completing primary grades, showed interest to be trained scribes. In a period of less than a year, each of the nine wards had four or five community literacy scribes already helping the neighbours not only with their official literacy needs but also to learn to read words from the available documents and forms.

As the project expanded its activities to ten mid and far western districts the local civil society organisations there showed great interest in Community Literacy Scribes. The good practice in this field, which was started at Dhankuta district, was later adapted by local women at Rupandehi district. Two grassroots level women (Amrita Thapa and Krishna Maya Karki), among others, continued with their pursuit to promote community literacy scribing through women who had dropped out of school and who they persistently trained and organised into a local network.

Local Literacy Materials

The production and use of local literacy instruction materials became a favourite activity of the 139 partner organisations from the ten mid and far western districts as the project scaled up its activities. The community interest-groups involved in varieties of group initiatives such as micro finance, honey production, community forestry, health service, combating domestic violence, social discrimination and bonded labour analysed their own literacy contexts with the help of CLP trained resource persons from the local support organisations. Material contents and learning modality were then decided. Unlike in the Tailor-Made Materials (TMM) development process at Dhankuta district during the initial phase, the design and production time was less lengthy, with less fuss made about the quality of paper and printing. Most of the materials were printed or photocopied locally not putting too much of emphasis on

making the content grammatically or linguistically 'correct', which otherwise would have delayed the use of the materials. The fundamental consideration remained to link literacy learning and use with the daily lives
of people and their group processes.

ISSUE OF INSTITUTIONALISATION AND MAINSTREAMING

Some hard lessons were learned with respect to the project institutionalisation process. The project's effort to mainstream its innovative practices in the national system of literacy and non formal education
programme were neither adequate nor entirely successful. There may
be lessons here for other projects following the approach in other parts
of the world.

Despite a heavy-weight project steering committee headed by senior
education ministry personnel (with membership from the National Planning Commission, Ministry of Finance and the donor representative
from the UK Department for International Development), the National
Non-Formal Education Centre did not mainstream any of the

Figure 5 Women using the 'tailor-made' materials.

approaches or methods developed by the project, despite these promising achievements.[5]

At the end of the project, most of the materials, reports and web-site of the project were left with the local management NGO. Although some of the project staff and NGO partners have continued to work in the education field, much of the information and resources developed by the project (including the information and reports stored on the web-site and written in Nepali) are no longer available for public access. Some of the approaches were adopted within a new donor project, but this largely retains the approach within the sphere of 'donor' control. The process and the politics of this 'closure' raises significant questions about the effectiveness of the project and the role of the donor community in supporting local ownership and sustainability of the approach and its resources.

CONCLUSIONS

The experience of the *Community Literacy Project* shows, nevertheless, that it is possible to respond to the expressed literacy tasks and needs of local communities while working with large populations. The use of ICT for flexible and responsive production of literacy learning materials enabled such responsiveness on a large scale. The willingness to listen and respond to the expressed literacy and communication needs of local groups and communities was the key principle that informed the approach. The focus on collective practice (of communities, institutions, self-help groups) enabled shared learning, support and mentoring that is noticeably lacking in conventional literacy programmes that focus on individuals. The focus on people's real life literacy texts and practices helped to make the project responsive to expressed needs and to improve the sustainability and impact of people's learning. Unlike many conventional literacy programmes, these activities had very low rates of 'drop-out' and a high level of application in people's daily lives.

The process of developing the approach was extremely challenging for a number of reasons. There were few role models on which the project could base the approach, and much of the early activities were conducted on a trial and error basis. The demands of being a 'development project' brought with them tremendous pressures—both in terms of delivering 'goods' to local communities and in terms of the donor and government's legitimate desire to have a wide-scale impact. It is

---

[5] The project's external evaluation report rated highly its performance and potential for scaling up the products it came up with.

questionable whether the government ever fully supported the ideas behind the project, and as a result, resistance from government and lack of buy-in and institutionalisation was an on-going factor that project staff had to deal with. The project staff often had to deal with the uncertainty and self-doubt associated with such a process of innovation, while attempting to protect themselves and the project from sometimes heavy criticism from outside. That was not always the ideal environment to ensure an open and deliberative process. As the project developed, a demarcation began to develop between the more radical politics and risk taking of popular education and attempts to control and manage the more 'risky' activities of the project (e.g., advocacy on language policy in governance, women's legal literacy activities, decentralised production of materials), which were often inherently political and did not conform to the conventional view of adult literacy.

On reflection, much of the resistance reflected the wider politics of education and communication within Nepal. Literacy and language are part of on-going aspects of inequality and social injustice, which the Nepali State and donor community have been either unable, or unwilling to effectively tackle. This became clear as the project became more integrated into civil society organisations and activities. What began as a community-based activity focused on local groups and organisations gained national resonance and as it did, it became clear that national and international politics are central in shaping communication practices and people's access to literacy.

In that sense, the term '*Community Literacy Project*' is both accurate and misleading. We can look at each of those terms, beginning with the concept of *community*. While the project always attempted to respond to the expressed needs of local communities, many of the 'dominant' literacy texts and practices people have to engage with are defined and given shape at the national or international level. As a space for social change the project was inevitably influenced by national and international concerns, development discourse, the concerns of government, overseas managers and donor organisations. As such, it could equally be described as the '*Global Literacy Project, in Nepal*'. At the same time, managing these multiple concerns, discourses and priorities was as much an issue of local organisations and communities as it was for the centrally funded project staff. Rather than a discrete entity, 'local' communities were always shot through with these national and international politics and institutional politics.

The term *literacy* is also only part of the picture. The activities of the project extended to other forms of communication media (numeracy, spoken and visual communication, radio, audio-tower). The literacy and numeracy activities were often embedded in wider social practices and were not always experienced as 'literacy' promotion. Examples such as the wall newspapers illustrate this point nicely, since there was a heavy literacy and literacy learning content, but the participants did not view the activity as being primarily one of 'literacy' learning.

Finally, the logic of the development *project* presented many difficulties, not least because of the expectations that it created about delivering development goods and the impact of ever changing donor agendas. Despite the agendas of poverty reduction and good governance, the development agenda can become depoliticised, and this created certain tensions within the project as we moved towards closer links with civil society groups more committed to social activism. This was clear as the project attempted to link local and national spheres by contributing to social movements in literacy and language policy. As an innovative project, such tensions were perhaps inevitable, and this itself should perhaps be one of the key learnings. Adult literacy promotion, as Paulo Friere has reminded us, is essentially a political project as one that challenges us to change the social and cultural norms, patterns and relations.

REFERENCES

Ahearn, L.: 2001, *Invitations to Love: Literacy Love Letters and Social Change in Nepal*, University of Michigan Press.

Chitrakar, R., Maddox, B., and Shrestha, B.: 2002, 'Literacy for livelihoods: Can CLP contribute to poverty reduction in Nepal?', in *Community Literacies*, Newsletter of the Nepal Community Literacy Project, Issue 7, July 2002, 7–13.

Chitrakar, R.: 2005, 'Nepali society, elitist thinking and education', in B. Phnuyal and T. Bhattrai (eds.), *Learning for Social Transformation: Resource Material for Popular Education Workers* (in Nepali language), Forum for Popular Education, Education Network Nepal, Kathmandu, 1–10.

Chhetri, A.: 2003, *Promoting Social Justice Through the Development of Community Literacy Scribes: The Experience of* (the NGO) *Mit Nepal of Bardiya* (Nepal). An unpublished article written for the Community Literacies Newsletter. World Education Nepal, Kathmandu.

Collins, J. and Blot, R.: 2003, *Literacy and Literacies: Texts, Power and Identity*, Cambridge University Press, Cambridge.

DFID: 2000, '*Literacy for Livelihoods*', Report of the Kathmandu Literacy for Livelihoods Conference, 4–6th December 2000.

Holland, D.: 1995, 'Contested ritual, contested femininities: (re) forming self and society in a Nepali women's festival', *American Ethnologist* 22(2), 279–305.

Ministry of Education and Sports: 2002, *Literacy Situation in Nepal: A Thematic Presentation*, Non-formal Education Centre, Sanothimi, Bhaktapur.

Mainali, M. (ed.): 2005, *The Foundations of Inclusive Democracy*, Social Science Baba (in Nepali), Lalitpur.

Maddox, B.: 2001, 'Literacy, communication and access to information: A multimodal approach to literacy development in rural Nepal', paper presented at the conference on Literacy and Language in Global and Local Settings, Cape Town, November 2001, Available on-line.

Maddox, B.: 2003, 'Language policy, modernist ambivalence and social exclusion: A case study of Rupendehi district in Nepal's Tarai', *Studies in Nepali History and Society* 8(2), 205–224.

Pigg, S.: 1992, 'Inventing social categories through place: Social representations and development in Nepal', *Comparative Studies in Society and History* 34(3), 491–513.

Robinson-Pant, A.: 2001, *Why Eat Green Cucumbers at the Time of Dying? Exploring the Link Between Women's Literacy and Development*, UNESCO, Institute of Education, Hamburg.

Rogers, A.: 1999, 'Improving the quality of adult literacy programmes in developing countries: the 'real literacies' approach', *International Journal of Educational Development* 19, 219–234.

Shrestha, A.: 2003, *Context Specific Literacy Learning Materials for Promoting Community Literacy* (in Nepali). An unpublished article written for the Community Literacies Newsletter, World Education Nepal, Kathmandu.

Street, B.: 1993, *Cross-Cultural Approaches to Literacy*, Cambridge University Press, Cambridge.

Street, B.: 1995, *Social Literacies: Critical Approaches to Literacy in Development, Ethnography and Education*, Pearson Education, Harlow.

TREVOR CAIRNEY

COMMUNITY LITERACY PRACTICES AND EDUCATION: AUSTRALIA

INTRODUCTION

Interest in community literacy practices is not new. Its consideration by administrators, schools and teachers has generally been driven by recognition that the literacy experiences of home and community have a significant impact on literacy success at school. But most interest has been in how families and their literacy practices serve school agendas with interest being driven by limited definitions of literacy and at times deficit views of learning (Cairney, 2003). This limited view of the relationship between literacy practices in and out of school has limited many attempts to build stronger relationships between schools and their communities. Prior to the 1980s most interest in non-school literacy was focussed on how parents support children's print literacy learning and to a limited extent how non-school literacy[1] has an impact on school literacy learning. This work paid little attention to variation in literacy practices within the community and appeared to assume that literacy was a unitary skill that needed to be supported in quite specific ways if children were to succeed at school.

However, research by Heath (1983) and others[2] helped researchers and educators to understand better the considerable variation that occurs in literacy across specific groups. Heath considered talk associated with literacy within the home and found that it is related to differences in culture and language. Motivated by this work, other researchers began to examine the literacy practices of home and school more closely and noted increasingly that the way teachers shape classroom discourse can be limited in scope and not reflective of the diversity of student language and culture (Breen, Louden, Barrat-Pugh, Rivalland, Rohl, Rhydwen, Lloyd and Carr, 1994; Cairney and Ruge, 1998; Cairney,

---

[1] This concern was primarily with how environmental print has an impact on early literacy development. See Cairney (2003) and Hall (1987) for a fuller discussion.
[2] There are numerous researchers whose work has contributed to the growing understanding of literacy diversity and its complex relationship to culture, ethnicity and class. See for example Bernstein (1964), Halliday (1975), Scribner and Cole (1981), Harste, Woodward & Burke (1984), Street (1984), Cook-Gumperz (1986), Cazden (1988) and Lareau (1989).

B. V. Street and N. H. Hornberger (eds), Encyclopedia of Language and Education,
2nd Edition, Volume 2: Literacy, 207–225.
© *2010 Springer Science+Business Media LLC.*

Lowe and Sproats, 1995; Cairney, Ruge, Buchanan, Lowe and Munsie, 1995; Freebody, Ludwig and Gunn, 1995; Gutierrez, 1993).

In parallel to the above work, two other key and related areas of inquiry began to inform home and community literacy research. One fruitful area has been concern with the variation in literacy practices that reflects the changing nature of communication and growth in multimedia and the need to reject limited definitions of literacy for the richer concept of multiliteracies (Cope and Kalantzis, 2000). This work has led researchers and practitioners to consider whether limited definitions of literacy effectively exclude a vast array of literacies that fall outside the boundaries of traditional school literacy practices.

A second area of related interest has been stimulated by the fields of critical theory, sociolinguistics and cultural studies and has stressed the need to recognise that power relationships are also part of literacy practices (see Freebody, Critical Literacy Education: On Living with 'Innocent Language', Volume 2). This work demonstrates that literacy is not value neutral and disconnected from other human activity, particularly the complex tapestry of relationships that characterise human existence. This theoretical work has highlighted that some families and individuals are disadvantaged (and others advantaged) by power relationships that fail to value the funds of knowledge that they bring to school (see Moll, 1992; Moll, Amanti, Neff and Gonzalez, 1992). This collective work has helped us to identify "the social practices by which schools, families and individuals reproduce, resist and transform hierarchies of social relations and their positions within them" (Solsken, 1993, p. 7). Furthermore, it has enabled research and educational initiatives concerned with family literacy to be critiqued in new ways.

What both these related areas of study indicate is that children from cultural and linguistic minority groups may continue to have difficulty in achieving school success because the dominant pedagogical approaches are based on "narrow understanding of school knowledge and literacy, which are defined and defended as what one needs to know and how one needs to know it in order to be successful in school and society" (Willis, 1995, p. 34).

Collectively these related fields of study demonstrate that while there is a relationship between community literacy and education, that there are many gaps in our understanding and the nature of their relationship to education. This chapter is a review of what research has taught us about this relationship, with a particular interest in Australian research and its relationship to wider research in this area. It is assumed for the purposes of the review that 'community literacy' refers to those social practices outside schools that involve the use of multiple sign systems to create meaning and that involve, in some way, the reading and/or writing of text. While not denying the importance and impact of informal education, education in this review is taken to mean 'formal' education administered by institutions[3].

In the review that follows there will be three major considerations. First, early foundational research efforts that explored community literacy practices as well as the relationship of this work to major theoretical traditions. Second, significant recent and current explorations that have acknowledged more complex definitions of literacy and community, with special consideration of work in Australia. Third, the need to problematise the existing research literature in this area and map out possible future directions.

A BRIEF LOOK AT EARLY RESEARCH OF
RELEVANCE

Early interest in community literacy practices was primarily motivated by a desire to enhance school success by ensuring that families supported school literacy. Some of the most significant early interest in the relationship between education and non-school literacy practices occurred in the United Kingdom. The Plowden report (Department of Education and Science, 1967) was one of a number of stimuli that encouraged schools to become more concerned with the relationship of home to school learning. Plowden argued strongly for partnership between home and school. Such notions of partnership were primarily concerned with what families could do to support schools and lacked the richness of more recent attempts to build partnerships between home, school and community (see Cairney and Munsie, 1992; Cairney and Ruge, 1998 for a fuller discussion of this issue).

The 1970s and 1980s saw a number of high profile program initiatives take place that were judged to be successful at supporting school literacy. Many of these were programs designed to help parents support children at home in relation to school learning, particularly those experiencing reading problems.[4] However, typically, these early projects assumed a deficit view of families and sought to rectify what were seen as barriers to children's educational success (Cairney, 2003). One well-known program, the Haringey Reading Project found that some of the children whose parents were involved in their program made significant gains in reading achievement irrespective of reading ability. This project

---

[3] This review does not attempt to address the significant work done in relation to adult literacy and workplace literacy. While each body of work is significant in understanding broader community literacy practices, a full discussion of each is outside the scope of this chapter that focuses primarily on the literacy worlds of children. For an interesting discussion of 'specialized' literacy populations and institutions see Quigley (2005).

[4] See Cairney (2000) for a more detailed review of this early work.

was to be a stimulus for other initiatives focussing on story reading strategies for parents and the provision of books to families (Tizard, Schofield, and Hewison, 1982).

While not wanting to dismiss these early attempts to address the relationship between school and non-school literacy practices, what is obvious is how such work was limited by the definitions of literacy that framed the work. Developments in other countries tended to parallel the UK experience. In the United States interest in considering the impact of home and community literacy practices on schooling was a little slower to emerge, but by the 1990s it was estimated that there were more than 500 family literacy programs alone in the USA (Nickse, 1993).

In Australia, the early interest in the literacy practices of home and community was again primarily to obtain support for school learning. Curriculum documents during the 70s and 80s stressed the importance of parents and a supportive home environment in children's learning. Common to these early efforts was a desire to encourage parents to become more involved in school and support school agendas, rather than building on the rich literacy practices of home and community.

In a federally funded review of Australian initiatives Cairney, Ruge, Buchanan, Lowe and Munsie (1995) identified 261 major initiatives and over 100 small-scale projects that showed an interest in using the relationship between the literacy of school and community to strengthen the school success of students who were struggling. This study showed that 76.3% of these projects were initiated by schools and were largely designed to fulfil school purposes and transmit information about schooling. The report concluded that more effort needed to be given to understanding the richness of family and community literacy practices and how this could be seen as a rich resource informing and supporting school-based literacy education.

As mentioned in the introduction to this chapter, one of the first researchers to seriously explore the complex relationship between the literacy practices of community and school was Heath (1983). She found that there was variation in the acquisition of oral language, and the manner in which parents introduced children to literacy and its purposes, and was able to document significant differences in community styles of literacy socialisation and the impact that this had on school success.

The work of Heath and others resonated well with earlier theoretical work on early language and literacy development[5] that had already challenged views on the role adults and families play in early literacy learning. The 1960s and 1970s had seen the emergence of important

---

[5] See for example Bernstein (1964), Clay (1966), Halliday (1975) and Vygotsky (1978).

changes in our understanding or oral language development that were eventually to lead to a number of significant literacy studies in the late 1970s and early 1980s. For example, Harste, Woodward and Burke (1984, p. 56) demonstrated that preschool children were actively attempting to understand the nature of the language spoken around them, making predictions and testing hypotheses about how language worked, and demonstrating rich literacy understandings embedded in everyday reading and writing experiences. This work was a serious challenge to maturational theories of child development that had previously confined literacy learning to the school years. Early literacy researchers embraced the term 'emergent' literacy to describe the significant literacy experiences that preschool children were encountering at home and in community settings.[6] These new insights helped researchers to begin to view non-school literacy experiences as relevant and significant to school success.

Almost in parallel to the development of emergent literacy was the emergence of constructivist theories based strongly on the work of Vygotsky (1978) and Bruner (1983). Rich literacy experiences, scaffolded support (Bruner, 1983, 1986; Rogoff, 1990) and encouragement of meaning making and risk taking were increasingly recognised as a vital part of child language learning. What this work again reinforced was the social foundations of literacy.

Sociolinguistic theories of language also contributed a great deal. Scholars like Bahktin (1935/1981), Gumperz (1986), Halliday (1975) and Hymes (1974), built upon the basic understanding that language is made as people act and react to one another. Cook-Gumperz (1986) argued that spoken language and literacy are cultural tools that shape individuals as they grow and transform behaviour as it is internalised. This work informed the view that people learn to be literate primarily in groups as they relate to others and seek to accomplish social and communicative functions. Literacy was seen as purpose driven and context bound, with people acting and reacting to the actions of others as well as to set patterns of group interaction.[7]

This work raised new questions about definitions of literacy and of how these definitions were being applied to community and family literacy. Street (1984) challenged what he called traditional 'autonomous' models that he saw as dominated by 'essay-text' forms of literacy, proposed

---

[6] Hall (1987) provided one of the earliest syntheses of the emergent literacy research and did much to translate this work into a form that could inform early childhood practice. However, this new view of preschool literacy had its roots in the work of many researchers including Clay (1966), Holdaway (1979), Wells (1982; 1986), Harste, Woodward and Burke (1984), Mason and Allen (1986), Teale and Sulzby (1986).

[7] There are many key studies and publications including the critical work of Bloome (1987); Cazden (1988); Cook-Gumperz (1986); Street (1984); and Wells (1986).

an alternative 'ideological' model. This model was concerned with the specific social practices of reading and writing, recognising the ideological and culturally embedded nature of literacy. He argued that the meaning of literacy depends upon the social institution within which it is embedded, and he called for the use of the term 'literacies' rather than literacy to recognise the social complexity of the practices. Street was one of a number of researchers seeking definitions that considered literacy as a set of social and cultural practices, not a unitary skill.

One final influence was the emergence of 'critical literacy' (Crawford, 1995). This perspective drew heavily on the work of critical theorists, sociolinguistics and cultural studies and attempted to critique and problematise the relationship between literacy and factors as diverse as school success, parental support, self-identity, gender and family life. The work argued that

- differences between the discourses of home and school can make a difference to the success of some children (Gee, 1990);
- an acceptance of cultural differences between home and school can lead to more responsive curricula that offer all children greater chances of success in learning;
- some people are disadvantaged by power relationships that fail to value the funds of knowledge that some children and their families bring to school, while others are advantaged (see Freire and Macedo, 1987; Gee, 1990; Luke, 1988; Moll, 1992; Moll, Amanti, Neff and Gonzalez, 1992; Street, 1995).

The combined and overlapping impact of the above quite disparate scholarly traditions was to bring about a significant shift in the way literacy was defined and studied and an increased understanding of the relationship between the literacy of home and school. In the following section major contributions to this emerging understanding are discussed.

MAJOR CONTRIBUTIONS

Studies that Describe Literacy Practices in the Home

While a great deal is known about early literacy development, there are few studies that have provided a detailed description of literacy practices within a wide range of families. Denny Taylor has conducted some of the most significant work in the last twenty years. Taylor's (1983) detailed ethnographic research spawned the term "family literacy", and provided some of the most detailed insights into the nature of literacy practices within homes. Her series of studies began in 1977 with a detailed description of a single family. By 1979 her ongoing observations had grown to include six white middle class families living in suburban New York City.

Taylor's close involvement in the families contributed a number of critical insights. She argued that literacy is implicated in the lives of family members and found that parents mediated literacy experiences in varied ways across and within families, and that older siblings helped to shape younger siblings' experiences of literacy (see Gregory, City Literacies, Volume 2). She also observed "shifts" in parents' approaches to the "transmission of literacy styles and values", coinciding with children beginning to learn to read and write in school (Taylor, 1983, p. 20). Literacy experiences within families she argued were rich and varied; surrounding family members as part of the fabric of life. Finally, she observed that children's growing awareness of literacy involved experiences that are woven into daily activities (Taylor, 1983, p. 56).

Taylor's early work informed a number of later studies, most notably her work with Dorsey-Gaines in conducting an ethnography of black families living in urban poverty (Taylor and Dorsey-Gaines, 1988). The combined work of Taylor and her colleagues challenged notions of what effective parent support of literacy involves, and attempted to move beyond white middle-class definitions of effective parenting. Their work showed that within the poor black families studied there was a richness of literacy experience that previous studies had not been able to recognise. This finding was later given support by the work of Auerbach (1989, 1995).

McNaughton's (1995) work in New Zealand is also relevant to this discussion. Based on case studies of 17 families in New Zealand he concluded that families are a critical determinant of children's early literacy development. His description of the literacy practices of Maori, Samoan and Pakeha families whose income earners were from non-professional occupations provided a picture of resourceful families able to support their children's early literacy learning. McNaughton was able to describe the complex ways in which families use time, space and varied resources to help preschool children to learn literacy. He noted that families used three different ways to support literacy learning: shared joint activities between the children and significant others; personal activities (e.g. scribbling or writing); and ambient activities where literacy was immersed in life.

Arguably the most extensive study conducted in Australia in the last decade was undertaken by Cairney and Ruge (1998) and sought to examine the relationship between home, school and community literacy. In a 2-year study, Cairney and Ruge (1998) conducted school and community-based case studies across four varied settings and subsequently conducted an ethnography of 37 children from 27 families, observing and describing their literacy practices at home and school. The focus children were of primary school age, but within the families there were approximately 20 additional preschool children. The participating families were asked to collect a range of data including, audio tape literacy events, an audit of home literacy resources, a log of all reading and writing activities, and photographs of significant literacy events in the home (using disposable cameras supplied by the researchers). One member of each family was also asked to act as co-researcher and was trained to help record a range of home literacy events.

Cairney and Ruge (1998) identified four distinct purposes for literacy in the homes and classrooms in their study: literacy for establishing and maintaining relationships; literacy for accessing or displaying information; literacy for pleasure and/or self-expression; and literacy for skills development.

One critical finding from this study was that specific literacy practices may contribute to, and constitute part of, different literacy events in different contexts depending on the understandings and purposes of the participants. For example, the intended purpose of a newsletter from school may be to give parents access to information about school policies or activities. Alternatively, the intended purpose may be to maintain communication between home and school and thereby develop the relationship between families and the school. However, in reading the newsletter at home, families may have very different purposes and 'use' the newsletter in different ways (e.g. one family used it for oral reading practice). This is consistent with the work of Barton (1994) and Street (1993) and their contention that different domains can place quite different demands on participants for literacy.

Cairney and Ruge (1998) also found that the families in their study differed greatly in the extent to which literacy was visible in everyday life. Similarly, families varied greatly in the amount and types of literacy resources available to them.

One of the striking features of literacy practices in the homes of many of the families in the Cairney and Ruge study was the extent to which 'school literacy' appeared to dominate family life. That is, the particular types and uses of literacy usually associated with schooling were prominent in many families. This prominence was manifest primarily in the amount of time spent on homework activities (up to 3 hours per day in some families) and, to a lesser extent, siblings 'playing schools'. As well, there was evidence to suggest that the literacy practices privileged right from the birth of a first child are strongly shaped by the parents' experience of school literacy as well as the desire to prepare the preschool child for later schooling (Cairney and Ruge, 1998).

Studies that Attempted to Bridge Home, School and Community Contexts

While there have been a significant number of studies that have observed literacy practices within the home, there is less evidence of research that has been able to tap into children's experiences of literacy outside the family and the school. Putting to one side a few seminal studies that have managed to tap the home, school and community contexts (e.g. Heath, 1983; Hull and Schultz, 2002; Schultz and Hull, Literacies In and Out of School in the United States, Volume 2) and studies of 'local' and 'heritage' literacies[8] that are concerned primarily with the maintenance of culturally unique adult literacy practices, what we do have falls into two main categories.

The first group contains cultural ethnographies that have provided insights into the role that written language and other sign systems play within community and family life. This body of work has also helped us to understand the cultural variation that occurs across communities and families. One of the most significant early studies to document cultural variations in literacy acquisition was the work of Scribner and Cole (1981), who found that the Vai people of Liberia used three different writing systems for different purposes. Arabic literacy was learned by rote as part of religious practices, English was learned as part of formal schooling, and finally, the Vai language was learned informally at home and in the community and for personal communication such as letters. Each of these 'literacies' was acquired and used for different social and cultural purposes.

Similarly, in an ethnography within the South Pacific, Duranti and Ochs (1986) found complexity, and that this had an impact on how children coped with literacy at school. They observed that the children of families in a Samoan village needed to cope with different forms of interaction across home and school settings.

However, while anthropology has been a major stimulus for new directions in literacy and culturally sensitive accounts of literacy within communities, Street (1995) argues that such work has often been framed by traditional limited definitions of literacy. He suggests, for example, that early ethnographies like that of Clammer (1976) in Fijian villages assumed 'autonomous' models of literacy in framing the study and failed to question the power relationships of the institution (in this the case the church) in introducing literacy, thus failing to problematise the role that literacy played in the colonisation of these people. However more recently ethnographies of literacy have adopted a broader social practice frame (as many contributions to this volume indicate).

---

[8] The term 'local literacies' has been used by Barton and others (see for example, Barton and Hamilton, 1998) to describe the literacy of everyday life. They observed that in everyday lives, people inhabit a textually mediated social world, bringing reading and writing into most activities. For an interesting discussion of 'heritage' literacies of immigrant families living literate lives in multiple languages see Maguire, Beer, Attarian, Baygin, Curdt-Christiansen and Yoshida (1995).

In Australia, the Federal government has funded a number of significant national studies over a ten year period that have sought to understand the complexity of literacy practices in specific contexts, with a particular concern for the implications of this work for school literacy success. The work by Cairney et al. (1995) and Cairney and Ruge (1998) discussed earlier was part of this broad sweep of projects. However, other studies have explored the literacy practices of children undertaking schooling by distance education (Louden and Rivalland, 1995), the experiences of children and families in the year prior to school as well as the first year of school (Hill, Comber, Louden and Reid, 1998), the literacy practices of urban and remote rural communities, and variations in literacy practices across rural and urban communities (Breen, Louden, Barratt-Pugh, Rivalland, Rohl, Rhydwen, Lloyd and Carr, 1994).

Breen et al. (1994), for example, conducted community-based case studies of 12 urban and 12 rural families and observed that "all children, regardless of specific language background, are very likely to enter school with different repertoires of language knowledge and use which express their initial communicative competence" (Breen et al., 1994, p. 35). They concluded that even when literacy practices across families appeared similar that they could have different meanings and values.

Similarly, Hill and colleagues (1998) found that Australian children come to school with diverse prior-to-school experiences. The 100 children who were studied were growing up in very different communities, families and homes. The researchers suggested that their observations indicated inequalities in contemporary Australia that have an impact on children's early lives. Schools they argued need to construct a more appropriate curriculum which explicitly builds on children's existing cultural capital and preferred ways of learning.

Studies of Indigenous Literacy

Australia's indigenous population has experienced special issues with literacy, with seven out of every ten Indigenous students in Year three performing below the national literacy standard, compared to just three out of ten for other Australians (DEST, 2000). Some of the earliest and most influential attempts to understand issues associated with Indigenous literacy were conducted by Harris (1980, 1984) and described traditional indigenous learning styles amongst communities in the Northern Territory of Australia. He found that learning styles were often context-specific and person-orientated and were dependent on observation and imitation, as well as personal trial and error.

Subsequent studies in this tradition (e.g., Gray, 1985, 1990) have pointed to the failure of existing pedagogy to accommodate Aboriginal learning styles. Malin (1990) was able to demonstrate that conflicts between Aboriginal home socialisation practices and teacher expectations had a significant effect on Indigenous success at school (cf. Susan Phillips' 1983 seminal study of the Warm Springs Indian Reservation in the US).

Other researchers have also highlighted the significant linguistic diversity of Indigenous learners and observed that Indigenous students in both urban and rural areas speak Aboriginal English in informal community contexts and then have to switch to standard English (Mattingley, 1992). Such work has argued for the valuing of the community English that Indigenous learners bring to school and the impact that such actions has on the central relationships between teachers, their students and communities (see e.g. Munns, Simpson, Connelly and Townsend (1999).

Understanding the Impact of Culture on School Achievement

Studies of Indigenous literacy in Australia reflect international research that acknowledges a new valuing of the richness of community and family literacy. Critical to this has been the growing understanding that literacies vary depending on purpose and life 'domains' (Barton, 1994). Researchers have begun to argue that there are many forms of literacy, each with specific purposes and contexts in which they are used. They conclude that to understand literacy fully, we need to understand the groups and institutions through which we are socialised into specific literacy practices (Bruner, 1986; Gee, 1990).

A key focus of research has been to identify why and how people learn through participation in the practices that make up specific groups and communities. How do communities organise their resources, and how does participation in the culture shapes identity? As Moll (1993) has suggested, this has represented a move away from viewing individual learners to viewing learning as participation in funds of knowledge as part of a community of practice. Consequently, a number of American researchers have explored differences in the suitability and impact of curricula and pedagogy on minority groups. For example, Foster (1992, p. 303) concluded that "... many of the difficulties African-American students encounter in becoming literate result in part from the misunderstandings that occur when the speaking and communication styles of their community vary from those expected and valued in the school setting" (p. 303).

Other researchers have investigated the impact of differences between the cultural beliefs and expectations of Native Americans, and those of mainstream cultures (Deyhle and LeCompte, 1994; Locust, 1988; McCarty, 1987; Phillips, 2002). For example, Locust (1988) examined traditional Native American belief systems, including their holistic approach to life and death, their emphasis on non-verbal communication, and their valuing of visual, motor and memory skills over verbal skills. She investigated the ways in which these beliefs conflict with the education system, and argued that traditional psychological education tests reflect the dominant culture resulting in native American children achieving low scores and being treated as learning disabled.

However, Cummins (1986) has argued that the educational success or failure of minority students is related to more than just curricula mismatches, suggesting that it is "a function of the extent to which schools reflect or counteract the power relations that exist within the broader society" (p. 32). As a result he has argued for the incorporation of minority students' culture and language in the education of their children (see Cummins, BICS and CALP: Empirical and Theoretical Status of the Distinction, Volume 2).

In a related Australian study Cairney and Ruge (1998) conducted case studies of four schools judged effective at acknowledging community language and cultural diversity. They found that within each of these schools five basic premises drove curriculum:

1. staff believed that all children could achieve school success irrespective of language or cultural background;
2. language was used in an integrated way across the curriculum;
3. curricula acknowledged that literacy development benefits from the maintenance of first language competence;
4. success was seen as critical to learning and students were given opportunities to succeed as they learnt new skills;
5. parents were seen as playing an important role in children's educational success and were actively involved in the activities of the school.

What the above research demonstrates is that an understanding of language and cultural diversity of a school's students and families is important. It also highlights the need to understand the complexity of community literacies in other than school terms and in ways that transcends 'autonomous' models.

In a related research study Street, Baker and Tomlin (2005) have considered how non-school factors affect school achievement. Adopting a sociocultural perspective on learning the Leverhulme Numeracy Research Program was a 5-year longitudinal project that sought to examine the meanings and uses of numeracy in school and community settings. Another focus was the language practices associated with numeracy, namely reading, writing, speaking and listening. A key concern was the influence of home contexts on school achievement. The

Leverhulme Programme attempted to develop ways of measuring pupil progression across a five-year period. The fieldwork involved observation of selected schools and classrooms and of informal situations in and out of school. It drew on interviews with teachers and pupils; analysis of texts from home and school, curriculum school policy documents, school programs and homework, and teacher feedback.

One of the most interesting insights from this research was that numeracy practices were often invisible to the researcher, with observations affected by how both the observers and the observed defined such practices. The question that this raised for the researchers was "what counts as numeracy"? The varied answers to this question impact not just on what is observed and recorded but what is valued and communicated between home and school. Street et al. (2005) found that when questions were asked of parents about numeracy that discussions often turned to school numeracy practices. The researchers were left with the key question "how are the borders between numeracy practices and other social practices constructed by researchers, schools and families?" This led the researchers to ask a related question, "How damaging are any omissions?" Such observations and questions have relevance to the observation already made in this chapter that researchers have noted that school literacy practices dominate home practices. One critical question that obviously needs to be explored is whether observations of school literacy or numeracy practices at home may involve (at least in part) a masking of other practices that researchers or participants simply don't count or define as literacy or numeracy. This topic requires further research.

New Literacies

One of the obvious gaps in community literacy research has been the failure to adequately tap and understand the richness of non-print literacy available to children outside school. Rarely have studies been able to identify, observe and document use of multiple sign systems, or even the relationship of multiple sign systems to print-based literacy. While early childhood studies have come closest to identifying the richness of children's early experiences[9], few studies have adequately tapped the diversity of literacy practices experienced day by day within communities.

The work of Kress and van Leeuwen (2001), Kress, Jewitt, Ogborn, and Tsatsarelis (2001) and Kress (2003) has done most to challenge views on the impact of visual literacy and its different demands for

---

[9] See for example Harste, Woodward and Burke (1984), Clay (1966), Holdaway (1979), Mason and Allen (1986), Teale and Sulzby (1986), and Wells (1982; 1986).

the learner. The New London Group (NLG) (Cope and Kalantzis, 2000) has also sought to re-theorise literacy, and challenge 'authoritarian' conceptions of unitary literacy (see Leander and Lewis, Literacy and Internet Technologies, Volume 2).

The NLG has proposed a metalanguage of multiliteracies based on the concept of 'Design' (Cope and Kalantzis, 2000). Multiliteracies for the New London Group are based on the understanding that "language and other modes of meaning are dynamic representational resources, constantly being remade by their users as they work to achieve their various cultural purposes." They suggest that meaning is made in ways that are increasingly multimodal, and our world is marked simultaneously by increasing local diversity and increasing global connectedness.

What we do know is that children are being exposed to richer opportunities to encounter written text in diverse digital as well as print forms, and that many of these have a relationship to visual, audio, spatial and behavioural experiences.

What this work promises to deliver is research that will demonstrate the increasingly demanding and diverse literacy practices that are encountered in community settings. The work of researchers like Lemke (2002) suggests that there is much that we need to explore and understand. Having investigated hypertexts, he has concluded that the there is great complexity in the processes required to combine words and images giving attention to sounds, music, graphics, hyperlinks, menu bars, hot spots, etc. If children are experiencing the richness of textual and visual forms outside the classroom then one suspects, that previous conceptions of the relationship between the literacy of home, school and community will need to be revised. There may be ever increasing hybridity of literacy practices as popular culture and new media merge with more traditional literary forms.[10]

PROBLEMS AND GAPS IN OUR UNDERSTANDING

What the above discussion should have demonstrated is that there is much that we still do not know about community literacy practices. While the studies discussed shed light on the topic there are a number of difficulties in moving forward.

One problem is that in trying to understand community literacy practices, it is difficult to separate out the impact of school literacy practices that have such a strong impact on families and attitudes towards what counts as literacy within the wider community (see Cairney and Ruge, 1998; and Freebody, Ludwig and Gunn, 1995). Alongside this must be

---

[10] The work of Dyson (1997) has much to say about these possibilities and how they are realised.

held the questions raised by Street et al. (2005) about the invisibility of some practices.

A second (and related) problem is the limitation of the methods that have been used to examine community literacy practices. Rarely, have studies of family and community literacy managed to achieve an 'insider' view of literacy practices. This should not surprise us as it is difficult to observe family and community literacy practices and the researcher's presence makes a difference to that which is observed. Rarely have in-depth observations been made of natural settings, and except for a small number of significant ethnographies and case studies, most research has involved limited time with small numbers of families. Getting at the 'invisible' literacy practices of home and community is one of the major challenges of researchers. The impact of multimedia and its prevalence poses special challenges for the researcher. What is counted? How is it observed? How are complex relationships between mutiliteracies to be uncovered and understood?

As well as these generic issues, there are many specific issues to explore. We need, for example, more studies that consider how gender, social class and culture interact with issues of literacy practice. Are the experiences of some students at home and school influenced by secondary factors such as language background, social class[11], gender[12] and so on. We also need considerable attention to be given to the impact of school literacy on home literacy as well as the reverse. Rather than simply examining family and community literacy to gain lessons for school literacy, we need to consider the synergistic relationship between the two contexts and the roles that students play as mediators between them. Some of the early intergenerational literacy work may be a useful starting point for this exploration (see Cairney and Ruge, 1998; Gregory, City Literacies, Volume 2).

Finally, we need to remember that literacy is not culturally and ideologically neutral (Street, 1995). Hence we need to examine what this means for literacy acquisition and the relationship of family literacy to life and, in particular, public institutions such as schools. It is important to understand how family literacy practices and their relationship to school literacy are implicated in power relationships that affect life chances.

The research reviewed in this chapter provides an incomplete picture of community literacy practices. While the literature is rich in its findings concerning the importance of the family as the first and perhaps

---

[11] One of the seminal works on this topic is the work of Lareau (1989).

[12] The issue of boy's education and falling literacy standards is a significant issue in its own right. Goldman's (2005) key publication provides an overview of this important issue.

most critical site for literacy acquisition, less is known about the literacy practices that are part of children's lives outside school, and how this relates to learning within school. Children experience a richness of literacy practices at home that is not replicated in school (Cairney and Ruge, 1998). This richness may be even more significant when children's involvement in complex communities outside the home is considered. Finally, we need to know much more about the impact of increased opportunities for multi-modal literacy experiences as we enter an increasingly digital age. Understanding how literacy varies across home, school and community contexts, and how these relate to other factors such as social disadvantage, gender and language diversity, is a significant area of research with implications for schools and communities.

REFERENCES

Auerbach, E.: 1989, 'Toward a social-contextual approach to family literacy', *Harvard Educational Review* 59, 165–181.

Auerbach, E.: 1995, 'Which way for family literacy: Intervention or empowerment?', in L.M. Morrow (ed.), *Family Literacy: Connections in Schools and Communities*, International Reading Association, Newark.

Bakhtin, M.: 1929/1973, *Problems of Dostoevsky's Poetics* (translated by R.W. Rotsel, 1973), Ardis, Ann Arbor.

Barton, D.: 1994, *Literacy: An Introduction to the Ecology of Written Language*, Blackwell Publishers, Oxford.

Barton, D. and Hamilton, M.: 1998, *Local Literacies: Reading and Writing in One Community*, Routledge, London.

Bernstein, B.: 1964, 'Aspects of language and learning in the genesis of the social process', in D. Hymes (ed.), *Language in Culture and Society*, Harper & Row, New York.

Breen, M.P., Louden, W., Barrat-Pugh, C., Rivalland, J., Rohl, M., Rhydwen, M., Lloyd, S., and Carr, T.: 1994, *Literacy in its Place: Literacy Practices in Urban and Rural Communities* (Volumes 1 & 2), DEET, Canberra.

Bruner, J.: 1983, *Child's Talk: Learning to Use Language*, Oxford University Press, Oxford.

Bruner, J.: 1986, *Actual Minds, Possible Worlds*, Harvard University Press, Cambridge, MA.

Cairney, T.H. and Munsie, L.: 1992, *Beyond Tokenism: Parents as Partners in Literacy*, Heinemann, Portsmouth, NH.

Cairney, T.H.: 2000, 'Beyond the classroom walls: The rediscovery of the family and community as partners in education', *Educational Review* 52(2), 163–174.

Cairney, T.H.: 2003, 'Literacy in family life', in N. Hall, Larson and J. Marsh (eds.), *Handbook of Early Childhood Literacy*, SAGE Publications, London, 85–98.

Cairney, T.H. and Ruge, J.: 1998, *Community Literacy Practices and Schooling: Towards Effective Support for Students*, DEETYA, Sydney.

Cairney, T.H., Ruge, J., Buchanan, J., Lowe, K., and Munsie, L.: 1995, *Developing Partnerships: The Home, School and Community Interface* (Volumes 1–3), DEET, Canberra.

Cazden, C.: 1988, *Classroom Discourse*, Heinemann, Portsmouth (NH).

Clammer, J.: 1976, *Literacy and Social Change: A Case Study of Fiji*, Leiden, Brill.

Clay, M.: 1966, *Emergent Reading Behaviour*, Unpublished PhD thesis, University of Auckland.

Cope, B. and Kalantzis, M. (eds.): 2000, *Multiliteracies: Literacy Learning and the Design of Social Futures*, Macmillan Publishers Australia Pty Ltd., Melbourne.

Cook-Gumperz, J.: 1986, *The Social Construction of Literacy*, Cambridge University Press, Cambridge.

Crawford, P.: 1995, 'Early literacy: Emerging perspectives', *Journal of Research in Childhood Education* 10(1), 71–86.

Cummins, J.: 1986, 'Empowering minority students: A framework for intervention', *Harvard Educational Review* 56, 18–36.

Department of Education and Science: 1967, *Children and heir Primary Schools: A Report of the Central Advisory Council for Education (England) Vol. 1: Report & Vol 2: Research and Surveys (Plowden Report)*, HMSO, London.

Department of Education, Science & Training: 2000, *The National Indigenous English Literacy and Numeracy Strategy*, Department of Science, Education & Training, Canberra.

Deyhle, D. and LeCompte, M.: 1994, 'Cultural differences in child development: Navajo adolescents in middle schools', *Theory into Practice* 33, 3, 156–166.

Duranti, A. and Ochs, E.: 1986, 'Literacy instruction in a Samoan village', in B. Schieffelin and P. Gilmore (eds.), *The Acquisition of Literacy: Ethnographic Perspectives*, Volume 21, Ablex Publishing Corporation, Norwood (NJ), 213–232.

Dyson, A.H.: 1997, *Writing Superheroes: Contemporary Childhood, Popular Culture and Classroom Literacy*, Teachers College Press, New York.

Foster, M.: 1992, 'Sociolinguistics and the African-American Community: Implications for Literacy', *Theory into Practice* 31, 4.

Freebody, P., Ludwig, C., and Gunn, S.: 1995, *Everyday Literacy Practices in and Out of Schools in Low Socio-Economic Status Urban Communities: A Descriptive and Interpretive Research Program*, DEETYA, Canberra.

Freire, P. and Macedo, D.: 1987, *Literacy: Reading the Word and the World*, Bergin & Garvey; Massachusetts.

Gee, J.: 1990, *Social Linguistics and Literacies: Ideology in Discourses*, The Falmer Press, London.

Goldman, R.: 2005, *Father's Involvement in their Education: A Review of Research and Practice*, National Family and Parenting Institute, London.

Gray, B.: 1985, 'Teaching oral English', in M. Christie (ed.), *Aboriginal Perspectives on Experience and Learning*, Deakin University Press, Geelong.

Gray, B.: 1990, 'Natural language learning in Aboriginal classrooms: Reflections on teaching and learning style for empowerment in English', in C. Walton and W. Eggington (eds.), *Language Maintenance, Power and Education in Australian Aboriginal Contexts*, NTU Press, Darwin.

Gumperz, J.: 1986, *Discourse Strategies*, Cambridge University Press, New York.

Halliday, M.A.K.: 1975, *Learning How to Mean: Explorations in the Development of Language*, Edward Arnold, London.

Hall, N.: 1987, *The Emergence of Literacy*, Hodder & Stoughton, London.

Harris, S.: 1980, *Culture and Learning: Tradition and Education in Northern Arnhem Land*, Professional Services Branch, Northern Territory Education Department, Darwin.

Harris, S.: 1984, 'Aboriginal learning styles and formal schooling', *Aboriginal Child at School* 12, 4, 3–22.

Harste, J., Woodward, V., and Burke, C.: 1984, *Language Stories and Literacy Lessons*, Heinemann, Portsmouth (NH).

Heath, S.B.: 1983, *Ways with Words: Language, Life and Work in Community and Classrooms*. Cambridge (UK): Cambridge University Press.

Hill, S, Comber, B, Louden, W., Rivalland, J., and Reid, J.: 1998, *100 Children Go to School, Volume 2*, Department of Employment, Education, Training & Youth Affairs, Canberra.

Holdaway, D.: 1979, *The Foundations of Literacy*, Ashton Scholastic, Sydney.

Hull, G. and Schultz, K. (eds.): 2002, *School's Out: Bridging Out-of-School Literacies with Classroom Practice*, Teachers College Press, New York.

Hymes, D.: 1974, *The Foundations of Sociolinguistics: Sociolinguistic Ethnography*, University of Philadelphia Press, Philadelphia.

Kress, G.: 2003, *Literacy in the New Media*, London, Routledge.

Kress, G. and van Leeuwen, T.: 2001, *Multimodal Discourse*, London, Arnold.

Kress, G., Jewitt, C., Ogborn, J., and Tsatsarelis, C.: 2001, *Multimodal Teaching and Learning. The Rhetorics of the Science Classroom*, London, Continuum.

Lareau, A.: 1989, *Home Advantage: Social Class and Parental Intervention in Elementary Education*, The Falmer Press, London.

Locust, C.: 1988, Wounding the spirit: Discrimination and traditional American belief systems. *Harvard Educational Review*, 55, 3, 315–330.

Lemke, J.: 2002, 'Travels in hypermodality', *Visual Communication* 1, 3, 229–325.

Louden, W. and Rivalland, J.: 1995, *Literacy at a Distance*, Department of Education Training & Employment, Canberra.

Luke, A.: 1988, *Literacy, Textbooks and Ideology*, Falmer Press, Brighton, UK.

Maguire, M., Beer, A., Attarian, H., Baygin, D., Curdt-Christiansen, X.L., and Yoshida, R.: 1995, 'The chameleon character of multilingual literacy portraits: Re-searching in "Heritage" language places and spaces', in J. Anderson, M. Kendrick, T. Rogers, and S. Smythe (eds.), *Portraits of Literacy across Families, Communities and Schools*, Lawrence Erlbaum Associates, Mahwah, NJ, 141–170.

McCarty, T.L.: 1987, 'School as Community: The Rough Rock Demonstration', *Harvard Educational Review* 59, 4, 484–503.

McNaughton, S.: 1995, *Patterns of Emergent Literacy*, Oxford University Press, Melbourne.

Malin, M.: 1990, 'The visibility and invisibility of Aboriginal students in an urban classroom', *Australian Journal of Education* 34, 3, 312–329.

Mason, J.M. and Allen, J.: 1986, *A Review of Emergent Literacy with Implications for Research and Practice in Reading*, Center for the Study of Reading, Champaign, IL.Technical Report No. 379,

Mattingley, C.: 1992, 'The authenticity of aboriginal English', in D. Myers (ed.), *The Great Literacy Debate*, Australian Scholarly Publishing, Kew.

Moll, L.: 1992, 'Literacy research in community and classrooms: A sociocultural approach', in R. Beach, J.L. Green, M.L. Kamil, and T. Shanahan (eds.), *Multidisciplinary Perspectives on Literacy Research*, National Council of Teachers of English, Urbana, IL, 179–207.

Moll, L.: 1993, 'Community-mediated educational practices', paper presented at the American Educational Research Association Annual Conference.

Moll, L., Amanti, C., Neff, D., and Gonzalez, N.: 1992, 'Funds of knowledge for teaching: Using a qualitative approach to connect homes and classrooms', *Theory into Practice* 31, 2, 132–141.

Munns, G., Simpson, L., Connelly, J., and Townsend, T.: 1999, '"*Baiyai* '. . . meeting place of two parties. . .'" (Wiradjuri)': The Pedagogical Literacy Relationship', in *Australian Journal of Language and Literacy* 22, 2, 147–164.

Nickse, R.: 1993, 'A typology of family and intergenerational literacy programmes; Implications for evaluation', *Viewpoints* 15, 34–40.

Phillips, S.: 1983, *The Invisible Culture: communication in classroom and community on the Warm Springs Indian Reservation*, Longman, New York.

Quigley, B.A.: 2005, '"First we must dream. Nothing is harder": Toward a discourse on literacy across the life span', in J. Anderson, M. Kendrick, T. Rogers, and S. Smythe (eds.), *Portraits of Literacy across Families, Communities and Schools*, Lawrence Erlbaum Associates, Mahwah, NJ, 321–337.

Rogoff, B.: 1990, *Apprenticeship in Thinking: Cognitive Development in Social Context*, Oxford University Press, New York.

Scribner, S. and Cole, M.: 1981, *The Psychology of Literacy*, Harvard University Press, Cambridge, MA.

Solsken, J.W.: 1993, *Literacy, Gender and Work: In Families and in Schools*, Ablex Publishing Corporation, Norwood, NJ.

Street, B.: 1984, *Literacy in Theory and Practice*, Cambridge University Press, Cambridge.

Street, B. (ed.): 1993, *Cross-cultural Approaches to Literacy*, Cambridge University Press, Cambridge.

Street, B.: 1995, *Social Literacies: Critical Approaches to Literacy Development, Ethnography and Education*, Longman, London.

Street, B., Baker, D., and Tomlin, A.: 2005, *Navigating Numeracies: Home/School Numeracy Practices*, Kluwer, Dordrecht.

Taylor, D.: 1983, *Family Literacy: Young Children Learning to Read and Write*, Heinemann, Portsmouth (NH).

Taylor, D. and Dorsey-Gaines, C.: 1988, *Growing Up Literate: Learning from Inner City Families*, Heinemann, Portsmouth (NH).

Teale, W. and Sulzby, E.: 1986, *Emergent Literacy: Writing and Reading*, Ablex, Norwood (NJ).

Tizard, J., Schofield, W., and Hewison, J.: 1982, 'Collaboration between teachers and parents in assisting children's reading', *British Journal of Educational Psychology* 52, 1–15.

Vygotsky, L.: 1978, *Mind and society: The Development of Higher Mental Processes*, Harvard University Press, Cambridge, MA.

Wells, C.G.: 1982, 'Some antecedents of early educational attainment', *British Journal of Sociology of Education* 2, 181–200.

Wells, G.: 1986, *The Meaning Makers*, Heinemann, Portsmouth (NH).

MARY R. LEA

ACADEMIC LITERACIES IN THEORY AND PRACTICE

INTRODUCTION

The term 'academic literacies' provides a way of understanding student writing, which highlights the relationship between language and learning in higher education. It draws upon applied linguistics and social anthropology for its theoretical framing and its orientation towards the social, cultural and contextualized nature of writing in the university. The work on academic literacies sits broadly within a body of research called New Literacy Studies (NLS), which takes a social and cultural approach to writing, in contrast to more cognitive perspectives. The use of the plural form, 'literacies', signals a concern with literacy as a range of social and cultural practices around reading and writing in particular contexts, rather than individual cognitive activity. Research findings suggest that in order to understand more about student writing it is necessary to start from the position that literacy is not a unitary skill that can be transferred with ease from context to context. The research points to the requirement for students to switch between many different types of written text, as they encounter new modules or courses and the writing demands of different disciplinary genres, departments and academic staff. It has unpacked this diversity primarily through ethnographic-type qualitative case study research, looking at students' and faculty experiences of writing for assessment, and the gaps between their expectations of the requirements of writing. In foregrounding the relationship between writing and learning, writing is conceptualized in terms of epistemology—rather than cognitive skill—and what counts as knowledge in the different contexts of the academy.

EARLY DEVELOPMENTS

In universities across the world academics publish books, journal articles and conference papers, while their students spend much of their time completing written assignments for assessment purposes. It is within this context that increased attention has been paid to student writing, in terms of how best to teach it and how best to support it. The longest tradition of student writing support in tertiary education has been in USA with the provision of freshman composition courses. According to Davidson and Tomic (1999) the first of these "began in

B. V. Street and N. H. Hornberger (eds), Encyclopedia of Language and Education,
2nd Edition, Volume 2: Literacy, 227–238.
©*2010 Springer Science+Business Media LLC.*

1806, when Harvard established the first Boylston Professorship of Rhetoric and Oratory" (p. 163). Later, alongside the compulsory freshman writing course, the expansion of US higher education in the 1960s led to the setting up of remedial or basic writing courses, for those students who were not deemed ready for the freshman courses. In tandem with the compulsory requirement for all American university students to follow a freshman writing course came the development of the College Composition movement which was well established from the 1960s in the USA, as practitioners, who were responsible for teaching these courses, also theorized their work in publications concerned with teaching writing (cf. Bartholomae, 1986; Bizzell, 1982). However, in the United Kingdom and other countries with similar educational traditions, there was little systematic attention paid to student writing in higher education before the mid-1980s (Ivanič and Lea, 2006).

Present day orientations towards theorizing academic literacies have their roots, in part, in the work which was carried out by practitioners supporting student writers in USA in the early 1980s. At this time a new direction had begun to emerge in the US literature which raised questions about the nature of academic discourse. This was informed by work in linguistics and literary theory, and contrasted with the more cognitive and psychological models of the individual learner which had come to dominate writing research. Bizzell (1982), for example, critiqued what she termed the 'inner-directed theorists', who were primarily concerned with the context-free cognitive workings of the individual mind. She contrasted their approach to writing with the 'outer-directed theorists', who, she suggested, were concerned with the social context of writing, and in particular with the influence of discourse communities in the use of language. She argued that the focus for student writers should be on discourse communities and the requirement to address their conventions; the task of freshman composition and basic writing teachers was to introduce students to academic discourse conventions.

Bartholomae (1986) also called for a social view of writing. He, too, was situated in the freshman composition context and concerned with basic writers and the ways in which inexperienced, novice writers wrote themselves into academic discourse and the different disciplinary conventions of the university. Coming from an English and humanities tradition, Bartholomae (op.cit) saw writing as both a social and political act, whereby students had to appropriate a specialized discourse; in Bartholomae's view this was often a matter of imitation. Both Bizzell (1982) and Bartholomae were concerned to find ways in which the student could be acculturated as smoothly as possible into both the broader discourse of the academy and the specific discourse conventions of particular disciplines.

At the same time that writers in the USA were focusing on the ways in which students could be helped to learn the conventions of academic discourse, similar approaches were also being taken by Ballard and Clanchy (1988), in Australia, and by Hounsell (1988) in the United Kingdom. These authors came from rather different disciplinary traditions and—in contrast to the US writers—they were not directly concerned with 'basic writers' or remedial writing classes. Their research was carried out with standard entrant 18-year-old students in traditional universities. Ballard and Clanchy adopted an anthropological approach in considering the issue of literacy in the university; their focus was upon the relationship between language and culture as a way of understanding more about literacy. Although situating their work within a rather different intellectual tradition from Bizzell (1982) or Bartholomae (1985), the arguments they rehearsed were remarkably similar to the US-based authors. That is, students lacked the experience and understanding of the linguistic traditions and conventions of higher education and they needed to be taught how to "read the culture" (Ballard and Clanchy, 1988, p.11). They argued that, if academics made the culture and its implicit ground rules of disciplinary writing explicit and accessible, students could grasp the way a discipline worked, and surface problems in their writing would disappear.

In the United Kingdom, Hounsell (1988) was one of the first to look in depth at the problems students encountered when confronted with the unfamiliar discourses of the university. He identified academic discourse rather than literacy as "a particular kind of written world, with a tacit set of conventions, or 'code', of its own." In common with Ballard and Clanchy (1988) he also conceptualized this code as 'crackable'. He illustrates how students need to be sensitive to different disciplinary ways of framing in their writing, and highlights the tacit nature of academic discourse calling for the features of academic discourse to be made more explicit to students. Although in many ways this work was the forerunner of 'academic literacies' research, it can be critiqued for its lack of attention both to the ways in which language is specifically implicated in the learning process and to deeper epistemological issues concerning the ways in which writing constructs disciplinary bodies of knowledge.

MAJOR CONTRIBUTIONS

New Literacy Studies

Against this backdrop a new body of work began to emerge. This offered a different explanation of students' struggles with writing and meaning making, which went further than the problems of acculturation into

disciplinary discourse—as evidenced in the work described earlier—
and explored the nature of power and authority in student writing
(Ivanič, 1998; Lea, 1994; Lillis, 1997). This particular orientation laid
the foundation for the contested approach which has become the hall-
mark of academic literacies research during the last decade. In 1996
Street published an innovative chapter on academic literacies which
both challenged academic convention (by incorporating the original
texts of others) and foregrounded questions of 'academic literacy'. The
perspective taken by Street (1996) in this publication sat within a body
of work which had become known as the 'New Literacy Studies'.
Street's seminal contribution to NLS had been made earlier when he distinguished between autonomous and ideological models of literacy
(Street, 1984). He had argued that whereas an autonomous model of literacy suggests that literacy is a decontextualized skill, which once learnt
can be transferred with ease from one context to another, the ideological
model highlights the contextual and social nature of literacy practices,
and the relationships of power and authority which are implicit in any literacy event. Literacy, then, is not something which once acquired can be
effortlessly applied to any context requiring mastery of the written word.
Writing and reading practices are deeply social activities; familiarity
with and understanding these practices takes place in specific social contexts, which are overlaid with ideological complexities, for example,
with regard to the different values placed on particular kinds of written
texts. Following this perspective NLS, with its roots in sociolinguistics
and linguistic anthropology, conceptualizes writing and reading as
contextualized social practices.

Challenge to Deficit Models of Student Writing

Until the mid-1990s this body of research had been concerned with
school-based, community and work-place literacies but had not paid
any attention to literacies in the university. Academic researchers had
concentrated in exploring other contexts for research purposes, rather
than the university context within which they themselves were situated.
Although early work by both Lea (1994) and Lillis (1997) had conceptualized writing as contextualized social practice and had explicitly
challenged deficit models of writing, neither situated their work explicitly in the NLS tradition nor made reference to 'academic literacies',
as such. However, Lea (1994) did illustrate the multiplicity of discourses in the academy, an important distinction from the use of the
term discourse in the singular. Ivanič also foregrounded the use of different and competing discourses in her study of mature students
(Ivanič, 1998). Overall, what characterized this emerging body of work
on student writing was its specific focus on writing as social practice

and recognition of the multiplicity of practices, whether these were conceptualized as discourses or literacies. The use of the term' literacies', rather than 'discourses' (the framing provided by US writers), gradually became more prevalent in the literature. This was not merely because of its association with a theoretical framing provided by NLS, but because the focus of concern was student writing, rather than spoken language; the term discourse being associated more commonly with the use of spoken rather than written language.

Research by Lea and Street (1998) introduced new theoretical frames to a field which was, at the time in the United Kingdom, still predominantly influenced by psychological accounts of student learning. Rather than frame their work in terms of 'good' and 'poor' writing, they suggested that there was a need to focus on understandings of faculty and students without making any judgements about which practices were deemed most appropriate. They examined student writing against a background of institutional practices, power relations and identities, with meanings being contested between faculty and students, and an emphasis on the different understandings and interpretations of the writing task. Findings from their research suggest fundamental gaps between students' and faculty understandings of the requirements of student writing, providing evidence at the level of epistemology, authority and contestation over knowledge, rather than at the level of technical skill, surface linguistic competence and cultural assimilation. Based on their analysis of their research data, they explicate three models of student writing: study skills; socialization; academic literacies. A study skills model is primarily concerned with the surface features of text, and is based on the assumption that mastery of the correct rules of grammar and syntax, coupled with attention to punctuation and spelling, ensure student competence in academic writing. An academic socialization model assumes that, in order to become successful writers, students need to be acculturated into the discourses and genres of particular disciplines. The third model, which is academic literacies, to some extent subsumes features of the other two, and is concerned with issues of meaning making, identity, power and authority in student writing. These three models and, in particular, the privileging of the academic literacies model, have been drawn upon widely in the literature on teaching and learning in higher education, calling for a more in depth understanding of student writing and its relationship to learning across the academy.

Methodological Considerations

Methodologically the research uses a mix of approaches for data collection and analysis although these tend to be dominated by ethnographic type and qualitative methods. Research in the field generally draws upon data from a number of different textual sources, frequently using interview transcripts alongside samples of students' writing and faculty feedback on that writing. Researchers have been particularly influenced by critical linguistics, which is concerned not only with the more obvious surface features of language but with the ways in which texts embed subtle relationships of power and authority. Researchers have found this approach to analysis particularly pertinent when examining how students make meaning in their writing. As a consequence of a methodological approach which focuses in detail on the relationship between texts and practices, ongoing research in the field has been influential in challenging dominant deficit models of student writing in higher education practice (cf. Jones et al., 1999; Lea and Stierer, 2000).

To date, much of the research in the field has been carried out amongst marginal groups of students. In her early work Lillis (1997) paid particular attention to the implications of the increasing diversity of the student body, exploring the implications of opening up higher education to previously excluded groups, such as mature women and black students. She uses detailed interview and data from students' essays to explore the ways in which such students make meaning through their academic writing. Methodologically similar perspectives are adopted by Ivanič, in her analysis of mature student writers and the distinctions she elaborates between four aspects of writer identity (Ivanič, 1998). Lea (1998) takes a similar stance in exploring how students studying at a distance construct knowledge through the texts they read and write. Despite the wide variety of contexts being studied, the findings concerning students' struggles with writing and the gaps between tutor and students' expectations and understanding remain remarkably constant. What links research in the field is the attention to the nature of situated practices and their associated written texts.

WORK IN PROGRESS

Academic literacies research has gone hand in hand with ongoing changes in global higher education, including increased diversity in the student body, the introduction of modular degree programmes, moves from traditional academic disciplines to vocational and professional courses, e-learning and the globalization of the tertiary sector. These are having profound influences on the kinds of texts that students are being asked to produce for assessment, and more recent research reflects the application of the principles of academic literacies to these changing contexts.

Research in the field has both reflected, and illuminated further, the changing nature of the context for today's academic writing. In this respect, authors have begun to address the implications of this research on student writing for educational development in tertiary education more generally (Lea and Stierer, 2000). One particularly significant aspect of this approach is related to the ongoing attention being paid in tertiary education to the use of reflective writing, particularly in professional and vocational courses. A number of researchers are examining the nature of the writing that is required in these contexts, both foregrounding and problematizing the relationship between the supposedly self-evident relationship between reflective practice and reflective writing (Baynham, 2000; Creme, 2000; Rai, 2004; Stierer, 2000).

Academic literacies research is also taking place against a backdrop of attention to the changing nature of texts themselves, a change first highlighted by the New London Group and their attention to multi-literacies. Arguing that increasing linguistic and cultural diversity and the multiplicity of channels of communication required new ways of understanding the literacy landscape in education, they suggested that language-based approaches alone were inadequate for addressing the changing environment. Their work has been taken forward in debates concerned with the nature of multimodal texts (Kress and Leeuwen, 2001). Thesen (2001) relates these more general debates on multimodality to the changing nature of higher education. Drawing on data from her research in a South African university, she provides evidence for the shifts that are taking place in the new contexts of higher education, which privilege multimodal texts over the essay. She suggests that these are likely to lead to intense struggles over what counts as powerful knowledge. Although this is a persuasive argument in some contexts, a tension, between the privileging of print and the increased use of multimodal texts, continues to surface, with ongoing claims being made for technologies bringing forth new kinds of literacies in educational contexts, in the face of the ongoing dominance of the authority of the written text in tertiary education (cf. Lea, 2004b).

In related debates, Street has critiqued approaches which appeared to align mode with particular types of literacy, for example, the use of terms such as computer literacy, visual literacy, arguing that it is the context rather than the mode which needs to be foregrounded in a social view of literacy (Street, 1996). In addressing this relationship further he uses the term 'new communicative order' to describe the complexity of literacy practices which are associated with screen-based technologies, multimodality, the use of hypertext and the web (Street, 1998). Snyder (2002) adds to these debates, arguing that being literate involves using different modalities, and that the challenge is to consider what technologies mean for educational practices in terms of the broader social, political, cultural and historical contexts. She suggests that texts are always informed by social and cultural practices and that new types of texts, new language practices and new social formations will develop as people find new ways of communicating with each other.

Despite these general developments, most of the work on literacies and technologies focuses upon school-based and informal contexts of learning (Lankshear et al., 2000; Snyder, 2002) and is not concerned with the contexts of higher education. One exception is a developing body of work which has been taking an academic literacies lens to the texts of online learning. Goodfellow et al. (2004) argue that the texts of computer conference discussion in online courses should be approached as academic writing, embedding relationships of power and authority in much the same way as any other writing in the academy. Despite being virtual environments, students still have to 'read off' the ground rules concerning what counts as knowledge, in a context given primarily by the university delivering the course. Goodfellow and Lea foreground the institutional context of virtual learning and the implications for student writing, whether on or off line. This builds upon their earlier research on a global online course, illustrating how students often struggle with, and have little opportunity to challenge, the dominant literacies and discourses embedded in the course design, thus foregrounding the nature of institutional practice (Goodfellow et al., 2001).

The focus on institutional context is particularly significant because the notion of academic literacies as institutional practice has been somewhat lost in the ways in which the literature of the field has been taken up recently, particularly in educational development circles. The importance of institutional context was first raised by Lea and Street (1998), and in separate publications both the authors have, more recently, returned to this as an essential element of an academic literacies framework (Lea, 2004a; Street, 2004). Street argues that we need to reconsider the whole notion of the university and the role of writing within that. He proposes a way of linking ideas from what he terms the new orders: that is the new work order, the new communicative order and the new epistemological order with academic literacies research.

PROBLEMS AND DIFFICULTIES

Academic literacies research has been highly successful in providing evidence for new approaches to student writing, which challenge more conventional deficit models and highlight the link between student writing and learning. Indeed, Haggis argues that this framing provides an alternative explanation to dominant approaches towards understanding student learning more generally in a mass higher education system (Haggis, 2003). However, the major challenge to the field, now, is to find ways of making the research findings relevant and central in pedagogic contexts. In this respect, some authors have raised questions about the relevance of this research to pedagogic practice. Lillis (2003) for example, argues that while 'powerful as an oppositional frame, that is as a *critique* of current conceptualizations and practices of student writing, academic literacies has yet to be developed as a design frame' p. 192. She argues that Bakhtin's work on dialogism provides an added dimension, providing a focus on dialogue rather than monologue as central to supporting student writing. Lea (2004a) raises concerns about the whole focus of the field upon student writing. She suggests that the 'tendency of the research in the field to concentrate on the non-traditional entrant and her writing, whether in terms of age, gender, race or language, at best might mask the implications of the research more broadly and at worst recreate a deficit model or study skills model'. She proposes a model of course design which is based on the findings from academic literacies research and takes more account of literacies across the university.

At present, therefore, the central body of research continues to be around issues of student writing and the applications of academic literacies as a research model to practice-based settings. In this respect, Creme and Cowan (2005) report some interesting research findings in a peer assessment project with students. They argue that it is not only academic teaching staff who have implicit models of 'good writing'. By the second semester of their first year of study, students, too, seemed to have internalized a view of 'the essay', and, in the action research project in question, appeared to be using this tacit knowledge in their response to the work of their peers. Creme and Cowan suggest that their students had already become acculturated, or academically socialized, into institutional ways of talking about essays; that is they seemed to implicitly 'know the rules'. This is a particularly interesting finding because it provides an alternative perspective to the dominant finding of academic literacies research concerning students' struggles with writing. Creme and Cowan conclude that their students had fairly fixed notions of other students' writing and suggest that this could form the basis for further exploration about students as both readers and writers. Academic literacies research has focused almost exclusively on writing and has not foregrounded what is to some extent a self-evident relationship between writing and reading. It may be time to redress this balance.

It is noticeable that the majority of publications in the field draw on research carried out in the United Kingdom, or countries with similar tertiary education structures, for example, South Africa and Australia. This reflects a troubling reality of research into academic and student writing; its national rather than international orientation. This might well be because research reflects local concerns which are not always understood across cultural divides, particularly when different educational priorities are at stake. We are beginning to see some exception in terms of a related area, the implementation of 'writing in the disciplines' programmes (Monroe, 2002). These foreground learning the discipline through writing and adopt principles which are closely related to the 'academic socialization and 'academic literacies' models of student writing. The distinctions and similarities between these two bodies of work remain a fruitful area of collaboration and research, with academic literacies researchers able to offer empirical methods of data collection and analysis, which are not generally evident in the literature in writing in the disciplines.

Methodologically, it could also be argued that the field has somewhat neglected social and cultural approaches to learning, which have their roots in disciplinary traditions other than those of social linguistics and anthropology. Lea (2005) has argued that academic literacies researchers should take account of the framing offered by work on communities of practice (Lave and Wenger, 1991), activity theory (Engestrom, 1987), and actor-network theory (Law, 1992). All these approaches can provide academic literacies researchers with additional methodological tools when analysing their research data.

FUTURE DIRECTIONS

This chapter has highlighted the varied and changing nature of the texts and practices found in academic contexts and the contribution made to our understanding of this from academic literacies research. However, to date, the focus has been primarily on writing. With the changing nature of textual practice in tertiary education, as explored in this chapter, it may now be an opportunity for researchers to pay more explicit attention to reading as part of writing, in both print based and virtual contexts. This development could be addressed in tandem with another limitation in the field, the lack of longitudinal ethnographic research in specific institutional settings. More research of this kind could provide evidence for comparison and contrast in different disciplinary contexts and take account of the changing status of knowledge, and its associated texts, in today's global higher education. A substantive body of work of this nature would establish the dominance of the field and its contribution to understanding how the academy of the twenty-first century is constructed through both its texts and practices.

See Also: *Kevin Leander and Cynthia Lewis: Literacy and Internet Technologies (Volume 2); Kwesi Kwaa Prah: Language, Literacy and Knowledge Production in Africa (Volume 2); Brian V. Street: New Literacies, New Times: Developments in Literacy Studies (Volume 2)*

REFERENCES

Ballard, B. and Clanchy, J.: 1988, 'Literacy in the university: An 'anthropological' approach', in G. Taylor, B. Ballard, Vic Beasley, H.K. Bock, J. Clanchy, and P. Nightingale (eds.), *Literacy by Degrees*, Society for Research into Higher Education/Open University Press, Milton Keynes.

Bartholomae, D.: 1986, 'Inventing the university', in M. Rose (ed.), *When a Writer Can't Write: Studies in Writer's Block and other Composing-Process Problems*, Guilford Press, New York.

Baynham, M.: 2000, 'Academic writing in new and emergent discipline areas', in M.R. Lea and B. Stierer (eds.), *Student Writing in Higher Education: New Contexts*, The Society for Research into Higher Education/Open University Press, Buckingham, 17–31.

Bizzell, P.: 1982, 'Cognition, convention, and certainty: What we need to know about writing', *PRE TEXT* 3(3), 213–244.

Creme, P.: 2000, 'The 'personal' in university writing: Uses of reflective learning journals', in M.R. Lea and B. Stierer (eds.), *Student Writing in Higher Education: New Contexts*, Society for Research into Higher Education/Open University Press, Buckingham, 97–111.

Creme, P. and Cowan, J.: 2005, 'Peer assessment or peer engagement? Students as readers of their own work', *Learning and Teaching in the Social Sciences* 2(2), 99–120.

Davidson, C. and Tomic, A.: 1999, 'Inventing academic literacy: An American perspective', in C. Jones, J. Turner, and B. Street (eds.), *Students Writing in the University: Cultural and Epistemological Issues*, John Benjamins, Amsterdam, 161–170.

Engestrom, Y.: 1987, *Learning by Expanding: An Activity Theoretical Approach to Developmental Research*, Orienta-Konsultit Oy, Helsinki.

Goodfellow, R., Lea, M., Gonzalez, F., and Mason, R.: 2001, 'Opportunity and e-quality: Intercultural and linguistic issues in global online learning', *Distance Education* 22(1), 65–84.

Goodfellow, R., Morgan, M., Lea, M., and Pettit, J.: 2004, 'Students' writing in the virtual university: An investigation into the relation between online discussion and writing for assessment on two masters courses', in I. Snyder and C. Beavis (eds.), *Doing Literacy Online: Teaching, Learning and Playing in an Electronic World*, Hampton Press, Hampton.

Haggis, T.: 2003, 'Constructing images of ourselves? A critical investigation into 'approaches to learning' research in higher education', *British Educational Research Journal* 29(1), 89–104.

Hounsell, D.: 1988, 'Towards an anatomy of academic discourse: Meaning and context in the undergraduate essay', in R. Saljo (ed.), *The Written World: Studies in Literate Thought and Action*, Springer-Verlag, Berlin, 161–177.

Ivanič, R.: 1998, *Writing and Identity: The Discoursal Construction of Identity in Academic Writing*, John Benjamins, Amsterdam.

Ivanič, R. and Lea, M.: 2006, 'New contexts, new challenges: The teaching of writing in UK higher education, in L. Ganobcsik-Williams (ed.), *Teaching Academic Writing in UK Higher Education: Theories, Practice and Models*, Palgrave/MacMillan, London.

Jones, C., Turner, J., and Street, B. (eds.): 1999, *Students Writing in the University: Cultural and Epistemological Issues*, John Benjamins, Amsterdam.

Kress, G. and Leeuwen, T.V.: 2001, *Multimodal Discourse: The Modes and Media of Contemporary Communication*, Arnold, London.

Lankshear, C., Snyder, I., and Green, B.: 2000, *Teachers and Techno-literacy: Managing Literacy, Technology and Learning in Schools*, Allen & Unwin, St, Leonards, New South Wales.

Lave, J. and Wenger, E.: 1991, *Situated Learning: Legitimate Peripheral Participation*, Cambridge University Press, Cambridge.

Law, J.: 1992, *Notes on the Theory of Actor Network Science*. http://ww.comp.lancs.ac.uk/sociology/soc054jl.html Retrieved 3rd February 2006: Science Studies Centre, University of Lancaster.

Lea, M.R.: 1994, '"I thought I could write until I came here": Student writing in higher education', in G. Gibbs (ed.), *Improving Student Learning: Theory and Practice*, Oxford Centre for Staff Development, Oxford, 216–226.

Lea, M.R.: 1998, 'Academic literacies and learning in higher education: Constructing knowledge through texts and experience', *Studies in the Education of Adults* 30 (2), 156–171.

Lea, M.R.: 2004a, 'Academic literacies: A pedagogy for course design', *Studies in Higher Education* 29(6), 739–756.

Lea, M.R.: 2004b, 'The new literacy studies, ICTs and learning in higher education', in I. Snyder and C. Beavis (eds.), *Doing Literacy Online: Teaching, Learning and Playing in an Electronic World*, Hampton Press, Hampton, 3–23.

Lea, M.R.: 2005, "Communities of practice in higher education': Useful heuristic or educational model', in D. Barton and K. Tusting (eds.), *Beyond Communities of Practice: Language, Power and Social Context*, Cambridge University Press, Cambridge/New York, 180–197.

Lea, M.R. and Stierer, B. (eds.): 2000, *Student Writing in Higher Education: New Contexts*, Society for Research into Higher Education/Open University Press, Buckingham.

Lea, M.R. and Street, B.V.: 1998, 'Student writing in higher education: An academic literacies approach', *Studies in Higher Education* 23(2), 157–172.

Lillis, T.: 1997, 'New voices in academia? The regulative nature of academic writing conventions', *Language and Education* 11(3), 182–199.

Lillis, T.: 2003, 'Student writing as academic literacies: Drawing on Bakhtin to move from critique to design', *Language and Education* 17(3), 192–207.

Monroe, J.: 2002, *Writing and Revising the Disciplines*, Cornell University Press, Ithica, London.

Rai, L.: 2004, 'Exploring literacy in social work education: A social practices approach to student writing', *Journal of Social Work Education* 40(2), 785–797.

Snyder, I. (ed.): 2002, *Silicon Literacies: Communication, Innovation and Education in the Electronic Age*, Routledge, London.

Stierer, B.: 2000, 'Schoolteachers as students: Academic literacy and the construction of professional knowledge within master's courses in education', in M.R. Lea and B. Stierer (eds.), *Student Writing in Higher Education: New Contexts*, Society for Research into Higher Education/ Open University Press, Buckingham, 179–195.

Street, B.: 1984, *Literacy in Theory and Practice*, Cambridge University Press, Cambridge.

Street, B.: 1996, 'Academic literacies', in D. Baker, C. Fox, and J. Clay (eds.), *Challenging Ways of Knowing: Literacies, Numeracies and Sciences*, Falmer Press, Brighton, 101–134.

Street, B.: 1998, 'New Literacies in theory and practice: What are the implications for language in education?', *Linguistics and Education* 10(1), 1–24.

Street, B.: 2004, 'Academic literacies and the new orders: Implications for research and practice in student writing in higher education', *Learning and Teaching in the Social Sciences* 1(1), 9–20.

Thesen, L.: 2001, 'Modes, literacies and power: A university case study', *Language and Education* 15(2&3), 132–145.

KATHERINE SCHULTZ AND GLYNDA HULL

LITERACIES IN AND OUT OF SCHOOL IN THE UNITED STATES

INTRODUCTION

Research on literacy practices separates into two strands. School-based research has focused on reading and writing in formal classrooms, often by examining teaching methods, curricula, learning, and assessment, its goal being to improve students' academic performance. Out-of-school research has documented the myriad literacy practices that occur in a range of institutions and social spaces with an interest in expanding conceptions of what counts as literacy. Important theoretical and conceptual advances in literacy studies have come from research within the second strand. Yet, a divide still exists between the engagement claimed for many youth in terms of their out-of-school literacy practices in contrast with their alienation from school-based reading and writing.

In this chapter, we sketch the major theoretical traditions that have shaped research on the relationships and borders of literacy in and out of school—the ethnography of communication, cultural historical activity theory, and the New Literacy Studies (Hull and Schultz, 2002)—and then introduce recent perspectives from cultural geography and semiotics. Research on literacy out of school continues to be an important and necessary corrective to unidimensional understandings of texts, processes, and contexts. However, the persisting challenge in an age of accountability and testing, narrowing conceptions of literacy, and growing socioeconomic disparities, is how to bridge out-of-school and in-school worlds in ways that make discernable, positive differences in youth's present circumstances and social futures.

EARLY DEVELOPMENTS

Arguably the most durable theoretical tradition to influence literacy studies has been the ethnography of communication, which traces its roots to the early work of Hymes (1964). Using this sociolinguistic approach, anthropologists and linguistics looked out of school at homes and communities to understand children's in-school difficulties, especially those from low-income families. Heath's (1983) decade-long study during the 1960s and 1970s of three contiguous communities in the Southern

B. Street and N. H. Hornberger (eds), Encyclopedia of Language and Education,
2nd Edition, Volume 2: Literacy, 239–250.
©*2010 Springer Science+Business Media LLC.*

USA is the best known and most influential of the bountiful empirical work in this tradition. Her research demonstrated how each community—a black working-class, white working-class, and a racially mixed middle class community—socialized its children into distinct language practices. It also explored, as did subsequent work, how teachers could rethink their pedagogies and curricula to use to advantage the fact that children are differentially socialized into patterns of language use.

A second theoretical tradition is built on the work of the Soviet psychologist Vygotsky and centered on investigating the mind in society or culture in the mind. Highlighting the notion of literacy as a socially organized practice, research in this tradition has emphasized the patterned interplay of skills, knowledge, and technologies within larger activity structures. Flagship literacy research from this perspective was carried out by Scribner and Cole (1981) in the early 1970s. They investigated the cognitive consequences of literacy for the Vai people in Liberia, where it was then possible to decouple the effects of literacy from the effects of schooling. Importantly, Scribner and Cole discovered that particular writing systems and literacy activities fostered specialized forms of thinking, which led them to conceptualize literacy as a multiple practice linked to specific contexts of use. This theoretical tradition, which later developed as "cultural historical activity theory," focused researchers' attention both inside and outside of schools.

Drawing on the ethnographic practice of documenting literacy in local communities and the characterization of literacy as multiple and situated, the third tradition, New Literacy Studies (NLS), emphasized the interplay between the meanings of local events and an analysis of broader cultural and political institutions and practices. A founder of the NLS, Gee (1996) popularized the construct of "Discourse," and literacy as usefully analyzed as part of that larger construct. Further, he drew attention away from a solitary focus on learning and language use in school settings and toward identity construction in and out of schools and across the life span. Gee's discussion of Discourses provided an important starting place for theorizing the connections between literacy, culture, identity, and power.

Brian Street, also a founder of NLS (1995), argued that schooling and pedagogy have narrowed ideas about literacy. Grounding his theoretical conceptions of literacy in his fieldwork in Iran in the early 1970s, Street (1984, 1995) defined literacy as a social practice rather than a set of neutral or technical skills, the customary definition in schools, adult literacy programs, and mass literacy campaigns. For Street literacy was embedded within ideologies and institutions—local belief systems, economic, political, and social and historical conditions—and he argued that research needed to make the varieties of everyday literacy practices visible. His work inspired a flowering of such studies as subsequent researchers followed his model of detailing literacy practices in different cultures and institutions, especially out of school.

MAJOR CONTRIBUTIONS

With the intersecting theories and methods associated with the ethnography of communication, cultural historical activity theory, and the NLS as its base, research on the relationships and borders of literacy practices in and out of school has contributed to our understanding of literacy and learning writ large in several important ways. First, through careful documentation of the learning that takes place in community-sponsored programs, we have learned a great deal about the nature of youth participation and engagement. For instance, in her research on community arts-based organizations, Heath (1998) discovered the importance of the collaborative nature of learning and teaching that occurs as youth draw on their own knowledge and skills through participatory projects.

Creating sustainable after-school activity systems for children, Cole (1996) and his colleagues investigated how learning and play can be combined as youth are provided with diverse starting points for learning and multiple paths to progress. In one such program, Gutiérrez, Baquedano-López, Alvarez, and Chiu (1999, p. 92) argued for the importance of creating contexts for learning where "hybridity" can flourish, "particularly in a time when English-only, anti-immigrant, and anti-affirmative action sentiments influence, if not dominate, educational policy and practice." Such programs can serve a range of important functions including helping us to reimagine classrooms and students. As Gutiérrez and others have shown, children often interact and learn in very competent ways after school, despite poor records and reputations within traditional classrooms (Hull and Schultz, 2002). After-school programs can reorganize learning, shifting typical student–teacher relationships and participant structures. The voluntary nature of these programs, however, can be crucial, and as Cole (1996) points out, these are contexts within which choice is balanced by discipline and learning is infused with play and imagination.

The turn to homes and communities has allowed us to notice and account for the vast, diverse, and often invisible repertoire of resources that youth bring to school. Using the generative term "funds of knowledge," Moll and Gonzalez (1994) illustrated how the expertise of parents and community members could be used to bridge home and school; they captured children's interest and investment in the school's curriculum by seeking out and drawing upon their own and their family's distinctive bases of knowledge and social practices. With a focus on language variation across community contexts, Lee (2000) identified community participation structures, for example, in African American hair salons, to draw on culturally relevant styles of speaking and arguing when she orchestrated classroom discussions about literature. Her research illustrates the potential for engaging students in high levels of reasoning about literary texts by putting to use their tacit knowledge about cultural forms found out of school.

Conducting her research within classrooms, but ever aware of the ways that children of necessity bring their home and peer culture to school, Dyson (1997) argued for the permeability of the classroom curriculum; it needed to include the linguistic and symbolic tools that children appropriate from popular culture and through social relations that extend beyond the school walls. More recently the term "third space" (Bhabha, 1994) has been used to demark the intersection of home, community, and school.

Learning in workplaces has been an important site for rethinking literacy and schooling. To be sure, there has long been interest in the USA in preparing particular students for particular kinds of jobs upon graduation from high school, but in economically tenuous times, that pressure redoubles, as has periodically been the case for the USA in recent years. But whereas the bulk of research and writing around these issues has typically focused on ascertaining exactly what skills workers need to keep the country competitive and themselves employed, research on literacy and work has also tended to complicate the picture. A case in point was Gee, Hull, and Lankshear's (1996) account of the contradictions at the heart of calls for a "new work order" that would elevate both skill requirements and the privileges, responsibilities, and rights of frontline workers. Hull and colleagues' studies of "high-performance" workplaces (Gee et al., 1996) linked literacy, identity, and power, revealing how opportunities to engage in particular literacy practices were distributed and constrained, as well as how new structures for participation created unexpected spaces for the exercise of new literacies, literate roles, and literate identities.

WORK IN PROGRESS

Current research on literacies in and out of school continues to draw generatively on anthropological and sociolinguistic theories and methods. For instance, researchers continue to describe literacy practices that occur in communities in rich ethnographic detail with attention to language use in social contexts. However, in recent years, the explosion of new technologies and the attendant new media have pushed literacy theory and conceptions of literacy practices in new directions with implications for reconceptualizing school practices. As new technologies and new media proliferate, scholars have turned to fields such as social semiotics (cf. Kress, 2003) and cultural geography (cf. Leander and Sheehy, 2004; Soja, 1996) to theorize these phenomena. New technologies make it possible for literacies to travel across space and time, complicating further the boundaries between school and out-of-school contexts. For instance, youth continue conversations and work on reading and writing with peers outside of school through instant messaging, bringing knowledge learned at school into their after-school pursuits; they bring internet games and communications begun at home into classrooms, drawing on these conversations and figures from games as they write literacy analyses; and they cross local, national, and international borders, communicating digitally with interlocutors at great physical removes through blogs, online interest groups, and assorted web sites.

As a result, rather than viewing literacy practices as socially situated, researchers have documented how discursive practices shape relationships in both time and space (Leander and Sheehy, 2004). Thus, youth are never really either simply in school or out of school: their identities and practices travel across those spaces. Further, the interaction between literacies and the production of identities, especially as students traverse the borders of school and communities and nation-states, has proven to be a critical area of study.

Current researchers have focused on the documentation of literacy practices across the boundaries of school and out-of-school contexts, noting the affordances of these new literacy practices and the implications for teaching and learning (e.g., Gee, 2003; Soep and Chavez, 2005). In her study of the popular genre of anime, Mahar (2003) found that instead of separating in- and out-of-school literacy practices, teachers used in-school tools to read out-of-school texts. She suggests that by learning about adolescents' worlds and popular cultures, teachers can become guides to helping them develop critical strategies for reading and assessing the truth of what they read. Knobel and Lankshear (2006) argue further that the investigation of youth blogs and the practice of blogging provides a window into what we might term "powerful writing," giving teachers access to the words and worlds of youth, shifting what we consider to be "powerful writing" from an individual to collective accomplishment, and from a local to a global practice. Finally, educators have usefully brought youth music (e.g., hiphop, beats) and youth media into classroom, hoping to capture student attention and interest in learning school material by paying respectful attention to youth cultural practices (cf. Morrell, 2004).

Documenting a Chinese immigrant youth's participation in an internet site that included a transnational group of peers led Lam (2000) to raise questions about literacies, transnational identities and "cultural belonging" (p. 457). Lam explains that the youth used the internet to develop a range of discourse practices and online identities with a "transborder" network of peers. While English spoken in his classroom seemed to contribute to his sense of marginalization, the English he acquired through the internet was the global English of adolescent pop culture and contributed to a sense of belonging. The textual and semiotic tools of the internet contributed simultaneously to the development of literacy practices that could be transferred to school tasks, while affording him new identities. Such work suggests a broader and critical conception of literacies in and out of school that reflect students' relationships with multiple target languages and communities (Lam, 2000).

Situating their work in the study of youth and media, Soep and Chavez (in press) explain that although much of the research in the past documented the deleterious effects of media on youth, more recently scholars, educators, and activists have investigated how media is conceptualized, produced, and distributed by youth. They conceptualize what they call the "pedagogy of collegiality" (Soep and Chavez, in press) or the shared responsibility youth felt to build community and accomplish media-related projects. In this pedagogy, youth and adults jointly frame and carry out the tasks with both groups accountable to an outside audience.

Hull and James (2007) bring together current work that connects recent research on literacy with theoretical understandings from semiotics and cultural geography in their work in the university–community based organization called Digital Underground Storytelling for Youth (DUSTY). A centerpiece of this work is the creation of what they call "identity texts," which are constructed through spoken word performances, written narratives, photo collections, storyboards, musical compositions, animations, or digital stories with a focus on fostering agency through a range of semiotic resources. Projects like DUSTY extend school-based definitions of literacy to include the visual and the performative. Drawing on notions of space and place (e.g., Soja, 1996) Hull and colleagues raise questions such as: "How is the construction of identities, both individual and collective, influenced by and enacted through spatiality?" In DUSTY, youth are provided with material tools and supportive social practices to construct new worlds and identities through multimedia and multimodalities. They conclude that learning to communicate with words, images, sound, and movement, and being able to produce artifacts that can traverse geographical, social, and semiotic boundaries brings us close to a new definition of literacy.

In her recent work, Heath (2000) has developed a new conception on schools based on her close study of learning outside of school contexts. Although this might not be an entirely realistic vision of schools given current constraints on curriculum and pedagogy, it represents a possibility based on what we have learned about youth, literacy, and learning from studies of literacy and learning in out-of-school contexts. Heath's proposal is to envision schools as an integrated system of learning environments explaining that schools should be "central nodes" within a web of learning contexts for children which might include museums, playgrounds, libraries, and the like that are open all day and all year. She writes:

> An ecology of learning environments would be the focus, rather than schools alone. In this way, societal members would reconceive young people as learners and recources for the learning of others rather than as passive students (p. 128).

This vision of what is possible suggests what we can—and indeed should-be learning from looking across schools and communities to understand the possibilities for literacy and learning that both suggest.

PROBLEMS AND DIFFICULTIES

At the same time that there is an explosion of new literacy practices in out-of-school spaces, learning and literacy in school has narrowed. In response to pressures for Adequate Yearly Progress (AYP) imposed by the federal No Child Left Behind (NCLB) legislation in the USA and comparable legislation and state-regulated curriculum in countries around the world, schools and districts have increasingly substituted test preparation for engaged learning, moving the curriculum further away from youth interests and knowledge so vividly displayed in out-of-school spaces. This creates a wide gulf between school pedagogies and what we know and have learned through the documentation of out-of-school literacy practices. As Carmen Luke (2003, p. 398) explains:

> When learning is no longer geographically tied to a desk, the school library, the book, or the teacher who demands 'all eyes up front,' then old-style transmission and surveillance pedagogy becomes less stable and less defensible but complementary to the out-of-school pedagogies and practices in households, communities and workplaces.

As a result, although schools and educators might recognize new literacy practices and technologies, this new knowledge has not fundamentally changed the structures of schools. Curriculum and content continue to be delivered in predictable ways and school knowledge and literacy practices tend to be valued over those used in everyday life. Out-of-school practices are used in service of school knowledge, to engage students in learning rather than to transform teaching, learning, and schooling.

Regulatory agencies at the federal, state, and local levels are strengthening the boundaries between school and communities, tightening control over what is taught in school. The demand for academic achievement that is narrowly defined has resulted in the disappearance of spaces for experimentation inside of school, marginalizing the opportunities to build on students' interests and knowledge based on their out-of-school practices. At the same time that researchers have usefully documented out-of-school literacy practices, juxtaposing youth's engagement with them to their alienation from school-based reading and writing, there has been a tendency to valorize such practices uncritically and to attribute to them too much agency (Hull and Schultz, 2002). For instance, we may overestimate how much youth know and learn through their engagement out of school with digital literacies, especially since these technologies are unevenly distributed across communities and there may be a social hierarchy among children in terms of knowledge and use (Moss, 2006). An additional concern is that, on the basis of erroneous assumptions about students' interests and identities, we constrain their opportunities to make choices that differ from perceptions of the norm. Why is it, Noguera (2003) asks, that we automatically assume African American boys are able to rap but not to debate?

Despite the plethora of research and documentation of out-of-school literacies, it seems clear to us that this work has not yet had the necessary impact on the ways schools are structured and the content of the curriculum in most countries and local districts. Instead, the norms associated with schooling have seemed to increase their reach, extending to nonschool learning spaces. For example, after-school programs in the USA and elsewhere have increasingly turned to schools as models, continuing the teaching during the school day after the school bell rings. The pressure for mastering content for tests has led to after-school programs based on test preparation and homework help. In many parts of the world, high-stakes national examinations lead parents and children to after-school programs that drill students in facts to prepare them for tests, which often determine whether or not youth can attend universities. Rather than a useful dialogic exchange between the academic and social content of learning that takes place inside and outside of school spaces, after-school programs, particularly those located in school buildings, are becoming extensions of schools. Teaching and learning is determined by examinations written by adults who are often at a far remove from the literacies and technologies that guide youth's lives.

A further challenge for research on literacies in and out of school is the design of research projects that might capture the movement and flow of literacy practices across boundaries such as those between school and community, but also across digital and print media and transnational boundaries. Multisited ethnography (Marcus, 1995) has guided researchers to document practices in multiple settings. Questions about methodology as well as ethics arise as researchers attempt to capture the wide range of literacy practices that youth engage in such as online conversations and text messaging. Although youth can inform their interlocutors that they are involved in a study, it becomes easy for outsiders to unknowingly become a part of a research project. At the same time, capturing the rich, complex nature of interactions and circulating literacy practices (Schultz, 2006) invites researchers to reimagine research methods and design.

FUTURE DIRECTIONS

Eyes focused on the computer screen and oblivious to the surrounding noise in her fifth grade classroom, Saima typed out the following poem that would become a centerpiece of her multimedia story:

I need an answer, for a question from deep inside.
Is life a hard journey, or just an easy ride?
I see this world as a big and open field,
Filled with opportunities and with problems to deal

A few days later Saima spoke these same words into a digital tape recorder to add to the soundtrack for her multimodal story. Once completed, the story was a bold statement about her life and her ambitions. It was an iMovie composed of family photographs, images from the internet, maps, and text. The final product included music from Saima's home country, Bangladesh, and her own soft voice reading two poems and a letter addressed to her teacher. The movie drew readers into the contours of Saima's life with wedding pictures and portraits of two sisters shyly posing for the camera. It also had a large embrace, addressing global issues such as conflict in the Middle East. Contributing more words to the classroom conversation than Saima had added all year, the movie had a loud presence. Its author, a small, shy girl who rarely spoke above a whisper and had only learned to speak English within the past year, seemed as awed by the process as her teachers (Schultz, 2006).

This vignette, drawn from research conducted over the past four years by Schultz and colleagues, illustrates the possibilities for introducing digital technologies into the school day to support a standardized core curriculum. As we look toward the future, we are well aware that it is impossible to imagine the new forms of literacy practices that will become available and the ways in which they will traverse home, community, and school spaces. The worry is that school curricula will continue to tighten, making it nearly impossible to incorporate new modes and media for expression, but the hope is that they will expand, providing the sorts of openings described here.

As these tensions play out, we expect and would encourage research on several fronts. Researchers can helpfully juxtapose the logocentric practices that dominate in schooling with opportunities to communicate in the multiplex combinations of modes and media that currently proliferate, sorting out the affordances and constraints of each. Attention can usefully be paid to ever-changing conceptions of space, place, and borders, rather than in-school and out-of-school dichotomies; after all, digital communication has the potential to bypass customary limitations of location, geography, and identity. In an age in which differences in an interconnected world grow more salient, even as we become increasingly aware of own identities as multiple, we hope for literacy research that enables students to imagine, access, and participate in the realties of others. And like the previous generation of researchers who pioneered the theoretical orientations that have proved so durable for studies of literacy across contexts, we urge the continuation of research that takes as its broadest goal the provision of opportunities to learn and thrive for all students.

We expect, however, that such studies will not proceed from the assumption that detailing differences in linguistic and social practices and celebrating diverse literacies, as helpful as this work has been, will necessarily or easily result in more equitable educational and social futures. Rather, the difficult lesson that researchers of in-school and out-of-school borders and relationships have learned, and their true challenge for the future, is the need now for new theoretical perspectives. These new theories will need to take into account the ways in which schooling and society are strongly bent toward social reproduction (Bourdieu and Passeron, 1977); they will need to assume just as vigorously the existence of intercultural, cross-cultural, and cross-national spaces where agency, resistance, and new identities grow (Appadurai, 1996); and of course, they will need to look expectantly and critically at the role of literacy, and as well as other semiotic systems, in this process.

REFERENCES

Bhabha, H.K.: 1994, *The Location of Culture*, Routledge, New York.
Bourdieu, P. and Passeron, J-C.: 1977, *Reproduction in Education, Society and Culture* (2nd ed.), Sage Publications, London.
Cole, M.: 1996, *Cultural Psychology: A Once and Future Discipline*, Harvard University Press, Cambridge, MA.
Dyson, A.H.: 1997, *Writing Superheroes: Contemporary Childhood, Popular Culture, and Classroom Literacy*, Teachers College Press, New York.
Gee, J.P.: 1996, *Social Linguistics and Literacies: Ideology in Discourses* (second edition), The Falmer Press, London.
Gee, J.P.: 2003, *What Video Games have to Teach us About Learning and Literacy*, Palgrave Macmillan, New York.

LITERACIES IN AND OUT OF SCHOOL 249

Gutiérrez, K., Baquedano-López, P., Alvarez, H., and Chiu, M.: 1999, 'A cultural-historical approach to collaboration: Building a culture of collaboration through hybrid language practices', *Theory into Practice* 38(2), 87–93.

Heath, S.B.: 1983, *Ways with Words*, Cambridge University Press, New York.

Heath, S.B.: 1998, 'Living the arts through language plus learning: A report on community-based youth organizations', *Americans for the Arts Monographs* 2(7), 1–19.

Heath, S.B.: 2000, 'Seeing our way into learning', *Cambridge Journal of Education* 30(1), 121–132.

Hull, G. and James, M.: 2007, Geographies of hope: A study of urban landscapes and a university–community collaborative. In Peggy O'Neill (Ed.), *Blurring Boundaries: Developing Writers, Researchers, and Teachers: A tribute to William L. Smith*, Hampton Press, Kresskill, NJ.

Hull, G. and Schultz, K. (eds.): 2002, *School's Out: Bridging Out of School Literacies with Classroom Practice*, Teachers College Press, New York.

Hymes, D.: 1964, 'Introduction: Towards ethnographies of communication', in J.J. Gumperz and D. Hymes (eds.), *The Ethnography of Communication*, American Anthropology Association, Washington, DC, 1–34.

Knobel, M. and Lankshear, C.: 2006, 'Weblog worlds and constructions of effective and powerful writing: Cross with care, and only where signs permit', in K. Pahl and J. Rowsell (eds.), *Travel Notes from New Literacy Studies*, Multilingual Matters, Clevedon, England.

Kress, G.: 2003, *Literacy in the New Media Age*, Routledge, London.

Lam, W.S.E.: 2000, 'L2 literacy and the design of self: A case study of a teenager writing on the Internet', *TESOL Quarterly* 34(3), 457–482.

Leander, K.M. and Sheehy, M. (eds.): 2004, *Spatializing Literacy Research and Practice*, Peter Lang, New York.

Lee, C.D.: 2000, *The Cultural Modeling Project's Multimedia Records of Practice: Analyzing Guided Participation Across Time*, Paper presented at the Annual Meeting of the American Educational Research Association, New Orleans.

Luke, C.: 2003, 'Pedagogy, connectivity, multimodality, and interdisciplinarity', *Reading Research Quarterly* 38(3), 397–403.

Mahar, D.: 2003, 'Bringing the outside in: One teacher's ride on the anime highway', *Language Arts* 81(2), 110–117.

Marcus, G.: 1995, 'Ethnography in/of the world system: The emergence of multi-sited ethnography', *Annual Review of Anthropology* 24, 95–117.

Moll, L.C. and Gonzalez, N.: 1994, 'Lessons from research with language-minority children', *Journal of Reading Behavior* 26, 439–456.

Morrell, E.: 2004, *Linking Literacy and Popular Culture: Finding Connections for Lifelong Learning*, Christopher-Gordon, Norwood, MA.

Moss, G.: 2006, 'Informal literacies and pedagogic discourse', in J. Marsh and E. Millard (eds.), *Popular Literacies, Childhood and Schooling*, Routledge, London, 128–149.

Noguera, P.A.: 2003, 'The trouble with Black boys: The role and influence of environmental and cultural factors on the academic performance of African American males', *Urban Education* 38(4), 431–459.

Schultz, K.: 2006, 'Qualitative research on writing', in C.A. MacArthur, S. Graham, and J. Fitzgerald (eds.), *Handbook of Writing Research*, Guilford Press, New York.

Scribner, S. and Cole, M.: 1981, *The Psychology of Literacy*, Harvard University Press, Cambridge, MA.

Soep, E. and Chavez, V.: 2005, Youth radio and the pedagogy of collegiality, *Harvard Educational Review*, 75(4), 409–434.

Soja, E.W.: 1996, *Thirdspace: Journeys to Los Angeles and Other Real—and Imagined—Places*, Blackwell Publishers, Malden, MA.

Street, B.V.: 1984, *Literacy in Theory and Practice*, Cambridge University Press, Cambridge, MA.
Street, B.V.: 1995, *Social Literacies: Critical Approaches to Literacy in Development, Ethnography and Education*, Longman, London.

DAVID BLOOME

LITERACIES IN THE CLASSROOM

INTRODUCTION

As teachers and children interact among themselves and with each other in classrooms, they use written language and related semiotic systems (such as text messaging and internet technologies) for a broad range of purposes. They acquire academic information and concepts, negotiate social relationships and social identities, engage in imaginary play, control others and themselves, and express their emotions and needs, among other functions. They also use written language to acquire competence in a select set of literacy practices (ways of using written language) labeled school literacy practices (more commonly described as learning to read and write) and academic literacies (ways of using written language in academic disciplines).

As a heuristic, literacy practices in classrooms can be categorized as official or unofficial literacy practices. Official literacy practices are promoted by the school and include learning to read and write literacy practices and academic literacies. Unofficial literacy practices are not sanctioned by the school (but may be tolerated) and occur in the classroom subrosa (e.g., Maybin, forthcoming). These include literacy practices such as passing notes, noninstructional game playing, and graffiti writing, among others. Here, we focus on official literacy practices.

Research on literacy practices in classrooms has been concerned with the nature of classroom literacy practices, the relationship of literacy practices outside of the classroom (in home and community) to literacy practices in classrooms, the use of classroom literacy practices for schooling, academic literacies, critique, and community action (cf. Schultz and Hull, Literacies In and Out of School in the United States, Volume 2).

NATURE OF CLASSROOM LITERACY PRACTICES

The warrant for describing literacies in classrooms derives from a conception of literacy as social practices involving written language (cf. Bloome, Carter, Christian, Otto, and Shuart-Faris, 2005; Heath, 1983; Pahl and Rowsell, 2005; Street, 1995) as opposed to defining literacy as a set of decontextualized, autonomous cognitive and linguistic processes. Literacy is inherently multiple; there are a broad range of

B. V. Street and N. H. Hornberger (eds), Encyclopedia of Language and Education, 2nd Edition, Volume 2: Literacy, 251–262.
©*2010 Springer Science+Business Media LLC.*

differing literacy practices. Literacy practices are embedded in and influence social situations and social events (e.g., face-to-face interactions) which are themselves embedded in broader cultural and social contexts including institutional contexts such as schooling. Thus, description of literacy practices in classrooms requires description of how those literacy practices are contextualized.

As a context for literacy practices, classrooms can be heuristically described as "cultural" communities. Within each classroom, teachers and students continuously negotiate a set of shared expectations and standards for the organization of events, how people will relate to each other, how meaning and significance are assigned to actions and materials, and how spoken and written language is to be used within and across classroom events, etc. Variation within and across classroom contexts and in the schools and communities in which classrooms are located implicate variation in the literacy practices within those classrooms. As such, key questions in the description of literacy practices in classrooms include:

1. What is (are) the nature(s) of classroom literacy practices given pedagogical contexts?
2. What literacy practices are constructed, and how, within and across classrooms?
3. How do teachers and students take hold of these literacy practices and change, and adapt them to new situations and goals?

Street and Street (1991) label pedagogically contextualized literacy practices as *school literacy practices* and describe their attributes as involving the objectification of language and an emphasis on metalinguistic practices. Thus, a distinction can be made between school literacy practices as described by Street and Street (1991) and literacy practices located in classrooms, per se. That is to say, school literacy practices do not necessarily constitute the entire set of literacy practices within classrooms. Some classrooms may eschew school literacy practices and foreground those that emphasize reading and writing for enjoyment and the expression of emotions and views.

Within the category of school literacy practices, there is variation both within and across classrooms. Borko and Eisenhart (1987) describe differences in reading practices across hierarchically organized instructional reading groups within a classroom. They show how students become socialized to the ways of using language and doing reading specific to their reading group making it difficult for students to move to another reading group. Similarly, uses of language and reading practices vary across classrooms organized by hierarchical tracks. Students acquire the literacy practices of their reading group or track with the accompanying consequence of acquiring a social identity associated with their reading group or track. Their social identity is both a result of their membership in the reading group or track and a result of using language and engaging in reading in ways consistent with that group's ways of using language and doing reading.

Some schools and classrooms may layer the pedagogical context with cultural ideologies that go beyond individual student achievement. For example, religious schools may emphasize learning to read as a nonhierarchical religious obligation; educational programs derived from political agendas may emphasize school literacy as part of a new nationalism or as revolutionary change, alternative schools may emphasize community pride, noncompetitive social relationships or other agendas as part of how they contextualize learning to read and write, etc. (cf. Cucchiara in Street, 2005). Such layering of cultural ideologies reframes how literacy practices in classrooms are understood and enacted by teachers, students, and others.

A distinction is needed between the surface level form of classroom literacy practices and deeper level functions and structuring of social relationships, knowledge, and ways of acting on the worlds in which teachers and students live. For example, Bloome, Carter, Christian, Otto, and Shuart-Faris (2005) showed how a teacher adapted what appeared on the surface to be traditional school literacy practices to help students engage in a "deeper" social agenda—to learn to use literary oriented literacy practices to question relationships between language and race relations.

THE RELATIONSHIP OF LITERACY PRACTICES OUTSIDE OF THE CLASSROOM (IN HOME AND COMMUNITY) TO LITERACY PRACTICES IN CLASSROOMS

The warrant for examining relationships among literacy practices outside of the classroom to those inside of the classroom derives from recognition that students have lives outside of the classroom that may affect how they engage in the literacy practices of the classroom. Students may bring their home and community based cultural models of how to use spoken and written language to classroom literacy practices. (cf. Maybin, forthcoming)

Cross-Cultural Contexts of Literacy Practices in Classrooms

A long-term ethnography of language and literacy practices by Heath (1983) in three culturally and economically different communities showed that the ways in which children use spoken and written language are derivative of both the communities' specific literacy practices and of broader cultural themes integral to each respective community.

As such, when children approach any social event, including social events in the classroom, the expectations and participatory frames they hold for what constitutes appropriate and effective use of spoken and written language derive from their experiences in analogous social events in their families and communities and in the broader family and community context. When the expectations and participatory frames for classroom events are foreign to the children—as may occur when their expectations and frames are derived from a different set of cultural experiences other than those on which classroom literacy practices are based, the children may not participate appropriately, effectively signal their competence with spoken and written language, or understand what is being expected of them, its import, or the basis for how their actions are being interpreted by the teacher. Such cross-cultural differences are especially likely for students from nondominant cultural and linguistic communities, potentially resulting in misevaluation and misinstruction (Cazden, John, and Hymes, 1972; Cook-Gumperz, 1986; Moss, 1994).

Taking a different view, Ogbu (1974; Ogbu and Simons, 1998) suggested that the historical and economic circumstances of minority groups' relationships with the dominant cultural and economic group fosters differential responses by students to engagement in classroom literacy practices. The existence of job ceilings on minorities influences how students view the efficacy of their participation in classroom instructional practices. In addition, Ogbu argued that there is a differential response to participation in school between those students who come from what Ogbu describes as voluntary minority communities versus those who come from an involuntary minority community. A voluntary minority community had voluntarily chosen to migrate to the target country and students from such communities adopt a stance of cooperation with the literacy practices of the classroom even if there are cross-cultural differences. An involuntary minority community has been forcibly brought to the target country through enslavement. Students from an involuntary minority community may adopt a stance of opposition to participation in the literacy practices of the classroom. The oppositional stance is viewed as fostering social solidarity and social identity of the students from that community and a distancing from the continued domination of the minority community.

Culturally Responsive Pedagogies as Context for Classroom Literacy Practices

Recognition of cross-cultural differences as well as the low-academic achievement of students from many cultural and racial minority groups (when compared to their white, middle-class counterparts), has raised questions about how classroom literacy practices as part of pedagogical practice might be organized. Shifts in the participatory organization of instructional practices so that they more closely resemble and take advantage of analogous practices with students' home communities have been shown to enhance participation and achievement (e.g., Au, 1980). Taking a broader perspective, Ladson-Billings (1994, 2005), Gay and Banks (2000) and others, have argued for culturally responsive pedagogies that include but go beyond the participatory organization of classroom literacy practices and incorporate broader cultural themes and interpersonal relationships consistent with students' home cultures. As such, classroom literacy practices are embedded in a broader cultural context focusing on interpersonal relationships among teachers, students, parents, and other community members; and this broader cultural context can be viewed as reframing the meaning and significance of participation in classroom literacy practices.

Part of the dynamic addressed by culturally responsive pedagogy involves eschewing *a priori* constructions of students as having a deficit cultural and linguistic backgrounds that make difficult students' effective participation in classroom literacy practices. The concept of funds of knowledge has been used to emphasize that the homes and communities of cultural and linguistic minority students are not deficit in social, linguistic and cultural capital, but rather that teachers need to design curriculum and instruction in ways that provide opportunities for students to bring to their participation in classroom literacy events the funds of knowledge available in their households and communities (Gonzales, Moll, and Amanti, 2005; Moll, Amanti, Neff, and Gonzalez, 1992). Similarly, Lee (1997) and Richardson (2003) argue for pedagogies for literacy learning that incorporate students' language and experiences in bridging to academic learning. Similarly, Willett, Solsken, and Wilson-Keenan (1999) describe how bringing parents into the classroom in ways that foreground the parents' cultural and vocational expertise, histories, and experiences, provides opportunities for students to engage in new forms of literacy practices by incorporating the cultural knowledge from across parents from diverse communities.

Bringing students' home cultures and languages to school literacy practices and academic learning provides opportunities for the students and the teacher to generate new understandings and heuristics. Gutierrez, Rymes, and Larson (1995) has labeled such a learning space, the third space, as it represents neither the dominant culture and language of the school nor those of the students, but one created by the dialectics involved in their juxtaposition. That is, activity in the third space is generative of new literacy practices and new understandings of academic knowledge for both the students and the teacher.

Central to the concepts of culturally responsive pedagogies, funds of knowledge, and teaching/learning in the third space is framing participation in classroom literacy practices and academic learning as not requiring cultural and linguistic minority students to make a choice between assimilation to the dominant culture and loss of cultural identity versus opposition to acquiring the literacy practices of the classroom. By building on the cultural and linguistic resources of students' home and community cultures and language, classroom literacy practices can strengthen students' connections and social identities with their cultural communities while they acquire school literacies and academic literacies.

USES OF CLASSROOM LITERACY PRACTICES FOR SCHOOLING, ACADEMIC LITERACIES, CRITIQUE, AND COMMUNITY ACTION

The range of opportunities for the writing of extended texts in classrooms are often limited (Applebee, 1984) and the instructional conversational contexts in which writing and reading occur often restrict extended response and opportunity to explore texts, topics and interpretations in depth (Nystrand, 2006). At issue is not merely expanding the range of opportunities for writing and reading nor simply restructuring instructional conversations to provide students with opportunities for topic initiation, extended response, and complex, higher level cognitive tasks. Rather, following Gee's (2004) critique of traditional schooling, shifting classroom literacy practices from an instructional context and from being about doing school (cf. Bloome, Puro, and Theodorou, 1989) to what Gee calls a cultural process. The example Gee (2004) uses below of learning physics applies equally well to learning to read and write.

> Besides natural and instructed learning processes, there are also what we can call "cultural processes." There are some things that are so important to a cultural group that the group ensures that everyone who needs to learns them ... What does it mean to learn physics as a cultural process? Masters (physicists) allow learners to collaborate with them on projects that the learners could not carry out on their own. ... Learners see learning physics as not just "getting a grade" or "doing school" but as part and parcel of taking on the emerging identity of being a physicist.... Children who learn to read successfully do so because, for them learning to read is a cultural and not primarily an instructed process... Children who must learn reading primarily as an instructed process in school are at an acute disadvantage (pp. 12–13).

Yeager, Floriani, and Green (1998) provide examples of teaching/learning the literacy practices of history and science as cultural processes in a middle school classroom by providing opportunities for students to engage in historical study as historians and scientific inquiry as scientists. But where Gee emphasizes work with "Masters," Yeager, Floriani, and Green engaged students in ethnographic study of what it means to be a historian and scientist and that ethnographic study was used by students to construct literacy practices and learning practices that incorporated the 'cultural processes' of those academic disciplines.

Academic Literacies

The literacy practices of academic disciplines and academic communities can be labeled academic literacies. Street (2005), drawing upon Lea and Street (1997) (cf. also Lea, Academic Literacies in Theory and Practice, Volume 2) identifies three heuristic models for acquiring the literacy practices of an academic discipline/academic community. The skills model focuses on instructing students in the skills needed to engage in the literacy practices of the academic discipline, often by isolating the skills and sequencing their mastery. The socialization model focuses on having students acquire literacy practices by engaging in those practices with more knowledgeable others (e.g., masters) within the context of the academic discipline/community. As the student becomes more adept at the set of literacy practices of the academic discipline and community, the student increasingly becomes a member of that academic discipline/community. The academic literacies model emphasizes acquisition of the literacy practices of an academic discipline/academic community in a manner similar to that of the socialization model, but also emphasizes critical reflection on those literacy practices and adaptation of those literacy practices based on what students bring to those literacy practices and the need to address new situations that are not necessarily bounded by that academic discipline/academic community. In the academic literacies model, neither the set of literacy practices nor the academic discipline/academic community are fixed and static, but both are continuously evolving and changing.

Critique and Social Action

One direction in classroom literacy practices has involved critical analysis of the worlds in which students live. Often finding roots in the literacy education theories and practices of Friere (2000), critical literacy practices focus attention on the power relations promulgated in and through texts (Baker and Luke, 1991; Comber and Simpson, 2001; Lankshear, 1997; Lankshear and Knobel, 2003; Morgan, 1997). An underlying assumption is that no text and no act of literacy is ever neutral with regard to cultural ideology and with regard to power relations. Critical literacy practices foreground interrogating texts in order to make visible those power relations. Similarly, attention is paid to the nature of literacy practices and literacy education practices themselves. Questions are asked about how a particular literacy practice or pedagogical practice structures relationships among people and how it privileges particular interpretations and understandings as opposed to others. Of special concern are those interpretations and understandings of texts and literacy practices that appear to naturalize inequitable distribution of privileges and advantage (Macedo, 1996).

Beyond critical analysis, in some classrooms literacy practices are organized to engage students in social and community action. In a series of studies reported in Egan-Robertson and Bloome (1998), students engaged in a series of ethnographic and linguistic studies of their own communities as a way to shift the context of classroom literacy practices from one which foregrounded instruction to one which foregrounded community action and purposeful inquiry. The literacy practices involved in those studies ranged from ethnographic note taking to letter writing to critical reading of community texts to report writing and presenting, among others. However, key to understanding the literacy practices was their orchestration within an ethnographic framework that enabled teachers and students to bring new epistemological understandings to constructing knowledge about their communities, identifying community issues, reporting on them to the community, and taking action. The actions taken often involved literacy practices that made visible people in the community who had made notable contributions to the community or that preserved a history and culture of a community (cf. also Larson, 2005).

FUTURE DIRECTIONS

Classroom literacy practices both influence and are influenced by the contexts in which they exist. Thus, as social, cultural, and economic contexts change, both at local levels and at broader levels, classroom literacy practices will both reflect those changes and will contribute to defining those changes. Here, three changes are considered that are likely to influence and be influenced by classroom literacy practices: the increasing integration of digital literacies into daily lives (cf. Leander and Lewis, Literacy and Internet Technologies, Volume 2; cf. Kress and van Leeuwen, 2001), increasing racial, cultural, and linguistic heterogeneity, and cultural and economic globalization.

As Lankshear and Knobel (2003) argue, it is not the increasing presence of digital literacies (what they call New Literacies) that constitutes a change in the social context, but rather that large numbers of people outside of schools (including large numbers of young people) have taken up these new literacies, adapted them to their own uses, needs, and interests, and created a series of cultural dynamics that are likely to influence the context of classroom literacies. Lankshear and Knobel note four dimensions of the change provoked by how people have taken up the new literacies:

1. Changes in "the world (objects, phenomena) to be known," resulting from the impact of digitization.
2. Changes in conceptions of knowledge and processes of "coming to know," contingent upon deeper incursions of digitization into everyday practices.
3. Changes in the constitution of "knowers," which reflect the impact of digitization.
4. Changes in the relative significance of, and balance among, different forms and modes of knowing, which are associated with the impact of digitization (p. 158).

How classroom literacy practices will respond to, contribute to, and refract those four dimensions is likely to be varied, depending as much on local contexts as on how the four dimensions above are mediated by various social institutions.

Increasing racial, cultural, and linguistic heterogeneity refers to demographic changes in geographies and social institutions, such as schools, in ways that make racial, cultural, and linguistic homogeneity less prevalent and more challenged (cf. Willis, Critical Race Theory, Volume 2). Again, it is not the heterogeneity itself that creates a changing social context of classroom literacy practices, but rather how that heterogeneity is taken up within local and broader contexts. Noting the changing demographics in the USA, Willis, Garcia, Barrera, and Harris (2003) argue for classrooms to adopt a multicultural literacy curriculum. Garcia (2003) explains that such a curriculum would foreground:

A complex understanding of culture and its relation to literacy, a strong commitment to social justice, a transformative mission, and implementation of the emancipatory paradigm (p. 2).

The taking up of a multicultural curriculum involves more than a surface level change in the nature of classroom literacy practices; it involves epistemological and ontological changes, social relationship and identity issues, changes in power relations, etc. (Enciso, 2003). Although, some classrooms have taken up a multicultural literacy curriculum as described by Willis, Garcia, Barrera, and Harris (2003), the degree to which a multicultural literacy curriculum will be taken up and redefine classroom literacy practices more broadly may depend on how changing demographics are incorporated in schools and how such incorporation is mediated by other social institutions at the local and broader level.

Globalization can be defined as a historical process through which there is increasing interaction among people globally across economic, cultural, and linguistic domains (cf. Luke and Carrington, 2002). Whether globalization involves increasing standardizing of cultural and linguistic practices and increasing centralizing of economic decision making and control is debatable. Regardless, as globalization extends even to remote rural areas, classroom literacy practices are influenced by the economic, cultural, and linguistic dilemmas, opportunities, and problems globalization entails. Within local contexts, people will increasingly have to struggle with how to balance maintenance of their local culture, community and ways of life with preparing their children for a world in which access to economic, intellectual, academic, cultural, and material resources will depend on being able to interact on a global level and address what people are doing elsewhere in the world (cf. Brandt and Clinton, 2002). Communities will variously choose to resist, to adapt themselves, to balance between the local and the global, to incorporate globalization within their own economic, cultural, and linguistic frames, or some combination. Such choices will affect classroom literacy practices as such choices shift the epistemological context and the context of social relationships.

REFERENCES

Applebee, A.: 1984, *Contexts for Learning to Write: Studies of Secondary School Instruction*, Ablex, Norwood, NJ.

Au, K.: 1980, 'Participation structures in a reading lesson with Hawaiian children', *Anthropology and Education Quarterly* 11(2), 91–115.

Baker, C. and Luke, C. (eds.): 1991, *Toward a Critical Sociology of Reading Pedagogy*, John Benjamins, Philadelphia.

Bloome, D., Puro, P., and Theodorou, E.: 1989, 'Procedural display and classroom lessons', *Curriculum Inquiry* 19(3), 265–291.

Bloome, D., Carter, S., Christian, B.M., Otto, S., and Shuart-Faris, N.: 2005, *Discourse Analysis and the Study of Classroom Language and Literacy Events – a Microethnographic Perspective*, Erlbaum, Mahwah, NJ.

Borko, H. and Eisenhart, M.: 1987, 'Reading ability groups as literacy communities', in D. Bloome (ed.), *Classrooms and Literacy*, Ablex, Norwood, NJ, 107–134.

Brandt, D. and Clinton, K.: 2002, 'Limits of the Local: Expanding perspectives on literacy as a social practice', *Journal of Literacy Research* 34(3), 337–356.

Cazden, C., John, V., and Hymes, D. (eds.): 1972, *Functions of Language in the Classroom*, Teachers College Press, New York.

Comber, B. and Simpson, A. (eds.): 2001, *Negotiating Critical Literacies in Classrooms*, Erlbaum, Mahwah, NJ.

Cook-Gumperz, J. (ed.): 1986, *The Social Construction of Literacy*, Cambridge University Press, New York.

Egan-Robertson, A. and Bloome, D. (eds.): 1998, *Students as Researchers of Culture and Language in Their Own Communities*, Hampton Press, Cresskill, NJ.

Enciso, P.: 2003, 'Reading discrimination', in S. Green and D. Apt-Perkins (eds.), *Making Race Visible: Literacy Research for Cultural Understanding*, Teachers College Press, New York.

Friere, P.: 2000, *Pedagogy of the Oppressed*, (thirtieth anniversary edition), Continuum International Publishing Group, New York.

Garcia, G.: 2003, 'Introduction: Giving voice to multicultural literacy research and practice', in A.I. Willis, G.E. Garcia, R. Barrera, and V. Harris (eds.), *Multicultural Issues in Literacy Research and Practice*, Erlbaum, Mahwah, NJ, 1–10.

Gay, G. and Banks, J.: 2000, *Culturally Responsive Teaching: Theory, Practice and Research*, Teachers College Press, New York.

Gee, J.P.: 2004, *Situated Language and Learning: A Critique of Traditional Schooling*, Routledge, New York.

Gonzales, N., Moll, L., and Amanti, C. (eds.): 2005, *Funds of Knowledge: Theorizing Practices in Households, Communities, and Practices*, Erlbaum, Mahwah, NJ.

Gutierrez, K., Rymes, B., and Larson, J.: 1995, 'Script, counterscript, and underlife in the classroom: James Brown versus Brown v. Board of Education', *Harvard Educational Review*, 65(3), 445–471.

Heath, S.: 1983, *Ways with Words*, Cambridge University Press, Cambridge, UK.

Kress, G. and van Leeuwen, T.: 2001, *Multimodal Discourse: The Modes and Media of Contemporary Communication*, Arnold, London.

Ladson-Billings, G.: 1994, *Dreamkeepers: Successful Teachers of African-American Children*, Josey-Bass, New York.

Ladson-Billings, G.: 2005, 'Reading, writing, and race: Literacy practices of teachers in diverse classrooms', in T. McCarty (eds.), *Language, Literacy, and Power in Schooling*. Lawrence Erlbaum Publishers, Mahwah, NJ.

Lankshear, C.: 1997, *Changing Literacies*, Open University Press, Buckingham and Philadelphia.

Lankshear, C. and Knobel, M.: 2003, *New Literacies: Changing Knowledge and Classroom Learning*, Open University Press, Philadelphia.

Larson, J.: 2005, 'Breaching the classroom walls: Literacy learning across time and space in an elementary school in the United States', in B. Street (ed.), *Literacies Across Educational Contexts*, Caslon Press, Philadelphia.

Lea, M. and Street, B.: 1997, "Student Writing and Faculty Feedback in Higher Education: an Academic Literacies Approach". in *Studies in Higher Education* Vol, 23 No.2.

Lee, C.: 1997, 'Bridging home and school literacies: Models for culturally responsive teaching, a case for African-American English', in J. Flood, S. Heath, and D. Lapp (eds.), *Handbook of Research on Teaching Literacy Through the Communicative and Visual Arts*, Simon & Schuster Macmillan, New York, 334–345.

Luke, A. and Carrington, V.: 2002, 'Globalisation, literacy, curriculum practice' in R. Fisher, G. Brooks, and M. Lewis (eds.), *Raising Standards in Literacy*, Routledge/Falmer; London.

Macedo, D.: 1996, 'Literacy for stupidification: The pedagogy of big lies', in P. Leistyna, A. Woodrum, and S. Sherblom (eds.), *Breaking Free: The Transformative Power of Critical Pedagogy*, Harvard Educational Review, Cambridge, MA, 31–58.

Maybin, J.: (in press), 'Literacy under and over the desk: oppositions and heterogeneity' *Language in Education* Vol, 21 No.6.

Michaels, S.: 1981, '"Sharing time": Children's narrative styles and differential access to literacy', *Language in Society* 10(3), 423–442.

Moll, L., Amanti, C., Neff, D., and Gonzalez, N.: 1992, 'Funds of knowledge for teaching: Using a qualitative approach to connect homes and classrooms', *Theory into Practice*, XXXI (2), 131–141.

Morgan, W.: 1997, *Critical Literacy in the Classroom: The Art of the Possible.* Routledge and Paul Chapman Publishing, London.

Moss, B. (ed.): 1994, *Literacy Across Communities*, Hampton Press, Cresskill, NJ.

Nystrand, M.: 2006, 'Research on the role of classroom discourse as it affects reading comprehension', *Research in the Teaching of English* 40, 392–412.

Ogbu, J.: 1974, *The Next Generation; An Ethnography of Education in an Urban Neighborhood*, Academic Press, New York.

Ogbu, J. and Simons, H.: 1998, 'Voluntary and involuntary minorities: A cultural-ecological theory of school performance and some implications for education', *Anthropology and Education Quarterly* 29(2), 155–188.

Pahl, K. and Rowsell, J.: 2005, *Literacy and Education: Understanding the New Literacy Studies in the Classroom*, Sage Publications, Thousand Oaks, CA, London.

Richardson, E.: 2003, *African-American Literacies*, Routlede, London.

Street, B.: 1995, *Social Literacies: Critical Approaches to Literacy in Development, Ethnography and Education*, Longman, London.

Street, B. (ed.): 2005, *Literacies Across Educational Contexts*, Caslon Press, Philadelphia.

Street, B. and Street, J.: 1991,'The schooling of literacy', in D. Barton and R. Ivanic (eds.), *Writing in the Community*, Sage, London, 143–166.

Willis, A.I., Garcia, G.E., Barrera, R., and Harris, V. (eds.): 2003, *Multicultural Issues in Literacy Research and Practice*, Erlbaum, Mahwah, NJ.

Willett, J., Solsken, J., and Wilson-Keenan, J.: 1999, 'The (im)possibilities of constructing multicultural language practices in research and pedagogy', *Linguistics and Education* 10(2), 165–218.

Yeager, B., Floriani, A., and Green, J.: 1998, 'Learning to see learning in the classroom', in A. Egan-Robertson and D. Bloome (eds.) *Students as Researchers of Culture and Language in Their own Communities*, Hampton Press, Cresskill, NJ.

Section 3

Living Literacies – Social and Cultural Experience

MARCIA FARR

LITERACIES AND ETHNOLINGUISTIC DIVERSITY: CHICAGO

INTRODUCTION

Chicago, in many ways an archetypal U.S. city, has become a global city, closely linked to other places in the world economically, culturally, and linguistically. Chicago has always had links to other places in the world through its large immigrant populations, but the rapid pace of recent globalization processes has intensified these connections. Globalization, however, yields pressures that move in two directions that have implications for literacy. Increased transnational communication, especially via mass media like satellite television, facilitates the development of a global monoculture, e.g., among youth worldwide who emulate African American musical and verbal style, thus spreading English literacy in the form of song lyrics. Yet global movements toward sameness are complemented by the marked differentiation of ethnic, class and other identities at local levels. Research in a variety of Chicago communities (Farr, 2004, 2005c), for example, has shown the resilience of such multiple ethnolinguistic identities and their accompanying languages and scripts. Such ethnolinguistic identities encompass verbal styles, both oral and written, that are closely associated with ethnic/ racial, gender, class, religious, and other identities.

Identities, in fact, are inseparable from the verbal styles that characterize them: as people speak or write, they construct themselves as particular kinds of people with particular ethnic, racial, class, gender, religious, or other identities. Verbal styles that construct identities are expressed both in speaking and in literacy practices in a wide range of contexts. Across Chicago's neighborhoods, for example, many different languages are spoken, written, and read in both public and private contexts: in stores, businesses, schools, homes, community centers, religious congregations, and workplaces. Signs in these neighborhoods are in English, Spanish, Polish, Arabic, Chinese, Italian, Greek, Hindi, Russian, Korean, Thai, etc., indicating either the residential or the commercial presence of people who speak, read, and write those languages. The notable multiplicity of ethnolinguistic styles reaffirms Chicago's reputation as a vibrant, multicultural and multilingual metropolitan area. Research on this ethnolinguistic diversity is relatively scant and recent, however.

B. V. Street and N. H. Hornberger (eds), Encyclopedia of Language and Education,
2nd Edition, Volume 2: Literacy, 265–282.
©*2010 Springer Science+Business Media LLC.*

EARLY DEVELOPMENTS

Historical research has documented that, from its beginnings, Chicago has been multicultural and multilingual (Holli and Jones, 1995). Most historical or current studies of Chicago, however, focus on ethnic populations or neighborhoods, rather than on languages or literacies, although insights can be inferred from such work. Chicago's earliest inhabitants, for example, were primarily Miami and Illinois Native American tribes in villages located along various waterways. In their indigenous languages, they called the area *Checagou*. The coming of the European fur trade between 1760 and 1800 profoundly changed local Indian cultures, resulting in cultural and linguistic loss as tribes merged into a pan-Indian culture. French and English were introduced at this time by French and Anglo-Saxon fur traders, the former notably including Jean Baptiste Point du Sable, a French- and African-descent French speaker from Haiti considered the founder of Chicago who undoubtedly spoke Haitian Creole as well as French, and possibly Potawatomi, the Native American language of his wife, as well (Cameron, 2006). Many European fur traders, especially the French, intermarried with Indian women, resulting in cultural and linguistic mixtures both among Indians and among whites. According to Jacqueline Peterson (1995, p. 24) "Most white traders ... blended into the pan-Indian culture developing in the Great Lakes region, learning Ojibway, the *lingua franca* of the trade, as their Indian counterparts learned a French *patois*." It is unclear how much of this trade was carried on only with oral language, or whether some literacy, perhaps with the French alphabet, was involved.

Another major change occurred when Yankee entrepreneurs from the east, notably John Jacob Astor and his American Fur Company, monopolized the region between 1811 and 1834. During this period Chicago was comprised entirely of "middlemen traders and their employees— clerks, *voyageurs*, and *engagés* of French, British, American, Indian, and mixed extraction" (Peterson, 1995, p. 25). Yankees, southerners from Virginia, French-Indian *métis* (of mixed race) and Indians shocked newly arrived easterners by socializing together in this frontier space, dancing and drinking to French fiddles. Clearly, if they socialized together, there must have been substantial bilingualism involving French, English, and Native American languages, most probably Ojibway. Moreover, the trading business clearly required not only the use of all these languages, but commercial literacy as well, at least in English, probably in French, and, using the French or English alphabet, possibly in Ojibway. After Chicago became an incorporated city in 1833, easterners continued to arrive, while most French, French-Indian *métis*, and Indians, faced with Anglo-Saxon control and attitudes of superiority, moved westward, the Indians having been coerced into signing a treaty that gave up their lands in return for acreage beyond the Mississippi. The fact that Indians signed a treaty clearly indicates some literacy, although it is not clear what "signing" meant—a mark indicating agreement, or a full written name.

From the 1830s onward, eastern businessmen promoted the city as a site for self-making and ambition (Spears, 2005, p. 8), and rapid population growth ensued throughout the 19th and early 20th century. In addition to easterners, the city attracted many migrants from the rural and small town Midwest, immigrants from Europe, and southern African Americans. Although the effort to establish Chicago as a cosmopolitan center both of the Midwest and of the nation was led by "the city's upper- and middle-class elites" (Spears, 2005, p. xv), this vision was crucially supported by the migrants who came to Chicago with hopes of social and economic mobility. Between 1860 and 1890, Chicago grew from 100,000 to 1 million residents, three quarters of whom were foreign-born. All these migrants provided labor for Chicago's "rapidly expanding industrial sector" (Howenstine, 1996, p. 32). A rare publication about language in early 20th century Chicago describes the city as "an unparalleled Babel of foreign tongues" (Buck, 1903, as quoted in Cameron, 2006, p. 114). German, spoken by 500,000 people, was the most dominant language in the city, followed by Polish, Swedish, Bohemian, Norwegian and Yiddish, Dutch, Italian, Danish, French, Gaelic, Serbo-Croatian, Slovakian, and Lithuanian, all of which had at least 10,000 speakers (Cameron, 2006). Print forms of these languages were extant also, primarily as newspapers, for example in German (Holli, 1995; Kloss, 1998[1977]) and Lithuanian (Markelis, 2004).

Southern African Americans began to settle on Chicago's near west side as early as the late 1860s, but large numbers, as part of the Great Migration to northern cities, only occurred around World War I, and even more rapidly after World War II, settling primarily on the south side of the city in an area called Bronzeville (Seligman, 2005), the end of the "blues trail" that began in New Orleans and Mississippi, and it fostered not only the Chicago Blues but many other musical innovations. Thus African American verbal, including musical, styles became an important part of Chicago, and much of the south side of the city, including both middle class (Braden, 1995) and working class neighborhoods, remains the cultural heart of this repertoire of ethnolinguistic styles and literacies.

African Americans, along with Mexicans and Appalachian whites, were recruited to work in Chicago's industries after World War I restricted the supply of European immigrants to the city, the previous source of labor. Thus, in addition to African American English, Appalachian

English (Wolfram, 1980; Wolfram and Christian, 1976) was added to the city's ethnolinguistic profile. The Mexicans brought Spanish, which in recent decades has emerged as a strong second language to English in Chicago, both in speech and print, with multiple Spanish-language newspapers, radio stations, and television channels.

After being recruited as labor around World War I, Mexicans began to arrive in larger numbers during the 1920s, settling in three neighborhoods on the south and southwest side (Kerr, 1977), and in dramatically larger numbers after the immigration law of 1965 abandoned national origin quotas and provided for family reunification. Puerto Ricans became a noticeable presence during the 1950s and continued to build in numbers through the 1960s, settling on the near Northwest side of the city (Padilla, 1987; Pérez, 2004). Although American citizens, they are the poorest Latino group in the U.S. and in Chicago. Chicago's Cubans, in contrast, are largely middle class, having fled Cuba after Castro's victory in 1957, leaving behind property and businesses. In the decades after 1965 a wider variety of Latin American populations (notably Dominicans and Guatemalans) and many other Asian populations filled the city's (and Cook County's) neighborhoods. Among the Spanish-speaking, Mexicans are by far the most numerous (Casuso and Camacho, 1995, p. 369). Thus Mexican Spanish, though not the only Spanish variety in Chicago, is the dominant variety. Over one quarter of the population speaks one or another of these varieties, and the younger generations speak a Latino variety of English that is as yet unstudied.

Chinese immigrants first migrated to Chicago from California in the wake of the Chinese Exclusion Act of 1882, but significant numbers of Chinese did not arrive until after the Communist victory in China in the late 1940s, leading to the development of Chicago's first "Chinatown" on the near south side of the city in the 1950s. These early immigrants were fairly homogeneous culturally and linguistically, having been primarily Cantonese-speaking peasants from southern China. After the end of the Vietnam war in 1975, however, another group of Chinese immigrants came to Chicago, this time largely entrepreneurial ethnic Chinese from Vietnam who spoke Cantonese and Mandarin, as well as Fukien, the Chinese province from which most of them originated. This group established a second "Chinatown" on the north side of the city.

Currently, the Chinese population in Chicago is quite heterogeneous, comprising Cantonese, Indo-Chinese, Taiwanese, mainland immigrants, American-born Chinese (referred to as ABCs), and racially-mixed Chinese (Moy, 1995, p. 408). The languages they speak are equally varied, and even the writing systems they use are differentiated. Earlier Chinese immigrants maintain the traditional Chinese writing system, with its thousands of complex characters, whereas more recent immigrants from the mainland use the modern simplified system of Chinese characters developed by the Chinese Communist government. Each group is quite attached to its writing system for reasons of familiarity, but also, importantly, for reasons of identity and politics (Rohsenow, 2004).

Like the Chinese, Japanese immigrants were primarily peasant farmers who first migrated to California, but they arrived there later, during the 1880s, replacing the excluded Chinese. By the early 1900s, however, they too experienced discrimination of increasing intensity, peaking with their internment in camps during World War II. After leaving the camps, many relocated in cities to the east like Chicago, although many of them returned to the West Coast before 1960 (Osako, 1995, p. 423). In contrast to stark anti-Japanese sentiments in California, Chicago was more open to Asian immigrants. Ultimately, many of this population became middle class and moved to the suburbs. A high percentage of the second generation intermarried with European Americans, perhaps "the first nonwhites to merge biologically into the dominant American society" (Osako, 1995, p. 432). Such intermarriage initially must involve some bilingualism and complex biliteracy, since Japanese writing involves three different scripts. It is unclear, however, to what extent the Japanese language and writing system have been maintained by Chicago-born or mixed-heritage Japanese. The demographics would suggest a shift to English among Japanese Americans, but Japanese literacy is maintained in Chicago by overseas Japanese who intend to return to Japan (Miller, 2004).

CURRENT DEMOGRAPHICS: ETHNICITY, LANGUAGE, AND LITERACY

As with the historical research literature, more information is available on current ethnic and linguistic diversity in Chicago than on diversity in literacy practices, although many of the newer immigrant groups bring distinct writing systems with them.

The 2003 American Community Survey by the U.S. Census Bureau indicated the city to be about 42% white, 37% African American, 26% Hispanic, and 4% Asian. Although the percentage of Asians is low, as a group they increased from 1980 to 1990 in the city by 50% and in the suburbs by 104%. The largest group in these percentages is Indian (who also showed the largest increase), followed by Filipino, then Chinese and Korean, then Japanese, Vietnamese, Cambodian, and Thai (Ahne, 1995, p. 483). These groups bring many different languages to Chicago, including at least one distinct variety of global English, Indian English. Moreover, many of these languages come with writing systems different from the alphabet used with English, Spanish, and many other European languages. For example, Chinese languages, grouped into seven major dialects, are written with Chinese characters that are part ideographic and part phonetic, being based on syllables and morphemes (Rogers, 2005). Two of these languages, Cantonese and Mandarin (the national standard taught in schools) are the primary Chinese languages in Chicago, and written Mandarin is used in newspapers, books (in bookstores and libraries), a Chinese Yellow Pages, and other media. Both languages are used on global television and radio and are taught in heritage language schools (Rohsenow, 2004). Korean and Japanese, genetically related to each other, but not to Chinese, adapted Chinese characters for their own writing systems. Today, written Japanese uses three sets of symbols and Korean uses an alphabet, Hankul, devised in the 15th century, although other forms of writing were already in use (Rogers, 2005). Both of these written languages, along with written Thai and other literacies, appear in signs and in printed material in several neighborhoods in Chicago and its suburbs.

The 2004 American Community Survey of the U.S. Census Bureau for the city of Chicago shows that slightly over a third of the population 5 years of age and older (34.3%) speak a language other than English. This number includes those who also speak English, but students entering Chicago Public Schools who do not speak English are entitled to 3 years of bilingual education at the level at which they enter school. Of non-English languages, which span all the continents of the world, the numerically important ones are Spanish (71%), Polish (6.3%), Chinese languages (3.8%), other Asian languages (3.1%), Tagalog (2.3%), languages of India—primarily Gujarati and Hindi—(2.1%), French (including creoles) (1.7%), and Arabic (1.5%). Although these figures show a wide range of languages and writing systems, clearly the predominant non-English language is Spanish, followed distantly, but significantly, by Polish, due to continuing immigration from Poland.

Spanish speakers, however, dominate these statistics, and roughly two-thirds of the Spanish speakers are of Mexican origin. Mexicans now move not only into traditional Mexican neighborhoods, but also into Puerto Rican and other Latino neighborhoods, and into "white ethnic" and some African American neighborhoods. The map, Latino Population by Community Area (see Figure 1), shows that Latinos can be found in almost all neighborhoods of the city, and they are a significant presence as well in the counties surrounding the city, north to the Wisconsin border, southeast to the Indiana border (and in northwest Indiana), and to the west of the city. Although numerically remarkable, the current preponderance of Spanish speakers is similar to that of German speakers over a century ago throughout

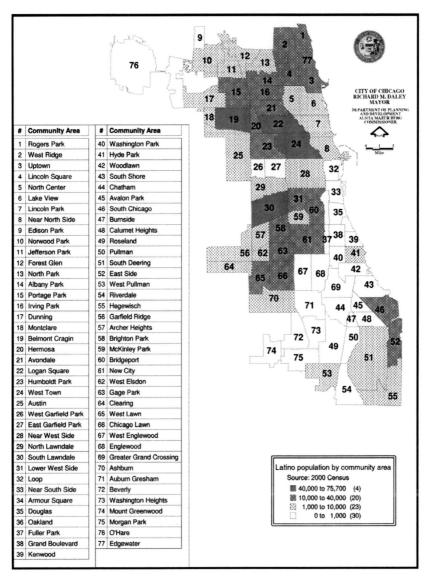

#	Community Area	#	Community Area
1	Rogers Park	40	Washington Park
2	West Ridge	41	Hyde Park
3	Uptown	42	Woodlawn
4	Lincoln Square	43	South Shore
5	North Center	44	Chatham
6	Lake View	45	Avalon Park
7	Lincoln Park	46	South Chicago
8	Near North Side	47	Burnside
9	Edison Park	48	Calumet Heights
10	Norwood Park	49	Roseland
11	Jefferson Park	50	Pullman
12	Forest Glen	51	South Deering
13	North Park	52	East Side
14	Albany Park	53	West Pullman
15	Portage Park	54	Riverdale
16	Irving Park	55	Hegewisch
17	Dunning	56	Garfield Ridge
18	Montclare	57	Archer Heights
19	Belmont Cragin	58	Brighton Park
20	Hermosa	59	McKinley Park
21	Avondale	60	Bridgeport
22	Logan Square	61	New City
23	Humboldt Park	62	West Elsdon
24	West Town	63	Gage Park
25	Austin	64	Clearing
26	West Garfield Park	65	West Lawn
27	East Garfield Park	66	Chicago Lawn
28	Near West Side	67	West Englewood
29	North Lawndale	68	Englewood
30	South Lawndale	69	Greater Grand Crossing
31	Lower West Side	70	Ashburn
32	Loop	71	Auburn Gresham
33	Near South Side	72	Beverly
34	Armour Square	73	Washington Heights
35	Douglas	74	Mount Greenwood
36	Oakland	75	Morgan Park
37	Fuller Park	76	O'Hare
38	Grand Boulevard	77	Edgewater
39	Kenwood		

CITY OF CHICAGO
RICHARD M. DALEY
MAYOR
DEPARTMENT OF PLANNING
AND DEVELOPMENT
ALICIA MAZUR BERG
COMMISSIONER

Miles

Latino population by community area
Source: 2000 Census
■ 40,000 to 75,700   (4)
▩ 10,000 to 40,000 (20)
▨ 1,000 to 10,000   (23)
□ 0 to 1,000   (30)

Figure 1 Latino population by community area. Source: 2000 census.

the Great Lakes states of Ohio, Indiana, Illinois, and Wisconsin.
Massive migrations of German speakers throughout the 19th century
vastly outnumbered the speakers of other languages, including English
in some places (Kamhoefner, Helbich, and Sommer, 1991; Trommler
and McVeigh, 1985).

Currently, Spanish speakers in Chicago comprise (in order of population size) Mexicans, Puerto Ricans, Guatemalans, Ecuadorians, Cubans, Colombians, Spaniards, Salvadorans, Hondurans, Peruvian, Dominicans, Argentineans, Nicaraguans, Chileans, Panamanians, Costa Ricans, Venezuelans, Bolivians, Uruguayans, and Paraguayans (Farr and Domínguez, 2005). These groups speak different varieties of Spanish, and some of them may speak indigenous languages such as Quechua or Zapotec as well. In many Caribbean varieties of Spanish, for example Cuban or Puerto Rican, speakers tend to aspirate *s*, as in *e'ta'* for *estas* (you are). No research has yet clarified if these varieties are blending in Chicago, or if speakers of other varieties adopt features of the dominant Mexican Spanish.

Even within national varieties of Spanish, vernacular and regional dialects differ from standard popular Spanish; for example, the group of rural Mexicans known as *rancheros* use archaic features in their speech and writing (Farr, 2005b, 2006), although this dialect is denigrated by educated Mexicans, and Spanish teachers in Chicago, as *español ranchereado* (ranch Spanish). For example, a woman who participates in a Catholic Charismatic prayer circle writes letters to God with some *ranchero* dialect features:

Padre Yavé	*Father Yahweh*
te pido que redames [derrames]	*I ask that you pour*
tus gracias el dia del	*your grace the day of the*
vautismo en el Espiritu	*baptism in the Holy*
Santo en tus hijos	*Spirit over your children*
que estamos en las	*who are in the*
claces de Evangelisación	*classes of Evangelization*

The above excerpt of a letter shows the use of the rural vernacular *redames* instead of the standard *derrames* (pour out), as well as non-standard spelling based on speech, as in *v* for *b* in *vautismo* (baptism) for *bautismo* (Guerra and Farr, 2002). Two years of primary school in rural Mexico did not "correct" these features of her oral language, but they did allow her to develop fluent religious literacy.

In fact, standard languages have rarely been used by immigrants to Chicago; Lithuanian (Markelis, 2004) and Swedish (Isaacson, 2004) immigrants, among others, spoke vernacular dialects of their respective languages, then learned standard varieties of these languages in Chicago in order to communicate with each other and to read ethnic newspapers. Moreover, as often happens with languages in contact (Winford, 2003), language mixing occurs naturally. English words appear in both oral and written Spanish; one sign above a *cantina* (bar) in a Mexican neighborhood boasts, *Tenemos* Via Satellite (We have satellite TV).

Code-switching between Spanish and English is common among Texas-origin Mexican Americans in Chicago (*tejanos*), and it is more frequent among Puerto Ricans than Mexicans. Although such "Spanglish" is often as denigrated as vernacular dialects are, in fact this is a common occurrence in all immigrant populations. In Chicago, for example, Greeks (Koliussi, 2004) and Swedes (Isaacson, 2004) used "Greeklish" and "Swinglish;" in a common pattern of code-mixing, Swedes borrowed English words into Swedish and used them with Swedish conjunctions, articles, and suffixes, as in *storet* (the store) rather than the standard Swedish *handel* or *affär* (Isaacson, 2004, p. 224). Such mixing of languages can be seen in both oral and written uses of language, as is evident in a Spanish conversation (for English translation, see Table 1 for transcript) in which Mexican women insert Polish and English words and in a photo of signs (see Figure 2) in Spanish and English in a Mexican neighborhood.

Today there is a rich variety of dialects in all languages used in Chicago, including a regional English in which whites, but not African Americans, pronounce The White Sox as "the white sacks" (Cameron, 2006). Morgan (2004), moving beyond pronunciation to discourse, describes how African American vernacular is used aesthetically to construct gender identities in south side neighborhoods of Chicago. Lindquist (2004) and Cho and Miller (2004), illustrate dialect diversity in the differing rhetorical styles used by Chicago's working and middle class white population. Thus language varieties differ both in terms of structural features such as pronunciation and syntax, and in their stylistic dimensions, what Hymes (1974) called "ways of speaking." Like ways of speaking, literacy practices also construct important aspects of identity, whether linked to class, race/ethnicity, gender, or other identities (such as religious or political). The next section reviews studies of such identity construction in both speaking and literacy practices across a range of ethnic populations.

MAJOR CONTRIBUTIONS AND WORK IN PROGRESS

Because most ethnolinguistic research in Chicago is so recent, and much of it is still ongoing, this section will combine these two sections, showing how people construct different aspects of their identities via a range of speech genres and literacy practices. Domínguez (2005, p. 77) shows how the use of proverbs constructs people in a Mexican transnational social network as having "sharp wit, facility of expression, and adherence to traditional values." The use of traditional Mexican proverbs affirms the solidarity of the network and approved social values, but it also distinguishes the individuals who use them as wise and

Table 1 Transcript, Playing with Race

1	D: *Yo no te veo delgada.*	D: I don't see you as slender.
2	B: *Pues no pero-*	B: Well, no, but—
3	L: *Pero ella quiere más-*	L: But she wants more—
4	B: *Estoy como la calidad del tordo al revés.*	B: I am like a bird, but in reverse.
5	D: {Laughs}	D: {Laughs}
6	L: *Ella quiere tener más...*	L: She wants to have more...
7	B: *Más piernas. Más/?/.*	B: More legs. More/?/.
8	W: *No, un poquito más pompis.*	W: No, a little more rear end.
9	L:*¿Tú sabes qué es dupa?*	L: Do you know what *dupa* is?
10	B:*¿Es qué?*	B: It's what?
11	L:*¿En qué idioma te estoy hablando?*	L: In what language am I speaking to you?
12	B: *No, no sé.*	B: No, I don't know.
13	L: *Polaco.* {laughs}	L: Polish. {laughs}
14	B: *Ay, en polaco es todo/?/.*	B: Oh, in Polish it's all/?/.
15	**L: *Fíjate nomás el progreso.* [ironic tone]**	**L: Just look at the progress. [ironic tone]**
16	**Women: {Much loud laughter}**	**Women: {Much loud laughter}**
17	B: *Ya de lo que–¿ya pasástes al qué?*	B: Now from that – now you've passed on to what?
18	L: *No, no todo.*	L: No, not really.
19	W:*¿A cómo/?/?*	W: How/?/?
20	B:*¿Cómo se dice en inglés pompi?*	B: How do you say in English *pompi*?
21	D: Butt.	D: Butt.
22	B: *Ya de eso ya pasástes a polaco y todo. Para el próximo año ya vas a hablar chino y* {laughter} *chan chan chan.*	B: Now from that you've passed on to Polish and everything. Next year you're going to speak Chinese and {laughter} chan chan chan.
23	D: *Como el novio de V dice "Yo sí se francés, yo sí sé frances" y le hace V bien callada, "Sí pero cuando se l–se le acaba el francés le entra el italiano."* {Laughter}	D: Like V's boyfriend says, "I can speak French, I can speak French," and V says real quiet, "Yes, but when the French finishes, the Italian begins." {Laughter}

Continued

Table 1 Continued

24	B: *¿Por qué¿De dónde es él?*	B: Why? Where is he from?
25	Young Women: *¡ES MEXICANO!*	Young Women: HE'S MEXICAN!
26	D: *Pero es puras mentiras, no sabe.*	D: But it's just lies, he doesn't know.
27	B: *Mexicano, hasta las cachas.*	B: Mexican, to the hilt!
28	L: *No, el mexicano va saber pero tarasco.*	L: No, the Mexican is going to know Tarascan.
29	D: **Oh *sí.***	D: **Oh yes.**
30	B: **Oh *sí.***	B: **Oh yes.**
31	D: *Pinche indios.* {Giggling}	D: **Damn Indians.** {Giggling}
32	B: *Ehi, calmada con los indios, yo soy india.*	B: **Hey, take it easy on the Indians, I am Indian.**
33	D: *Todos nosotros, todos. {pause} No me ves el pinche nopal/?/que me sale una tuna ahí.* {laughs}	D: **All of us, all. {pause} Don't you see the damned nopal/?/that the fruit comes out here {laughs}**
34	B: *El nopal* {laughing}.	B: **The nopal {laughing}.**
35	W: *Ay ay ay.*	W: Ay ay ay.
36	L: *Ay, como son tremendas.*	B: Oh, how audacious you all are.

knowledgeable. Farr (2005a) shows how Mexicans from a *ranchero* background construct themselves as independent individuals with a frank speech style that is direct, candid, and down-to-earth. Inasmuch as this speech style constructs the *ranchero* ideology of liberal individualism, it contrasts sharply with the communal identities attributed to non-*ranchero* Indian Mexicans. Both studies of transnational families, then, show Mexicans constructing identities of personhood via sanctioned ways of speaking. Domínguez (2002) develops the implications for literacy by showing how the complex cognitive processes required to correctly interpret a proverb used in context can be utilized in the teaching of writing. The link between proverbs and literacy goes back centuries, since, as Pérez (1988) points out, proverbs are quite likely the oldest surviving texts of Western and other civilizations.

Lindquist (2001, 2004) also links oral rhetoric to literacy; she shows how class identities can conflict when working class students learn to write at the university, arguing that "the domain of argument itself is a site of class struggle" (Lindquist, 2001, p. 262). The verbal style of academic argument is culturally and historically specific (Farr, 1993),

Figure 2 Chicago bilingual and biliterate street scene.

and using it as "real work" strikes those from working class cultures as oddly privileged, especially since work for them is action-oriented and productive, and verbal argument a matter of play, not work. Cho and Miller (2004) similarly distinguish white working class and middle class verbal styles, showing how "working class families privilege personal storytelling in a way that middle class families do not" (Cho and Miller, 2004, p. 99). They also note that working class mothers co-narrating young children's experiences are more direct and forthright than middle class mothers. This linking of a direct verbal style with working class speakers evokes the *franqueza* of the rural Mexicans in Farr's study (Farr, 2005a, 2006). Herrick's (2005) study of workplace communication at a factory in Chicago also shows how class differences can emerge in literacy practices. While translating a brochure into Spanish to initiate new workers, Mexican workers of different class backgrounds (rural *ranchero* vs. urban educated) argue vehemently about whether to use "correct" Spanish or the language of the "people on the [factory] floor" (Herrick, 2005, p. 372).

Moss (2003, 2004) shows how the verbal style of African American sermons (for example, using the pronoun *we* rather than *you* and personal testimonials) constructs the minister as a humble member of the community, rather than one who is superior to it. The genre of sermons is particularly interesting, in that it seems to be both a speech and a literacy event: delivered orally, sermons are sometimes prepared in writing, and they are often based on religious text (cf. Besnier, 1995). Reynolds (2004) also focuses on a religious genre: prayers at Ibo association meetings that coalesce the physical distance between Chicago and Nigeria. Here prayers are used both to build transnational solidarity and to distinguish the individual creating the prayer as verbally astute, like the user of proverbs in Dominguez's (2005) Mexican families. Finally, as discussed above, literacy practices that construct a religious identity are found in Guerra and Farr (2002) and Farr (2005b), which discuss how a Mexican woman constructs herself as authoritative both in her oral religious discourse and in the letters she writes to God as part of her Charismatic prayer circle. As she builds an ideology of personhood with her frank *ranchero* dialect of Mexican Spanish, she simultaneously creates a gendered, religious, and political identity.

Nardini (1999, 2004) analyzes Italian women's use of *bella figura* (literally, beautiful figure, or good impression) in their discourse at a social club. Here women use verbal art to perform in ways that are consonant with the Italian cultural construction of verbal and visual beauty, but that also construct gender identities that are not submissive. Cohen (2005) also focuses on gender identities, but with literacy practices. She shows how second-generation Mexican high school girls experiment with both gender and ethnic identities on the internet by participating in chat rooms and developing relationships online. Computer and internet literacy allows these girls to try out possible selves from the safety of their homes: they "get out of the house" without disobeying parental restrictions that keep them, but not their brothers, at home.

Del Valle (2005) contrasts the verbal practices of two families, one of which experiences more social and economic success than the other. The family that uses literacy regularly for religious and political purposes (much of it in Spanish) and emphasizes Puerto Rican oral traditions, e.g., *rosarios cantados* (sung rosaries), also achieves some upward mobility that involves specific work literacies. The other family, using primarily English and leisure time literacy (e.g., reading magazines), seems unable to move out of their precarious economic position. Interestingly, although both families appear demographically similar, one of them illustrates "the behaviors, values, and literacy practices" of more mainstream populations (Heath, 1983). This cautions against making facile generalizations about entire demographic groups and indicates that literacy practices that construct religious, political, and cultural identities can have positive effects in life trajectories.

Many of these studies of ethnolinguistic diversity in Chicago bring transnational relations into sharp relief. Cohen (2003), for example, describes how high school girls in Chicago who pretend to be *chilangos* (residents of Mexico City) in Internet chat rooms have their true identities discovered through the "lexical and morphologic variations" (Cohen, 2005, p. 196) in the Spanish that they write. Thus people online recreate national, gender, and other identities solely through the available clues in literacy. This is yet another example of how literacy practices construct identity, although on this occasion inadvertently. Similarly, Hurtig (2005) shows how adult women construct gendered Mexican identities and thus resist assimilation through the pieces they write and publish in a locally-produced magazine.

Both Rohsenow (2004) and Markelis (2004) discuss political identities as constructed by literacy practices. Rohsenow (2004) shows transnational influences on literacy practices among Chicago's Chinese populations: earlier immigrants read and write the traditional Chinese writing system, refusing to use the simplified characters devised during the 1950s by the People's Republic of China, arguing that this move on the part of the then-new Communist government was a "deliberate attempt to cut off China's people from thousands of years of traditional Chinese culture and values" (Rohsenow, 2004, p. 338). Markelis (2004) describes the considerable efforts by Lithuanians in Chicago to maintain their language, both oral and written, through Lithuanian parochial schools, mass media, and ethnic churches. Migrating in large numbers from 1881 to 1920, the Lithuanian press only ceased operating in Chicago in the late 1970s. Markelis attributes this to the fact that "Concerns about the possibility of linguistic annihilation were widespread among Lithuanian immigrants, who had experienced suppression of their language during the 42 years of the czarist press ban" (Markelis, 2004, p. 282). Having been forced to use (and go to school in) Russian instead, and having secretly fought to use Lithuanian, Lithuanians in the diaspora refused to give it up when they had the freedom to speak and publish it freely. Lithuanian newspapers published both in Chicago and in Lithuania especially served to connect people in this transnational ethnic community by reporting on events and circulating in both places.

Thus both historically and currently, ethnolinguistic practices in Chicago are inextricably linked to events, people, and institutions in their places of origin. Politics, educational practices, local linguistic characteristics, religious traditions, class relations, gender orders, and cultural values in the "homeland" do not determine, though they do influence, what happens in Chicago, and these, as well as other dimensions of life "back home," are necessary to understand transnational (and internal migrant) communities in Chicago. From its beginnings, ethnic diversity in Chicago implies linguistic diversity in both oral and written forms. The world's languages and dialects, used alone and mixed with each other or English, create vibrant communities with a range of oral and written genres.

PROBLEMS AND DIFFICULTIES

As is typical of new research directions, studies of ethnolinguistic diversity in Chicago explore the subject with a variety of approaches and findings. Unlike the early historical research on ethnic diversity in Chicago, which traced the historical trajectories of various populations in similar ways, language-focused research has yielded understandings as diverse as the populations and languages or dialects under study. Although united under the general framework of the ethnography of communication (Hymes, 1974; Saville-Troike, 2003), some studies focus on oral genres such as sermons, prayers, proverbs, arguments, and personal narratives; others focus on written genres such as letters, newspapers and magazines, books, workplace brochures and reports, and journal narratives; and yet others focus on how language, oral or written, constructs various aspects of identity. Eventually, a more theoretically-focused set of studies across populations would be useful.

FUTURE RESEARCH DIRECTIONS

In addition to developing a more shared theoretical and content focus, future research could expand the range of populations studied. Although research has begun to describe the myriad ways in which people in Chicago use various languages in speaking, reading, and writing, this research is quite recent and does not include, for example, Polish, Indian, Korean, and Native American language and literacy practices, even though these populations have a notable presence in Chicago. Such studies could explore not only Chicago-based varieties of languages and their accompanying literacies, but also the varieties of English that have evolved among various groups in Chicago (e.g., Latino English, Indian English, etc). Finally, studies of groups that are limited to Chicago could be extended globally to include comparative sites: Does the *bella figura* of Italians in Chicago differ from that expressed in Italy? Does the English used by Ibos in Chicago differ in significant ways from the African English used in Nigeria? This final example suggests yet another direction for future research: how much interaction is there among the various ethnolinguistic groups in Chicago, and does interaction lead to yet newer varieties of language and/or new, hybrid literacy practices?

REFERENCES

Ahne, J.: 1995, 'Koreans of Chicago: The new entrepreneurial immigrants', in G. Holli and P. d'A. Jones (eds.), *Ethnic Chicago: A multicultural portrait*, Eerdmans, Grand Rapids, MI, 463–500.

Besnier, N.: 1995, *Literacy, emotion, and authority: Reading and writing on a Polyne-sian atoll*, Cambridge University Press, Cambridge.

Bousfield, M. *Map of Latino Population by community area based on 2000 U.S. Census.*

Braden, W.: 1995, 'Chatham: An African-American success story', in M.G. Holli and P.d'A. Jones (eds.), *Ethnic Chicago: A multicultural portrait*, Eerdmans, Grand Rapids, MI, 341–345.

Cameron, R.: 2006, 'Words of the windy city (Chicago, IL)', in W. Wolfram and B. Ward (eds.), *American voices: How dialects differ from coast to coast*, Blackwell Oxford, 113–117.

Casuso, J. and Camacho, E.: 1995, 'Latino Chicago', in M.G. Holli and P.d'A. Jones (eds.), *Ethnic Chicago: A multicultural portrait*, Eerdmans, Grand Rapids, MI,346–377.

Cho, G. and Miller, P.: 2004, 'Personal storytelling: Working-class and middle-class mothers in comparative perspective', in M. Farr (ed.), *Ethnolinguistic Chicago: Language and literacy in the city's neighborhoods*, Erlbaum, Mahwah, NJ, 79–101.

Cohen, J.: 2003, *Creativity within constraints: Language, identity, and U.S.-born Mexican girls in Southeast Chicago*, Unpublished dissertation, University of Illinois at Chicago.

Cohen, J.: 2005, 'Global links from the post-industrial heartland: Language, Internet use, and identity development among U.S.-born Mexican high school girls', in M. Farr (ed.), *Latino language and literacy in ethnolinguistic Chicago*, Erlbaum, Mahwah, NJ187–215.

Del Valle, T.: 2005, ''Successful' and 'unsuccessful' literacies of two Puerto Rican families in Chicago', in M. Farr (ed.), *Latino language and literacy in ethnolin-guistic Chicago*, Erlbaum, Mahwah, NJ, 97–131.

Domínguez, E.: 2005, 'Sociocognitive aspects of proverb use in a Mexican transnational social network', in M. Farr (ed.), *Latino language and literacy in ethnolinguistic Chicago*, Erlbaum, Mahwah, NJ, 67–95.

Elias Dominguez.: 2002, *Reconciling cognitive universals and cultural particulars: A Mexican social network's use of proverbs*, Unpublished dissertation, University of Illinois at Chicago.

Farr, M.: 1993, 'Essayist literacy and other verbal performances', *Written Communica-tion*, 10(1), 4–38.

Farr, M. (ed.): 2004, *Ethnolinguistic Chicago: Language and literacy in the city's neighborhoods*, Erlbaum, Mahwah, NJ.

Farr, M.: 2005a, '¡A mí no manda nadie! Individualism and identity in Mexican ranchero speech', in M. Farr (ed.), *Latino language and literacy in ethnolinguistic Chicago*, Erlbaum, Mahwah, NJ, 35–65.

Farr, M.: 2005b, 'Literacy and religion: Reading, writing, and gender among Mexican women in Chicago', in M. Farr (ed.), *Latino language and literacy in ethnolin-guistic Chicago*, Erlbaum, Mahwah, NJ, 305–321.

Farr, M. (ed.): 2005c, *Latino language and literacy in ethnolinguistic Chicago*, Erlbaum, Mahwah, NJ.

Farr, M.: 2006, *Rancheros in Chicagoacán: Language and identity in a transnational community*, University of Texas Press, Austin.

Farr, M. and Domínguez, E.: 2005, 'Latinos and diversity in a global city: Language and identity at home, school, church, and work', in M. Farr (ed.), *Latino language and literacy in ethnolinguistic Chicago*, Erlbaum, Mahwah, NJ, 3–32.

Guerra, J. and Farr, M.: 2002, 'Writing on the margins: The spiritual and autobio-graphical discourse of two *mexicanas* in Chicago', in G. Hull and K. Schultz (eds.), *School's out! Bridging out-of-school literacies with classroom practices*, Teachers College Press, New York, 96–123.

Heath, S.B.: 1983, *Ways with words: Language, life, and work in communities and classrooms*, Cambridge University Press, Cambridge.

Herrick, J.W.: 2005, 'What it means to speak the same language: An ethnolinguistic study of workplace communication', in M. Farr (ed.), *Latino language and literacy in ethnolinguistic Chicago*, Erlbaum, Mahwah, NJ, 351–377.

Holli, M.G. and d'A. Jones, P. (eds.): 1995[1997], *Ethnic Chicago: A Multicultural Portrait*, William B. Eerdmans Publishing Co., Grand Rapids.

Holli, M.G.: 1995, 'German American Ethnic and Cultural Identity from 1890 Onward', in M.G. Holli and P.d'A. Jones (eds.), *Ethnic Chicago: A Multicultural Portrait*, William B. Eerdmans Publishing Co., Grand Rapids, 93–109.

Howenstine, E.: 1996, 'Ethnic change and segregation in Chicago', in C.C. Roseman, H.D. Laux, and G. Thieme (eds.), *EthniCity: Geographic perspectives on ethnic change in modern cities*, Rowman and Littlefield, New York, 31–49.

Hurtig, J.: 2005, 'Resisting assimilation: Mexican immigrant mothers writing together' in M. Farr (ed.), *Latino language and literacy in ethnolinguistic Chicago*, Erlbaum, Mahwah, NJ, 3–32.

Hymes, D.: 1974, 'Ways of speaking', in R. Bauman and J. Sherzer (eds.), *Explorations in the ethnography of speaking*, Cambridge University Press, Cambridge, UK.

Isaacson, C.: 2004 'They did not forget their Swedish: Class markers in the Swedish American community' in M. Farr (ed.), *Ethnolinguistic Chicago: Language and literacy in the city's neighborhoods*, Erlbaum, Mahwah, NJ, 223–249.

Kamhoefner, W.D., Helbich, W., and Sommer, U.: 1991, *News from the land of freedom: German immigrants write home*, Cornell University Press, Ithaca, NY.

Kerr, L.A.N.: 1977, 'Mexican Chicago: Chicano assimilation aborted, 1939–54', in M.G. Holli and P.d'A. Jones (eds.), *Ethnic Chicago*, William B. Erdmans Publishing Co., Grand Rapids, MI, 269–298.

Kloss, H.: 1998[1977], *The American bilingual tradition*, Center for Applied Linguistics and Delta Systems, Washington, DC. and McHenry, IL.

Koliussi, L.: 2004, 'Identity construction in discourse: Gender tensions among Greek Americans in Chicago' in M. Farr (ed.), *Ethnolinguistic Chicago: Language and literacy in the city's neighborhoods*, Erlbaum, Mahwah, NJ, 103–133.

Lindquist, J.: 2001. 'Hoods in the polis'. *Pedagogy: Critical approaches to teaching literature, language, composition, and culture*, 1(2), 261–274.

Lindquist, J.: 2004, 'Class identity and the politics of dissent: The culture of argument in a Chicago neighborhood bar', in M. Farr (ed.), *Ethnolinguistic Chicago: Language and literacy in the city's neighborhoods*, Erlbaum, Mahwah, NJ, 295–319.

Markelis, D.: 2004, 'Lithuanian and English language use among early twentieth century lithuanian immigrants in Chicago', in M. Farr (ed.), *Ethnolinguistic Chicago: Language and literacy in the city's neighborhoods*, Erlbaum, Mahwah, NJ, 275–293.

Miller, L.: 2004, 'Consuming Japanese print media in Chicago', in M. Farr (ed.), *Ethnolinguistic Chicago: Language and literacy in the city's neighborhoods*, Erlbaum, Mahwah, NJ, 275–293.

Morgan, M.: 2004, 'Signifying laughter and the subtleties of loud-talking: Memory and meaning in African American women's discourse', in M. Farr (ed.), *Ethnolinguistic Chicago: Language and literacy in the city's neighborhoods*, Erlbaum, Mahwah, NJ, 51–76.

Moss, B.J.: 2003, *A community text arises: A literate text and literate traditions in African-American churches*, Hampton Press, Cresskill, NJ.

Moss, B.J.: 2004, 'A literacy event in African-American churches: The sermon as a community text', in M. Farr (ed.), *Ethnolinguistic Chicago: Language and literacy in the city's neighborhoods*, Erlbaum, Mahwah, NJ, 137–159.

Moy, S.: 1995, 'The Chinese in Chicago', in M.G. Holli and P.d'A. Jones (eds.), *Ethnic Chicago: A multicultural portrait*, Eerdmans, Grand Rapids, MI, 378–408.

Nardini, G.: 1999, *Che bella figura! The power of performance in an Italian ladies' club in Chicago*, University of New York Press, Albany.

Nardini, G.: 2004, 'Italian patterns in the American Collandia ladies' Club: How do women make *bella figura*?', in M. Farr (ed.), *Ethnolinguistic Chicago: Language and literacy in the city's neighborhoods*, Erlbaum, Mahwah, NJ, 251–273.

Osako, M.: 1995, 'Japanese Americans: Melting into the All-American melting pot', in M.G. Holli and P.d'A. Jones (eds.), *Ethnic Chicago: A multicultural portrait*, Eerdmans, Grand Rapids, MI, 409–437.

Padilla, F.: 1987, *Puerto Rican Chicago*, Notre Dame Press, Notre Dame.

Pérez, G.: 2004, *The Near northwest side story: Migration, displacement, and Puerto Rican families*, University of California Press, Berkeley.

Pérez M.H.: 1988, *Por el refranero mexicano*, Universidad Autonoma de Nuevo Leon, Nuevo Leon, Mexico.

Peterson, J.: 1995, 'The founding fathers: The absorption of French-Indian Chicago, 1816–1837', in M. Holli and P.d'A. Jones (eds.), *Ethnic Chicago: A multicultural portrait*, Eerdmans, Grand Rapids,, 17–56.

Reynolds, R.: 2004, ' "Bless this little time we stayed here": Prayers of invocation as mediation of immigrant experience among Nigerians in Chicago', in M. Farr (ed.), *Ethnolinguistic Chicago: Language and literacy in the city's neighborhoods*, Erlbaum, Mahwah, NJ, 161–187.

Rogers, Henry.: 2005, *Writing Systems: A Linguistic Approach*, Blackwell Publishing, Maiden, MA.

Rohsenow, J.S.: 2004, 'Chinese language use in Chicagoland' in M. Farr (ed.), *Ethnolinguistic Chicago: Language and literacy in the city's neighborhoods*, Erlbaum, Mahwah, NJ, 321–355.

Saville-Troike, M.: 2003, *The Ethnography of Communication: An Introduction*, third edition, Basil Blackwell Publishing, Malden, MA.

Seligman, A.I.: 2005, *Block by block: Neighborhoods and public policy on Chicago's west side*, University of Chicago press, Chicago.

Spears, T.B.: 2005, *Chicago dreaming: Midwesterners and the city, 1871–1919*, University of Chicago Press, Chicago.

Trommler, F. and McVeigh, J.: 1985, *America and the Germans*, University of Pennsylvania Press, Philadelphia.

U.S Census Bureau: 2003, *Population by race*. Retrieved January, 24, 2006, from http://egov.cityofchicago.org/city.

U.S Census Bureau: 2004, *Non-English language in Cook county, Illinois*. Retrieved January 24, 2006, from http://www.census.gov/acs/www/.

Winford, D: 2003, *An Introduction to Contact Linguistics*, Blackwell, Oxford.

Wolfram, W.: 1980, '*A*-prefixing in Appalachian English', in W. Labov (ed.), *Locating language in time and space*, Academic Press, New York.

Wolfram, W. and Christian, D: 1976, *Appalachian speech*, Center for Applied Linguistics, Washington, DC.

INGE SICHRA

LANGUAGE DIVERSITY AND INDIGENOUS LITERACY IN THE ANDES

INTRODUCTION

The Andes mountains extend across the entire length of the South American continent. Traditionally in the social sciences and in pre-colonial studies in particular, the Andean space refers to the Inca Empire's sphere of influence (Cerrón-Palomino, 1985). Following that usage, this chapter focuses on the entire region spreading from the south of Colombia to the north of Argentina and Chile, encompassing coastal areas, mountain ranges and the high plateaus or *altiplano*.

This review of indigenous literacy in the Andes centres on Andean languages that have managed to survive Spanish language rule and maintain certain functional spaces in national societies. It is commonly accepted that indigenous languages had some sort of graphic or notational, non-alphabetical, system. From this, the tendency is to call the indigenous societies illiterate; yet this deficit terminology hinders acknowledgment of different literacies such as textile writing or 'other forms of textual expression and graphic representation' (López, 2001).

In recent decades, speakers of Andean languages increasingly raise them up as symbols of ethnic and political vindication in their efforts to secure prestigious and public spheres for these languages (King, 1997; López, 2001; Sichra, 2005). From this perspective, literacy acquires a driving role in the social participation of sectors traditionally marginalized by their societies, i.e. it could be an empowerment mechanism for the individual, the community and the group (Hornberger, 1997). This chapter focuses on the literacy of languages characterized by their orality and adheres to the ideological model in which literacy comprises concrete social practices whose purposes depend on underlying political and ideological factors (Street, 1984). Literacy events, that is, activities in which literacy plays a social role, can help us observe said practices (Barton and Hamilton, 1998).

EARLY DEVELOPMENTS

Early chroniclers, like the Jesuit Acosta in 1588, expressed their admiration for the 'veritable language jungle' found by Spanish invaders

B. V. Street and N. H. Hornberger (eds), Encyclopedia of Language and Education,
2nd Edition, Volume 2: Literacy, 283–297.
©2010 Springer Science+Business Media LLC.

upon their arrival in 1532 to the current Peruvian territory. Cieza de León in 1550 gave an account of a process of 'Quechuification' *(quechuización)* established by Inca Huaina Capac at the beginning of the fifteenth century as a unifying policy for the Inca Empire which nevertheless also upheld and fostered pluridialectism and plurilingualism. Chroniclers thus record Quechua as a general language superimposed on so-called 'natural languages' like Aymara, Puquina and 'other languages they understand and speak, and call hahuasimi, which means language apart from the general one' (Monzón, 1586/1965, p. 221). A century later, late chroniclers like Cobo would still register a profusion of languages within any particular town or valley (Cerrón-Palomino, 1988).

The linguistic diversity was partly a consequence of the archipelago system, in which each community established settlements on several ecological niches, thereby dispersing languages and dialects across non-contiguous territories (Mannheim, 1991). This linguistic diversity can likewise be attributed to the Inca policy of *mitmas*, whereby Quechua speakers were forced to migrate in order to secure newly conquered peoples and territories. There were, during the Inca Empire, six linguistic families in the current Peruvian territory (Cerrón, 1988); Moya (1997) reports various languages, without mentioning their specific linguistic affiliation, in what is today Ecuador.

Another surprising observation extensively commented on by Spanish chroniclers of the late sixteenth century, such as the Jesuit José de Acosta or the monk Fray Martín de Morúa, were the records, or *khipus*, that the vast empire's administration kept. According to Blas de Valera in 1578, the system of knots in multi-coloured wool was read in the manner of a poetic text. Despite the abundance of studies on this topic, it has yet to be confirmed if khipus were in effect text documents, or rather accounting and mnemonic instruments (Ascher and Ascher, 1997). In any case, even though alphabetical decoding has not yet been proven, the readers of this register, the *khipukamayuq*, narrated historical facts and mythical stories that legitimized Inca power. New studies of this system of communication are incorporating the contexts in which khipus were used and the intervention of the khipukamayuq as producer and interpreter (Platt, 1992a). Salomon (2004a) also provides evidence for the use of khipus until the latter part of the twentieth century in the Province of Huarochirí, Department of Lima in Peru, and for the coexistence of khipus and writing as complementary records for at least four centuries.

On the other hand, it was initially written text in the form of a book that came to epitomize the historical confrontation between Spaniards and indigenous people. Several chronicles of the encounter between

Europeans and the last Inca, in Cajamarca in 1534, highlight the Inca Atahuallpa's amazement at the object that bore God's word, the Bible. The Inca's anger and frustration with an object 'that said nothing to him' have defined a scene that would later be mythologized and incorporated into Andean imagery as a trauma borne from the conquest: a symbol of subordination to the invader, of the Inca's death and the empire's defeat (MacCormack, 1988). As instruments of death and punishment, writing and its bearers—paper, letters, memorials and edicts—fascinated and astounded for their unexplainable magic power and foretelling effects (Mignolo, 1995). Platt (1992b) asserts that indigenous people attested to the shamanic powers of European alphabetic writing, finding it analogous to their own experience of representing visual patterns, generated by hallucinogenic visions, in graphic designs for shamans to interpret.

At the outset of the conquest, with the First Council of Lima in 1552, Quechua saw a new period of expansion when it was declared, along with Aymara and to a lesser degree Puquina, the means for evangelization and colonial administration. The Third Council of Lima in 1583 established evangelization in these languages, and for that purpose undertook to print—inaugurating the use of the press in Peru and South America—the *Doctrina cristiana* and *Confessionario* in 1584 and the *Tercero Cathecismo* a year later in a Quechua variety constructed for a broad audience as a written lingua franca. The first pieces of descriptive and interpretative linguistic work followed soon thereafter; monumental lexical-grammatical studies of Quechua by Spanish missionaries like Domingo de Santo Tomás in 1560 and González Holguín in 1608; and of Aymara by Ludovico Bertonio in 1612. In this period of Quechua and Aymara studies, Quechua professorships were created at the Lima Cathedral in 1551 and at San Marcos University in 1579, where writing received particular attention.

Beginning in 1770 with the Bourbon reforms, specifically those of Charles III, a decisive policy of *castellanización* was established 'to achieve once and for all the extinction of the different languages used (. . .) so that only Spanish be spoken' (Rivarola, 1990, p. 108). Thirteen years later, the Quechua professorship at San Marcos University closed down. Constant indigenous uprisings between 1780 and 1782 were decisive in the rigorous enforcement of this change in language policy. In the nineteenth century, languages like Mochica, Culli and Cholón on the Peruvian coast also disappeared. This led to linguistic displacement in the Peruvian coastal area and northern sierra, and equally to an unstoppable process of social and political marginalization and progressive neglect of the major indigenous languages, Quechua and Aymara, in the newly formed Republics.

MAJOR CONTRIBUTIONS

At the beginning of the seventeenth century, an indigenous assistant of the mestizo priest Francisco de Avila wrote the Huarochirí Quechua Manuscript, the first compilation of Andean literature transcribed into a vernacular language (Taylor, 1988). Forced evangelization and cult banning, the so-called extirpation of idolatries, as well as the rupture of the territorial organization that safeguarded indigenous cultural and religious practices, prompted the need to use writing in order to preserve memory (ibid). De Avila advocated educating local rulers' children 'so they would not conceal or protect native rites' (Glave, 1990, p. 460). To educate these youngsters in Spanish language and culture and make of them intermediaries between the indigenous and the Spanish worlds, the Jesuits founded Schools for Caciques (local rulers) in Cusco, Lima and Quito. The physical extermination of the indigenous intellectual class in power centres at the end of the eighteenth century brought about the cultural and linguistic decline of Quechua and Aymara. The very same indigenous aristocracy, that is, the local rulers and principals who began the process of independence from the Spanish crown, themselves used only Spanish to summon anti-colonial rebellion (Godenzzi, 1995).

The only extant written sources date from the earlier mid sixteenth to the mid seventeenth century period, 'the golden era of written Quechua' (Durston, 2003, p. 210). In addition to the aforementioned Quechua writings, there are other Quechua texts appearing in Spanish books, written by indigenous chroniclers such as Felipe Guamán Poma de Ayala (*El Primer Nueva Corónica y Buen Gobierno* in 1615) and Joan de Santa Cruz Pachacuti Yamqui Salcamaygua (*Relación de antigüedades deste reyno del Perú* in 1613); mestizo chroniclers like Inca Garcilaso de la Vega (*Comentarios Reales de los Incas* in 1609 and 1617); and mestizo monks like the Jesuit Blas de Valera (*Historia de los Incas* in 1596) and Cristóbal de Molina 'El Cuzqueño' (*Ritos y Fábulas de los Incas* in 1574). Poma de Ayala's work is specially worth mentioning. Written as correspondence to the King, it included Quechua and Aymara texts that combined alphabetic writing with illustrations of festive and daily scenes. This exemplary piece of multiple literacies allowed the writer to express veiled meanings of resistance and denunciation before the Spanish authority (Dedenbach-Salazar, 2004).

Fragments pertaining to widely circulating lyric genres, important during the Inca period for their ceremonial and ritual purposes permeating everyday activities, are today studied for their historical and literary meanings and reproduced for circulation among contemporary readers (Murra and Adorno, 1980; Sichra and Cáceres, 1990). Historical sources that include these oral traditions as songs do not on the other hand record any prose texts, with the exception of two epic fragments in Fray Martín de Murúa's *History of the Origin and Royal Genealogy of the Peruvian Inca Kings* (1590), collected from khipukamayuq who had survived the Spanish invasion.

The above-mentioned educated native literature (Beyersdorff, 1986), written by descendants of the indigenous nobility commissioned by the Crown or the Church, contrasts with another area of Quechua literature which has come to light only in the last two decades (Adelaar and Trigoso, 1998; Durston, 2003; Itier, 1991; Taylor, 1985). These are documents from the era when Quechua flourished, between the sixteenth and seventeenth centuries, consisting of judicial complaints written by notaries and letters or petitions of indigenous authorship, in several cases by indigenous elite women. The documents were written in the Quechua variety promoted by the aforementioned Third Council of Lima. After several centuries, it is extremely difficult to find this type of daily, spontaneous writings in neglected and isolated parish or archbishopric archives. Nevertheless, these documents are precious evidence of how much social validity Quechua writing must have had among the indigenous population, reaching beyond legal and administrative realms, and becoming a means of communication among speakers. According to Itier (1991), this is proof that Quechua had the status of a written language.

Gradually, literary Quechua began to be cultivated and its importance increased with the use of the Cusco variety in which the colonizing minority of Spaniards and creoles produced religious and secular literature in a European style, and even came to consider it as their own (Itier, 1987). This literature includes theatrical works with which the landholding elites, usurpers of indigenous lands, attempted to establish a Quechua literature that would legitimize them politically. Mannheim (1990) calls the revival of Spanish literary styles in Andean languages during the eighteenth century 'the golden century of literary Quechua'. Nonetheless, it generated an adverse process for Quechua as a means of communication in that the creole and mestizo elite cultivated the language for its importance in the glorious Inca empire rather than its significance as a language of the contemporary majority (Itier, 1995). These plays, targeted to an erudite creole audience, continued to flourish until the Republican period in the nineteenth century. One exception is the Quechua poetry of Juan Wallparimachi of Potosi, Bolivia who wrote at the beginning of the nineteenth century and whose poems have survived in part in popular culture as anonymous writings (Sichra and Cáceres, 1990). Over the course of two centuries (mid-eighteenth to mid-twentieth), Andean languages ceased to be written means of communication for indigenous users, with literary creation being maintained solely through oral tradition in stories and songs regarded as folklore while in a parallel process languages were gradually being confined to low-prestige social roles and functions.

Although the work of the Summer Institute of Linguistics beginning in the first half of the twentieth century in the Amazonian and the Andean regions sought to assimilate indigenous populations through evangelization (Stoll, 1984), SIL linguists initiated truly pioneering work in systematizing indigenous languages and establishing them in writing. They also contributed to speakers' awareness of the feasibility of writing in their languages (Landaburu, 1998). The last third of the twentieth century reveals a profusion of linguistic descriptions and studies of languages and varieties of Quechua and Aymara, accompanied by protracted debates about their respective alphabets, debates which generate recurring confrontations despite the languages having achieved official status in Bolivia, Peru and Ecuador in the 1980s.

WORK IN PROGRESS

The diversity of Andean languages began to be acknowledged and promoted as anti-authoritarian political currents swept the continent from Ecuador to Argentina, and also as a result of the accelerating phenomenon of globalization. Confronting the authoritarian regimes that had been established during the 1960s to the 1980s, movements with social and later ethnic demands questioned the state's homogenizing and unifying character and challenged nation-building aims that adopt a 'one language, one culture' ideology.

A remarkable fact is that the efforts to spread Quechua during the Inca regime and during the first century of Spanish rule, displacing regional and local languages including even a major language such as Aymara, nevertheless failed to impose a supra-regional Quechua variety. Despite the Republican language policy of forced imposition of Spanish, languages and varieties of the Quechua family have been maintained to a great degree in the entire Andean region—although with a tendency towards shift—with the exception of the now extinct languages of the central coast of Peru. Aymara, the most preserved language of the Aru family, is confined to the Peruvian–Bolivian high plateau. López (2001) estimates there are 12 million Quechua speakers and 2.5 million Aymara speakers, mostly Spanish bilinguals. In the Bolivian high plateau, there are still some few Chipaya speakers of the Arawak family. In all Andean countries, migration from the countryside to cities and capitals is transforming urban areas into spaces of increasingly greater reproduction of Andean cultures and languages (Sichra, 2005).

Another revelation, in these times when indigenous organizations and peoples are rising up as active interlocutors with the state in their struggle for legal recognition and territorial rights, is the re-emergence of multi-ethnicity among peoples traditionally subsumed under the term Quechuas (in Peru and Bolivia) or Quichuas (in Ecuador), and to a lesser degree Aymaras. Oral traditions such as myths, stories and songs, common law (*usos y costumbres*), records and maps in chronicles or judicial writings, community demarcation and land titles and other oral and written documents are brought forward by indigenous communities (*originarios* or 'aborigines' in Bolivia, peoples or 'nationalities' in Ecuador) as historical evidence of their collective identity and rights. In the 1990s, all of the Andean constitutions were modified or created to incorporate adjectives like 'pluriethnic', 'multilingual', formulations like 'ethnic and cultural diversity', and terms like 'ethnic groups', 'nationalities', 'indigenous peoples' and 'native peoples'. Amidst this constellation, asserting one's belonging to indigenous peoples has ceased to necessarily be a stigma, as can be seen for example in Bolivia, where the proportion of the population claiming indigenous identity increased between the census of 1992 and that of 2001.

Among the most notable effects of the constitutional realignments are educational reforms in the Andean region that seek to include indigenous languages in primary education in order to develop decoding skills and literacy through them (López, 2001), under the rubric of intercultural bilingual education, indigenous education or ethno-education (see López and Sichra, Intercultural Bilingual Education Among Indigenous Peoples in Latin America, Volume 5). This is an arduous and paradoxical process, given the difficulty of erasing a long, painful history of discrimination towards everything indigenous; something that characterized—and still does—public schools in charge of 'civilizing' through Spanish literacy (Hornberger, 2000; Oliart, 2004). Nowadays, sustained by the diglossic relation between Spanish and indigenous languages prevalent in Andean societies despite constitutional and political changes, 'writing and literacy are closely associated with the hegemonic language' (López, 2001, p. 211).

The Freirean (1970) pedagogical current in Latin America of the 1970s and 1980s established the idea that writing can be an instrument of political participation, permitting processes of self-affirmation through reading the reality of the world. Raising awareness of a subordinate condition (in those times, of the popular sectors) went in tandem with introducing literacy. This was originally conceived of as Spanish literacy targeting the working population and the urban proletariat. From various scenarios and with the contribution of several actors—NGOs, indigenous intellectuals, rural union organizations, universities—a rich vein of literacy in Andean languages has been developing along the lines of 'reading reality to write history' (Pereson, Cendales and Cendales, 1983, p. 152). The fact that oral history and life testimonies became crucial in this process of establishing literacy during the decades of de facto governments, political oppression and social exclusion is not coincidental. Raising silenced voices in order to narrate history through testimony not only updates historical awareness but 'can also have a political role in the sense of wanting to influence the present, transform the order of things, and project towards a different future' (Howard-Malverde, 1999, p. 341).

In La Paz, Aymara-Spanish bilingual transcriptions of community history, indigenous and union struggles, indigenous leaders and schools and oral tradition and life stories, all of indigenous authorship, were sought out using ethnographic methods and published by the *Taller de Historia Oral Andina* (THOA), the *Instituto de Historia Social de Bolivia* (HISBOL) and the History Department of the Universidad Mayor de San Andrés. Participants included Aymara intellectuals and descendants of local rulers' representatives or *caciques apoderados*, who had launched a movement in Bolivia at the end of the nineteenth century to recover and secure original community lands from state plundering by obtaining old titles signed by the Spanish Crown. Focusing on action-research in Cochabamba, the *Centro de Comunicación y Desarrollo Andino* (CENDA) generated bilingual publications in Quechua and Spanish, collecting oral history and literature on peasant survival strategies in health, agricultural wisdom, community leadership and union struggles. In all these cases, publications were targeted as much to indigenous activists and authors, adults and children in rural areas, as to urban mestizo readers.

For 20 consecutive years now, CENDA has been editing the rural bilingual magazine CONOSUR *Ñawpaqman* (Southern Cone *Forward*). Its contents, relevant to peasant life and political and social movements in Cochabamba, Bolivia, are collected periodically from its own rural readers and returned to them as registered oral discourse (Garcés, 2005). This work is therefore engaged in 'generating new styles and new usages, (with) the grand art of letting people feel that this is their language, that there is nothing artificial in it' (Albó, 2001, p. 9). Stories collected for two decades and regularly appearing in the newspaper have been republished as full-colour editions, along with other material in indigenous language, for school libraries established by the Bolivian Educational Reform at the end of the nineties.

In Peru, the Andean Centre for Education and Promotion (*Centro Andino de Educación y Promoción*, CADEP) publishes traditions and narratives in bilingual editions that recuperate contents related to myths, to the era of the *hacienda*, and aspects of culture; they also preserve some of this material as audio-recorded oral testimony. The Bartolomé de las Casas Andean Regional Studies Centre in Cusco has published several bilingual texts of oral history and oral literature.

In this line of literacy aimed at political empowerment, there is also considerable documentation in Ecuador of community and individual histories of participation in struggles of the 1960s and 1970s to recover lands occupied by hacienda owners and large landowners. Cayambe in the north of Quito, Chimborazo in the central sierra, and Cañar in the south were centres of peasant indigenous movements that stood out in their struggle to advance recognition of their rights to their own education, territory, organization and political participation. These issues came to light in bilingual texts collected and published by the Catholic University of Quito and the undergraduate course in Andean Linguistics and Bilingual Education at the University of Cuenca.

In all three of these countries, between the 1980s and 1990s, scholars, writers, and academics, Andean and foreign alike, compiled oral tradition, stories, legends, riddles, and songs in a wide range of texts for diffusion, cultural affirmation and study, but principally in order to recover and preserve them in writing so they would not disappear as oral patrimony. The Experimental Project for Bilingual Education in Puno, Peru, sponsored by the German Technical Cooperation, also produced texts in Quechua and Aymara. In all these cases, indigenous authorship, although situated in a local or regional context, is anonymous (commonly known as popular cultural wealth).

PROBLEMS AND DIFFICULTIES

Ironically, problems in indigenous literacy do not spring from a failure to recognize Andean languages and cultures, but from ideological notions embedded in Andean governments' lack of political will to face the promotion of writing and literacy in indigenous languages as instruments of power in the broadest sense. It is crucial to keep in mind the almost absolute weight granted everything related to Spanish literacy, writing and decoding skills, promoted by the globalizing and development-oriented current that underlies current state policies. National societies voluntarily assume this sort of dogma, with hegemonic sectors transmitting it to indigenous communities and individuals. Principles sustaining all types of international and national policies are therein crystallized and can be summarized as follows: Spanish decoding skills have intrinsic instrumental value in overcoming poverty and Spanish literacy is an inalienable right to participate as a citizen and a requisite for democracy. This strongly internalized faith, materialized in development through written Spanish and the consequential hierarchical differentiation between those who know how to write and those who do not, has been well documented in several Quechua speaking communities (Hornberger and King, 1996; Salomon, 2004b; Zavala, 2002). Contradictory as it may seem, this ideological current is spreading among the indigenous organizations themselves, and is being fostered as state policy by the new Bolivian government (January 2006) that has an indigenous and popular orientation.

Linguists, education specialists and indigenous organizations continue to place enormous importance on problems concerning alphabets and orthography for indigenous languages, yet invest very little consideration to writing and literacy issues. Establishing written indigenous language was probably important per se to exemplify its equality and its potential equivalence with the dominant language. On the other hand, the policy and practice of public bilingual education has promoted a normative notion of writing that hinders and distances written practice of a daily nature (King, 2001). In the same vein, literacy in Andean languages in rural areas may actually undermine the very languages meant to be preserved and reaffirmed (Arnold and Yapita, 2000). With regard to this 'technical' vision of writing that, far from approaching literacy remains at the level of decoding, the vicious circle is closed by evidence that 'alphabetic non-literacy remains widespread and is a common focus of governmental and non-governmental development projects in Bolivia, Peru and Ecuador' (Arnold and Yapita, 2000).

Even where there are attempts to transcend the orthographic issue in order to promote writing as a useful tool in daily life, efforts in adult education and in primary school education tend to present literacy as the only medium to create and transmit cultural knowledge, ignoring or nullifying other Andean linguistic and cultural media (Howard-Malverde, 1998). Indigenous cultures are cultures of orality and of argumentation that grant central value to spoken words, a crucial characteristic that cannot be denied or ignored by failing to articulate a connection between orality and writing. If indigenous peoples have not appropriated writing, it is because it has been introduced without taking into account its relation to existing social practices in the community. Writing must cease to be a form of acculturation and rather be incorporated into indigenous social practices, without implying a loss of value for the spoken word or their own writings. It is a matter of recognizing writing's social value and ceasing to understand it as a merely educational or technical skill.

At the same time, this means recognizing the wealth Andean cultures exhibit in their diverse textual expressions. For example, Franquemont (1994, p. 362) wonders, 'How is it that textiles could represent information and ideas so effectively that the sophisticated Andean civilizations never felt the need to develop writing?' From this perspective, our failure to understand the textile system condemns us to perpetual illiteracy in Andean thought. Close inquiry into what

was and is present in the textile arts, pottery and music would further
our understanding of the cultural, social and political meanings of the
various textual practices. As Desrosiers (1994, p. 361) specifies, 'textile techniques have probably constituted a means of resistance to
acculturation, which would explain both their preservation in numerous
communities and their sudden abandonment by those seeking to partake of a new system of social relations pertaining to urban life."

FUTURE DIRECTIONS

Considering the above in the light of the ideological model that 'con-
centrates on the overlap and interaction of oral and literate modes rather
than stressing a 'great divide" (Street, 1984, p. 3), a couple of promising viewpoints emerge for the future. On the one hand, understanding
and promoting indigenous literacy must take as point of departure the
indigenous languages themselves and their characteristic orality. On
the other hand, multiple, complementary modes of literacy (alphabetic,
graphic, textile) must be taken into account.

Within formal education, this integrated perspective of literacy
would build on the mutual influences among cultural, discursive and
writing practices, in order to develop local, not universal, teaching
and learning methods (Arnold and Yapita, 2000). Childhood literacy
within the community realm is undoubtedly the most promising path,
entailing the fostering of diverse writings, beyond imposition of a
standardized norm or of school contents and topics. Existing experiences along these lines display great creative, stylistic and graphic
wealth, where social meanings compete with those of identity, affect
and self-esteem.

As for the development of indigenous language practice and func-
tionality in academic spaces, the challenge implies overcoming the traditional narrative genres of stories, myths and legends, and penetrating
into informative, descriptive, argumentative and other genres. For this,
however, the starting point would not be Spanish discourse models, but
rather the discourse forms and resources of the oral languages, such as
metaphor, rhetoric, textual inference and ambiguity, and non-linear
argument structure. In order to advance this task of respecting the
structural particularity of orality, Calvo (1993) proposes a pragmatic
grammar that responds to the specificities of orality, in which, for
example, the circular organization of narrative text might be described.
Sichra (2001) refers to the recognition of oral language discursive
resources to stimulate indigenous students' creativity in formal scholarly events, such as the production of academic texts in the Masters
program in Bilingual Intercultural Education at PROEIB Andes in

Cochabamba, Bolivia. In this way, the pedagogic practice of writing texts in indigenous languages according to Spanish molds, a consequence of an imposed literacy, could begin to be overcome (Ivanic and Moss, 1991). Paraphrasing these authors, the proposal is to go beyond a literacy where the permitted style and content range are set by external social institutions *of the Spanish learned culture*, and promote a self-generated literacy stemming from peoples' own interests, needs and purposes, where there is freedom to adopt the very content and styles of *oral indigenous cultures*. Elaborating, among others, academic, technical and pedagogical texts *in* Quechua and Aymara, and not only *on* Quechua and Aymara languages and cultures would further this line (Von Gleich, 2004).

The fact that Andean cities and capitals are becoming indigenous, and that formal spaces like higher education or the written mass media are being conquered for the use of indigenous languages, will no doubt encourage biliteracy in accordance with the interculturality evident in Latin American societies (Hornberger, 1997). Literacy events in which two languages intervene will probably exceed monolingual events in indigenous languages, given the advance of bilingualism in cities and the expansion of Spanish to rural areas.

As for multimodal writing, textiles have until recently been studied mostly as historical or modern products from three perspectives: firstly, to understand the cognitive and cultural meaning of their structure and techniques; secondly, to discover their semiotic meaning and related visual and cognitive grammar; and thirdly, to explore their use as clothing, for ritual purposes, and as means to transmit collective memory. Currently, attention is being drawn to the ability and practice of weaving as a process of acquiring socially relevant knowledge (Crickmay, 2002). There is evidence that, during their primary socialization stage, indigenous children learn through the language of textiles the repertoire of textual practices cherished by the community, such as narratives, songs and music (Arnold and Yapita, 2000). A very promising vein is for indigenous professionals to study these indigenous literacies from the perspective of the users themselves (Castillo, 2005). This perspective on indigenous pedagogy reclaims indigenous peoples' sociocultural childrearing and socialization processes for producing, systematizing and spreading their own knowledges and literacies.

REFERENCES

Adelaar, W. and Trigoso J.: 1998, '"Un documento colonial quechua de Cajamarca"', en Sabine Dedenbach-Salazar (ed.), *50 años de estudios americanistas en la Universidad de Bonn: Nuevas contribuciones a la arqueología, etnohistoria, etnolingüística y etnografía de las Américas*, Seminar für Völkerkunde Universität Bonn, Bonn, 641–651.

Albó, X.: 2001, *Periódico Conosur Ñawpaqman* Nr. 93, July. Cochabamba.
Arnold, D. and Yapita J. de D.: 2000, *El rincón de las cabezas. Luchas textuales, educación y tierras en los Andes*, ILCA/Facultad de Humanidad y Ciencias de la Educación UMSA, La Paz.
Ascher, M. and Ascher, R.: 1997, *Mathematics of the Incas, Code of the Quipu*, Dover Publications, New York.
Barton, D. and Hamilton, M.: 1998, *Local Literacies. Reading and Writing in One Community*, Routledge, London.
Beyersdorff, M.: 1986, '"La tradición oral quechua vista desde la perspectiva de la literatura"', *Revista Andina* Año 4, Nr. 1. 213–236.
Calvo, J.: 1993, *Pragmática y Gramática del Quechua Cuzqueño*, CBC, Cuzco.
Castillo, M.: 2005, *Aprendiendo con el corazón: El tejido andino en la educación quechua*, Plural/PROEIB Andes, La Paz.
Cerrón-Palomino, R.: 1985, '"Panorama de la lingüística andina"', *Revista Andina*, Año 3, Nr. 2. 509–572.
Cerrón-Palomino, R.: 1988, '"Unidad y diferenciación lingüistica en el mundo andino"', in L.E. López (ed.), *Pesquisas en lingüística andina,* CONCYTEC/GTZ/UNAP.121–152, Lima-Puno.
Crickmay, L.: 2002, '"Transmission of knowledge through textiles: Weaving and learning how to live"', in H. Stobart and R. Howard (eds.), *Knowledge and Learning in the Antes*, Liverpool University Press, Liverpool, 40–55.
Dedenbach-Salazar, S.: 2004, '"El lenguaje como parodia: Instancias del uso particular del quechua de Guaman Poma y de Pachacuti Yamqui Sacamaygua"', *Revista Andina* Nr. 39. 227–255.
Desrosiers, S.: 1994, '"Comentario"', *Revista Andina*, Año 12, Nr. 2. 359–362.
Durston, A.: 2003, '"La escritura del quechua por indígenas en el siglo XVII"', *Revista Andina* Nr. 37. 207–236.
Franquemont, E.:1994, '"Comentario"', *Revista Andina*, Año 12, Nr. 2. 362–364.
Freire, P.: 1970, *Pedagogía del oprimido*, Siblo XXI, México.
Garcés, F.: 2005, *De la voz al papel. La escritura quechua del periódico CONOSUR Ñawpaqman*, Plural/CENDA, La Paz.
Glave, L.M.: 1990, '"Grito de pueblos silenciados. Intermediarios lingüísticos y culturales entre dos mundos: Historia y mentalidades"', *Allpanchis* Año XXII Nrs. 35/36. 435–513.
Godenzzi, J.C.: 1995, '"Discurso y actos de rebelión anticolonial: Textos políticos del siglo XVII en los Andes"', in C. Itier (comp.), *Del siglo de oro al siglo de las luces: lenguaje y sociedad en los Andes del siglo XVIII*, CBC, Cusco, 59–88.
Hornberger, N.: 1997, '"Quechua literacy and empowerment in Peru"', in N. Hornberger (ed.), *Indigenous literacies in the Americas. Language Planning from the Bottom up*, Mouton de Gruyter, Berlin/New York, 3–16.
Hornberger, N. and King, K.: 1996, '"Language revitalisation in the Andes: Can the schools reverse language shift?"', *Journal of Multilingual and Multicultural Development* 17(6), 427–441.
Hornberger, N.H.: 2000, 'Bilingual education policy and practice in the Andes: Ideological paradox and intercultural possibility, *Anthropology and Education Quarterly* 31(2), 173–201.
Howard-Malverde, R.: 1998, '"Grasping awareness': Mother-tongue literacy for Quechua speaking women in Northern Potosi, Bolivia", *International Journal of Educational Development* 18(3), 181–196.
Howard-Malverde, R.: 1999, '"Pautas teóricas y metodológicas para el estudio de la historia oral andina contemporánea"', in J.C. Godenzzi (ed.), *Tradición oral andina y amazónica. Métodos de análisis e interpretación de textos*, CBC, Cusco, 339–385.
Itier, C.: 1987,'"A propósito de los dos poemas en quechua de la crónica de fray Martín de Murúa"', *Revista Andina* Año 5, Nr. 2. 11–227.

Itier, C.: 1991, '"Lengua general y comunicación escrita: cinco cartas en quechua de Cotahuasi—1616"', *Revista Andina* Año 9, Nr.1. 65–107.

Itier, C.: 1995, '"Quechua y cultura en el Cuzco del siglo XVIII"', in C. Itier (comp.), *Del siglo de oro al siglo de las luces: lenguaje y sociedad en los Andes del siglo XVIII.* CBC, Cusco, 89–112.

Ivanic, R. and Moss, W.: 1991, '"Bringing community writing practices into education"' in D. Barton and R. Ivanic (eds.), *Writing in the Community*, Sage, London, 193–223.

King, K.: 1997, '"Indigenous politics and native language literacies: Recent shifts in bilingual education policy and practice in Ecuador"', in N. Hornberger (ed.), *Indigenous Literacies in the Americas.* Language Planning from the Bottom up, Mouton de Gruyter, Berlin/New York, 267–283.

King, K.: 2001, *Language Revitalization Processes and Prospects. Quichua in the Ecuadorian Andes*, Multilingual Matters LTD, Clevendon.

Landaburu, J.: 1998, '"La situación de las lenguas indígenas de Colombia: Prolegómenos para una política lingüística viable"', in M. Trillos (ed.), *Educación endógena frente a educación formal*, CCELA, Bogotá, 293–314.

López, L.E.: 2001, '"Literacy and intercultural bilingual education in the Andes"', in D. Olson and N. Torrance (eds.), *The Making of Literate Societies*, Blackwell Publishers, Oxford, 201–224.

Mannheim, B.: 1990, '"La cronología relativa de la lengua y literatura quechua cusqueña"', *Revista Andina* Año 8, Nr.1. 139–178.

Mannheim, B.: 1991, *The Language of the Inka Since the European Invasion*, University of Texas, Austin.

MacCormack, S.: 1988, '"Atahualpa y el libro"', *Revista de Indias* XLVIII (3). 693–714.

Mignolo, W.: 1995, *The Darker Side of the Renaissance: Literacy Territoriality and Colonization*, University of Michigan Press, An Arbor.

Monzón, L.: (1586) 1965, *Relaciones geográficas de Indias* I, Ediciones Atlas, Madrid.

Moya, A.: 1997, *Ethnos. Atlas etnográfico del Ecuador*, P-EBI, Quito.

Murra, J. and Adorno, R.: 1980, *El primer nueva corónica y buen gobierno por Felipe Guaman Poma de Ayala*, Siglo Veintiuno, México.

Oliart, P.: 2004, '"Leer y escribir en un mundo sin letras. Reflexiones sobre la globalización y la educación en la Sierra rural"', in C.I. Degregori and G. Portocarrero (ed.), *Cultura y Globalización*, Red para el desarrollo de las ciencias sociales en el Perú, Lima, 203–223.

Pereson, M., Cendales, G., and Cendales, L.: 1983, *Educación popular y alfabetización en América Latina*, Dimensión Educativa, Bogotá.

Platt, T.: 1992a,'"Writing, shamanism and identity, or voices from Abya-Yala"', *History Workshop Journal* 34 (comp. Bill Schwartz), Oxford University Press, Oxford.

Platt, T.: 1992b, '"The sound of light. Speech, script and metaphor in the Southern Andes"', in S. Arze et al. (comps.), *Etnicidad, economía y simbolismo en los Andes*, HiISBOL/IFEA/SBH-ASUR, La Paz, 439–466.

Rivarola, J.L.: 1990, *La formación lingüística de Hispanoamérica*, Fondo Editorial Pontificia Universidad Católica del Perú, Lima.

Salomon, F.: 2004a, *The Cord Keepers. Khipus and Cultural Life in a Peruvian Village*, Duke University Press, Durham.

Salomon, F.: 2004b, '"Literacidades vernáculas en la provincia altiplánica de Azángaro"', in V. Zavala, M. Niño-Murcia, and P. Ames (eds.), *Escritura y sociedad. Nuevas perspectivas teóricas y etnográficas*, Red para el Desarrollo de las Ciencias Sociales en el Perú, Lima, 317–345.

Sichra, I.: 2001, '"Huellas de intraculturalidad en un programa intercultural en el ámbito de educación superior"', in M. Heise (ed.), *Interculturalidad. Creación de un concepto y desarrollo de una actitud*, Programa FORTE-PE, Lima, 193–202.

Sichra, I.: 2005, '"Trascendiendo o fortaleciendo el valor emblemático del quechua: identidad de la lengua en la ciudad de Cochabamba"', in S. Coronel-Molina and L. Grabner-Coronel (eds.), *Lenguas e identidades en los Andes: Perspectivas ideológicas y culturales*, Abya Yala, Quito, 211–250.

Sichra, I. and Cáceres A.: 1990, *Poésie quechua en Bolivie*. Edition Trilingue, Patiño, Géneve.

Stoll, D.: 1984, *Pescadores de hombres o fundadores de imperios*, Quito, Abya Yala.

Street, B.: 1984, *Literacy in Theory and Practice*, Cambridge University Press, Cambridge.

Taylor, G.: 1985, '"Un documento quechuia de Huarochirí-1607 (sic)"', *Revista Andina* Año 5, Nr.1. 157–185.

Taylor, G.: 1988, '"La tradición oral andina y la escritura"', in L.E. López (ed.), *Pesquisas en lingüística andina*, CONCYTEC/GTZ/UNAP, Lima-Puno, 181–190.

Von Gleich, U.: 2004, '"New Quechua literacies in Bolivia"', *Int. J. Soc. Lang.* 167, 131–146.

Zavala, V.: 2002, *(Des) encuentros con la escritura: Escuela y comunidad en los Andes peruanos*, Red para el Desarrollo de las Ciencias Sociales en el Perú, Lima.

JABARI MAHIRI

LITERACIES IN THE LIVES OF URBAN YOUTH

INTRODUCTION

A period of approximately 30 years from the late 1970s through 2006 frames the discussion in this chapter of out-of-school literacy practices. Young people born during this period can be seen as "natives" of the digital age. A key feature of this age is that "new media" enabled by digital computer technologies greatly increased the mobility, inter-changeability, and accessibility of texts and signs while magnifying and simplifying processes for their production and dissemination. Video games, instant or text messages, blogs, zines, email, ipods, ichat, and Internet sites like myspace are digitized places that many young people inhabit. Importantly, these new media have enabled "new literacies" (see also Leander and Lewis, Literacy and Internet Technologies; Street, New Literacies, New Times: Developments in Literacy Studies; Schultz and Hull, Literacies In and Out of School in the United States, Volume 2). Another consideration for this period is its overlap and reciprocal influences with the hip-hop generation—youth around the world who utilize particular styles of music, language, dress, and other practices linked to hip-hop culture for core representations of meaning and identity. During the early part of this period, ways that youth were framed in public discourse contrasted with ways young people have begun to use new media to enact alternative frames. Finally, this period reflected fundamental changes in how literacy itself was conceptualized, moving from traditional literacy models that focused on writing and speech as the central forms of representation to new literacy and new media models that explore multimodal and multi-textual representational practices and forms "situated" in specific social contexts.

EARLY DEVELOPMENTS

Earlier theories of literacy as static skills that had pervasive cognitive consequences by scholars like Jack Goody and Ian Watt, David Olsen, and Walter Ong began to encounter challenges in the late 1970s and early 1980s from a number of scholars like Ruth Finnegan, Sylvia Scribner, Michael Cole, Denny Taylor, and Marcia Farr who reported ethnographic research on actual literacy practices in various social contexts. Heath (1983) was a classic example of these studies that described

B. V. Street and N. H. Hornberger (eds), Encyclopedia of Language and Education,
2nd Edition, Volume 2: Literacy, 299–307.
©*2010 Springer Science+Business Media LLC.*

the range of literacy events and practices of different participants acting together in social situations. She explored the language socialization of children in two communities she called Trackton and Roadville and compared these processes in conjunction with a third community of townspeople. Among other things, she found very different literacy events occurring.

Storytelling, for example, varied considerably from community to community. The black residents of Trackton saw the facts of a story very differently from the white residents of Roadville. Although Trackton storytellers may have based their stories on actual events, they liberally fictionalized the details such that the outcome of the story might bear no resemblance to what really happened. These highly elaborated tales were greatly valued. However, parents in this community almost never read stories to their children. In Roadville, on the other hand, stories were read to children and stories would also stick to the facts. There residents usually waited to be invited to tell their stories where in Trackton stories were self-initiated in order to reveal personal status and power. These literacy events had different functions and different social meanings in the different communities. This work by Heath and others during the late 70s and early 80s made early contributions to re-conceptualizing non-school literacy practices by delineating distinct and culturally specific ways of making and receiving meaning in a variety of textual mediums.

Extending the re-conceptions of literacy that were emerging from various ethnographic studies, Street (1984) argued that earlier theories claiming that literacy was a universal and decontextualized set of skills that did not change significantly from one social setting to another reflected an "autonomous model" that was severely limited for understanding actual literacy practices. He put forth an "ideological model" as an alternative framework for understanding literacy in terms of concrete social practices embedded in and given meaning through different ideologies. He chose the term "ideological" to denote that these practices were aspects of power structures as well as of cultures. In further developing this framework, Street (1993) began to outline a "new literacy studies" approach to focus more comprehensively on how literacy is linked to social and cultural contexts. In this edited volume, Street brought together research from a variety of world cultures to investigate and demonstrate the different meanings and uses of literacy in different cultures and societies. This work globalized what Heath (1983) had done with local communities and families in one geographical region.

One early revision of the autonomous model of literacy was a "continuum model" that challenged the notion of a great divide between orality and written texts. Yet, this model also tended to reify "literacy in itself at the expense of recognition of its location in structures of power and ideology" (Street, 1993, p. 4). Street co-founded a group of international scholars (see Gee, 1990; Barton and Hamilton, 1998; Barton, Hamilton and Ivanic, 1999; Pahl and Rowsell, 2006; etc.) called the New Literacy Studies Group who took the view that literacies were multiple rather than a monolithic concept, and that they should be studied as variably and historically "situated" practices within social, cultural, economic, and political contexts. The contributions reviewed in the following section reflect this new literacy perspective.

MAJOR CONTRIBUTIONS

A wave of qualitative research and critique influenced by the early developments in studying and theorizing non-school literacy practices began to explore sociocultural contexts like transnational communities (Guerra, 1998, 2004; Gutierrez, 1997; Lam, 2004), families (Cushman, 1998), churches (Moss, 1994), sports (Mahiri, 1994), youth social and peer groups (Finders, 1996; Smith and Wilhelm, 2002; Willis, 1990) youth organizations (Heath and McLaughlin, 1993; Maira and Soep, 2005), gangs (Cowan, 2004), rap music and spoken word venues (Miller, 2004; Rose, 1994), and digital mediated spaces like the Internet (Alvermann, 2002), video games (Gee, 2004), and other electronic media (Johnson, 2005). This work documented and analyzed literacy practices and built additional, grounded theories about learning and literacy in non-school settings.

For example, Guerra's (1998) transnational fieldwork with a Mexicano social network of several hundred people residing both in Chicago and in a rural *rancho* in Mexico further problematized notions of dichotomies between orality and literacy. His research indicated that both were highly overlapping linguistic (rhetorical) practices that resisted any clear characterization of fixed boundaries between them. Furthering this analysis, he used the literacy practices of one young woman in this social network to demonstrate her use of overlapping, situated literacies and a "nomadic consciousness" (shaped by continual physical and linguistic border crossings) to enact what he termed "transcultural repositioning" – a rhetorical ability to productively move back and forth between different languages, literacies, dialects, social settings, and ways of seeing and thinking (Guerra, 2004). Transcultural repositioning elides the simplicity of dichotomous models of literacy and can be connected to Gutierrez (1997) and her collaborators' notion of a "third space" for language and literacy learning. Moving beyond discourses that position literacies as oppositional and hierarchical, these researchers posited a third space in which less distinction is placed on formal versus informal learning and more emphasis is placed on normalizing multiple pathways and literacies as learning resources. Lam (2004) utilized a slightly different third space metaphor in her

research on the transnational discourse of Chinese youth to illuminate
the nature of their reading and discussion of international comic books
as a fundamental social practice linked to literacy learning and the
transformation of their cultural identity. Here the third space was
the site of new or emerging frames of reference and processes of
signification afforded between cultures of transnational youth.

A number of significant contributions followed leads from Heath
(1983) to look further at community literacy practices revealed in
families, churches, youth social groups, and neighborhood based organizations serving youth. Cushman (1998) showed the rich repertoire of
literacy practices that poor black women exhibit as they interact with
societal institutions from which they need to get resources. Moss's
(1994) work on black sermons delivered from full, partial, or no texts
continued the complication of intersections between oral and written
language. Mahiri (1994) described and assessed an array of spontaneous
and adaptive literacy practices of preadolescent African American
males linked to their involvement in a community sports program.
Smith and Wilhelm (2002) looked at boys and young men from a variety of backgrounds to investigate why males disproportionately under
perform in literacy and found wide-ranging practices of literacy that
usually do not get valued in schools. Cowan (2004) researched the lowrider car culture of some Latino males (who are often assumed to be
gang members) and found unique literacy practices associated with
constructing reading cars as symbolic texts and powerful identity markers. By contrast, Willis (1990) noted that traditional conceptions of
symbolic creativity "have no real connection with most young people
or their lives" (p. 1). Focusing on adolescent girls, Finders (1996) captured both visible and "hidden" literacies that girls use to construct
personal identity and to maintain friendship groups. All of these studies
or critiques acknowledged the contrast of their copious findings of
complex and expansive practices of literacy to how little is known or
utilized from these practices in schools and other societal institutions.

Other more recent contributions have explored the workings and
implications of novel literacy practices connected to and often enabled
by digital technologies. Manovich (2001) described how earlier visual
media eventually converged with (or was consumed by) digital computer
technologies through the expanding capability of computers to translate
all existing media into numerical data. The result was a "new media"
that incorporated graphics, moving images, sounds, shapes, and other
forms of texts into data that was computable and thereby interchange-
able. These qualities allowed for new forms of authorial assemblage
through re-mixing, sampling, and cutting-and-pasting of highly muta-
ble and (through the Internet) highly accessible texts. It created what
Miller (2004) termed a "gift economy" that supplies abundant textual

raw materials that allow consumers of all kinds of literacy texts to easily become producers of them. Johnson (2005) argued that as these kinds transformations in meaning making are taking place, "the culture is getting more intellectually demanding, not less" (p. 9). Gee (2003), in his analysis of how these transformations play out specifically in the domain of video games noted that the theory of learning reflected in these digital environments actually "fits better with the modern, high-tech, global world today's children and teenagers live in than do the theories (and practices) of learning that they see in school" (p. 7).

A number of studies have attempted to understand how and what intellectual demands and literacy practices are engaged by youth in digital environments. For the studies in her edited volume Alvermann (2002) broadened "the term *literacies* to include the performative, visual, aural, and semiotic understandings necessary for constructing and reconstructing print-and-nonprint-based texts" (p. viii). Chapters in this volume describe the new "attention" economy that is becoming increasingly pervasive; they portray literacies in the lives of people defined as "millennial" adolescents or "Shape-Shifting Portfolio People"; and, they argue that youth participation in digital technologies offers dramatically new ways of constructing meanings and identities.

An illuminating example of the some of these considerations was provided in a study by Fleetwood (2005). Her description and analysis of the production process for a narrative video about youth life in San Francisco's Mission District that was to be shot from the youth's perspective revealed provocative issues connected to practices of literacy and the creation and representation of identity through digital visual media. The question this study raised was could this visual media be utilized by youth for "authentic" projections, or did the larger community and organizational context surrounding the use of this media inherently work to mainly racialize and contrive youth identity? It was a question of could practices of literacy associated with visual media production work to transform rather than merely conform perceptions of youth. Fleetwood concludes that youth media production does provide possibilities for alternative representations of youth, but it does not resolve the complicated problems of youth being represented authentically.

WORK IN PROGRESS

In attempting to apprehend more authentic youth practices and representations, recent research has worked to counter characterizations of youth in mainstream media and political discourse as a "transitional" category and often marked as violent, or dangerous, or weird: "the devious computer hacker, the fast-talking rapper, the ultra-fashionable Japanese teenager teetering on platform heels. Youth in these incarnations personify a given society's deepest anxieties" (Maira and Soep, 2005, p. xv). The on-going work of these researchers attempts to capture and critique "the transnational imaginaries of youth culture" facilitated by the global reach of technology, but "always in dialectical tension with both national ideologies and local affiliations" (p. xxvi).

Other on-going research on learning and literacy of youth outside of schools attempts to capture their authentic textual productions and symbolic representations at the intersection of new or alternative digital media and the local and global manifestations of hip-hop culture. Miller (2004) continues to demonstrate the cross-fertilizing connections between hip-hop and technology noting, for example, that rap artists were quickest to exploit digital samplers and sequencers when these and other technologies suited their cultural purposes. A decade earlier Rose (1994) had argued that "hip hop transforms stray technological parts intended for cultural and industrial trash heaps into sources of pleasure and power. These transformations have become a basis of digital imagination all over the world" (p. 22). Now, contemporary youth in the U.S and globally are utilizing technological resources to sample, cut and paste, and re-mix multimedia and multimodal texts for replay in new configurations, just as hip hop DJs reconfigure images, words, and sounds to play anew (see Richardson, African American Literacies, Volume 2).

Work by Mahiri and a group of collaborators (2007) is one example of research at the intersection of digital media and hip-hop culture. One of the originators of hip-hop, DJ Herc, claimed that it "has given young people a way to understand their world" (Quoted in Chang, 2005, p. xi). It is widely considered to be a salient voice of contemporary youth – a voice that is electrified, digitized, and spoken through rappers' mikes, DJ music mixes, dance styles, and graffiti. The mic of the music DJ or the rap and spoken word MC is a potent symbol at the intersection of power and pleasure on hand inside this dynamic and comprehensive aspect of youth culture. The mic also marks the intersection and interaction of production and consumption of hip-hop texts and styles. Mahiri and his collaborators are documenting and analyzing the wide-ranging practices of literacy inside hip-hop culture focused on how these practices are manifested on both sides of the mic by producers and consumers who are writing and reading the world though vibrant, provocative, music-centric lenses.

Other work in progress by a group of distinguished literacy researchers under the direction of Banks (2007) is focused on understanding and theorizing the nature of learning that is "life-long, life-wide, and life-deep." This research is comprehensively addressing the nature of learning in the multiple contexts and valued practices of everyday life across the life span and attempting to connect the different and continuously changing "whats" of learning to the different and continually changing "whos" of learners. One strand of this research contends that for youth particularly, the complexity of rapidly changing repertoires of practice might be best understood as "semiotic domains" that Gee (2003) noted as "any set of practices that recruit one or more modalities (e.g., oral or written language, images, equations, symbols, sounds, gestures, graphs, artifacts, etc.) [to create] and communicate distinctive types of meaning" (p. 18). This research on learning for youth that is life-long, life-wide, and life-deep is attempting to understand semiotic domains that are increasingly linked to interactive, web compatible, digital technologies like cell phones, ipods, video games, audio and video recording and playback devices, as well as computers.

PROBLEMS AND DIFFICULTIES

Traditional conceptions of print-based literacy do not account for the richness and complexity of actual literacy practices in young people's lives enabled by new technologies that magnify and simplify access to and creation of multimodal texts. Similarly, traditional research processes (that intimately link to traditional conceptions of print-based literacy) are not well suited to capture these widely variable, highly changeable, temporal, and local acts of meaning making and identity construction. The novel, diverse, and transient text production and utilization we attempt to document, analyze, and publish are only realized long "after the fact" and thereby increase the possibility that the fact has significantly changed.

How do we bridge the generational divide between researchers and researched? If our informants are digital natives, we are more like digital tourists who are recognized immediately as if we were wearing fanny packs and white running shoes. I have tried to circumvent this problem by working with young graduate student researchers, but even they are quickly reminded that they are "old school." More importantly, how do we bridge conceptual divides that distort our views of youth practices as they are filtered through our more static cultural models? Particularly the primacy of modes of meaning making and representation for youth seem to have shifted from written texts to more dynamic and interactive visual, tactile, and sonic texts, yet the primacy of modes for attempting to report these shifts seems not to be affected at all by these changes.

FUTURE DIRECTIONS

A key challenge for the future seems to be to imagine and implement new ways to more fully and more accurately capture and reflect the significance of everyday practices of youth in part through their textual productions. Willis (1990) noted, "that there is a vibrant symbolic life and symbolic creativity in everyday life, everyday activity and expression—even if it is sometimes invisible, looked down on or spurned. We don't want to invent it or propose it. We want to recognize it—literally re-cognize it" (p. 1).

One of thing that needs to be "re-cognized" in research on the literacy and learning of youth is the centrality of practices of meaning making and representation through musical texts the selection of which enact narratives—sonic significations—that are increasingly enabled by digital technologies. "Sound," Miller (2004) claimed, "has become a digital signifier whose form adjusts its shape in front of us like an amorphous cloud made of zeros and ones" (p. 5). His point and intent (that more literacy researchers may also need to engage) is to create a "rhythm science"—"a forensic investigation of sound as a vector of coded language that goes from the physical to the informational and back again" (pp. 4–5).

REFERENCES

Alvermann, D.E. (ed.): 2002, *Adolescents and literacies in a digital world*, Peter Lang Publishing, New York.
Chang, J.: 2005, *Can't stop won't stop: A history of the hip-hop generation*, St Martin's Press, New York.
Banks, J.: 2007, Learning: Life-long, life-wide, life-deep. Center for Multicultural Education, University of Washington.
Barton, D. and Hamilton, M.: 1998, *Local literacies: reading and writing in one community*, Routledge, London.
Barton, D., Hamilton, M., and Ivanic, R. (eds.): 1999, *Situated literacies: Reading and writing in context*, Routledge, London.
Cowan, P.: 1994, 'Devils or angels: Literacy and discourse in lowrider culture', in J. Mahiri (ed.), *What they don't learn in school: Literacy in the lives of urban youth*, Peter Lang Publishing, New York, 47–74.
Cushman, E.: 1998, *The struggle and the tools: Oral and literate strategies in an inner city community*, State University of New York Press, Albany, New York.
Finders, M.: 1996, *Just girls: Hidden literacies and life in junior high*, Teachers College Press, New York.
Fleetwood, N.R.: 2005, Authenticating practices: Producing realness, performing youth, in S. Maira and E. Soep (eds.), *Youthscapes: The popular, the national, the global*, University of Pennsylvania Press, Philadelphia, PA 155–172.
Gee, J.P.: 1990, *Social linguistics and literacy: Ideology in discourses*, Falmer Press, London.
Gee, J.P.: 2004, *What video games have to teach us about learning and literacy*, Palgrave Macmillian, New York.
Guerra, J.: 1998, *Close to home: Oral and literate strategies in a transnational Mexicano community*, Teachers College Press, New York.
Guerra, J.: 2004, 'Putting literacy in its place: Nomadic consciousness and the practice of transnational repositioning', in C. Gutierrez-Jones (ed.), *Rebellious reading: The dynamics of Chicana/o cultural literacy*. Center for Chicana/o Studies, Santa Barbara, CA.

Gutierrez, K.D., Baquedano-Lopez, P., and Turner, M.G.: 1997, 'Putting language back into language arts: When the radical middle meets the third space', *Language Arts* 74(5), 368–378.

Heath, S.B.: 1983, *Ways with words: Language life and work in communities and classrooms*, Cambridge University Press, Cambridge.

Johnson, S.: 2005, *Everything bad is good for you: How today popular culture is actually making us smarter*, Riverhead Books, New York.

Lam, E.: 2004, 'Border discourses and identities in transnational youth culture', in J. Mahiri (ed.), *What they don't learn in school: Literacy in the lives of urban youth*, Peter Lang Publishing, New York, 79–98.

Mahiri, J.: 1994, 'Reading rites and sports: Motivation for adaptive literacy of young African American males', in B. Moss (ed.), *Literacy across communities*, Hampton Press, Cresskill, NJ.

Mahiri, J., Ali, M., Scott, A., Asmerom, B., and Ayers, R.: 2007, 'Both sides of the mic: Digital natives in the age of hip-hop', in J. Flood, D. Lapp, and S.B. Heath (Vol. II Eds.), *Handbook of Research on Teaching Literacy through the Communicative, Visual, and Performing Arts*, Lawrence Erlbaum, Mahwah, NJ.

Maira, S. and Soep, E. (eds.): 2005, *Youthscapes: The popular, the national, the global*, University of Pennsylvania Press, Philadelphia.

Manovich, L.: 2001, *The language of new media*, MIT Press, Cambridge, MA.

Miller, P.: 2004, *Rhythm science*, MIT Press, Cambridge, MA.

Moss, B.: 1994, Creating a community: Literacy events in African American Churches, in B. Moss (ed.), *Literacy across communities*, Hampton Press, Cresskill, NJ.

Pahl, K. and Rowsell, J. (eds.): 2006, *Travel notes from the New Literacy Studies: Case studies in practice*, Multilingual Matters Ltd, Clevedon.

Rose, T.: 1994, *Black noise: Rap music and black culture in contemporary America*, Wesleyan University Press, Middletown, CT.

Street, B.: 1984, *Literacy in theory and practice*, Cambridge University Press, Cambridge.

Street, B. (ed.): 1993, *Cross-cultural approaches to literacy*, Cambridge University Press, Cambridge.

Smith, M.W. and Wilhelm, J.D.: 2002, *"Reading don't fix no Chevys": Literacy in the lives of young men*, Heinemann, Portsmouth, NH.

Willis, P.: 1990, Symbolic Creativity, in *Common culture: Symbolic work at play in the everyday cultures of the young*, Westview Press, Boulder, CO, 1–83.

PIPPA STEIN

LITERACIES IN AND OUT OF SCHOOL
IN SOUTH AFRICA

INTRODUCTION

I imagine another universe, not beyond our reach, in which
[we] can jointly affirm our common identities (even as the
warring singularists howl at the gate). We have to make sure,
above all, that our mind is not halved by a horizon. Amartya
Sen (2006) *Identity and Violence*

Literacy learning in South Africa has never been value-free. Since
print-based literacy was introduced in mission schools in the nineteenth
century, through the apartheid era of Bantu Education (1948–1994), the
idea of literacy has been constructed by social groups and governments
as a marker of power and control, of exclusion and inclusion: between
'literates' and 'illiterates', 'Christians' and 'heathens', between the
'civilised' and the 'barbaric', between 'traditionalists' and 'modern-
ists', between 'English' and 'indigenous languages'. The advent of
democracy in South Africa in 1994 brought with it a new dispensation
based on human rights, social justice, equality and multilingualism.
Since then, attention has turned to what a more inclusive, culturally
responsive literacy curriculum might look like: what does it mean, in
practice, to design a curriculum which works towards integrated understandings of South African identities, despite the diversity of races,
cultures, languages, religions and histories? There is a progressive,
learner-centred curriculum in place, but paradoxically, the autonomous
model of literacy still prevails in most South African classrooms
(Chisholm, 2004; Kell, 2001), where multilingual children are learning
through the medium of English, their second or third language. Although
there are pockets of good literacy instruction in some schools, not
enough children are attaining the necessary literacy levels required
for success in school. What counts as literacy is, in the main, constructed within very narrow bands: 'in school' literacy learning in the
early stages is often the meaningless performance of phonic drills and
practice, whether children are learning literacy in their home languages,
or in English. At higher levels, literacy is taught as a set of decontextu-
alised, technical skills, with a focus on written language in its standardised forms. There is little attention to literacy as a technology for the

B. V. Street and N. H. Hornberger (eds), Encyclopedia of Language and Education,
2nd Edition, Volume 2: Literacy, 309–320.
©*2010 Springer Science+Business Media LLC.*

interpreting and designing of meaning for diverse purposes, discourses and audiences. As a result, there is evidence of low literacy
achievement and high dropout rates in the majority of schools.

This chapter presents a selected overview of research projects in
South Africa, which investigate alternative ways of conceptualising
literacy learning: here, literacy is constructed as a multiple semiotic
practice, used, inserted and transformed by agentive human beings
across local and global sites, contexts and spaces, discourses, languages and genres. In these multiple forms of crossings (Street,
2005), the relationship between learning in everyday lives and school
learning, and what might be an effective relationship between them,
is explored (Hull and Schultz, 2002). In doing so, it attempts to
reconfigure taken for granted assumptions about what constitutes rich
locations for literacy and learning.

EARLY DEVELOPMENTS

The study of literacy is an under-developed but emerging field of
enquiry in South African scholarship. An important body of work in
post-colonial, cultural and historical studies (Comaroff and Comaroff,
1993; Harries, 2001; Hofmeyr, 1993) explores the relations between
indigenous cultural and linguistic forms in Southern Africa, which
were predominantly oral and performative in nature, and their interaction with western cultural forms and epistemologies, including literacy.
The orientation of much of this work views literacy as a socially situated practice which African people appropriated for their own visions
of modernity and embedded in multiple symbolic systems. This interactive relationship between African and western forms of knowledge
positions African intellectual agency as central to these processes.

In her study of oral historical narrative in a Transvaal chiefdom that
was radically transformed by colonialism and capitalism, Hofmeyr
(1993) explores the dynamic relationship between orality and literacy
in the history of this community. She traces the impact of mission
school literacy, through its production of primary basal readers, on
out-of-school indigenous oral storytelling practices, and vice versa.
She argues that the overall impact of the agencies of colonialism on
oral performance was ambiguous. It was not literacy per se which
transformed oral forms: rather it was the political intervention of
literate institutions like the church, state or school, which shaped and
asserted how literacy was to be used and understood. Drawing on a
classic study of Xhosa oral storytelling practices by Scheub (1975),
Hofmeyr reveals the gendered nature of oral storytelling practices
in African households and challenges the idea of indigenous or
'traditional' oral genres as fixed and stable: rather, she demonstrates

how they shift and transform in response to social and political dynamics and pressures. The instability and hybridity of cross-cultural forms, modes and practices is an important idea which underpins this chapter.

In the field of educational scholarship, the political struggle against apartheid injustices provides the backdrop against which the major critical debates in educational theory and practice have taken place (Christie, 1992). There has been little attention, until more recently, to focusing on literacy education and pedagogy per se, except in the field of adult basic literacy education. Kallaway's (1984) edited volume of essays, *Apartheid and Education,* explores the origins and evolution of black educational policy, including education beyond schools in the radical adult education night school movement during the first-half of the twentieth century. Most of the investigation into school-based literacy has taken place within the context of wider debates on language-in-education policies within the context of the relative status and positions of English, Afrikaans and the indigenous African languages (Heugh, Siegruhn and Pluddermann, 1995). This is particularly the case in relation to the debates around the language of choice for early literacy, in essence, the impact of mother-tongue literacy instruction and English literacy instruction on children's initial literacy learning. Hartshorne (1992) points out that during the apartheid era, decisions about language-in-education policy were intended to divide African communities and limit their social mobility and access to higher education. Since 1994, in spite of the political will to promote multilingualism, and declare all South African languages equal, official languages, English is rapidly monopolising powerful domains like government, the media, schools and business. The dominance of English needs to be seen in relation to the struggle to establish a body of literature in African languages, the absence of which has a direct impact on the range and availability of written materials for early literacy learning.

MAJOR CONTRIBUTIONS AND WORK IN PROGRESS

In 1994, the ANC government, under the leadership of Nelson Mandela, initiated a new era in South African education. Nineteen departments of education, previously divided along racial lines, were combined into one national department of education. Faced with the challenges of producing educational policies which would address the inequities of the past and enable young people to enter the globalised world of the twenty-first century, the government introduced curriculum reform in 1998 through a national curriculum, Curriculum 2005, an outcomes-based model of education. This was later revised as the Revised

National Curriculum Statement in 2002. The South African model of outcomes-based education (OBE) differs from its international counterparts in its explicit emphasis on constitutionally enshrined values of redress, equity, the development of a democratic culture based on social and environmental justice, fundamental human rights and inclusivity, multilingualism and multiculturalism. The curriculum is 'learner-centred' and promotes participatory, interactive models of learning, emphasising the important role of the learner's interests, prior knowledge, history and identity in the learning process.

It was in this context of political and social transformation that a number of important initiatives in the area of literacy research took place. The government set out to redesign the assessment framework for education and training and a concern for literacy and Adult Basic Education was included. A major contribution to re-thinking literacy education within a social practice perspective in South Africa and influencing research traditions, was the path-breaking *Social Uses of Literacy* (Prinsloo and Breier, 1996), a collection of ethnographic case studies on the reading and writing practices of ordinary people in the Western Cape, who had little or no schooling. This volume formed part of the first wave of ethnographic research into local literacies research in the tradition of the New Literacy Studies (Barton, 1994; Heath, 1983; Street, 1984, 1993). This research aimed to make an intervention in adult basic education policy discussions, and challenge the universalism of most policy research by providing detailed accounts of the social uses and meanings attached to literacy in a range of contexts, from informal urban settlements to family farms, from townships to the taxi industry. Whilst the planners of the 1994 parliamentary elections considered 'illiteracy' to be a major barrier to knowing about the election and voting, only 1% of the votes cast were spoilt ballots, despite the fact that the ballot form was complex and lengthy. The work challenges the rhetorical 'literate'/'illiterate' divide operating in many educational and policy circles, that without schooling, adults are a homogenous mass of socially disabled people. The research demonstrates how people are able to draw effectively on local forms of knowledge, literacy mediators and forms of apprenticeship learning, in order to participate in processes and actions which affect their everyday lives.

There is a growing awareness in South Africa of the need for more ecological models of literacy education (cf. Barton, 1994) in which teaching young children to read and write has to be linked into much broader chains of sustainability. In a project focused on early childhood literacy learning, Tshidi Mamabolo an early literacy educator working with children from impoverished communities on the outskirts of Johannesburg, changed her 'autonomous' model of literacy pedagogy through reconfiguring the boundaries between home and school (Stein and Mamabolo, 2005). She set 'in school' activities which built on children's indigenous knowledges, identities and multilingual practices outside of school. However, she discovered that 'pedagogy was not enough': the effects of hunger, poverty and HIV/AIDS on her children's lives forced her to cross the boundary between school and home backgrounds, to try to 'get everyone on board'—households, families and communities—in order to sustain early literacy development across multiple sites and contexts. In remaking the conditions for reading, Mamabolo recognised that 'home background' rather than being in 'deficit', needs to be positively referenced as a matrix of social relations, social conditions and potentials for social action.

In a different version of an ecological model, Janks (2003) describes a whole school environmental educational development project in a poor school on the outskirts of Pretoria, in which critical literacy was nested within other projects, and contributed to the changes produced in the school. One of these classroom projects involved the children in collecting, explaining and illustrating their everyday games for children in Australia. This project drew on their out-of-school literacies and used their multilingualism as a pedagogic resource (see Freebody, Critical Literacy Education: On Living with 'Innocent Language', Volume 2).

It has been argued that the separation of early childhood development and Adult Basic Education and Training in different sites of delivery and curricula can undermine the potential of learning within the household or family. Culturally sensitive, organic models of family literacy in which meaningful partnerships are formed with family members, have much to offer in enhancing literacy in households. Pioneering work in this field was carried out in the early 1990s by Letta Mashishi (2003), who worked with parents and children in Soweto in the Parents and Schools Learning Clubs Programme (PASLC). These programmes were initially developed on the basis of requests from different communities of parents, who did not possess the requisite literacy skills to providing support to their children in school. The aim of these clubs was twofold: to encourage family members to share their experiences, knowledge of languages and cultural knowledge with their children and other members of the family; and to involve families in the effort to entrench reading, writing and learning as part of the culture of African homes. The PASLC curriculum which evolved over 10 years was based on a model of collaborative action research, allowing for high levels of democratic participation and resulted in synergies which directly impacted on parents' and children's engagement with literacy practices. A central focus of this work was discussion and research into African identities and traditional ways of life, including aspects of genealogy and kinship, musical and oral traditions such as praise poetry, family totems, family and community histories, which then became the content around which different genres of written texts were produced, in extended family chains of collaboration. Building on the fact that the majority of parents indicated that they had not considered that cultural factors such as family trees and praise poems could be relevant to their children's education, this programme was highly political and challenging in its assertion of the importance of African cultural issues and indigenous knowledges within the realm of family literacy. In this organic, contextualised model of family literacy, parents and children, together, forged an alternative set of texts and concerns to those operating in mainstream schooling.

Another example of a successful intergenerational family literacy programme is the Family Literacy Project, which works with groups of women from remote rural areas in Kwazulu-Natal (Desmond, 2004). This model explores ways in which mothers can support the development of their children's early literacy learning. Through the process of broadening the women's horizons through developing a culture of reading, the women come to understand the importance of their own role in relation to their children's healthy development. In 2003, a home-visiting scheme was launched where group members visited other families, took out books and read to children, and at the same time discussed child development with the parents.

The Children's Early Literacy Learning Project (CELL) is an ethnographic research project in the tradition of the New Literacy Studies, investigating the literacy practices of children across homes, schools, streets and communities. This project is trying to understand the key shaping influences which enable some children, and not others, to read and write in South African schools. This research observes children from a range of socio-economic backgrounds in their home and school environments. In a study of children in their everyday play in the Western Cape, Prinsloo (2004) describes how, in contexts where children's resources for representation are not strictly regulated by adults, the children drew in imaginative and creative ways on multiple semiotic resources from their official school world, peer social world, the world of the media and the home. Their games are characterised by a mix of languages, hybrid narrative resources, images and artefacts from local popular culture, including 'traditional' Xhosa and Christian church influences, from the mass media (TV and radio) and from schooling (see Leander and Lewis, Literacy and Internet Technologies, Volume 2). In their home language, isiXhosa, they used rich sources of image, metaphor and music. These practices were in direct contrast to the kinds of literacy pedagogy they encountered in school, which was mainly in the form of highly directed skill and drill teaching. Prinsloo argues that in the absence of meaning making activities in school which are connected to their social worlds, the children's chances of developing careers as successful readers and writers were limited by the narrowness of their school experience, rather than by their home experiences.

Stein and Slonimsky (2006) present data from the CELL project in their ethnographic study of multimodal literacies involving adult family members and girl children, all of whom are high achievers in school literacy, and who come from a range of socio-economic backgrounds. They investigate the microcultures in each family in relation to its ideological nature (Street, 1984): what kinds of textual practices count, by whom and for what ends, in relation to how different roles and identities for the child both as reader and as subject are constituted and projected. Through an analysis of particular family literacy events in each household, Stein and Slonimsky show how what counts as 'good reading practices' are not the same in each family. At the same time, they demonstrate how each adult family member uses the practice of literacy to project and orientate the child towards certain forms of worldliness. Each adult uses the practice of literacy to develop each girl's capacities to self-regulate, to map pathways of access in relation to aspirations and possible futures. These pathways include how to get access to various forms of linguistic, educational, cultural and economic resources. These pathways are both real and imaginary—the dusty roads which lead out of the 'shacks' and the 'townships' to the city of Johannesburg and beyond. The authors argue that the different ways in which adult family members shape and reshape the 'stuff' of literacy (Kress, 2003) with and for their children has deep effects on children's orientations to the future both as readers and as subjects.

In multilingual South Africa, a culturally responsive literacy curriculum has to include bilingual/multilingual literacy. In spite of new language-in-education policies which actively promote functional multilingualism, most parents want their children to have access to English as the language of power and internationalism (Granville, Janks, Mphahlele, Reed and Watson, 1998). The work of Project for the Study of Alternative Education in South Africa (PRAESA) (Bloch and Alexander, 2003) is committed to promoting African languages and developing African literature in African languages in the face of what they call 'the self-defeating language attitudes of the majority of people'. They argue that full functional use of indigenous languages at all levels of education is central to economic development and the development of democracy in South Africa. They propose that all South African schools should become dual-medium institutions in which the home language is sustained as a language of teaching and learning for as long as possible, alongside a second language of teaching and learning, and in which additional languages are offered as

subjects. An important part of PRAESA's work is enabling and supporting teachers to carry out an additive approach to bilingualism and
biliteracy in early childhood classrooms. In order to do this meaning-
fully and effectively, the project develops multilingual learning materials and story readers for teachers and parents to use in children's initial
literacy development.

In an attempt to understand the relationship between school learning
and students' learning in their everyday lives, the Wits Multiliteracies
Project (Stein and Newfield, 2004) has developed classroom-based
pedagogies which are multimodal, multilingual and involve different
kinds of 'crossings'—across languages, discourses, popular youth
cultural forms, indigenous knowledges and performance arts. The work
is based on an application of the New London Group's Pedagogy of
Multiliteracies (Cope and Kalantzis, 2000) to a South African context
(see also Leander and Lewis, Literacy and Internet Technologies,
Volume 2). These pedagogies attempt to move beyond literacy in the
form of written language only. Members of the project argue that
school literacies exclude the life worlds of those who participate in
them and they work with indigenous knowledge systems, cultural practices and languages within a critical framework that takes account also
of school and global literacies. Brenner and Andrew (2004), working in
a university context, explore the relationship between visual literacy,
identity and knowledge, in their class assignments which focus on local
craft forms, such as the *minceka*, a traditional cloth inscribed with
narrative forms, worn by women in Limpopo Province. Mamabolo's
Grade 1 children at Olifantsvlei Primary School made dolls based on
traditional South African fertility figures, as part of a project exploring
history, culture and neighbourhood.

Similar work which explores the contribution of multimodality to
designing culturally responsive curricula at the tertiary level is Archer's
(2006) research which demonstrates how pedagogies which incorporate multimodality and indigenous knowledges can yield successful
results for students from diverse language and cultural backgrounds,
who are studying academic literacy in an engineering foundation
course at university.

In an attempt to engage 'at risk' students in a Soweto secondary
school, an English teacher, Robert Maungedzo consciously worked with
multimodal pedagogies to stimulate his disaffected Grade 11 students
into creative production, hoping that this might stimulate them to
returning to poetry, which they had abandoned in the school because
it was 'too difficult' (Newfield and Maungedzo, 2006). In this project,
the students collectively made a cultural identity text, a large cloth
stitched with maps of South Africa, ethnic dolls, praise poems and
contemporary poems. They made this cloth to send to teenagers in

China in an international exchange project. The mixed media, multi-modal cloth they called TEBUWA, which means 'to speak'. Since this time, they have returned to poetry and written a collection of their poems which have been published. Their poems experiment in playful and original ways with forms of rap, text messaging and different South African languages, including township idiom, youth slang and the rhythms of kwaito, a genre of local popular music (see Richardson, African American Literacies, Volume 2).

PROBLEMS AND DIFFICULTIES

South Africa is engaged in a sustained process of recovery and recon-struction after centuries of racism, violence and oppression. The extremely damaging effects of generations of appalling apartheid edu-cation and poverty live on in people's psyches, senses of identity and selfhood. They also continue to affect people in very material ways, in terms of grossly unequal access in the society to quality education, and therefore to successful literacy learning. This is especially the case for the rural poor (Nelson Mandela Foundation, 2005). Whilst major gains have been made in overhauling apartheid education, with com-pulsory, improved access to schooling, free schooling for the poor, accelerated provision of school infrastructures, more equitable distribu-tion of resources, school-feeding programmes, better teacher–learner ratios, and better quality textbooks in all schools, the fact remains that the majority of South African children are struggling to become suc-cessful readers and writers in school, *in any language*. There are many structural, social and educational reasons for this, some of which have been outlined earlier. A key area of concern is literacy pedagogy: the new national curriculum allows for a range of meaningful literacy activ-ities, which incorporate and build on learner's knowledges, semiotic resources and multilingualism. However, teachers find this difficult to implement, for historical, cultural and pedagogical reasons (Adler and Reed, 2002). Educators have only recently begun to note the differ-ences in the long-standing international debate between phonics and whole language literacy pedagogies. Teacher education programmes, both pre-service and in-service, which focus on literacy as a social practice can work with teachers on how to sustain and develop learn-ers' literacies in ways which make sense to learners and which draw on their everyday worlds. Part of such programmes involve the devel-opment of teachers' own multiple literacies, as most teachers were educated in the impoverished apartheid model. This seems to me an important way forward to improving literacy pedagogies. Another area of concern is resources: learners all over the country need access to literacy materials in different South African languages, in print-based and electronic forms. These materials are more readily available in urban areas: hopefully, more sustained attention will be given by the government to adults and children in remote, rural areas, who live in conditions of extreme deprivation and hardship.

FUTURE DIRECTIONS

As researchers in the New Literacy Studies have powerfully demonstrated, literacy learning is part of much broader chains of sustainability and social development. In a developing country like South Africa, which straddles first and third world economies simultaneously, it is important to 'get everyone on board' to raise public awareness around the value and importance of literacy in sustaining democracy and human rights. Families, households, communities, the business sector and the government need to support the development of literacy as one of the enabling conditions for the practice of freedom, at all levels and in all sectors of the society. Culturally responsive models of family literacy can have positive benefits to all participants. At the same time, rigorous, ongoing academic research into literacy practices across educational contexts needs to continue and be part of education programs at tertiary levels. Whilst this chapter has mainly concentrated on research investigating out-of-school literacies, it is fair to say that very little research has actually been conducted into 'in' school literacies: it is time to look in much deeper ways into children's actual experience of literacy learning across the curriculum. This involves getting a better sense of children's engagement with literacy at different grades and levels, across discourses, genres and technologies.

REFERENCES

Adler, J. and Reed, Y. (eds.): 2002, *Challenges of Teacher Development: An Investigation of Take-up in South Africa*, Van Schaik, Pretoria, South Africa.

Archer, A.: 2007, 'Opening up spaces through symbolic objects: Harnessing students' resources in developing academic literacy practices in engineering', *English Studies in Africa* Vol. 49, No. 1.

Barton, D.: 1994, *Literacy: An Introduction to the Ecology of Written Language*, Blackwell, Oxford.

Bloch, C. and Alexander, N.: 2003, 'Aluta continua: The relevance of the continua of biliteracy to South African multilingual schools', in N. Hornberger (ed.), *Continua of Biliteracy: An Ecological Framework for Educational Policy, Research and Practice in Multilingual Settings*, Multilingual Matters, Clevedon, UK.

Brenner, J. and Andrew, D.: 2004, 'Identity and visual literacy in South Africa', *Visual Communication* 3(2), 177–188.

Chisholm, L. (ed.): 2004, *Changing Class: Education and Social Change in Post-Apartheid South Africa*, HSRC Press, Cape Town; ZED Books, London.

Christie, P.: 1992, *The Right to Learn: The Struggle for Education in South Africa*, SACHED/Ravan, Johannesburg.

Comaroff, J. and Comaroff, J.: 1993, *Of Revelation and Revolution: Christianity, Colonialism and Consciousness in South Africa*, Vol. 1, University of Chicago Press, Chicago.

Cope, B. and Kalantzis, M. (eds.): 2000, *Multiliteracies: Literacy Learning and the Design of Social Futures*, Routledge, London and New York.

Desmond, S.: 2004, 'Literacy for now and for the future: Working with parents and children', *Language Matters: Studies in the Languages of Africa* 35(2), 348–362.

Granville, S., Janks, H., Mphahlele, M., Reed, Y., and Watson, P.: 1998, 'English with or without g(u)ilt: A position paper on language in education policy for South Africa', *Language and Education* 12(4), 254–272.

Harries, P.: 2001, 'Missionaries, marxists and magic: Power and the politics of literacy in South-East Africa', *Journal of Southern African Studies* 27(3), 405–427.

Hartshorne, K.: 1992, *Crisis and Challenge: Black Education 1910–1990*, Oxford University Press, Cape Town.

Heath, S.B.: 1983, *Ways with Words*, Cambridge University Press, Cambridge.

Heugh, K., Siegruhn, A., and Pluddermann, P. (eds.): 1995, *Multilingual Education for South Africa*, Heinemann, Johannesburg, South Africa.

Hofmeyr, I.: 1993, *'We Spend Our Years as a Tale that is Told': Oral Historical Narrative in a South African Chiefdom*, Witwatersrand University Press, Johannesburg; Heinemann, Portsmouth; James Currey, London.

Hull, G. and Schultz, K. (eds.): 2002, *School's Out! Bridging Out-of-School Literacies with Classroom Practice*, Teachers College Press, Columbia University, New York and London.

Janks, H.: 2003, 'Seeding change in South Africa: New literacies, new subjectivities, new futures', in B. Doeke, D. Homer, and H. Nixon (eds.), *English Teachers at Work*, Wakefield Press and the Australian Association for the Teaching of English, South Australia. http://www.unisa.edu.au/hawkeinstitute/cslplc/documents/SEEDing/pdf.

Kallaway, P. (ed.): 1984, *Apartheid and Education*, Ravan Press, Johannesburg.

Kell, C.: 2001, 'Ciphers and currencies: Literacy dilemmas and shifting knowledges', *Language and Education* 15(2–3), 197–211.

Kress, G.: 2003, *Literacy in the New Media Age*, Routledge, London and New York.

Mashishi, L.: 2003, 'Reviving a culture of teaching and learning through Parents and Schools Learning Clubs', in A.E. Arua (ed.), *Reading for All in Africa: Building Communities where Literacy Thrives*, IRA publication, Newark, DE, 43–50.

Nelson Mandela Foundation/HSRC: 2005, *Emerging Voices: A Report on Education in South African Rural Communities,* HSRC Press, Cape Town.

Newfield, D. and Maungedzo, R.: 2007, 'Mobilising and Modalising Poetry in a Soweto Classroom', *English Studies in Africa*, Vol. 49, No. 1.

Prinsloo, M.: 2004, 'Literacy is child's play: Making sense in Kwezi Park', *Language and Education* 18(4), 291–304.

Prinsloo, M. and Breier, M. (eds.): 1996, *The Social Uses of Literacy: Theory and Practice in Contemporary South Africa*, SACHED Books, Bertsham, South Africa; John Benjamins Publishing Co., Amsterdam, Philadelphia.

Scheub, H.: 1975, *The Xhosa Ntsomi*, Oxford University Press, Oxford.

Sen, A.: 2006, *Identity and Violence: The Illusion of Destiny*, W.H. Norton & Company, New York, London.

Stein, P. and Mamabolo, T.: 2005, '"Pedagogy is not enough': Early literacy practices in a South African school', in B. Street (ed.), *Literacies across Educational Contexts: Mediating Teaching and Learning*, Caslon Inc., Philadelphia.

Stein, P. and Newfield, D.: 2004, 'Shifting the gaze in South African classrooms: New pedagogies, new publics, new democracies', *Thinking Classroom* 5(1), 28–36. International Reading Association, Newark, DE, www.readingonline.org.

Stein, P. and Slonimsky, L.: 2006, 'An eye on the text and an eye on the future: Multimodal literacy in Three Johannesburg families' in K. Pahl and J. Rowsell (eds.),

Travel Notes from the *New Literacy Studies: Instances of Practice*, Multilingual Matters, Clevedon, UK.

Street, B.: 1984, *Literacy in Theory and Practice*, Cambridge University Press, Cambridge.

Street, B.:1993, *Cross-Cultural Approaches to Literacy*, Cambridge University Press, Cambridge.

Street, B. (ed.): 2005, *Literacies across Educational Contexts: Mediating Teaching and Learning*, Caslon Inc., Philadelphia.

JUDY KALMAN

LITERACIES IN LATIN AMERICA

INTRODUCTION

Latin America is a heterogeneous region with deep cultural, social, economic and linguistic differences. International agencies such as UNESCO, World Bank, and the Economic Commission for Latin America (CEPAL) refer to the region as Latin America and the Caribbean in order to include not only the land mass stretching from Mexico to Argentina but also the small English, Spanish, and French-speaking islands as well. Disparities in class, race, language, and ethnicity shape literacy in Latin America. In 2000, 20% of the region's income was earned by 5% of the population and 46% of all families were identified as living below the poverty line. Countries such as Brazil, Dominican Republic, El Salvador, Guatemala, Honduras, and Haiti still have illiteracy rates above 10% and this figure tends to increase among indigenous peoples. As a region, Latin America has high educational gender equality. Male and female enrollment is nearly equal and the difference between genders in adult literacy statistics is just 4%. However, indigenous peoples are more likely to be illiterate than other groups. Indigenous women are more likely to be illiterate than indigenous men and although illiteracy in urban centers tends to be 6%, it is twice that in rural areas. Any discussion of literacy in Latin America needs to contemplate this socioeconomic reality as well as the history of literacy in the region, the role of schooling in the dissemination of reading and writing, and education policies promoted by international agencies (La Belle, 2000; Prins, 2001; Rivero, 2000; Seda Santana, 2000).

EARLY DEVELOPMENTS

School is the social institution traditionally responsible for the education of readers and writers. Starting as early as the 1950s, Latin American countries made universal literacy a national goal and began expanding their school systems in order to guarantee all children a place in a classroom. As a result, literacy rates climbed to 70% in the 1970s, reaching 89% region wide in 2005 (La Belle, 2000; Socialwatch.org, 2005). While most children enroll in school, many fail the early grades and/or drop out before finishing their primary education, creating a potential population for adult education and literacy programs (Ferreiro and

B. V. Street and N. H. Hornberger (eds), Encyclopedia of Language and Education,
2nd Edition, Volume 2: Literacy, 321–334.
©*2010 Springer Science+Business Media LLC.*

Schmelkes, 1999). However, the role of formal schooling of children should not be underestimated. Latapi and Ulloa (1993) studied the relationship between schooling and the dissemination of literacy. After considering the expansion of the Mexican public school system and adult literacy programs and policies, they concluded that declined illiteracy rates were due more to the growth of formal education, rather than programs designed to teach adults to read and write given the steady increase in school attendance and terminal efficiency and the disappointing outcomes of adult literacy programs.

By the late 1960s, official programs linked literacy to economic development and employment. Seda Santana (2000, p. 41) notes that "the general premise was that industrialized countries have high levels of literacy and therefore reading and writing were necessary conditions for national development." Adult literacy curricula tended to emphasize *alfabetización* or the learning of letters and sounds and then *postalfabetización,* the development of so-called complex skills and abilities considered necessary for the job market. However, many organizers of nonformal education programs associated literacy with Paulo Freire's theories of consciousness raising and oriented their efforts towards building a more socially and politically aware population. Perhaps the best-known endeavor of this type was the literacy campaign in Nicaragua. Before the revolution of 1979, clandestine educational activity persisted for many years. Following the fall of Somoza, the National Literacy campaign, involving 150,000 student volunteers was launched. Employing Freire's methodology, the campaign used short narratives based on the nation's recent struggle as the basis for their program. The organizers claim to have reduced illiteracy in 3 months from 50.3 to 12.98, although there is not a clear picture of the types or depth of literacy achieved (Freeland, 1995; Hornberger, 1997; La Belle, 2000; Lankshear, 1988; Miller, 1985).

The dominant language in continental Latin America is Spanish, except for Brazil where Portuguese is spoken. Over 400 indigenous languages exist in the region, some of them with fewer than 10,000 speakers. In countries such as Bolivia, Paraguay, Ecuador, Guatemala, Mexico, and Peru, the rate of illiteracy among the indigenous population is much higher than the nonindigenous population. One clear example of this phenomenon is Guatemala, a multilingual country with 15 languages having 10,000 or more speakers each. Data from 1993 put illiteracy among the indigenous population at 79%, as compared to 40% among the nonindigenous population (Psacharopoulos and Patrinos, 1993). Most of the literature on illiteracy and indigenous languages centers on bilingualism and national identity, the importance of literacy for development, the right to education in the mother tongue, and educational programs and policies. Shirley Brice Heath's 1972 publication of *La Politica del lenguaje en México: De la colonia a la nación* is one of the earliest in-depth studies of the issues from a sociolinguistic perspective (Heath, 1972).

It is important to note that not all prehispanic languages were unwritten. While Quechua, the lingua franca of the Inca empire was agraphic, several Mesoamerican languages were not. In Mexico, writing developed around 600 B.C. and was passed on from one culture to another. At the time of the Spanish conquest, for example, the Mayans engraved stone and wrote glyphs on folded sheets of *amate*, a paper made from the bark of a local tree. Scribes and priests used writing to record historical events, sacred texts, almanacs, astronomical calculations, and mathematics. The Spanish destroyed the *amate* codices and prehispanic literacy as part of their policy to impose social and cultural dominion in the New World (King, 1994). While local literacy was shattered, the conquerors introduced their writing system and uses of written language as an instrument of authority, still associated by many with colonial power and domination (Zavala, 2005).

Education programs developed for speakers of indigenous languages have historically been based on transition models and cultural assimilation policies aimed at building a homogeneous national identity. Schooling for indigenous children and education for adults has involved either teaching the colonial language and then reading and writing or creating a written representation of local languages and using it to teach reading and writing as an intermediate step towards literacy in the dominant language (Freeland, 2003). Programs designed for adults have had different outcomes but most have been unsuccessful. Adults often do not register for programs, and if they do, they tend to drop out before completing them. Cutz and Chandler (2001) have noted that ethnic identity requires adults to adhere to standards of behavior that identify them with their communities. This may include working in the fields or the forests, dressing in typical clothing, and speaking their language. Literacy and/or the learning of Spanish may be seen as a sign of disrespect.

Research during the 1970s and the 1980s was mostly instrumental in nature, oriented towards material development and program design and description. However, there are some notable exceptions. The most prominent literacy theorist in Latin America is Paulo Freire (Freire, 1970), well known for his book *Pedagogy of the Oppressed*, ideas about banking education and his advocacy for *conscientizaçao*—conscious raising learning processes. His work is still widely referenced by adult literacy program designers, informal education programs, and grassroots organizations and is used as a theoretical basis for the development of pedagogical actions in Latin America and beyond. Another early contribution was made by Ferreiro and Teberosky with the publication of their book (Ferreiro and Teberosky, 1979). Using a Piagetian framework, these two researchers from Argentina unearthed the process of conceptualization involved in understanding the alphabetic principle. This work has been the basis for rethinking emergent literacy throughout the region.

MAJOR CONTRIBUTIONS

During the 1970s and 1980s, various countries in Latin America were ruled by military dictatorships and authoritative regimes or engaged in civil war. The impact of these extreme circumstances on human rights, combined with the general decline in living standards, fostered social movements during these years. According to La Belle (2000), women were protagonists of these social movements. Their momentum was assisted in 1980 by the United Nations declaration of the Decade for Women. Many of the activities that women engaged in combined various forms of social action with literacy efforts (Prins, 2001). Recent publications explore women's literacy learning and experiences within community-based organizations, official programs, and religious organizations (Aikman and Untehalter, 2005; King, 1998; Medel-Añonuevo, 1997; Prins, 2001; Purcell-Gates and Waterman, 2000). A recurring theme in this literature is the role literacy classes play as spaces for socialization (Kalman, 2005; Stromquist, 1997). Women tend to be confined to their households and hindered by domestic responsibilities and oppressive family structures with few opportunities to interact with other women. Stromquist observes that "the literacy classes constitute very desirable social spaces. The classroom emerges as a setting that is socially approved for women and can offer services that are not available elsewhere" (p. 90). These services function as a site for social distractions, a self-help group and an informal social club.

There is consensus in the literature that the majority of current literacy research continues to be instrumental, what Arnove and Torres (1995) call "under-funded and under-theorized." Jáuregui, Jeria and Retama (2003) note that a great wealth of work has been done on curriculum design and evaluations of performance and quality. Seda Santana (2000, p. 49) points out that "in the midst of multiple demands, research has not been a major priority for Latin American countries." The applied nature of literacy research is due, at least in part, to its close ties to education programs and the sense of urgency to understand and solve what are conceived to be obstacles to obtaining the long-standing goal of universal literacy. Furthermore, adult literacy tends to be divorced from other areas of educational research and perceived basically as a problem of remediation (Kalman, 2005).

In the late 1990's, UNESCO supported research on the characteristics of functional literacy. The study, published under the title *Functional Illiteracy in Seven Countries in Latin America* (Infante, 2000), was carried out in Argentina, Brasil, Colombia, Chile, Mexico, Paraguay, and Venezuela. Using standardized tests for reading and mathematics, the study aimed to measure adults' abilities to comprehend texts with various degrees of difficulty, to do arithmetic calculations, read graphs, and understand numeric information. One of the most important conclusions was that all those tested showed some knowledge about reading and writing, leading the author to question the widespread belief in a literacy–illiteracy dichotomy. Adults classified in the lower levels of literacy had approximately 6 years of schooling while those with higher reading levels had at least 11 years. This led the researchers to conclude that functional literacy is correlated with at least 6 years of schooling. It should be noted that this finding did not consider more qualitative factors such as opportunities to read and write in everyday contexts or the availability of print materials.

Several studies have recently contributed a more qualitative perspective to a small but growing body of research on literacy, schooling, and social practice in Latin America. A study from Mexico documenting the dissemination of literacy in a semiurban township recently won the UNESCO International Literacy Research Award (Kalman, 2004). In this analysis, the author makes a conceptual distinction between availability (the material conditions for reading and writing) and access (the social conditions for appropriating written culture). She first draws on historical and interview data to portray the development of the town over the last 50 years as a context for using written language. Then she describes in detail a literacy class for some of the townswomen where the local history and culture were backdrops for learning to read and write. She notes that for those whose lives are basically confined to their town, their opportunities for accessing literacy are limited to the reading and writing contexts they encounter there. She concludes that opportunities to interact with other readers and writers are intrinsic in becoming literate.

Rockwell (2001) has also made important contributions to the study of literacy as cultural practice in classroom settings. She draws on Chartier's notion of written culture based on shared practices, artifacts, meanings, and attitudes. Her study centers on reading in a rural school in Mexico analyzing how the layout of the textbook and the ways in which reading was accomplished influenced the outcome of the lesson. She then discusses how students construct changing relationships to the written language through schooling. Zavala (2002) published an ethnographic study of Umaca, a small Quechua community of 70 families in the Andes. There she studied the different ways the townspeople perceive written language, how they associate different meanings to reading and writing and struggle with literacy in both their relationship with their traditional culture and with their efforts to relate to the dominant culture. Because written culture has been associated with Spanish and perceived as foreign to Umaca life, people there have never considered literacy as necessary or found its' integration into their lives particularly desirable. Not only did the participants not use literacy in Spanish, they found reading and writing in Quechua cumbersome and pointless.

All of these studies offer a different perspective on the study of literacy. Their goal is to further the understanding of the factors and processes that contribute to the dissemination of written culture, explain why literacy is not always rapidly embraced and recognize the complexity of literacy practices. Overall, this line of research contributes to a growing body of knowledge about literacies in Latin America and beyond. The value of these studies is not the potential for their immediate application in a given program, but the specificity of the cases that they examine.

WORK IN PROGRESS

One of the ongoing discussions in Latin America and the Caribbean is around the meanings of the term literacy and its representation in different languages. In Spanish, *alfabetización* (*alfabetização* in Portuguese) refers to both the process of learning to read and write and the presence of written language in a given society. Until the 1990s, the notion of literacy as divided into two phases prevailed. This concept claimed that an initial phase involved learning the most rudimentary aspects related to encoding and decoding written language, followed by a second phase of learning how to use written language known as *postalfabetización*. The majority of programs for unschooled and under-schooled youths and adults were built on this principle directing their efforts toward the acquisition of an isolated set of mechanical skills. Those unable to recognize the alphabet, name letters, read and write their names, or read and write simple messages were referred to as *analfabetos absolutos*. Those deemed as lacking in the abilities related to reading, writing, oral expression, and basic arithmetic thought necessary for employment were considered to be *analfabetas funcionales*. It should be noted that during the last decade these definitions have come under scrutiny. Broader notions of literacy and what it means to be literate have become subjects of dispute. These concepts have been debated in international meetings, academic publications, and among educators and policy makers in the region linking their arguments with similar debates in the international context (cf. Rogers, 2006; Street, 2006; UNESCO, 2005).

Researchers and educators have expressed concerns about the narrowness of the term *alfabetización* and its tendency to conceal the use of written language as social practice. In Brazil, for example, the term *letramento* has been used to analyze literacy as social practice and examine its pedagogical implications (Kleinman and Moraes, 1999; Masagao Ribeiro, 2003) whereas in Mexico *cultura escrita* is currently in use to broaden the concept of *alfabetización* to include both culture of reading and writing and the culture found in written text. The definition of literacy as social practice (cf. Section 1 of this volume; cf. Street, 2001) now has widespread acceptance, as shown by its recent inclusion in the curriculum for language arts in countries such as Argentina, Mexico, and Chile. However, this does not imply that it has been easily integrated into teaching practices.

In the 1990s, the term "youth" was officially introduced to region-wide adult education and literacy and education efforts to explicitly refer to the large number of young people who leave school before finishing their basic education. During this period, Latin America has witnessed the proliferation of education programs aimed at reincorporating learners of 15–30 years of age (or more) back into the education system. These programs tend to be more flexible, focusing on the social, economic, and cultural issues young adults face (Jaureguí, Jeria and Retama, 2003). An example of this type of *approach* is the recent program developed by the Instituto Nacional de Educación para Adultos (INEA) in Mexico. The accelerated basic education program based on academic subjects such as mathematics, science, language arts, and social studies also includes courses based on health, family, domestic violence, child rearing, and employment issues.

The *Centro de Cooperación Regional para la Educación de Adultos en América Latina* (CREFAL) published in 2003, a theme issue of its journal *Decisio* on the topic of written culture and Adult Education. This collection of papers, written for literacy practitioners and program designers, emphasized the relationship between written and oral language, the notion of multiple literacies (Robinson-Pant, Women, Literacy and Development: Overview, Volume 2; Rogers, Informal Learning and Literacy, Volume 2), the use of writing as a vehicle for learning and self-expression, and the complex relationship between those who read and write well and those who want to read and write well. All of these notions extend the traditional boundaries of the concept of *alfabetización*.

In this discussion of the significance and accomplishment of literacy, the exchange of ideas among researchers, policy makers, and practitioners has become crucial. An ongoing host for this kind of dialogue is the *Comunidad E-ducativa,* run by Rosa María Torres of the organization Fronesis. This group serves as a permanent forum for exchanging articles, announcing events, proposing measures and region-wide declarations. Along with the Fronesis web page http://www.fronesis. org/, it has become one of the principal resources for keeping up with current literacy and education-related events.

International agencies continue to play a major role in shaping literacy policies and related programs. As part of the policy aimed at achieving universal primary education (UPE) for all children, UNESCO currently promotes the development of libraries, the publication and distribution of books, and access to information, themes partly articulated through the shift of focus from individuals to 'literate environments' signaled in the Global Monitoring Report (Street, 2006; UNESCO, 2005). In Latin Amercia, this has been translated to a series of programs referred to as *fomento del hábito de la lectura* (promoting reading habits). Currently 19 Latinamerican countries have national reading plans with similar objectives and schemes of action. *The Centro Regional para el Fomento del Libro en America Latina y el Caribe* (CERLALC), an offspring of UNESCO, provides countries technical support for running their programs, organizing events, training teachers, librarians and other literacy personnel, and circulating information. It is not coincidental that these programs have developed simultaneously: the region is currently facing what has been called an education crisis, provoked at least in part, by the recent concern caused by the low achievement scores that students are obtaining on standardized tests and their poor rating in comparison with students in other countries, even after most Latin American nations have given priority to expanding their school systems over the last 45 years (Peña and Isaza, 2005).

The national reading programs are very similar in approach. They are based on the premise that reading is necessary for the development of democracy, the fight against poverty, the advancement of science and technology and, in general, a higher standard of living (Peña and Isaza, 2005). The idea that reading is essential for personal development, instills morals and values, and contributes to democracy by strengthening national identity and social economic development, is ideologically reminiscent of the 1960s literacy campaigns. The various ministries of public education seek to promote reading beyond the usual language arts curriculum, through book distribution programs for neighborhood groups, schools and public libraries; publishing programs to support the production of reading materials for young people; and working closely with teachers and school.

However, the programs do not exist without critics. Both Hernández (2005) and Zavala (2005) note that they operate from a single notion of reading and do not contemplate realities of people in Latin America struggling to get by. Kalman (2006) questions the idea that becoming a reader is a matter of habit and argues that written language use is deeply embedded in other communicative processes. Citing Rodriguez (1995) Seda Santana (2000) noted that legislating literacy often comes up against the conditions and variations of cultures. Becoming "a region of readers" will only be possible when the social world of diverse groups and cultures are taken into account. All authors agree that the distribution of books alone will not turn people into readers. The appropriation of literacy requires opportunities to interact with other readers and writers and participate in social situations where written language is key to communication (Kalman, 2004; Robinson-Pant, Women, Literacy and Development: Overview, Volume 2; Rogers, Informal Learning and Literacy, Volume 2).

PROBLEMS AND DIFFICULTIES

One problematic situation for countries in this region is the heavy influence that international agencies have in shaping policies and programs. From 1981 to 2000, UNESCO organized and directed its education policies for the region through the Principal Education Project for Latin America and the Caribbean (PPE). From 1981 onward, the main thrust was to promote primary education for children (Ames, 2003; Torres, 2004). Despite the importance official policies gave to literacy and basic educations for adults, few resources were channeled toward these areas. In countries where two-third of the rural population were illiterate, only 1% or 2% of their education budgets are/were directed to adult education (Arnove and Torres, 1995; Jauregui et al., 2003). This is partially due to the emphasis in international policy directives on UPE and the following reluctance of national governments to fund to adult literacy and basic education (cf. Rogers, Informal Learning and Literacy, Volume 2). The World Bank has also promoted the idea that investing in education programs for children brings a higher rate of return investing in adults (UNESCO, 2006; World Bank, 2003), although the Global Monitoring Report has scope for reintroducing emphasis on youth and adults (Street, 2006; UNESCO, 2005).

This policy has had several impacts on the direction of literacy work with communities and target populations. It has led educators in the region to separate literacy for children and adults, based on the premise that they could not learn together or from each other. As a result, many opportunities for intergenerational learning may have been missed despite the important findings on parent–child interactions around literacy from research in other contexts (cf. Ames, 2003; Rogers, Informal Learning and Literacy, Volume 2). It has also contributed to adult programs being second rate, depending on untrained volunteers, improvised spaces, and low social prestige. The poor funding and status of adult literacy and basic education has led to the dismantling of important state-funded organizations previously responsible for designing and coordinating learning opportunities. While many adult literacy initiatives have often been criticized for their irrelevancy, inefficiency, and compensatory nature, these policies have been a major obstacle to professionalizing literacy teachers, systematically documenting programs, and improving practice (Rivero, 1999). The current tendency in Latin America is to think of literacy policy as a two pronged agenda: preventive measures to provide high-quality education for children and keeping them in school, and the development of programs for marginalized youth and adults (Torres, 1998). In order for this approach to be translated into action, international agencies and lenders will have to reconsider their policies and create mechanisms for more local participation.

Although countries in the region are making efforts to provide education opportunities, both oral and written, to indigenous populations in their own language, literacy in indigenous communities continues to be problematic and insufficiently understood. Today, even with the development of some alphabetic representations, most of these languages are unwritten. The issue of literacy and illiteracy among speakers of indigenous languages poses important questions for the conceptualization of what it means to be literate (King, 1998; Freeland, 2003; Jones and Martin-Jones, 2000). In the strictest sense, one would have to conceive these cultures and peoples as agraphic, without writing, rather than illiterate, unknowledgeable of writing. In school contexts, indigenous languages continue to be used mostly as a bridge to the dominant language. What is needed is that the local languages be used as a means of communication and reflexion as well as the language of instruction. For writing to thrive, literacy policies will need new strategies that promote the use of writing and the development of indigenous writers who can create written texts from and for their cultures (Ferreiro, 1993). Currently, countries such as Mexico, Nicaragua, Colombia, Bolivia, Ecuador, and Peru are developing programs that emphasize the need to develop a strong sense of identity among learners in addition to learning to speak, read, and write both the dominant and indigenous languages. If the context allows it, this would also include teaching indigenous languages to nonindigenous speakers (Schmelkes, 2006).

Research in literacy has been characterized as dispersed and weak: it is permeated by a sense of immediacy that overrides other agendas. In general, universities and other institutions of higher education lack the infrastructure, the funding, and qualified personnel in this field. For this reason, much of what is available in local publications is centered on immediate program applications, program evaluations, material development, and policy analysis. There is an urgent need for a broader research agenda, graduate programs for training of new researchers, and increased collaboration and academic exchanges among researchers.

FUTURE DIRECTIONS

Globalization has caused important changes in national economic policies. One of the results of the incursion of Latin American countries into international markets has been economic growth during the 1990s, in some cases as high as 6.9%. Despite this statistic, the impact for local employment has been devastating (Hernández, 2005). Formal jobs are scarce and increasingly replaced by the rapid expansion of the informal economy: jobs located outside the formal social structures of work that do not adhere to labor laws, wage conditions, or social security and benefit regulations. They often include exchange mechanisms involving bartering, and activities such as household-based domestic work, day laborers, street vendors, and social services based on self-help. It is currently estimated that 40% of the work force in Latin America is informally employed, and the number is rising (La Belle, 2000).

Young adults in contexts of poverty are likely to end up in the informal sector. Often unschooled or under-schooled, they are ill-prepared for other types of employment. Recent research has reiterated that for survival in this job market, workers need to know how to read and write, make decisions in situations of great uncertainty, negotiate with customers, and calculate costs. For education programs to be relevant for young people and adults working in this environment, planners will have to contemplate the types of literacies and knowledges workers mobilize in this rapid expanding sector. Some activists would also argue that what we should really be doing is working to change this economic structure but that is beyond the scope of literacy programs alone and of this paper. The recent election of more governments with a stronger social agenda such as Michel Bachelet in Chile and Evo Morales in Bolivia is a reflection of these concerns.

Over the last four decades, urban spaces have been decorated with slogans and graffiti sprayed on walls, facades, or under bridges. Even the most unreachable spaces are turned into public displays of youngsters' loyalties and group affiliations. Murals exhibit common cultural icons that have been resignified to account for globalized urban identities (Valenzulea Arce, 1997). These and other types of representations are currently all but absent from research or considerations for literacy planning. Knowledge about people's meaning-making processes is important for thinking about their inclusion in written culture. Everyday literacy practices, alternative sources of text, popular literature, and symbolic representations form a fertile ground for both research and development.

New directions in literacy research should also include the use of Information and Communication Technologies (ICTs) (see Leander and Lewis, Literacy and Internet Technologies, Volume 2). Present efforts are concerned with the distribution of equipment and "technological readiness" while the ways in which ICTs shape literacy use (how people learn to use these technologies, the place they play in everyday communication, or how new formats and connectivity are inserted into the language life of communities) are still unexplored. The impact of handheld devices and the types of transformations in reading and writing messages has not been investigated. While there have been some experiences in using computers in classrooms in Mexico, Chile, Brazil, and other parts of the region, there is an assumption that their mere presence in schools will improve learning. It is often assumed that past curricular contents of literacy will continue to be essential for the future. As a result, computers have been installed in classrooms without much thought given to how teachers and learners will use them.

In the last decades, literacy in Latin America has been contextualized by tensions for educators, policy makers, and researchers. Literacy has been seen as a step towards the labor market and at the same time as part of the road to liberation. It has been promoted as a means of cultural assimilation as well as the means for preserving local cultures. It has been prioritized for children yet almost abandoned for adults; and efforts to understand literacy have been so instrumental in nature that many questions remain unanswered. A deeper view of literacy in everyday life, the emergence of ICTs, the role of symbolic representations in identity building among youth, indigenous people, women and other historically marginalized groups will contribute to the development of a broader notion of literacy in Latin America. In turn, this understanding can help frame new courses of action for shaping literacy in this part of the world.

REFERENCES

Aikman, S. and Untehalter, E. (eds.): 2005, *Beyond Access. Transforming Policy and Practice for Gernder Equality in Education*, Oxfam, Oxford.

Ames, R.P.: 2003, *Multigrade Schools in Context: Literacy in the Community, The Home and the School in the Peruvian Amazon*, Thesis submitted for DPhil, Institute of Education, University of London, London.

Arnove, R. and Torres, C.: 1995, 'Adult education and State Policy in Latin America: the contrasting cases of Mexico and Nicaragua', *Comparative Education* 31, 311–326.

Cutz, G. and Chandler, P.: 2001, 'Emic–etic conflicts as explanation of nonparticipation in adult education among the Maya of Western Guatemala', *Adult Education Quarterly* 51, 64–75.

Ferreiro, E.: 1993, 'Alfabetización de los niños en America Latina', *Boletin del Proyecto Principal de Educación en América Latina y el Caribe* 25–30.

Ferreiro, E. and Schmelkes, S.: 1999, 'Literacy in Mexico and Central America', in D. Wagner, R. Venezky, and B. Street (eds.), *Literacy: An International Handbook*, Westview Press, Boulder, Colorado, 444–447.

Ferreiro, E. and Teberosky, A.: 1979, *Los sistemas de escritura en el desarrollo del niño [Literacy before schooling]*, Siglo XXI Editores, Mexico City.

Freeland, J.: 1995, *The Literacy Campaign on the Atlantic Coast of Nicaragua*, World University Service, London.

Freeland, J.: 2003, 'Intercultural–bilingual education for an interethnic-plurilingual society? The case of Nicaragua's Carribean Coast', *Comparative Education* 39, 239–260.

Freire, P.: 1970, *Pedagogía del oprimido*, Siglo XX1 Editores, Mexico City.

Heath, S.B.: 1972, *La Política del lenguaje en México: De la colonia a la nación*, Instituto Nacional Indigenista, Mexico City.

Hornberger, N. (ed.): 1997, *Indigenous Literacies in the Americas*, Mouton de Gruyter, Berlin, New York.

Infante, I.: 2000, *Alfabetismo funcional en 7 paises de América Latina [Funcional Literacy in 7 Latinamerican Countries]*, UNESCO, Santiago de Chile.

Jáuregui, M., Jeria, J., and Retama, G.: 2003, *La educación de Jóvenes y Adultos en América Latina y el Caribe, Hacia un estado del arte*, Orealc/UNESCO, Santiago de Chile, 291.

Jones, K. and Martin-Jones, M. (eds.): 2000, *Multilingual Literacies: Comparative Perspectives on Research and Practice*, J. Benjamins, Amsterdam.

Kalman, J.: 1993, 'En búsqueda de una palabra nueva: La complejidad conceptual y las dimensiones sociales de la alfabetización' [In search of a new word. The conceptual complexity and social dimensions of literacy], *Revista Latinoamericana de Estudios Educativos* XXIII, 87–97.

Kalman, J.: 2004, *Saber lo que es la letra: una experiencia de lecto-escritura con mujeres en Mixquic*, Secretaría de Educación Publica-UIE-Siglo XXI Editores, Mexico, DF.

Kalman, J.: 2005, 'Mothers to daughters, pueblo to ciudad: women's identity shifts in the construction of a literate self', in A. Rogers (ed.), *Urban literacy. Communication, Identity and learning in Development Contexts*, UNESCO Institute of Education, Hamburg, Germany, 183–210.

Kalman, J.: 2006, 'Ocho preguntas y una propuesta', in Daniel Goldin (ed.), *Encuesta National de Lectura, Informs y Evaluaciones*, Conaculta, Mexico, DF, 155–172.

King, L.: 1994, *Roots of Identity. Language and Literacy in Mexico*, Standford University Press, Standford, California, 193.

King, L. (ed.): 1998, *Reflecting Visions. New Perspectives on Adult Education for Indigenous Peoples*, UNESCO Institute for Education and The University of Waikato, Germany, 224.

Kleinman, A. and Moraes, S.: 1999, *Lectura e interdisciplinariedad:* Mercado de Letras, Campinas. [Mercado de Letras is the Publisher, Campinas is the city-its in Brazil].

La Belle, T.: 2000, 'The changing nature non formal education in Latin America', *Comparative Education* 36, 21–36.

Lankshear, C.: 1988, *Literacy, Schooling and Revolution*, Falmer Press, London.

Latapi, P. and Ulloa, M.: 1993, *Diagnostico educativo nacional*, Centro de Estudios Educativos, Mexico City.

Masagao Ribeiro, V.: 2003, *El concepto de letramento y sus implicaciones pedagógicas*, Decisio, 10–13.

Medel-Añonuevo, C. (ed.): 1997, *Negotiating and Creating Spaces of Power: Women's Educational Practices Amidst Crisis*, UNESCO Institute of Education, Hamburg.

Messina, G.: 1993, *La Educación Básica de Adultos: La Otra Educación.* UNESCO, Regional Office of Latin America and the Caribbean, Santiago de Chile.

Miller, V.: 1985, *Between Struggle and Hope. The Nicaraguan Literacy Crusade*, Westview Press, Boulder and London.

Prins, E.: 2001, 'Critical perspectives on womens literacy in Latin America', *Adult Education Quarterly* 52, 55–69.

Psacharopoulos, G. and Patrinos, H.: 1993, *Indigenous People in Latin America*, HRO dissemination notes, Human Resources and Development Operations Policy, No. 8, World bank.

Purcell-Gates, V. and Waterman, R.: 2000, *Now We Read, We See, We Speak*, Lawrence Erlbaum Associates, Mahwah, New Jersey.

Rivero, J.: 2000, 'Reforma y desigualdad educativa en América Latina', *Revista Iberoamericana de Educación* 1–23.

Rogers, A.: 2006, 'DFID experience of adult literacy,' *International Journal of Educational Development* 26, 339–346 (www.sciencedirect.com).

Seda Santana, I.: 2000, 'Literacy research in Latin America', in M. Kamil, P. Mosenthal, P. Pearson, and R. Barr (eds.), *Handbook of Research in Reading*, Lawrence Erlbaum Associates, Mahwah, 41–52.

Socialwatch.org.: 2005, *Control Ciudadano*. Indicadores Sociales: Mapas, Tablas y Gráficas.

Stromquist, N.: 1997, *Literacy for Citizenship: Gender and Grassroots Dynamics in Brazil*, State University of New York Press, Albany, New York, 248.

Street, B. (ed.): 2001, *Literacy and Development: Ethnographic Perspectives*, Routledge, London.

Street, B. (ed.): 2006, *Fresh Hope for Literacy? A Critical Reflection on Literacy for Life*, EFA Global Monitoring Report, Balid/UKFIET, London.

Torres, R.: 1998, *qué y cómo aprender*, Secretaría de Educación Pública, Mexico City.

Torres, R.: 2004, *El laberinto de la cooperación internacional para la educación mirado desde America Latina y el Caribe [The Laberythn of International Cooperation for Education Viewed from Latin America and the Caribbean]*, Fronesis.org

UNESCO: 2005, *Global Monitoring Report*, http://portal.unesco.org/education/en/ev. php-URL_ID=23023&URL_DO=DO_TOPIC&URL_SECTION=201.html

Valenzulea Arce, J.: 1997, *Vida de barro duro. Cultura popular juvenil y graffiti [Life of Hard Clay. Popular Youth Culture and Graffiti]*, Universidad de Guadalajara y Colegio de la Frontera Norte, Guadalajara, Mexico.

Zavala, V.: 2002, *Desencuentros con la Escritura*, Red para el desarrollo de las ciencias sociales en Perú, Lima, Perú.

Zavala, V.: 2005, *La lectoescritura como práctica social; una reflexión desde la problemática educativa peruana [Literacy as Social Practice: Reflections on Education Issues in Peru]*, Presented at V International Conference on Reading and Development, Feria Internacional del Libro, Guadalajara, Mexico.

ELAINE RICHARDSON

AFRICAN AMERICAN LITERACIES

INTRODUCTION

African American literacies refers to the concept that African American
cultural identities, social locations, and social practices influence ways
that members of this discourse group make meaning and assert themselves sociopolitically in subordinate as well as official contexts.
This definition includes but goes beyond making meaning out of and
producing print and language in their strict and broadly defined
senses, to include the contemporary context rooted in technological
dominance which promotes multimodal meaning making. The term
African American literacies encapsulates the sociocultural approaches
to African American literacy education advanced by the various subfields: including sociolinguistics, rhetoric and composition, and New
Literacies Studies. As Americans of African descent had been enslaved
and marginalized within American society, the early scholarly thinking
about Black language and culture reflected the common prejudices of
the time: Blacks were culturally and intellectually inferior. Since the
1940s, scholars presented the systematicity, the West African background, the history and development of what is currently referred to
by linguists as "African American Vernacular English," with many language educators advocating inclusion of African American language
histories, structures, and discourse practices alongside those of the
dominant culture's to make literacy education socially just by repositioning students as knowledge-making language resources. Other societal domains should have an awareness of African American literacies.

EARLY DEVELOPMENTS

One of the basic goals of the Civil Rights and Black Liberation Movements of the 1950s and 1960s was for African Americans to gain
access to institutions and begin the project of a more multicultural
America. The 1954 Brown versus Board of Education of Topeka,
Kansas Supreme Court case won by the NAACP's Legal Defense Team
symbolized America's granting of completely equal societal status to
African Americans. This victory brought about the entrance of Black
students into America's previously segregated public schools, which

B. Street and N. H. Hornberger (eds), Encyclopedia of Language and Education,
2nd Edition, Volume 2: Literacy, 335–346.
©2010 Springer Science+Business Media LLC.

were not prepared to change their pedagogies or their ideas about the inferiority of African American language and culture. Early work in linguistic anthropology (Herskovits, 1941; Turner, 1949) and (socio) linguistics (Bailey, 1965; Labov, 1972; Smitherman, 1977) focused on the origins and development of Black English Vernacular (BEV) or "Negro Dialect" and its relation to other languages that have their origin in similar contact situations such as Gullah and Jamaican Creole. These experts uncovered significant West African language and cultural commonalities. The work of Labov (1969; 1972), Dillard (1972), and Smitherman (1977) urged educators to apply linguistic knowledge to improve Black literacy education. Smitherman emphasized the importance of Black language to Black culture, identity, and history along with knowledge of discourse modes, rhetoric, and linguistic surface features.

Labov's (1972) work investigated whether or not "dialect differences" had anything to do with reading failure: and if so, could educator knowledge of the differences between the two systems be useful in curricula design and delivery of services to speakers of BEV. Labov concluded that the conflicts between BEV and standardized American English were symbolic of the cultural conflict and racism that is inherent in the society at large, and played out in the classroom. Such work discredited the idea that African American students were culturally deficient and lacked verbal stimulation in the home (Bereiter and Engleman, 1966). Subsequent scholars focused on factors associated with the trend of literacy underachievement among African American students. They noted mismatch between schools' and students' language and culture, (Heath, 1983, in linguistic anthropology; Shaughnessy, 1977, in composition studies), teachers' negative attitudes toward Black students, (Goodman and Buck, 1973, in reading) Black communities' mistrust of schools, Blacks as involuntary minorities and their opposition to imposed ways of being (Ogbu, 1979, 1983, in educational anthropology).

Researchers have sought to develop literacy curricula using well-documented research on African American language and culture as the basis of instruction. (See Rickford, Sweetland, and Rickford, 2004 for a fuller listing.) For example, Baxter and Reed (1973) developed composition curricula. Simpkins C., Simpkins G., and Holt (1977) developed reading materials or "dialect" readers. In 1974, The College Conference on College Composition and Communication (CCCC) developed the "Students' Right to Their Own Language" policy, promoting the development of theories and practices for linguistic diversity in education. In 1979, a Michigan judge ruled that AAVE was a legitimate system of speech and that teachers needed to have knowledge of it to facilitate their students' literacy achievement in the "Ann Arbor King School 'Black English' Case." Yet, as a general rule, American literacy education operates on sanctioned autonomous models of language and literacy, whereby subordinated peoples are made to submit to the dominant official language (variety) along with its received ways of using language and reading the world.

The ideas of vernacular literacy (UNESCO, 1953), later expanded to vernacular literacies (Camitta, 1993) converge with African American literacies, where it is understood that the subordinated culture has literacy practices and values that may conflict with the dominant culture's and that the subordinate culture should define its own empowering literacy agenda.

MAJOR CONTRIBUTIONS

Ethnographers of literacy have uncovered African American literacies that are not acknowledged or built upon by educational institutions as they are evaluated negatively. For example, Gilmore (1983) observed Black adolescent girls on school grounds "doin' steps," involving rhyming and spelling of words while doing rhythmic body movements. Because of their participation in these routines, school officials denied them access to full participation in school sanctioned literacy activities. School officials as well as some Black middle-class parents interpreted these performances as oppositional to school culture. As such, school officials labeled these girls as bad girls and they tracked them as lower ability. Officials never considered the value in the girls' rhymes, for example, their employment of homonyms, their spelling abilities, and their display of embodied social knowledge. In the college context, researchers have identified such culturally biased educational experiences and note the development of adverse literacy practices within some Black students such as employing White supremacist discourse in their compositions or classroom talk (the use of "fronting," for example) because they think they will be rewarded [and oftentimes are]. (See, e.g., Canagarajah, 1997; Fine, 1995 [in Gadsden and Wagner] among others)

From historical, intellectual, sociolinguistic as well as social justice perspectives, the literacy experiences of African Americans must be taken into account in literacy education. Documented history attests to Blacks' struggle for literacy and education as a means of upliftment and liberation. (See Engs, 1987; Beavers and Anderson, in Gadsden and Wagner, 1995; Harris, 1992; Royster, 2000; among others) Gates' (1988) study traced an intertextual chain of distinct tropes, themes, and oral-written patterns in the African American canon of imaginative literature, wherein Black authors repeat and revise themes to point to their shared experience and cultural identity. Among these are the "freedom through literacy" and the "Talking Book" trope in which writers speak their voices into the Western text through their use of Black discourse patterns. Lee's (1993) work on the application of the Black discourse genre of signifying to literary interpretation is instructive. Lee drew on students' knowledge of the African American Language practice of signifying, which is based on indirection and shared knowledge to teach them how to interpret literature. Ball's (1995) work showed that some high achieving urban African American high school students preferred certain Black culturally based design patterns in their writing. This finding corresponds to the National Assessment of Educational Progress (NAEP) essays that Smitherman (1994, reprinted in 2000) studied where she found that raters highly evaluated Black students' writing as powerful and fluent when it evinced higher use of a Black discourse style. Both Ball and Smitherman recommended that educators build on these cultural strengths to enhance students' literacy education (see also Gilyard, 1991).

Such research within the milieu of African American literacies has substantiated that written literacy cannot exist without orality, literacy is informed by an array of socially constituted practices, understandings, and ways of being in the world, literacy is not a set of isolated skills that can be taught, acquisition of language, and literacy is socialization into particular discourses and worldviews. An important work by Gee (1989) surveys key studies with regard to literacy that inform scholars' theorization of African American literacies. Crucial ideas in these studies are the "the great divide" between literate and oral cultures [that literacy itself (without schooling) restructures thought and societies]; that oral practices are necessarily more bound up in group identity than "objective" written practices (Ong, following Havelock, Goody). One problem as Gee shows is how the literate/nonliterate debate evolved from the civilized/noncivilized conceptions of orally based cultures. Gee's (1989, p. 45) observation of this is an important one: "In modern technological societies like the United States, something akin to the oral/literate distinction may apply to groups (usually of lower socioeconomic status) with "residual orality" or "restricted literacy" and groups (usually middle and upper class) with full access to literacy taught in the schools. Levi-Strauss' recasting of the primitive/civilized distinction in terms of a contrast between concrete and abstract thought, now explained by literacy, comes then to roost in our 'modern' society." Gee rejects this line of thought, and along with scholars now identified with the New Literacies Studies hold that literacy is a social construction and what counts as literacy varies with context and is bound up in relations of power (for an overview see Street, 1999).

The decades-long literacy underachievement of African American students as documented in periodic reports such as the NAEP and other US Department of Education publications is not the result of massive cognitive deficiency among Black students. Research has presented evidence which suggests that a host of factors contribute to the so-called achievement gap. Among them are: low parent educational level, low social economic status, poor school resources, to name a few. One response to counteract the problem of parents' educational level is the institution of community and family literacy programs to promote higher levels of literacy and to help "at risk" students of color to excel academically. The theory behind this movement and others (e.g. vouchers, charter schools, school choice) is that access to well-funded schools, with lower teacher–pupil ratios and highly skilled teachers, will provide teachers with adequate resources to help students. This is a start but avoids the politics of language and literacy education for Black and poor people. One of the major roots of African American literacy underachievement is the ideology of White supremacist and capitalistic-based literacy practices that undergird curriculum construction and reproduce stratified education and a stratified society, which reproduce the trend of African American literacy underachievement. White supremacist ideology is insidious because it is entangled with the discourse of American meritocracy, which says that individuals are responsible for their own success, which is not entirely false. However, the value of individualism is consonant with White supremacy when large groups of students of color fail to achieve under its account. White supremacy in this usage refers to practices that confer privileges to white-skinned Anglo Americans and their norms, values, and ways of being at the expense of disprivileging people not of white skin, a form of racism. The percentage of students suffering under this paradigm is far beyond that of a smattering of lazy and cognitively deficient individuals who cannot measure up. The failure is not individual, but ethnic and cultural groups are underachieving under the present (decades-long) practices. This indicates that the problem is structural.

Characteristics of the ideology of White supremacist and capitalistic-based literacy include consumption, consent, obedience, fragmentation, singularity (as opposed to multiplicity), and positivism. The educational practices associated with this autonomous conception of literacy (Street, 1993) are naturalized in the system and taught to students as a set of isolated skills divorced from social context, politics, culture, and power. Teaching standardized English, a narrowly conceived academic discourse, and the "academic essay," are examples of the "neutral skills" needed to succeed in the corporate educational system and the market driven capitalistic society (Berlin, 1996).

Works such as that of Hoover (1982) and Ladson-Billings (1995) argue convincingly for culturally appropriate and culturally relevant literacy education, at the college and pre K-12 levels, respectively. Culturally appropriate and relevant approaches focus on integrating African American perspectives, along with those from the dominant culture, in a way that empowers students. Such teachers employ diverse teaching methods and become partners with the community.

Lanehart's (2001) state-of-the-art collection of essays by scholars entitled *Sociocultural and Historical Contexts of African American English* contains chapters by Wyatt, Foster, Baugh, Labov, and Spears which address the role of African American English (AAE) in education. In that work, Wyatt discusses the wide diversity of language use among African Americans even within the same socioeconomic class and how this is not usually factored into theories of language acquisition and literacy education. Foster's research explores the instructional uses of call-response to engage students in higher order thinking, whereas Labov addresses AAVE with regard to reading development. He reports on research with the Oakland Unified School District and holds that reading difficulty can be overcome if the profession and educators apply what we know. Baugh's work details what it is that the profession knows and how all concerned can apply this knowledge, whereas Spears contributes new understandings of directness in African American speech practices and how this should be dealt with in educational settings. Spears makes the point that the terms set for African American Language are "rooted in non-black discursive practices" (p. 243). Many social interactions which would be judged negatively in White-mainstream-culture dominant classrooms would not be judged as such in spaces where all Black norms prevail. Black teachers and administrators in schools in which Black values predominate can use direct speech in ways that build educational achievement and community among the students and the families of the school.

Drawing on sociolinguistics, African American studies, rhetoric and composition, literacy research and critical race theory, Richardson (2003) constructed a theory and pedagogy of African American literacies, attending to discourse forms and functions as well as what it means to teach and learn within these discourse practices. This approach locates African American literacies in a tradition of negotiation of vernacular and standard epistemologies and ontologies. Literacy for people of African descent is the ability to accurately read their experiences of being in the world with others and to act on this knowledge in a manner beneficial for self-preservation, economic, spiritual, and cultural uplift. In the work, *African American Literacies Unleashed: Vernacular English and the Composition Classroom*, Ball and Lardner (2005) cover significant issues which teachers of

AAVE-speaking students must confront. Teachers must face their subjective knowledge about AAVE and become willing to go against the grain as many have internalized unconscious negative racial beliefs and attitudes and educational institutions have set us in motion to gatekeep. Ball and Lardner approach the problem through building teachers' sense of efficacy and reflective optimism. Ball and Lardner define this important approach to literacy education as such:

> Efficacy acknowledges affect as an essential element in teacher's constructs of knowledge. Efficacy therefore pushes us to theorize unspoken dimensions of teaching practices, for example, its felt reality, and to trace them to their sources. Efficacy refers not just to what teachers know about linguistically and culturally diverse students but what teachers believe about their ability to teach students from various cultural and linguistic backgrounds. Reflective optimism as the correlate perception of those students' ability to achieve is reflected in the expectations teachers hold for their students' achievement. (p. 65)

Ball & Lardner work with teachers to help them develop culturally relevant pedagogy and to transform their identities as teachers who can teach all students.

An important review article by Alim (2005) revisits many of the issues and theoretical orientations outlined earlier, coupled with the current defacto segregation or resegregation of many urban cities and schools. Alim argues that critical language awareness pedagogies are desperately needed. In this view, it is not enough to teach unequal power relations and standardized English. Language and literacy educators use students' own discourse practices, their Hiphop literacies, for example, to critically engage them in research and action, to confront and change racist discourse practices and institutions that promote them (see Mahiri, Literacies in the Lives of Urban Youth, Volume 2).

WORK IN PROGRESS: NEW THOUGHT IN AFRICAN AMERICAN LITERACIES—POPULAR CULTURE AND GLOBAL LITERACIES

Morgan's (2002) work helps scholars to understand how Black youth inscribe their identities through urban, working class and Black language use, how they mark public space therewith, the worldviews they bring to bear on their gendered, sexed, classed, racialized, and otherwise embodied readings of the world. As Black youth culture provides grist for the mill of popular culture in digital media and a wide array of industries, scholars have taken up these understandings of Black youth language and applied them to their documentation of the development of global literacies.

Pennycook (2003) and Androutsopolous (2004) show that certain Black discourse and literacy practices have been incorporated into Japanese and German youth Hiphop, for example, language in offline and online contexts, respectively. Following this line of inquiry, Richardson (2006) explores Hiphop literacies of Black youth, the ways in which those who participate in Hiphop cultural practices manipulate as well as read and produce language, gestures, images, material possessions, and people, to position and protect themselves advantageously. Richardson attempts to locate strands of Hiphop discourse within global, dominant and vernacular contexts and relate these to the lived experiences of Black people, emanating from their quest for self-realization, their engagement in a discursive dialectic between various vernacular and dominant discourses and semiotic systems. Such lines of study underscore motivation for language acquisition, language change, identity negotiation, globalization and the conflicting evaluations of Black representations, how Black symbols are representative of power and powerlessness, the resilience, identification, and commodification of the global youth village. Such issues provide a complex view of African American Language and its potential in the larger scheme of things. Several scholars have advocated Hiphop or popular culture pedagogies at lower and higher levels of schooling, enlisting the rich knowledge that youth have about the world they live in and how these can be enlisted in literacy education (e.g., Alim, 2006; Haas Dyson, 2003; Jackson, Michel, Sheridan, and Stumpf, 2001; Morrell and Duncan Andrade, 2002; Yasin, 2003).

PROBLEMS, DIFFICULTIES, AND FUTURE DIRECTIONS

Though there has been significant support for application of knowledge of African American language and literacy in educational institutions, there are a range of problems of which institutions and instructors must be aware. A question that often arises is how will educational institutions become a site where no single historic group dominates the core experience in a dominating society? Further, as cultural practices and identities are always in flux so are literacies. This situation requires that educational institutions become more open to helping students adapt their literacies to an ever changing world, while simultaneously recognizing the role of identity, history, and context in literacy. This should not be understood as using students' home discourse to indoctrinate them into "traditional literacy." Recent work geared toward the gendered aspects of literacy for Black males and females (as well as to other groups) demonstrates this sensitivity (Lanehart, 2002; Richardson, 2003, Tatum, 2005, See the chapters of Slaughter-Defoe and Richards; and Fine in Gadsden and Wagner, 1995, for example).

Culturally centered approaches to literacy education emphasize a holistic view. In other words, comparative/contrastive measures should not be understood to mean emphasis on only the grammatical surface level, but rather on the totality of different discourses as different ways of being in the world, the conflicts, coincidences, possibilities for change. Another factor that must be considered in improving literacy education is the role of institutional language policies and philosophies. Blake and Cutler (2003) report on a study of five (5) New York City public schools and their teachers' attitudes toward "African American English" (AAE) and language policies or lack thereof for AAE-speaking students. This work suggests that schools' philosophies influenced teachers' disposition toward AAE-speaking students. For example, the school with the large bilingual population had a philosophy that promoted linguistic diversity and its teachers had greater sensitivity to issues of AAE-speaking students. Baugh (1995) underscores significant problems that need to be addressed to reform delivery of educational services to African American students. Teachers along with the larger society harbor misinformed and racist beliefs about African American English though linguists have proved otherwise. In theory, all languages and varieties are equal, but in practice, they are not. Societal beliefs influence institutions, especially the law, which does not recognize African American English-speaking students as language minorities. This predicament denies AAE-speaking students funding which could be used to improve education. Another problem is that speech pathology is used to refer African American English-speaking students to special education, though AAE is not pathological. Further, sometimes schools place AAE-speaking students in classes with students for whom English is not their "native" language, which presents a different set of problems, though both groups experience barriers to an equitable education. Baugh argues that there is a need for policies and programs that address the literacy needs of linguistically diverse students.

FUTURE RESEARCH DIRECTIONS

Heightening awareness of the politics of literacy education of African American students cannot be overstated. The most recent Ebonics Controversy of 1996 revealed not only the continued devaluation of Black culture and racist positions held by the general public but by the U.S. government as well. Research has continued to plumb the language and literacy acquisition of African American students, much of it providing fodder for comparative studies of literacy in various contexts

and how the various strengths of Black students, their families, and
their teachers can be built on for successful delivery of literacy education. Investigation of school policies and attitudes toward Black students is another important area that deserves continued study. In the
current era of high stakes testing and national standards, critical
research on teaching, reading, and writing as well as assessment will
continue to be invaluable. Though we must pay attention to the ever
evolving condition of globalization, emigration, and continued cultural
contact and shift as these affect the literacy development of our students, I agree with Auerbach (2005): It is abundantly clear that major
global forces, not individual competence, shape life possibilities, and
that to promote new multimodal literacies as the key to participation
in the globalized world risks becoming a new version of the literacy
myth. (p. 369)

There is a continued need for research that strives to contribute to
more democratic literacy education and a better world.

REFERENCES

Auerbach, E.: 2005, 'Connecting the local and the global: A pedagogy of not-
    literacy', in J. Anderson, (eds.), *Portraits of Literacy Across Families, Commu-
    nities, and Schools: Intersections and Tensions*, Lawrence Erlbaum Associates,
    Mahwah, NJ.
Alim, H.S.: 2006, *Roc the Mic: The Language of Hip Hop Culture*, Routledge, New
    York and London.
Alim, H.S.: 2005, 'Critical language awareness in the United States: Revisiting issues
    and revising pedagogies in a resegregated society', *Educational Researcher* 34.7,
    24–31.
Androutsopoulos, J.: 2004, 'Non-native English and sub-cultural identities in media
    discourse', in H. Sandøy (ed.), *Den Fleirspråklege Utfordringa*, Novus, Oslo,
    83–98. http://www.fu-berlin.de/phin/phin19/p19t1.htm
Bailey, B.: 1965, 'Toward a new perspective in negro English dialectology', *American
    Speech* 40, 171–7.
Ball, A. and Lardner, T.: 2005, *African American Literacies Unleashed: Vernacular
    English and the Composition Classroom*, Southern Illinois University Press,
    Carbonade, IL.
Ball, A.: 1995, 'Text design patterns in the writing of urban African American stu-
    dents: Teaching to the cultural strengths of students in multicultural settings',
    Urban Education 30.3, 253–289.
Baugh, J.: 1995, 'The law, linguistics, and education: Educational reform for African,
    American language minority students', *Linguistics and Education* 7, 87–105.
Baxter, M. and Reed, C.: 1973, *Teachers Manual for Teaching Standard English Writ-
    ing to Speakers Showing Black English Influences in Their Writing*, Language
    Curriculum Research Group, Department of Educational Services, Brooklyn
    College, Brooklyn, NY.
Bereiter, C. and Engelmann, S.: 1966, *Teaching Disadvantaged Children in Pre-
    school*, Prentice-Hall, NJ, New York.
Berlin, J.: 1996, *Rhetorics, Poetics, and Cultures: Refiguring College English Studies*,
    National Council of Teachers of English, Urbana, IL.

Blake, R. and Cutler, C.: 2003, 'AAE and variation in teachers' attitudes: A question of school philosophy', *Linguistics and Education* 14.2, 163–194.

Camitta, M.: 1993, 'Vernacular writing: Varieties of literacy among Philadelphia high school students', in B. Street (ed.), *Cross-Cultural Approaches to Literacy*, Cambridge University Press, Cambridge.

Canagarajah, A.S.: 1997, Safe houses in the contact zone: Coping strategies of African American students in the academy, *Journal of the Conference on College Composition and Communication* 48.2, 173–96.

Dillard, J.L.: 1972, *Black English: Its history and usage in the United States*, Random House.

Engs, R.F.: 1987, Historical perspectives on the problem of black literacy, *Educational Horizons* 66.1, 13–17.

Gadsden, V.L., and Wagner, D. (eds.): 1995, *Literacy Among African American Youth: Issues in Learning, Teaching, and Schooling*, Hampton Press, Creskill, NJ.

Gates, H.L.: 1988, *The Signifyin(g) Monkey: A Theory of African American Literary Criticism*, Harvard University Press, Cambridge, MA.

Gee, J.: 1989, Orality and literacy: From the savage mind to ways with words, *Journal of Education* 171.1, 39–60.

Gilyard, K.: 1991, *Voices of the Self: A Study of Language Competence*, Wayne State University Press, Detroit, MI.

Goodman, K. and Buck, C.: 1973, 'Dialect barriers to reading revisited', *Reading Teacher* 27.1, 6–12.

Haas Dyson, A.: 2003, *The Brothers and Sisters Learn to Write: Popular Literacies in Childhood and School Cultures*, Teachers College Press, New York.

Harris, V.: 1992, 'African American conceptions of literacy: A historical perspective', *Theory into Practice* 31.4, 276–286.

Heath, S.B.: 1983, *Ways With Words: Language, Life and Work in Communities and Classrooms*, Cambridge University Press, Cambridge, UK.

Herskovits, M.: 1941, *The Myth of the Negro Past*, Harper & brothers, New York and London.

Hoover, M.: 1982, A culturally appropriate approach to teaching basic (and other) critical communication skills to black college students, *Negro Educational Review*, 33.1, 4–27.

Jackson, A., Michel, T., Sheridan, D. and Stumpf, B.: 2001, 'Making connections in the contact zones: Towards a critical praxis of rap music and hip hop culture', *Black Arts Quarterly*, 6.2; H. Samy Alim (ed.), *Hip Hop Culture:Language, Literature, Literacy and the Lives of Black Youth*. Committee on Black Performing Arts-Stanford University, Stanford, CA (Special Edition).

Labov, W.: 1969, *The Study of Nonstandard English*, Center for Applied Linguistics, Washington, DC.

Labov, W. 1972, *Language in the Inner City: Studies in the Black English Vernacular*, University of Pennsylvania Press, Philadelphia, PA.

Ladson- Billings, G.: 1995, 'Toward a theory of culturally relevant pedagogy', *American Educational Research Journal*, 32.3, 465–491.

Lanehart, S. (ed.): 2001, *Sociocultural and Historical Contexts of African American English*, John Benjamins, Philadelphia, PA and The Netherlands.

Lanehart, S.: 2002, *Sista Speak!: Black Women Kinfolk Talk about Language and Literacy*, University of Texas Press, Austin, TX.

Lee, C.D.: 1993, *Signifying as a Scaffold to Literary Interpretation: The Pedagogical Implications of an African American Discourse Genre*, NCTE, Urbana, IL.

Morgan, M.: 2002, *Language, Discourse, and Power in African American Culture*, Cambridge University Press, New York.

Morrell, E. and Duncan-Andrade, J.: 2002, Promoting academic literacy with urban youth through engaging hip hop culture', *English Journal* 89–92.

Ogbu, J.: 1979, Social stratification and the socialization of competence, *Anthropology and Education Quarterly* 10.1, 3–20.

Ogbu, J.: 1983, Minority status and schooling in plural societies, *Comparative Education Review* 20.2, 168–190.

Pennycook, A.: 2003, 'Global Englishes, Rip Slyme, and Performativity', *Journal of Sociolinguistics* 7(4), 513–533.

Richardson, E.: 2006, *Hiphop Literacies*, Routledge, New York and London.

Richardson, E.: 2003, *African American Literacies*, Routledge, New York and London.

Rickford, J., Sweetland, J., and Rickford, A.: 2004, 'African American English and other vernaculars in education: A topic-coded bibliography', *Journal of English Linguistics* 32.3, 230–320.

Royster, J.: 2000, *Traces of a Stream: Literacy and Social Change Among African American Women*, University of Pittsburgh Press, Pittsburgh, PA.

Simpkins, C., Simpkins, G., and Holt, G.: 1977, *Bridge, A Cross-Culture Reading Program: Study Book*, Houghton Mifflin, Boston, MA.

Smitherman, G.: 1977/1986, *Talkin and Testifyin: The Language of Black America*. Hougton Mifflin, Boston, MA; reissued, with revisions, Wayne State University Press, Detroit.

Smitherman, G.: 2000, 'The blacker the berry, the sweeter the juice', in *Talkin that Talk: Language, Culture, and Education in African America*, Routledge, New York and London, 176–191.

Street, B. (ed.): 1993, *Cross-Cultural Approaches to Literacy*, Cambridge University Press, New York.

Street. B.: 1999, 'The meanings of literacy', in D. Wagner, R.L. Venezky, and B. Street (eds.), *Literacy: An International Handbook*, Westview Press, Boulder, CO and UK, 34–40.

Tatum, A.: 2005, *Teaching Reading to Black Adolescent Males: Closing the Acheivement Gap*, Stenhouse Publishers, Portland, ME..

Turner, L.D.: 1949, *Africanisms in the Gullah Dialect*, University of Chicago Press, Chicago, IL.

UNESCO: 1953, *The Use of Vernacular Language In Education*. UNESCO, Paris.

Yasin, J.: 2003, 'Hip Hop meets the Writing Classroom', in C. Coreil and A. Moulton (eds.), *Multiple Intelligences, Howard Gardner and New Methods in College Teaching*, New Jersey City University, New Jersey City, NJ, 75–82.

EVE GREGORY

CITY LITERACIES

INTRODUCTION

'Until then, I had thought each book spoke of the things . . . that lie out-side books. Now I realised that, not infrequently, books speak of books; it is as if they spoke amongst themselves. It (the library) was, then, the place of a long . . . murmuring, an imperceptible dialogue between one parchment and another, a living thing, a receptacle of powers not to be ruled by human mind, a treasure of secrets emanated by many minds, surviving the death of those who produced them or their conveyors . . .' (Eco 1980: p. 286)

Cities, the home of many of the world's great libraries, have traditionally been recognised as a hub of both literacy and illiteracy; proudly boasting literacy excellence in their wealth and variety of resources and practices and sadly acknowledging high levels of literacy failure in their inner-city schools. Below is a review of existing literature documenting the history and development of 'city literacies', translated into 'literacies in cities'. This is followed by a more detailed account of recent major contributions to the field and trends in research in progress with special reference to individuals growing up and becoming literate at the beginning and the end of the twentieth century in London, one of the largest and most ethnically diverse cities in the world.

EARLY DEVELOPMENTS

A number of historical studies include literacy in cities as part of a more general history of literacy. A comprehensive account of the history of literacy by Levine (1986) stresses the importance of Athens as the first city with widespread institutionalisation of literacy around 500 BC. However, although literacy made possible the wide diffusion of Greek ideals throughout the Mediterranean world, there was still a strong preference for oral dialectic (Havelock, 1976). Throughout history, however, it is clear that city life gradually facilitated and fostered the written mode and that literacy competences were generally more developed in cities (Clanchy, 1979). London was particularly advanced in this respect. Thus, wills were officially listed in London from 1258 and records kept by royalty of personnel in the state chancery etc. from the early Middle Ages (Levine, 1986). Papal documentation in Rome

B. V. Street and N. H. Hornberger (eds), Encyclopedia of Language and Education, 2nd Edition, Volume 2: Literacy, 347–355.
©*2010 Springer Science+Business Media LLC.*

reveals 300 writs in 1130 (Clanchy, 1979), a similar concentration of literacy to the city of Rome.

From the Renaissance on, cities were regularly populated by a higher proportion of literates and attracted more literate immigrants. They also held more formal and informal opportunities for learning and literacy education. Among other studies, Cressy (1980) documents impressively high rates of literacy amongst the merchant classes of late medieval London where literacy had a practical value for most professions and crafts. Cressy stresses that sixteenth century London women were precocious readers—something unknown in the rest of England—and highlights the fact that seventeenth century Londoners were unique in Britain whereby only 22% made marks as opposed to 70% who were unable to sign outside the capital. Studies of similar cities, for example Florence, show rates of literacy far exceeding more rural parts of Italy. As Graff (1987) stresses, not only were people in cities more likely to be in trades and professions needing literacy, they were also more likely to understand national vernaculars than rural folk, giving them not only an additional stimulus for acquiring literacy but also access to more materials. According to Graff, cities across Europe were hosting groups of readers, whereby books would be read out loud to both literates and illiterates.

Social historians focus on the importance of literacy as a means for galvanising workers, often in cities, into rebellion against oppression. In 'The History of the Working Class' (1963), Thompson stresses the uniqueness of 'Radical London' for 200 years (from the seventeenth to the nineteenth centuries), which was always more heterogeneous and fluid in its social and occupational definition than the Midlands or northern towns which were clustered into two or three staple industries. The population of London read more widely and was more sophisticated in its agitations. However, as the city grew, not all were able to be so literate. Altick (1957) stresses the contrasts between the literate artisans of London's West End who were 'almost to a man red-hot politicians' (p. 267) and the unskilled labourers of East London who remained 'a different class of people' who, through their lack of literacy 'have no political opinions at all' (p. 51).

The nineteenth century, indeed, saw a huge expansion of industrialisation in cities in Europe and USA leading to two very separate developments which would later influence late twentieth century and early twenty-first century research into literacy and illiteracy. Both took place within the context of the burgeoning of industry leading to the necessity for a literate workforce and both reveal opposite sides of the coin of literacy and illiteracy resulting from this. In Britain, for example, although basic literacy was offered to all children through the 1870 Education Reform Act which paved the way for free elementary schooling in 1891, it was clear that the government aim was for workers only to be literate enough to be able to follow instructions rather than being literate enough to begin to question the conditions in which they were forced to work (Inwood, 1998).This tension between the growing demands of industry and the low standard of literacy delivered to and achieved by workers was to be the subject of a number of more recent large-scale studies on illiteracy in cities. On the other hand, literacy for poorer urban workers was generally improving. In smaller as well as larger cities, people were rapidly developing their literacy skills by turning to the radical press to further their case for more humane working conditions. Thompson (1963) documents working-class radical papers, such as 'The Gauntlet', 'The Poor Man's Advocate' and 'The Working Man's Friend' highlighting the spurt in working-class urban literacy as well as noting that Cobbett's Second Register sold between 40 and 60,000 copies in 1817.

Historical studies, therefore, leave us with contrasting views of literacies in cities; of both a lively and radical reading public encompassing not only the wealthy and artisans but also the newly urban working-class, as opposed to a large group of illiterates from the unskilled or unemployed labouring urban populace.

MAJOR RECENT CONTRIBUTIONS

During the last decades of the twentieth century, considerable concern was growing over the poor literacy skills of inner-city children as well as the 'functional illiteracy' (Vélis, 1990) of adults in urban European contexts. In a short document published by UNESCO, Vélis argues passionately for a greater understanding of the complexity of what he terms 'functional illiteracy' in Europe. He cites the 1986/7 study carried out at the University of Lancaster in the UK on behalf of ALBSU (adult literacy and basic skills agency) based on the data gathered from the National Child Development Study of 10,000 children born from 3rd to 9th March 1958 who were monitored until reaching the age of 23, which indicated that 13% of the group encountered difficulties with reading and writing. Extrapolating, this would put the number of functional illiterates in the UK at about 6 million, a figure allowing The Guardian (27/11/1987) to announce 'Illiterate Six Million: Only Tip of the Iceberg'. Parallel to government action in setting up more comprehensive adult literacy and family literacy programmes, a Literacy Research Group was formed at Lancaster University who were also founder members of a national network linking practitioners and researchers in Adult Basic Literacy, known as RAPAL (research and practice in adult literacy).

During the 1990s, members of RAPAL set out to put the insights and perspectives of literacy learners and users themselves at the centre of research about literacy. The resulting 'Worlds of Literacy' (1994) edited by Hamilton, Barton and Ivanic, opened readers' eyes to the literacy lives of a number of urban readers setting out to improve their own literacy skills. These studies set out to question the notion, hitherto accepted, of literacy as an autonomous cognitive skill. Instead, they drew upon an 'ideological model' of literacy as outlined by Street (1984), whereby literacy is culturally and socially embedded in peoples' lives. Thus, instead of referring to 'literacy' it becomes more appropriate to refer to 'literacies' or 'literacy practices' (Scribner and Cole, 1981) in which people engage and of which they become 'members', using the materials, methods, participation structures and mediators that are appropriate. Within the framework of 'literacy practices' or habitual usage of certain types of literacy (e.g. Bible reading, shopping, playing monopoly, choirs, etc.) that include specific 'literacy events' or one-off occurrences of literacy, ethnographers were able to detail a particular cultural or learning practice and its importance in the individual's life.

Two in-depth studies of urban literacies written at the end of the twentieth and the turn of the twenty-first centuries were 'Local Literacies: Reading and writing in one community' by Barton and Hamilton (1998) and 'City Literacies: Learning to read across generations and cultures' by Gregory and Williams (2000). 'Local Literacies' provides an in-depth study of literacies in the lives of ordinary people in Lancaster, a city in north-west England. Data were collected from over 100 participants in the study in the form of interviews, case studies and a survey and these are embedded in a social history of the city, photographs, original literacy documents and information on the scope and variety of literacy resources in the community. The theory of literacy put forward is 'an ecological approach where literacy is integral to its context' (p. 4), whereby different chapters provide first the context (past and present) of literacy in the city before offering in-depth case studies of four different participants. These are followed by chapters analysing (i) the range of practices (ii) the patterning of practices (iii) the web of literacies in local organisations (iv) literacy and sense-making and (v) vernacular literacies. The whole study is designed within an ethnographic framework, where the authors explain the purpose of their work in empowering the literacies of ordinary people. Integral to the study is the aim to provide an emic perspective (literacy as viewed by the participants themselves) and part of this is the use of photographs of original documents, for example notes on horses for information at the betting shop as well as a residents' committee newsletter composed by one participant. Overall, the study provides an intimate yet broad picture of literacy lives in one city, revealing a wide range of practices, spanning the predictable, such as library visits, reading newspapers, bills, working on the computer etc. to the less predictable, such as those tied up with the 25 local groups listed, as diverse as the Quiz League, Machine Knitting Club and People Opposed to Noxious Gases (PONG)!

'Local Literacies' is focussed on home and community literacy practices and on adults rather than children or the role of the school as part of the community it serves. In contrast, 'City Literacies' uses as its focus two Primary schools, one set within the square mile boundary of the City of London and the other, just to its east, in the area of Spitalfields, Tower Hamlets. Using a similar ethnographic approach to 'Local Literacies', this study presents a tableau of literacy in the lives of different generations of pupils attending or with children attending the two schools. Similar to 'Local Literacies', 'City Literacies' aims to 'make visible the lives of people whose lives are not normally told' (p. 16). In this case, those lives represent a heritage that is ethnically much more diverse than the Lancaster participants. The authors of 'City Literacies' interviewed over 50 people, aged between 3 and 93, whose origins could be traced back to the French Huguenots, East European Jewish, Bangladeshi British or Anglo London backgrounds. Again, set within the context of the area, past and present, participants relate their memories of learning to read in one of the two focus Primary schools, at home and in their community language or religious classes. The last section of the book presents classroom-reading experiences for children at the end of the twentieth century and contrasts these with their very different literacies in Qur'anic and Bengali classes. Throughout, the argument is made that 'contrasting literacies' (hitherto regarded as a cultural clash leading to school failure), instead are a strength and that emergent bilingualism and biliteracy equips children with advantages rather than problems.

WORK IN PROGRESS

'City Literacies', written on the cusp of the twenty-first century, was beginning to reveal a major new development and area for research on literacies in cities: that of multilingual literacies. The end of the twentieth and the early years of the twenty-first centuries have witnessed a massive exodus of people from both economically and politically unstable countries to live in cities across Europe, Australia and USA. It is now clear that many children in urban contexts across the world enter school speaking a different language from that in which tuition will take place. Detailed demographic documentation on the scope of this in Europe and USA is given in *Urban Multilingualism in Europe: Immigrant Minority Languages at Home and School* edited by Extra and Yağmar in 2004. This collection draws together findings from the Multilingual Cities Project, a project based at Tilburg University, The Netherlands, that investigated the scope and breadth of multilingual literacies as well as language choice in Gőteborg, Hamburg, The Hague, Brussels, Lyon and Madrid at the beginning of the twenty-first century. The collection of papers highlights ways in which migrants are often, although not always, highly literate in their mother tongue and take with them numerous literacy practices from their country of origin. These practices or 'unofficial literacies' (Gregory and Williams, 2000) may remain separate from the 'official literacies' in school in their new country. With time, however, and for younger children, both heritage and adopted literacies may syncretise, forming a new and dynamic whole.

A number of ethnographic studies falling into the former category, showing dual or parallel literacy practices in the lives of migrants, can be found in Martin-Jones and Jones' (2000) edited volume 'Multilingual Literacies. Reading and Writing different Worlds'. This book provides a collection of largely ethnographic studies of multilingual literacy practices, largely in cities in Britain. Thus we learn of the different heritage literacies of, amongst others, Sylheti/Bengali speakers both in Spitalfields, East London and Birmingham; Gujarati speaking women in Leicester and children in London; Punjabi speakers in Southall, London; Mandarin speakers in Reading; Arabic speakers in Sheffield and Punjabi and Urdu speakers in Manchester. Most of these studies signal on-going work on a new and fascinating phenomenon taking place in cities, where people are operating in different languages and using different literacies according to the group within which they find themselves.

Studies falling into the latter category, showing very young children who are able to 'syncretise' or blend practices into a new form, can be found in 'Many Pathways to Literacy: Young Children learning with Siblings, Peers, Grandparents and Communities', edited by Gregory, Long and Volk (2004). Different studies in this volume show the cognitive and linguistic flexibility of young children in different cities across UK and USA as they go about making meaning from print in different languages and using different scripts. The authors argue that these children do not live in parallel but in simultaneous worlds (Kenner, 2004). The studies include 6-year old Puerto-Rican children in a Midwestern city in USA; a 3-year old Punjabi/Pahari child in Watford, near London, as well as Samoan-American children, Pueblo children in USA and Chinese children in London.

Studies on urban literacies in school settings during the first decade of the twenty-first century tend to focus on the classroom as an active site for negotiating cultures, including definitions of teacher/student knowledge and values, etc. A variety of examples showing ways in which this is happening across the globe are presented in 'Portraits of Literacy across Families, Communities and Schools' edited by Anderson Smythe and Shapiro (2005). Authors in this volume explore the intersections and tensions between 'unofficial' and 'official' literacies in multilingual cities such as Johannesburg and Cape Town, South Africa; Vancouver, Canada; London, UK; Australia; Quebec, Canada and USA. In every case, literacies are multilingual and, as in Gregory, Long and Volk (2004), children show themselves as able to live in simultaneous worlds. The subtitle of this volume 'Intersections and Tensions' highlights the very contrasting experiences faced and managed by children as they confront different practices, styles and interpersonal relationships as well as languages from those of their parents. In some cases, children manage these very positively, practising with their siblings or other cultural and language mediators (Gregory, 2005; Maguire et al., 2005). In others, particularly for example where indigenous groups have been ostracised within their native country, shown by the example of First Nation children in Canada (Anderson, Kendrick, Rogers and Smythe, 2005) and aboriginal families in Australia (Cairney, 2005), the task is more complex and by no means resolved.

One major group of urban literacy practices in which early twenty-first century multilingual children are engaged, can be grouped under the umbrella of 'community classes'. These are the subject of interest by a number of linguists and educationalists and may involve both religious and secular literacy classes. Community classes have, of course, long existed in cities, usually entailing both religious and heritage language classes. However, research studies now reveal a shifted interest from simply the factual and historical to the ways in which community classes might enhance both cognitive and literacy skills as well as the effect they might have on children's identities. A number of studies in this field at the beginning of the twenty-first century are focusing on the multiple identities of children participating in community classes as well as the notion of identity choice (Creese and Martin, 2006; Chao-Jung, 2006; Robertson, 2006).

PROBLEMS AND DIFFICULTIES AND FUTURE DIRECTIONS

There are a number of problems and difficulties for future research on literacies in cities. Some of these are listed here, together with some possible directions for future studies in order to tackle these:

- There have always been (and still are) contradictions concerning the extent of illiteracy existing in cities. Different research approaches produce different data. In UK, for example, on the one hand surveys conducted among employers as well as Universities appear to reveal considerable cause for concern at the standard of literacy. Most of this concern centres on the standard of children in urban contexts. On the other hand, however, national examination results improve year by year. Immense problems have always existed in measuring standards of literacy and illiteracy, and this is most apparent in city contexts;

- What is found tends to reflect the research methodology employed. Performance in national tests may well fail to reveal the breadth of urban children's 'unofficial literacies'. Ethnography has begun to open up insights into these but we still lack knowledge of the literacy practices of many multilingual and/or urban groups. For this knowledge to improve, we shall, at the very least, need:
- Life histories of those who have migrated so that the role and scope of different literacies in life as well as the way in which these link with changing and/or multiple identities are uncovered. We also need life-histories of those becoming literate for the first time later in life;
- Longitudinal studies showing how peoples' membership of different literacy practices changes over the years and the effect of these changes (particularly where the language in which the literacy takes place also changes) on the identities of individuals;
- A greater range of ethnographic studies on different local literacies, showing particularly what people are actually reading, the materials they use and the purpose for which they are used;
- Studies that trace the influence and importance of religious literacies in children's lives;
- The huge effect of computer and text messaging literacies—not only found in cities but having a major impact on urban youth cultures.

The quotation opening this chapter linked literacy with libraries and libraries with cities. It is clear that libraries are no longer the sole or even the major repository of reading materials. Even the most rural environment can often be connected via satellite or internet to a wealth of literacies, both oral and written, in numerous languages. Nevertheless, cities still remain a hub of literacy. Through facilitating face-to-face interaction for people of all nations and backgrounds they will always provide a haven for the development of new and dynamic literacies.

REFERENCES

Adult Literacy and Basic Skills Agency (ALBSU): 1986/7, Literacy, Numeracy and Adults—Evidence from the National Child Development Study, ALBSU, London.

Altick, R.D.: 1957, *The English Common Reader: A Social History of the Mass Reading Public 1800–1900*, University of Chicago Press, Chicago.

Anderson, J., Kendrick, M., Rogers, T., and Smythe, S.: 2005, *Portraits of Literacy across Families, Communities and Schools. Intersections and Tensions*, Lawrence Erlbaum Associates, Mahwah, NJ and London.

Anderson, J., Smythe, S., and Shapiro, J.: 2005, 'Working and learning with families, communities and schools: A critical case study' in Anderson, J. et al (op. cit.)

Barton, D. and Hamilton, S.: 1998, *Local Literacies. Reading and Writing in One Community*, Routledge, London.

Cairney, T.: 2005, 'Literacy Diversity: Understanding and Responding to the Textual Tapestries of Home, School and Community' in Anderson, J. et al (op. cit.).

Chao-Jung, W.: 2006, 'Look Who's Talking: Language Choices and Culture of Learning in UK Chinese Classroom', *Language and Education. An International Journal*, 20(1), 62–75.

Clanchy, M.T.: 1979, *From Memory to Written Record: England 1066–1307*, Edward Arnold, London.

Creese, A. and Martin, P.: 2006, 'Interaction in complementary school contexts: Developing identities of choice—An introduction, *Language and Education. An International Journal*, 20(1), 1–4.

Cressy, D.: 1980, *Literacy and the Social Order: Reading and Writing in Tudor and Stuart England*, Cambridge University Press, Cambridge.

Eco, U.: 1980, *The Name of the Rose*, Picador, London.

Extra, G. and Yağmar, K.: 2004, *Urban Multilingualism in Europe. Immigrant Minority Languages at Home and School*, Multilingual Matters Ltd. Clevedon, Avon.

Graff, H.: 1987, *The Labyrinths of Literacy. Reflections on Literacy Past and Present*, The Falmer Press, London.

Gregory, E.: 2005, 'Guiding lights: Siblings as literacy teachers in a multilingual community' in Anderson, J. et al. (op. cit.).

Gregory, E. and Williams, A.: 2000, *City Literacies: Learning to Read across Generations and Cultures*, Routledge, London.

Gregory, E., Long, S., and Volk, D. (eds.): 2004, *Many Pathways to Literacy. Young Children Learning With Siblings, Grandparents, Peers and Communities*, Routledge, London.

Hamilton, S., Barton, D., and Ivanic, R.: 1994, *Worlds of Literacy*, Multilingual Matters Ltd., Clevedon, Avon.

Havelock, E.A.: 1976, *The Origins of Western Literacy*, Ontario Institute for Studies in Education, Ontario.

Robertson, H.L.: 2006, 'Learning to read 'properly' by moving between parallel literacy classes, *Language and Education. An International Journal*, 20(1), 44–61

Inwood, S.: 1998, *A History of London*, Macmillan, London.

Levine, K.: 1986, *The Social Context of Literacy*, Routledge & Kegan Paul, London and New York.

Maguire, M., Beer, A.J., Attarian, H., Baygin, D., Curdt-Christiansen, and Yoshida, R.: 2005, 'The Chameleon character of multilingual literacy portraits: Re-searching in "heritage" language places and spaces' in Anderson, J. et al (op. cit.).

Martin-Jones, M. and Jones, K. (eds.): 2000, *Multilingual Literacies. Reading and Writing Different Worlds*, John Benjamins, Amsterdam/Philadelphia.

Scribner, S. and Cole, M.: 1981, *The Psychology of Literacy*, Cambridge University Press, Cambridge.

Street, B.V.: 1984, *Literacy in Theory and Practice*, Cambridge University Press, Cambridge.

The Guardian: (27/11/1987), 'Illiterate Six Million: Only Tip of the Iceberg'

Thompson, E.P.: 1963, *The Making of the Working Class*, Penguin, London.

Vélis, J.P.: 1990, *Through a Glass, Darkly. Functional Illiteracy in Industrialised Countries*, UNESCO, Paris.

SUBJECT INDEX

NAME INDEX

TABLE OF CONTENTS

VOLUME 1: LANGUAGE POLICY AND POLITICAL ISSUES IN EDUCATION

TABLE OF CONTENTS

VOLUME 3: DISCOURSE AND EDUCATION

TABLE OF CONTENTS

VOLUME 4: SECOND AND FOREIGN LANGUAGE EDUCATION

TABLE OF CONTENTS

VOLUME 5: BILINGUAL EDUCATION

Section 1: 21st Century Bilingual Education: Advances in Understanding and Emerging Issues

TABLE OF CONTENTS

VOLUME 6: KNOWLEDGE ABOUT LANGUAGE

Section 3: Knowledge about Language, the Curriculum, the Classroom and the Teacher

Section 4: Knowledge about Language, Bilingualism and Multilingualism

TABLE OF CONTENTS

VOLUME 7: LANGUAGE TESTING AND ASSESSMENT

TABLE OF CONTENTS

VOLUME 8: LANGUAGE SOCIALIZATION

TABLE OF CONTENTS

VOLUME 9: ECOLOGY OF LANGUAGE

TABLE OF CONTENTS

VOLUME 10: RESEARCH METHODS IN LANGUAGE AND EDUCATION

Lightning Source UK Ltd.
Milton Keynes UK
29 March 2011

170051UK00003B/20/P